D0844798

PACE COLLEGE
OPPORTVNITAS
ARS COMMERCIVM CIVITAS
MCMVI
NEW YORK

Principles of Administrative and Supervisory Management

Principles of Administrative and Supervisory Management

JAMES E. MORGAN, JR.

Director of Training
Williams Division
Georgia-Pacific Corporation

Prentice-Hall, Inc., Englewood Cliffs, New Jersey

Library of Congress Cataloging in Publication Data

Morgan, James E., Jr.
Principles of administrative and supervisory management.

Includes Bibliographies.
1. Management. 2. Supervision of employees.
I. Title.
HD31.M629 658.4 72-8848
ISBN 0-13-709386-1

10 9 8 7 6 5 4 3 2 1

Printed in the United States of America

PRENTICE-HALL INTERNATIONAL, INC., *London*
PRENTICE-HALL OF AUSTRALIA, PTY. LTD., *Sydney*
PRENTICE-HALL OF CANADA, LTD., *Toronto*
PRENTICE-HALL OF INDIA PRIVATE LIMITED, *New Delhi*
PRENTICE-HALL OF JAPAN, INC., *Tokyo*

To my wife, Earline

Contents

III
Supervisory Skills 179

IV
Management Techniques 271

Preface

This text is designed to furnish the potential or working manager with the fundamental principles that he or she needs to know to do the job. Although it is especially appropriate for the college student, the material is also suited to be used as a reference book by the working midmanager or first-line supervisor, as supplementary material in a manager-training program, as a guide for training directors for in-plant management or supervisory training, or as a text for adult education courses in management or supervision.

Although management is too complex a subject to be exhausted in a single text, the widest coverage possible was sought by treating management as a universal process applying to any field; only material that can be applied universally is included. Specifically, the text covers the four areas in which a manager has to be proficient to be an effective manager. Part I—The Management Process—presents the fundamental principles that are needed to develop a management-minded point of view. Part II—Human Relations—is designed to help develop an employee-oriented philosophy. Part III—Supervisory Skills—outlines the experience-tested skills that make the close relationship between manager and employees effective. Part IV—Management Techniques—covers the work patterns that help manage the job efficiently and handle the situations that cannot be handled by supervisory skills alone. These four areas are a balance between theory and application—Parts I and II stress knowledge accumulation, and Parts III and IV stress knowledge application.

The instructor's guide for the text includes suggestions for a course outline, instructional methods, class assignments, outside reading, and a film list; answers to case studies; a fifty-question objective examination for each of the four parts; and answers to the objective examination.

Because no one man can produce a text on a broad subject such as management without relying on the works and the indirect contributions of others, I would like to acknowledge my gratitude to the countless authors, administrators, consultants, supervisors, and students whose accumulated knowledge and philosophies contributed immeasurably in shaping this book. I am especially grateful to the management of the many companies that assisted me in giving balance to this book. Also, I wish to acknowledge my indebtedness to Mrs. Blanche Heifner for research assistance and to Mrs. Dixie Hill for assisting in the preparation of the manuscript.

James E. Morgan, Jr.

Principles of Administrative and Supervisory Management

I

The Management Process

From the first day on the job, a person occupying a management position is expected to act like a manager, speak like a manager, and represent management's point of view. In short, he or she must be management-minded. Although developing this attitude is a continuous process, every manager should begin with a fundamental understanding of the management process. In other words, he should become aware of how the system that underlies all organizations works. Not only will this provide the manager with the background for developing a management-minded philosophy but it will also furnish him with the necessary frame of reference for executing the functions and duties of management. Consequently, it is the purpose of this part of the book to present and discuss the essential factors necessary for understanding the management process. Major topics included are:

Introduction to Management
The Functions of Management
Organizations
Communications in Management
Economics in Management

1

Introduction to Management

The field of management has been described as a theory jungle.[1] Accumulated literature on the subject of management contains a seemingly bewildering hodgepodge of precepts, concepts, principles, practices, procedures, methods, techniques, and a variety of approaches, philosophies, and points of view. Therefore, before management can be studied as a general subject, attention must be given to bringing these various factors into focus and reducing them to a level at which they can be universally applied. To do this, it is necessary to realize that management is both a science and an applied art. The scientific approach aims at formulating certain principles and laws and a statement as to their possible application. The applied approach aims at developing an operational system that produces results. Both approaches have contributed substantially to the field of management. The scientific approach has produced the body of principles that underlies all management effort. The applied approach has supplied the skills and techniques that the manager can use in obtaining results. Although there is wide disagreement among both scientists and practicing managers as to which approach is best, most generally agree that certain management factors are common to all managers, at all levels, regardless of their particular fields or the nature of the organization. This simply means that while techniques and skills are ever changing to meet the social and technological demands of our society, certain fundamental management principles remain constant and can be adapted to almost any situation. This allows management to be discussed as a general subject and to be viewed as a universal process. It is the

[1] Harold Koontz, "The Management Theory Jungle," in *Readings in Management,* 3rd ed., Max D. Richards and William A. Nielander (Cincinnati, Ohio: South-Western Publishing Co., 1969), p. 3.

purpose of this chapter to further clarify this concept and at the same time present some basic information that can be used in developing a perspective—a balanced and consistent point of view—of management. This can be done by examining the following major topics: (1) what management is, (2) the requirements of a manager, (3) administration and supervision, (4) management philosophy, and (5) development of managers.

WHAT MANAGEMENT IS

The term *management* has several meanings that can be applied in different ways. First, the term is used to define the broad area of activities that make up the control of an organization. In this sense, it is used to distinguish between management and labor. Second, *management* is used to describe, collectively or separately, the level of authority within an organization. Collectively, the term is applied to all levels of authority above the worker. Separately, the term is used to divide levels of management into top management, middle management, and first-line management. Each of these definitions is useful in forming a perspective of management. But more important is the functional definition. For the purpose of this book, the functional definition of *management* is the process of organizing and employing resources to accomplish a predetermined objective with and through people. This definition is functional in that it implies certain actions and proposes certain results. It implies that all management actions are undertaken for a purpose (normally to provide a service or make a profit), and to accomplish this purpose, resources (money, manpower, machines, material, time, space) must be arranged and allocated in a skillful way and used in a process to obtain results. This definition can be best understood by examining two basic approaches to management: (1) the management process approach, and (2) the human behavior approach.

The Management Process Approach

This approach sees management as a process of getting things done through and with people operating in organized groups. Stemming from the pioneer work of Henri Fayol, a French industrialist, and Frederick W. Taylor, the father of scientific management, this approach regards management as a universal process, regardless of the type of enterprise or the level of management in the organization. Essentially, this means that management is management regardless of the level of the manager and the kind of operation he manages.

A basic point in visualizing management as a universal process is to understand the close interdependence of all activities in an organization in reaching an objective. In most organizations, regardless of their type, specific activities are closely interrelated. Carrying out one activity of the organization influences or is influenced by another. This may be viewed as the integration of objectives and the allocation and use of resources by the various levels of management. Each level of management (top, middle, and first-line) corresponds to different levels of objectives. Each level of management involves the integration of the several objectives of each level below. Although levels of the operation differ in size, importance, and type of activity, the nature of each is essentially the same. Their managers *manipulate* the nonhuman resources and *motivate* the human resources immediately below them in an effort to carry out their operation in an integrated system adapted to using available resources to achieve their objectives.

Top management is concerned with the overall objectives of the organization and employing resources available to the organization to meet these objectives. To do this, certain specific objectives are assigned to the various middle managers along with a share of the resources.

Middle management assigns certain objectives and a portion of the resources to first-line management.

First-line management assigns certain objectives to individuals (workers, specialists, technicians, salesmen, and so on) or groups of individuals in the form of tasks. These individuals or groups, through one of the several working processes, use the resources to produce an end product consistent with the overall objective of the organization.[2]

Management viewed from this perspective can be studied as a dynamic process of developing and blending various activities to meet the overall objectives of an organization rather than as a series of static functions and duties. Moreover, this approach permits the functional definition of management to apply at each management level and to all types of organizations.

The Human Behavior Approach

This approach to management is based on the central idea that since managing involves getting things done with and through people, management must be centered on interpersonal or human relations. This approach brings to bear existing and newly developed theories, methods, and techniques to help the manager understand and get the best results from people by meeting their needs and responding to their motivation. In other words, this approach concentrates on the "people" part of management, and rests on the principle that since people work together in order to accomplish objectives, people

[2] This concept will be developed further when management by objectives is discussed in Chapter 2.

should understand people.[3] As this implies, human relations is an art that all managers should understand and practice.

Basically, the two approaches discussed above support the functional definition of *management* and the process of management mentioned in the introduction to the chapter. This is not to say, however, that the two approaches will not be applied differently. The way that the management process is adapted will vary somewhat according to the manager's field and the level and nature of his operation. On the other hand, although the basic principles for understanding people in general are universal, each employee is unique and must be treated differently. Nonetheless, the two approaches are useful in developing a universal perspective of the principles of management.

THE REQUIREMENTS OF A MANAGER

Having discussed a universal approach to the management process, attention is now given to applying this approach to the requirements of the person who uses the process: the manager. The requirements of a manager will vary according to his particular circumstances. Basically, however, the general requirements are the same for all managers, and vary only in degree.

What a Manager Is

As the above discussion indicates, management implies working with people. Therefore, a *manager* is defined as a person who makes things happen through the efforts of other people. This definition applies to executives and supervisory personnel at all levels, whether it is the president of the company or the foreman of a production unit. Managers are classified according to the level of the management position they occupy.

Top managers are those people who are responsible for carrying out the overall objective of the organization. They occupy the top executive jobs in the organization. For example, the top manager of a corporation is the president. On the other hand, the top manager of a manufacturing plant is the general manager. Both are top managers since they occupy the highest executive position in their organization.

Middle managers are those people in an organization who are responsible for a department or division within an organization. They are normally charged with a specific activity such as personnel, purchasing, manufacturing, production, quality control, marketing, sales, and so on. Their

[3] See Koontz, "The Management Theory Jungle," p. 8.

titles vary according to the jobs they hold, such as Personnel Manager, Head of Purchasing, or Office Manager.

First-line managers are those people in an organization who are responsible for carrying out the policies and procedures of the organization through the efforts of the workers. This is basically a man-to-man relationship in getting the job done. Foremen and supervisors are titles commonly given to first-line managers.

Figure 1 shows the management group by level and rank order above

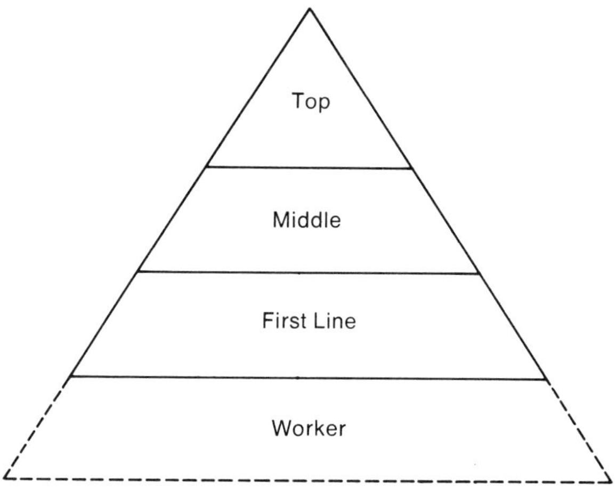

Figure 1 Management Levels

the worker. Here and throughout this book the term "worker" applies to those individuals who use nonhuman resources to produce a product or provide a service regardless of skill level. Doctors, lawyers, scientists, engineers, professors, teachers, instructors, craftsmen, and technicians do not belong to the managment group unless they occupy a position that meets the definition of manager.

The Duties of a Manager

The specific duties and responsibilities of a manager vary according to the particular job and the level of management. Despite this, however, certain duties and responsibilities are fundamental to all managers:

1. Setting or interpreting goals and objectives for the operation.
2. Determining priority of claim as to resources (money, manpower, machines, time, and space).

3. Determining and directing the best use of resources consistent with economy, effectiveness, and efficiency.
4. Being particularly mindful of human resources (manpower) by developing a keen awareness of human behavior and personal interactions.
5. Integrating resources into a well-developed pattern or system of operation.

These duties and responsibilities are essentially universal in that they represent general areas rather than specific position functions. Therefore, they apply to all managers regardless of their particular function or managerial level.

The Functions of a Manager

The means by which managers carry out their managerial duties and responsibilities are referred to as the functions of management. These functions are classified as planning, organizing, coordinating, directing, and controlling. Management functions will be discussed more fully in the next chapter, but a brief examination of these five key words will indicate a simple breakdown of the steps necessary in carrying out the management process.

Planning is the initial step of any action. It consists of understanding the assignment and objective, gathering related information, discovering abilities and inabilities, exploring possibilities, and listing resources. It relies heavily on knowledge of the situation and sound judgment.

Organizing consists of assembling the resources and arranging them in a manner most likely to result in effective completion of the objective. In its broad sense, the assembling of resources includes recruiting, selecting, and placing the "right man for the right job." This important phase of organizing is referred to as staffing, and is discussed in some detail in Chapter 10.

Coordinating is the concern of securing cooperation of those inside and outside the manager's control to assure that the other management functions can be executed smoothly.

Directing is the orientation of the activity toward the established objective. It is the actual supervision of the work and people to assure that objectives are achieved and results produced.

Controlling is the final phase and consists in checking up on the activity to assure that it is going according to plan and the desired results are produced.

While the five functions of management are performed by all managers at all levels, they are not performed equally at all levels. As a general rule, top and middle managers perform the functions of planning and organizing more than do managers at the first-line level. On the other hand, first-line managers are more concerned with the functions of directing and controlling. (Coordination is basically a communications process and is applied about equally at all levels.) The approximate relationship is shown in Figure 2.

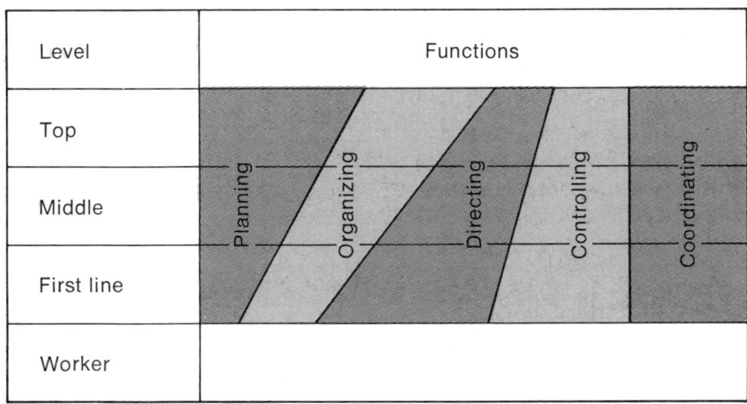

Figure 2 Approximate Relationship between Levels of Management and Functions of Management (Adapted from Leonard J. Kazmier, *Principles of Management,* 1st Edition, p. 240. Copyright 1961 McGraw Hill Book Company, Inc.)

The Qualifications of a Manager

Because qualifications involve a combination of personal characteristics, traits, and abilities, unlike the requirement factors discussed previously, the exact qualifications of a manager cannot be pinned down. Through a wide array of studies, however, a considerable amount of information has been compiled over the years. Whereas this information varies and is by no means conclusive, it is generally agreed that certain qualifications are common in some degree to most successful managers. Some common indicators are as follows:

1. Ability to analyze
2. Ability to communicate ideas
3. Ability to organize
4. Ability to plan
5. Ability to inspire others
6. Ability to gather and interpret information
7. Ability to instruct others
8. Ability to solve problems and make decisions
9. Ability to influence others, individually and in groups
10. Ability to recognize individual strength and weakness
11. A sense of responsibility
12. A liking for people
13. Courage of convictions
14. A sense of loyalty, both to employees and organization
15. A will and drive for achievement (ambition)
16. Emotional balance

17. Social consciousness and understanding
18. Awareness for economy
19. Technical competency

It is important to note that most of the qualifications indicated above can be learned. *Therefore, it can be stated that managers are made, not born.*

ADMINISTRATION AND SUPERVISION

The terms *administration* and *supervision* are often the source of confusion in attempting to form a perspective of management. Both operationally and in management literature, the word *administration* is often defined as those people who are primarily concerned with developing and implementing overall policy, formulating plans, and assuming responsibility for the whole or a major element of the organization. When applied in this way, the term *administration* applies only to top and middle managers, and the term is used synonymously with management. On the other hand, the word *supervision* is often used to describe the lower element of the management group, which is directly responsible for the daily, face-to-face, immediate operation and is treated separately from management. Are supervisors a part of management? Perhaps the confusion implied by this question stems from the word *supervision,* which means oversee or watch over. As originally used, it was applied to those who oversaw or watched over the work for someone else. Those overseers were the gang bosses, section chiefs, and the like who watched over the work of others for others. As overseers they were not considered a part of management, but hired hands employed to do a job. Today, this situation has changed. Although the first-line manager is still referred to as a supervisor, he is definitely a part of management. Not only is he considered as such in labor laws, but modern organizations recognize that the supervisor is part of the management team. He is the vital link between the worker and the other management levels of the organization.

Moreover, the watching over process is not restricted to the first-line manager. Supervision is a major part of every manager's job. Top managers supervise the work of their subordinates; middle managers oversee the employees who work immediately for them; and in small organizations where management levels are less distinct, the top manager may directly supervise most of the employees of the organization. Conversely, administration is not restricted only to the executive level of a firm. Although as shown earlier, the first-line manager is not concerned as much with planning, goal setting, and the like, he nevertheless participates in performing certain administrative functions. Therefore, the approach taken here is that administration and supervision are not separate functions but management can be divided into two parts: administrative management and supervisory management.

Administrative management is the process involved in using processes, principles, and practices to establish or develop goals, policies, and procedures necessary to achieve the objective of an organization or elements of an organization and to provide general guidance and direction to the organization.

Supervisory management is the process involved in using processes, principles, and practices to oversee an organization or elements of an organization in the direct operation in achieving established objectives.

This approach permits the terms *management* and *manager* to be used to describe all functions and all levels of an organization involved in executing the management process, and still allow for a distinction to be made between functions and levels.

Level	Type Management	
Top	Administrative	
Middle	Management	Supervisory
First line		Management
Worker		

Figure 3 Approximate Relationship between Types of Management by Levels of Management (Adapted from William R. Spriegel and Richard H. Lansburgh, *Industrial Management*, 5th Edition, p. 1.9. Copyright 1955, John Wiley and Sons.)

This distinction is only one of degree, as shown in Figure 3. For example, a plant or store manager will spend most of his time in planning, organizing, establishing goals, and giving general guidance to the organization (administrative management). However, he will still be involved to a much lesser extent in the direct supervision of his immediate subordinates (supervisory management). On the other hand, a foreman of a production unit or a supervisor of a specific department will spend most of his time in the direct process of getting the work out through face-to-face contact with his workers (supervisory management). He will also, however, spend some time planning and organizing his work (administrative management).[4]

[4] For a modified version of this concept, see Dalton E. McFarland, *Management Principles and Practices* (New York: The Macmillan Company, Inc., 1958), p. 11.

MANAGEMENT PHILOSOPHY

The guiding force for carrying out the management process is the philosophy of the manager. Although this topic will be discussed in various sections elsewhere, the importance of developing a philosophy is essential in forming a perspective of management and is a major object of this book, and so it is introduced at this time. In their book, *Elements of Managerial Action,* Michael J. Jucius and William E. Schlender summarize the need and essence of management philosophy very well:

> Perhaps the most important aspect of management is the philosophy that underlies all of its activities. This has reference to the basic thinking that guides the actions of a manager. It determines which course he will take when faced with a number of fundamental choices. For example, should he consider himself to be primarily a representative of the owners of the business? Primarily concerned with protecting the continuity of the business? Primarily interested in the welfare of the employees? Primarily responsible for producing a service for the customers of the enterprise? Primarily a servant of the community in which the business operates?
>
> These are very fundamental questions. How they are answered determines the way all activities in the enterprise are directed and emphasized. From the top of an organization to the very bottom, pressure is exerted to move in the direction indicated by the basic answers. That is why it has been said, for example, that an organization is but the shadow of one man. And this is so because a group must work together or else it works against itself to its own defeat.[5]

Discovering answers to the questions posed above involves a considerable amount of experience coupled with a realistic appraisal of the overall situation in which the manager is involved. But the approach taken here is that the manager can use two fundamental principles to guide his actions: responsibility to his organization and responsibility to his employees.

First, the manager is responsible to his organization for achieving its particular objectives or goals. As a part of management the manager must keep this factor foremost in his mind. This means that he must support his organization's policy, project it in the best possible light, and represent it fairly in his dealings with employees, labor, customers, and the general public. In short, he must be *management-minded.*

Second, the manager is responsible to the people in his part of the organization for helping them achieve their individual goals and objec-

[5] See Michael J. Jucius and William E. Schlender, *Elements of Managerial Action,* rev. ed. (Homewood, Illinois: Richard D. Irwin, Inc., 1965), p. 15.

tives. He knows that if he is to obtain cooperation he has to be able to help these people relate individual goals to organizational goals. He must know about human behavior and human motivations; about why people work; about causes and effects in human behavior; about ways to foster and stimulate human improvement, both individually and in groups.[6] In short, he must become *people-minded.*

These two factors—management-mindedness and people-mindedness—are the basic elements of a sound management philosophy. In applying this philosophy, the manager should remember that he must strike a proper balance between the two by looking at both sides of the coin. Striking this balance is that elusive factor called leadership through which the manager's philosophy is manifested.

DEVELOPMENT OF MANAGERS

In recent years, much attention has been given to manager development. Management literature is abundant on the subject. Almost every educational institution conducts seminars and offers courses for all levels of managers. More and more organizations, both large and small, at least pay lip service to the idea. Despite this, however, there has yet to be devised a formula for manager development that assures success. The reason for this is that both manager development and success are predicated on a host of varying and changing circumstances that cannot be predicted or controlled. Economic, political, technological, and social conditions change rapidly, causing entire career fields to be all but abolished and less in demand. This makes it difficult for manager development to be planned. On the other hand, the manager who is right for one situation may be totally wrong for another. Consequently, managerial success is more an art of adapting to changing circumstances than following a predetermined plan. An insight as to how successful managers adapt and learn from circumstances can be gained from a study made by Thomas H. Patten, Jr., for the School of Labor and Industrial Relations, Michigan State University.[7] In this study Mr. Patten conducted in-depth interviews with seventy-nine middle and top managers of a large firm employing more than 100,000 persons. In response to the question: "What do you think has made the most important contributions to your career success and personal development?" the following were the most frequent responses:

[6] See Elmore Petersen, E. Grosvenor Plowman, and Joseph M. Trickett, *Business Organization and Management,* 5th ed. (Homewood, Illinois: Richard D. Irwin, Inc., 1962), p. 17.

[7] *Organizational Process and Development of Managers: Some Hypotheses,* Reprint No. 95 (East Lansing, Mich.: Michigan State University, 1967–1968).

Luck. In nearly every case, the managers interviewed mentioned that at least once in their careers, they were exposed to what they considered an opportunity that made their work visible to organizational superiors. This they considered as being in the right place at the right time, or—luck.

Observation of Superiors at Work. The managers interviewed generally agreed that a second factor that contributed to their development was the chance to observe organizational superiors at work. They used both the superior's negative and positive behavior patterns to model their own later actions by rejecting the negative and accepting the positive patterns they had observed.

Work Assignments. A third factor mentioned as contributing to their success was the challenge of work assignments. Most indicated that being given assignments with broad responsibilities where they could develop the specific details to accomplish the objective, and being offered the challenge to resolve problems of increasing difficulty and complexity had contributed to their personal development.

Experience in Other Organizations. The value of having worked in other organizations was a factor mentioned as contributing to their development. This had given them exposure to different management techniques that could be used in their overall development.

Although no concrete conclusions can be drawn from these factors, they are useful as a guide for personal development.

Although as this indicates, manager development is more the art of adapting to changing circumstances than following a predetermined plan, five universal factors considered to be fundamental to manager development should be understood. First, it is generally agreed that a manager must be competent in a particular field. For example, to be a sales manager, he must know something about the principles and practices of selling; to be a supervisor of a retail outlet or of a production unit, he must know his particular field; or to be a personnel manager, he should know personnel administration. Second, because it has been established that management is carried out through a process, this process should be understood. Not only will this assist the manager in developing the management-minded philosophy, which is essential to managerial success, but it will allow him to make better use of his resources. Next, it has been said that the manager works with and through people and that developing a people-minded philosophy is an essential ingredient to management. This makes it apparent that all managers should understand the principles of how and why people behave as they do and the interrelations of people in an organization. Fourth, because the manager's efficiency is based on the way in which he manages his people to obtain results, he must learn certain supervisory skills. Finally, he must develop the management techniques necessary for the overall management of the workers and the work of his department.

The four areas pertaining to management are covered in this book. The management process is discussed in Part I; Part II covers human relations; supervisory skills are covered in Part III; and Part IV includes management techniques. Obviously, no single textbook can possibly cover these four areas in detail, nor can the academic study of management alone make a person a manager. Manager development requires the assimilation of many points of view tempered and molded through experience. Moreover, since it is equally obvious that no textbook can possibly illustrate by example the application of the principles to the many particular fields that the manager manages, examples in this book should be viewed as being representative only and not to orient the material toward a particular type of activity. One of the major advantages of management being a universal process is that the principles apply to all fields.

KEY POINT SUMMARY

1. Management is both a science and an art.
    a. The scientific approach provides the laws and principles.
    b. The applied approach provides the skills and techniques.
2. Because certain fundamental principles remain constant, the scientific approach allows management to be studied as a universal process, which means:
    a. That although techniques and skills vary, certain principles remain constant.
    b. That these principles can be applied regardless of the level of management or the operation being managed.
3. The functional concept of management is defined as a process of organizing and employing resources to accomplish a predetermined objective with and through people. The universal application of this definition is supported by two fundamental approaches to management.
    a. The management process approach
    b. The human behavior approach
4. A manager is a person who makes things happen through the efforts of others. This definition applies to all managers at all levels. The universal approach to management can also be applied

to the requirements of a manager. While manager requirements vary, it is only a matter of degree.

5. Managers are classified by levels of management as:
   a. Top
   b. Middle
   c. First-line
6. Certain managerial duties and responsibilities are universal since they are common to all management levels. These include:
   a. Setting or interpreting goals and objectives
   b. Determining priority of claim to resources
   c. The use of resources consistent with economy, efficiency, and effectiveness
   d. Developing an awareness of human behavior and personal interaction
   e. Integrating resources into a pattern or system of operation
7. A manager performs certain functions that are characteristic of all managers. These are:
   a. Planning
   b. Organizing (to include staffing)
   c. Coordinating
   d. Directing
   e. Controlling
8. These functions are performed by all managers, at all levels, but some functions are performed by one level of management more than by others.
   a. Top and middle managers perform more planning and organizing.
   b. First-line managers perform more directing and controlling.
   c. Coordinating is performed about equally by all levels of management.
9. Manager qualifications involve certain characteristics, traits, and abilities that are common to most leaders. (*See* page 9.)
10. While the terms *administration* and *supervision* can be applied at all levels, there are two types of management:
    a. Administrative management
    b. Supervisory management
11. All levels of management perform both administrative and supervisory functions:
    a. Top and middle managers are concerned more with administrative management.

b. First line managers are concerned more with supervisory management.

12. While manager development is more the process of adapting to changing circumstances than a well-developed plan, five fundamental factors are common to manager development. These are:
    a. Be knowledgeable in a certain technical field.
    b. Understand the management process.
    c. Understand human relations.
    d. Develop certain supervisory skills.
    e. Develop certain management techniques.

DISCUSSION QUESTIONS

1. Why is management both an art and a science?
2. Why is management essentially a universal process? How does the management process and human behavior approach support the universal concept of management?
3. Why are the requirements of a manager essentially universal?
4. Who is a manager? Is the buyer of a major department store, the technician working primarily on research, or the executive secretary to a vice president of a firm a manager?
5. How are managers classified? What classification should be given to these personnel: (a) the manager of a shoe department who supervises five people; (b) the owner of a small business; (c) the manager of a major department such as personnel; (d) a senior engineer working primarily on research.
6. What are the fundamental duties of a manager? How would a program to reduce cost through the better use of manpower relate to the fundamental duties of a manager?
7. What are the functions of a manager? What is the relationship of these functions to the three levels of management?
8. What are the qualifications of a manager? Is there any relationship between these qualifications and managerial duties? managerial functions?
9. What is the relationship of administration and supervision with management? Which management level is concerned with administrative management? Supervisory management?
10. What is meant by management philosophy? What are two principles a manager can use in developing a philosophy? Is there a relationship between developing a management philosophy and the following: (a) The human behavior approach to management? (b) Duties of a manager? (c) Qualifications of a manager?
11. What are the fundamental factors that constitute the framework for manager development? What is the relationship between the four management

factors and developing a management-minded and people-minded management philosophy?

CASE PROBLEM

Case 1–1

Due to increased operation, a company is organizing a second department, and is in the process of selecting a supervisor for the new operation from the company's existing employees. The choice has been reduced to two men: Jack Clark and Bill Jones.

1. Jack Clark is considered an expert in his field. He is thoroughly reliable and has the highest production rate and the lowest number of rejects of any man in his department. He is reserved and works best when shown what to do and left alone to do it. He rarely participates in company activities, preferring to go directly home after work. He complies with company policy without question. His technical advice is often sought by his co-workers.

2. Bill Jones is an average employee. His technical know-how is adequate, and his product and quality work record is good, but not outstanding. He has an outgoing personality and occasionally leaves his job to talk with other workers. He likes company activities and is the coach of a Little League baseball team that he helped to organize in his community. He often questions company policy, but when he has had his say, he gives the policy his support. His co-workers often discuss their personal problems with him and seek his advice on these matters.

Questions

1. *Which man should be selected for supervisor of the new department? Why?*
2. *What is the contrast of the philosophy between the two men?*
3. *In performing his supervisory duties, with which management functions would the man selected be most concerned?*
4. *Would the man selected be more concerned with administrative management or supervisory management?*
5. *In developing his career, what factors should the man selected consider?*

SELECTED REFERENCES

ALLEN, LOUIS A., *Management and Organization,* Chap. 1. New York: McGraw-Hill Book Company, Inc., 1958.

AMRINE, HAROLD T., JOHN A. RITCHEY, and OLIVER S. HULLEY, *Manufacturing, Organization, and Management* (2nd ed.), Chap. 2, Englewood Cliffs, N.J.: Prentice-Hall, Inc., 1966.

JUCIUS, MICHAEL J., and WILLIAM E. SCHLENDER, *Elements of Managerial Action* (rev. ed.), Chaps. 1 and 2. Homewood, Ill.: Richard D. Irwin, Inc., 1965.

Koontz, Harold, "The Management Theory Jungle," in *Readings in Management* (3rd ed.), Chap. 1, Sec. 1. Cincinnati, Ohio: South-Western Publishing Company, 1969.

McFarland, Dalton E., *Management Principles and Practices,* Chaps. 2 and 3. New York: The Macmillan Company, 1958.

Patten, Thomas H., Jr., "Organizational Processes and the Development of Managers: Some Hypotheses," Reprint No. 95. East Lansing, Mich.: School of Labor and Industrial Relations, Michigan State University, 1967–1968.

Petersen, Elmore, E. Grosvenor Plowman, and Joseph M. Trickett, *Business Organization and Management* (5th ed.), Chap. 1. Homewood, Ill.: Richard D. Irwin, Inc., 1962.

Pfiffner, John M., and Frank P. Sherwood, *Administrative Organization,* Chap. 19. Englewood Cliffs, N.J.: Prentice-Hall, Inc., 1960.

2

The Functions of Management

In the previous chapter, the functional approach to management was introduced as a logical series of steps that the manager could use to carry out the management process. These steps or functions were identified as planning, organizing, coordinating, directing, and controlling. In this chapter, each of these functions will be examined separately. It should be kept in mind that while this static step-by-step approach is a convenient way to discuss each function separately, both in the study of management and in actual operation, the functions are not as clear-cut as they appear on paper. They tend to overlap and become interwoven, often making it impossible to identify when a person is studying or performing only one function, or where one function ends and the next one begins.

It was also pointed out that although the functions are performed by all managers, they are not performed equally by each management level. Carrying this a step further, it should also be understood that managers, regardless of level (top, middle, first-line), seldom if ever perform these functions in their entirety. In other words, each function is an integrated process within itself. This means that when viewed as a whole, the manager only performs a part of the planning function, a part of the organizing function, a part of the coordinating function, a part of the directing function, and a part of the controlling function; and when applied to the organization, each function is shared with someone else. Nevertheless, understanding the basic elements of each function is essential in building a frame of reference for understanding the management process and the application of this process on the job. With this purpose in mind, this chapter will examine the following major topics: (1) the role of objectives, (2) the essentials of planning, (3) the essentials of organizing, (4) the essentials of coordinating, (5) the essentials of directing, (6) the essentials of controlling, and (7) the interrelation and application of functions.

THE ROLE OF OBJECTIVES

Since the management process is undertaken to achieve predetermined objectives, it is only logical that preceding any discussion of the functions of management the role of objectives be clarified. Essentially, the role of objectives is to provide general guidance and specific directions to the management process by furnishing the manager at each level with a compass bearing for his activities.

Types of Objectives

Objectives are of two basic types: broad and specific.

Broad Objectives. These spell out or imply the general purpose of the organization and provide the basis for all managerial action. These objectives are normally set by top management or are inherent in the nature of the organization. For example, the broad objective of a plant manufacturing tires may be a stated objective of producing *X* number of tires in a specific period of time within a certain cost factor. On the other hand, service organizations such as hospitals or schools may have the inherent objective of providing a category of service to a certain population in a limited geographical area. Still further, a broad objective of a department store may be stated in gross volume of sales. All are broad objectives since they provide direction and establish purpose.

Specific Objectives. Within an organization, there are several major components responsible for carrying out a specified segment of the total operation of the organization. These components are normally departments such as personnel, manufacturing, sales, budget, and finance, and are made up of lesser components to include the individual workers. The contributions of each of these segmented components at each level constitute specific objectives. In other words, specific objectives are the results that each component and each member of the organization are expected to achieve toward the broad objectives of the organization.

Management by Objective

To provide guidance in carrying out the management process, objectives must be meaningful. For objectives to be meaningful, they must be stated in measurable terms, compatible at all levels of the organization and integrated at all levels of the organization. The process of making objectives meaningful is called *management by objective.* Ideally, the management by objective concept should apply to the total organization. When this is not the case, the process is effective when used separately by individual managers. This is how the process works:

1. To start with, each manager at each level develops clearly spelled out objectives for his department, units, and individuals in his department. These objectives are stated in results expected in measurable terms. Agreement is sought in establishing the desired results, and a commitment is made by all concerned that the results agreed upon will be diligently sought.

2. Next, the required resources are committed to accomplish the established objectives.

3. Third, a system of reporting is designed to provide a way in which individual or departmental performance can be measured by comparing actual performance against expected results.

4. Finally, procedural adjustments are made where required to bring performance in line with the predetermined objectives.

With the role of objectives in mind, the functions of management can be discussed with the understanding that when these functions are performed, as a whole or as separate entities, they are done so to reach the broad objectives of the organization by establishing and achieving a series of individual and departmental goals.

The overall (broad) objectives of the organization are established or interpreted by top management and discussed with the managers of each major department. From the broad objectives, several specific objectives that apply to each particular department may be identified and stated. These specific objectives are discussed using the four basic steps indicated above. This cycle is repeated at each lower level until the worker level is reached. Here, the supervisor and the worker relate the objectives to specific jobs and tasks. Thus the objectives are integrated at all levels: organization, departments, subunits, and jobs. Each manager then uses his resources by applying the functions of management (planning, organizing, coordinating, directing, and controlling) to reach his specific objectives, which collectively should satisfy the broad objectives of the organization.

THE ESSENTIALS OF PLANNING

As a function of management, planning is the first step in the management process. *Planning* has been defined in many ways, but simply stated, it is deciding what is to be done and determining the best way to do it.

Basically, planning is the process of developing a blueprint or a set of specifications to achieve either a broad or a specific objective. In this respect, planning can be long range or short range. Long-range plans include the overall instructions for reaching objectives or goals in the future; short-range plans usually consist of instructions for accomplishing an immediate specific assignment. For example, a company anticipating an expansion of its operations should properly develop a long-range plan. On the other hand, an assignment to fill a certain order within a certain time would require only a short-range plan. Within the framework of this definition, the function of planning can be reduced to these essentials: (1) understanding the assignment, and (2) developing a plan.

Understanding the Assignment

Normally, planning is necessitated by the manager being given an assignment. The assignment may derive from the inherent nature of his operation in the form of implied or predetermined objectives, or one that is given to him by his superior. In either case, assignments are often vaguely stated and poorly defined. Because the effectiveness of planned action is predicated on the planner having a clear perception of the factors involved, the first step in the planning process is for the manager to obtain a clear understanding of the assignment. Other things being equal, the better the understanding, the better the chances of his plan obtaining the expected results. This understanding can be obtained by systematically analyzing the assignment in the following terms:

1. The specific purpose of the assignment
2. Its relationship to the overall objective of the organization and the specific objectives of the appropriate managerial unit
3. The reason for undertaking the assignment
4. Its relationship to current policies, procedures, and instructions
5. Its priority over other assignments and its claim to existing and potential resources such as money, manpower, materials, time, and space
6. Specific results expected

Once the assignment is clarified, a course of action can be determined and a plan developed to carry it out. Normally, the manager will gain some idea of what his course of action will be in the process of clarifying the assignment. However, for the manager to adapt his action to the assignment, he must of course have a thorough knowledge of the broad objectives of his organization and the specific objectives of his particular operation. Because planning is the initial step of any action, as indicated earlier, objectives give direction to these activities. After the objectives have been clearly established, the manager can use his overall knowledge of this operation to determine how this assignment can be accomplished. Of course, this depends on a combination of circumstances, and there may be any number of courses of action available to him. Regardless of what his course of action may be, he should develop a plan.

Developing a Plan

A plan is a statement indicating what has to be done and how to do it. This statement should answer the questions: *why, what, who, when,* and *how.* The plan may be in the form of a policy, a procedure, or a method; or, it may be a combination of all three. Also a plan may be in the form of a specified document such as a budget or a forecast. Still further, a plan may be self-supporting or a part of a larger plan or a series of plans to form a system. Common categories of plans are identified and briefly discussed below:

POLICY. A policy is a verbal, written, or implied overall guide that sets up the limit and direction in which management action can take place. Unlike objectives, policy describes the principles and rules for action rather than what is to be accomplished. A policy may be as simple as a *No Smoking* sign or as involved as the total foreign policy of the United States. Also, policy may pertain to a certain area or activity such as personnel policy, financial policy, sales policy, and the like, or it may be more restrictive, such as the supervisor of a department telling a new employee that it is his policy that no one eats lunch at his desk. Whether simple or complex, policy establishes the boundaries and the base for action.

PROCEDURE. A procedure describes a series of related tasks that make up the chronological sequence and established way for performing the work to be done. Procedures are more specific than policy, and include step-by-step routine instructions concerning how an operation should be carried out. Like a policy, a procedure can be verbal or written, permanent or temporary. For example, if an employee is asked to go to the front office, pick up the mail for the department, and return it to the supervisor's desk, this of course would be a one-time verbal procedure. However, if this routine were to be an everyday occurrence, it would be developed into a permanent operating procedure.

METHOD. While procedures describe step-by-step instructions for an operation, methods prescribe the manner in which a specific task is to be performed. They outline the specific way and means that a job is to be accomplished. An example of a simple method is when a task like filling out a form is reduced to a certain prescribed way: Line 1: Enter company name; Line 2: Enter company address; Line 3: Enter name of person preparing the form, and so on. This is a method, since the person performing the operation is instructed specifically how to do a certain task.

Forecast. Forecasting is the systematic attempt of looking into the future and drawing certain conclusions based on past experience and facts. This recorded conclusion is a forecast. While a forecast is a form of plan, it is also a tool of planning. Managers find that they can plan more effectively if they first make an assessment of future events. Forecasts are especially applicable to sales, but they can be used for other activities as well.

Budget. Another type of specified plan is a budget. A budget is a statement appropriating certain resources over a specified period against their expected use. Often considered as applying only to money, budgets can be used to allocate time, materials, space, and manpower. Like a forecast, a budget is both a plan and a tool for planning. Also, when actual use is compared to that which was allocated, the budget is a good control device.

When a series of plans are combined, a system is formed. A system is a set of related and interlocking procedures designed to interrelate various elements of an organization in achieving a specific goal. Systems may be contained in one document, or in a series of specific documents or plans. The term *system* as used here is not to be confused with the total system of operations of an organization. Whereas the total operational system includes plans, it also involves the assembly and use of resources for attaining the desired goal of the operation.

THE ESSENTIALS OF ORGANIZING

Organizing has been defined as the arrangement of human and material resources to effect the carrying out of a plan in the most efficient manner possible. Whenever two or more individuals begin to work together toward a common goal, a certain amount of organizing becomes necessary. Even if the goal is a relatively simple two-man task, such as pulling a stump or moving a desk, some organizational procedure or pattern is evident: a plan is followed, efforts are coordinated, and a division of labor is made. Usually, one of the two workmen will take charge of even such simple operations. As the number of persons concerned increases, the relations between these individuals become proportionately more complicated. In large groups of workmen, or in small groups engaged in complex tasks, organizing becomes a basic essential if the goal is to be reached in a reasonable period of time. *Organizing,* reduced to its simplest essentials, is concerned primarily with the process of establishing a pattern and developing a structure by which people can work together to carry out planned activities to attain established goals. It should be obvious, then, that good organization is the foundation upon which proper management must stand. This being so, organizations are discussed separately in the next chapter.

THE ESSENTIALS OF COORDINATING

The third function of management, coordinating, is often treated as an objective of management rather than as a function.[1] Although there is some merit in treating coordinating in this way, for our purpose it can best be understood by including it as one of the management functions. As a function of management, *coordinating* can be defined as the process of communicating with others inside and outside the manager's control to get their cooperation whenever they influence or are influenced by the manager's operation.

As this definition indicates, coordinating is establishing good working relations with those on whom the manager may depend to assist him in achieving the objectives of his operation. This may include both those within or without his organization. Within the organization, a manager has a close relationship with his immediate supervisor, his employees, other managers and supervisors, and the staff members of the organization. Outside the organization, he may need to establish working relations with professional groups and institutions such as community leaders, the clergy, schools and colleges, governmental agencies, and so on. Coordinating permits the manager to cut across organizational lines when the support of others is necessary in carrying out his assignments. It provides for clearance and balance. Whereas there are no set principles for the manager to follow in performing the function of coordinating, this pattern may prove useful:

1. Determine whether and to what extent operations are influenced by internal or external persons or activities.
2. When internal or external people or activities are involved, communicate with them to:
   a. Inform, or get information
   b. Obtain understanding of common purpose
   c. Obtain active support and aid when required
3. Establish means of resolving conflict.
4. Continue to maintain good working relations to further the goal of the management team.

[1] See Leonard J. Kazmier, *Principles of Management,* 2nd ed. (New York: McGraw-Hill Book Company, Inc., 1969), p. 34.

It should be noted that the ways and means of coordinating are also the ways and means of communications. Therefore, this function can be more fully understood when the subject of communications is discussed in Chapter 4.

THE ESSENTIALS OF DIRECTING

The function of *directing* is the process of implementing the planned activities of the organization and using resources in the actual operation. The function of directing is often discussed only in terms of guiding and directing people. Although directing people is obviously a substantial part of the directing function, it should be recognized that directing also involves the manager assuming responsibility for his total operation. This includes assuring that the work goes according to plan by maintaining a steady flow of work, using resources properly, and assuming the responsibility for the end product of his operation being delivered in quality and quantity and within the schedule consistent with the objectives. These tasks are all broadly related to human performance, but none of these is directly transferable to pure manager-subordinate relationships only. The essential factors of direction can be summarized as follows:

1. Transmit through organizational channels:
   a. Organizational objectives
   b. Plans of operation
   c. Procedures and directives
   d. Local policies
2. Implement or determine policy for:
   a. Establishing individual practices
   b. Resolving conflict between plans and actual operation
3. Make decisions and issue orders required to:
   a. Assure a flow and maintenance of resources in proper relation to each other
   b. Maintain integrated procedures
   c. Assure that the end results are consistent with objectives
4. Develop ways and means for improving operations.

As this summary indicates, directing involves both motivating people toward the achievement of the objective and the manipulation of resources aimed at achieving end results. The two, taken together, comprise the overall function of directing, and like other management functions these elements are performed by all managers at all levels of an organization.

THE ESSENTIALS OF CONTROLLING

Controlling, the final function of management, is the process of comparing present and recent operations with some measurable criteria to determine if activities are going according to plan. It is the function of management that requires an operation to be assessed in terms of results.

Because controlling relies heavily on a set of criteria by which performance can be compared and a system by which mistakes and deviations become immediately apparent, essentials of controlling can be expressed and discussed as *performance standards* and *control systems.*

Performance Standards

The criteria by which the effectiveness of an organization is measured are called *standards.* Standards can be administrative or technical, simple or complex. They can be in the form of norms or ratios based on past experience, or they can be established by more precise methods such as testing or exacting measuring. However, to be effective as a means of control, they have the common requirement of serving as a yardstick by which performance can be measured to detect deviations. The means by which performance is measured apply differently at each level of an organization.[2]

At the top level, performance is measured by how well the organization as a whole meets its objectives. The standards used here are of an administrative or psychological nature and are used to measure the long-range performance of the organization. In large organizations, deviations at this level are not readily detected; in smaller ones, deviations become apparent in a shorter period of time.

At the middle level, performance can be more specific, and standards can be more useful in spotting deviations from the planned action. In profit-oriented organizations, standards concern output and results such as sales volume, production increases, profit ratios, growth rate and other measurable entities that directly affect the successful performance of the organization. In nonprofit organizations, standards are concerned with the service provided by the organization. Standards at the middle level can be used to detect deviations on a much shorter range basis, and thus are more effective as a means of control.

At the bottom level, performance is measured on a more specific and individualized basis. Standards for such things as worker output, manpower

[2] Stanley E. Seashore, "Criteria of Organizational Effectiveness, *Michigan Business Review,* July 1963, pp. 26ff.

turnover, machine downtime, salesman quotas, and number of people served can be developed. At this level, standards can be used by the manager to spot deviations almost immediately, thereby increasing their effectiveness.

In viewing standards by organizational level, it becomes apparent that standards closely approximate the objectives of the organization. This being so, standards can also be used to provide the measurable criteria for applying the management-by-objective concept discussed earlier.

Control Systems

Whereas standards provide the manager with the means to measure performance, in order to be used as a control, a system is needed to bring exceptions to the manager's attention so action can be taken. Basically, there are two types of systems by which this can be done. One is by personal observation, where the manager is in direct contact with the operation, knows what is going on, and may enter into the operation at any step that requires redirection. This type of system is obviously possible only in relatively small groups that are located in one place. On the other hand, whenever operations are widespread and of such magnitude that the manager is unable to watch them directly, the manager must rely on records and reports.

CONTROLLING BY EXCEPTION. Regardless of the system, it should bring to the attention of the manager those performances that are not in accordance with the established standard or norm. This is called controlling or managing by exception. It suggests that only exceptional situations be brought to the manager's attention. It further suggests that he should be concerned with such things as unmet schedules, breakdowns in operations, and quality standards not being reached rather than with the details of the operation that are going according to plan.[3] The controlling-by-exception concept has the obvious advantage of freeing the manager's time so that he can concentrate on those things that cannot be resolved by his subordinates. It may be a disadvantage, however, if the manager relies so heavily on controls that he isolates himself from his operation. Despite this possible disadvantage, controlling by exception is a valued concept, and when taken with standards, is an essential part of the controlling process.

BUILT-IN CONTROLS. As stated above, controlling relies heavily on deviations from the established standards being brought to the attention of the manager. This can best be accomplished when controls are built into the operational plan where they will function automatically. Built-in con-

[3] When these exceptions are brought to the manager's attention, they may be corrected on the spot or through the problem-solving process discussed in Chapter 16.

trols serve as a thermostat, signaling the manager when some part of the operation is unsatisfactory. Built-in controls may be a report or some other type of statistical data, a checklist, or, with the use of data processing and automated or mechanical equipment, controls may be a part of the operational design of the equipment. Built-in controls are not feasible for many operations, but they should be considered in all control systems.

OVER-CONTROLLING. In developing or applying a control system, a manager should be very cautious not to over-control his operation. The manager who insists on "seeing everything before it goes out," or requires information that makes little or no contribution to the effectiveness of his operation, runs the risk of stifling the initiative of his employees and becoming overburdened with the process of analyzing and interpreting information at the expense of more important matters. One means of avoiding over-controlling is to periodically question the need for all controlling devices and to devise a way in which only exceptional matters are brought to the attention of those who have a need to know, or who are required to take action.

INTERRELATION AND APPLICATION OF FUNCTIONS

Viewing the functions of management as discussed in the preceding sections is useful in understanding the management process and in gaining a perspective as to how the management personnel of an organization work together in achieving the organization's objectives. Also, this can serve as a fundamental guide for the individual manager when carrying out his duties and responsibilities. However, as pointed out in the introduction to the chapter, when applied on the job, the function becomes interrelated and integrated since no manager performs all of the functions in their entirety, nor in the sequence in which they are given. This is particularly true at the work management level. When applied in the process of getting the work out, functions become less distinct and more integrated. This is not to say that the functions of planning, organizing, coordinating, directing, and controlling are not performed, only that they lose their identity and become cross-sectional in their application. For the purpose of this book, work management is identified as the supervisory process and consists of five activities.[4] These five activities and their relationship to the functions of management are identified and briefly discussed below.

[4] This concept was adapted from Elmore Petersen, E. Grosvenor Plowman, and Joseph H. Trickett, *Business Organization and Management,* 5th ed. (Homewood, Illinois: Richard D. Irwin, Inc., 1962), pp. 7ff.

Clarifying and Stating Purpose

It is the supervisor's job to work within the limits of his assignment and the policies of his organization to meet a predetermined objective according to established standards. This means that although the supervisory manager does not normally establish the overall guidelines for the operation of his unit or department, it is the supervisor's job to clarify these policies, standards, and objectives to his workers. This means that they must be translated in meaningful and, where possible, measurable terms. These statements (oral or written) then serve the manager as a basic and functional guideline for the management of his department. To do this the manager must have a thorough understanding of the assignment, be knowledgeable of the policies of his organization and the standards pertaining to his particular work, and be keenly aware of the objectives of his department in particular and his organization in general. This activity is related both to objectives and to the function of planning.

Allocating and Scheduling Resources

To achieve the objectives of his department, the manager must allocate and schedule his resources in such a way that they can be efficiently, effectively, and economically used. This requires assigning employees where their skills will be best used, developing procedures, methods, and an overall system (normally in the form of a work plan) that will assure that deadlines are met, resources are properly used, and the work of his department progresses in an orderly and consistent pattern. Obviously, this activity is related to both planning and organizing.

Taking Action and Getting Results

This is the very heart of supervisory management. Results are not produced in a vacuum. Action must be taken to bring them about. Employees must be motivated, resources manipulated, control exercised, and human and nonhuman resources integrated and directed toward the objective. In taking action, the interrelations of the various functions are exhibited better than in any other activity. Although this step can be classified under the general function of directing, other functions come into play. To obtain results, procedures may have to be changed, on-the-spot corrections made, resources rescheduled and reallocated, and the activity coordinated within and outside the manager's department. In addition, in carrying out this activity, the manager must be keenly aware of the policies, standards, and objectives of his department. In short, taking action and getting results is not only the heart but the "guts" of supervisory management as well.

Gathering Information and Measuring Performance

In this activity, the manager is in the constant process of observing his operation and reviewing records to detect deviations from the norm established by the standards. In this process, the manager evaluates, assesses, and reconciles the difference between what the performance actually is and what it should be by taking whatever action necessary to bring the two into alignment. While gathering information and measuring performance is basically a controlling function, taking corrective action is more closely related to directing.

Improving Work Performance

An important activity of the supervisory process is improving the performance of the manager's department. This involves counseling and training employees, improving and simplifying work methods, developing and implementing cost-reduction programs, and a host of technical and managerial activities that the manager takes to improve the overall performance of his department in general and each employee in particular. Performance that needs improvement is normally detected during the controlling process, but there may be shred outs from the other functions as well.

To sum up, it can now be seen that the functions of management are useful not only in understanding the management process but in serving as a fundamental guide for managerial action as well.

KEY POINT SUMMARY

1. In studying the functions of management, it should be understood that although planning, organizing, coordinating, directing, and controlling can be discussed as separate entities, in both the study of management and in actual practice they are often interrelated, making them practically operationally indistinguishable.
2. Objectives have an important role in management since they give the manager direction in carrying out the management process.
3. Objectives are of two types: broad and specific.
    a. Broad objectives are those that spell out or imply the general purpose of the organization.
    b. Specific objectives are the results each component and each member are expected to make toward the broad objective of the operation.

4. The process of stating objectives in measurable terms, making them compatible at all levels of the organization and an integrated part of the organization is called management by objective.

5. The process of deciding what is to be done and determine the best way to do it is planning.

6. The essentials of planning involve understanding the assignment and developing the plan. Plans can be divided into five categories:
   a. Policy
   b. Procedure
   c. Method
   d. Forecast
   e. Budget

   When plans are combined to interlock and interrelate various elements of an operation, they form a system.

7. The function of organizing is defined as the process of establishing a pattern and developing a structure in such a way that planned activities can be carried out. (This function is discussed in the next chapter.)

8. The function of coordinating is the process of communicating with those inside and outside the manager's control to obtain their cooperation.
   a. Within the organization these include: immediate supervisor, employees, other managers, and staff personnel.
   b. Outside the organization, the manager may want to contact persons in professional groups and organizations.

9. Directing includes implementing the planned activities of the organization and using resources in the actual operation. It includes both directing people and directing the manager's operation.
   a. Directing people is the process of motivating the manpower resources toward the achievement of objectives.
   b. Directing operations is the process of manipulating nonhuman resources aimed at achieving end results.

10. Controlling is the process of comparing present or recent operations with some measurable criteria to determine if activities are going according to plan. Essentially, effective controlling consists of:
    a. Standards
    b. Control systems

11. Standards are criteria that serve as yardsticks by which performance is measured to detect deviations.

12. Control systems are of two basic types:
    a. Personal observation—used in small groups that are in one place
    b. Records and reports—used when the operation is widespread
13. Controlling by exception means that only exceptional situations be brought to the manager's attention for his consideration and action.
14. Controls that are built into operational plans are effective in controlling since they function automatically by signaling the manager when parts of the operation are unsatisfactory.
15. When applied to work management, the five functions of management become interrelated and make up a series of activities that can be viewed as the supervisory process. These activities include:
    a. Clarifying and stating purpose
    b. Allocating and scheduling resources
    c. Taking action and getting results
    d. Gathering information and measuring performance
    e. Improving work performance

DISCUSSION QUESTIONS

1. What is the role of objectives in management? Explain the two types of objectives and discuss the purpose of each.
2. As a concept, what is management by objectives and how is this concept applied?
3. What is planning and what are the essentials of this management function?
4. In clarifying an assignment, what are the factors to be considered?
5. What are the five categories into which plans can be classified and what are the characteristics of each? What is a system?
6. What is organizing and what is the essential element?
7. Essentially, what does the concept of controlling include? What are its basic functions?
8. What two factors are involved in directing? Explain.
9. What is a standard and how are standards used?
10. Is controlling by exception a valid concept? What are the advantages and disadvantages of this method of control?
11. Built-in controls serve what useful purpose?
12. What is the relationship between the supervisory process and the functions of management? Relate each function to the five activities that make up the supervisory process.

CASE PROBLEM

Case 2–1

A small business engaged in the manufacture, sales, and service of a calculating device was organized as indicated below:

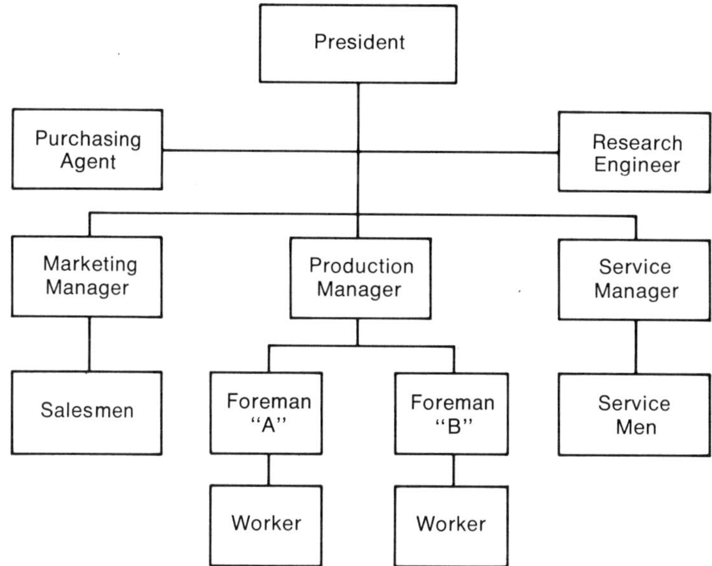

Questions

1. *What is the overall objective of this organization?*
2. *What is the specific objective of each element of the organization?*
3. *What role does each play in achieving the overall objective?*
4. *How could the various elements be classified as to top, middle, and first-line managers, and workers?*
5. *In regard to the five functions of management, which element would be most concerned with each function?*
6. *Which element would be most concerned with administrative management? Supervisory management?*
7. *Discuss the following:*
   a. *How each manager could integrate the objective of his department with the broad objective of the organization.*
   b. *How the essentials of each function of management would be applied by each level of management.*

SELECTED REFERENCES

ALLEN, LOUIS A., *Management and Organization,* Chap. 2. New York: McGraw-Hill Book Company, Inc., 1958.

AMRINE, HAROLD T., JOHN A. RITCHEY, and OLIVER S. HULLEY, *Manufacturing, Organization, and Management* (2nd ed.), Chap. 26. Englewood Cliffs, N.J.: Prentice-Hall, Inc., 1966.

DALE, ERNEST, and L. C. MICHELON, *Modern Management Methods,* Chap. 1. Cleveland, Ohio: The World Publishing Company, 1966.

KAZMIER, LEONARD J., *Principles of Management* (2nd ed.), Unit 2. New York: McGraw-Hill Book Company, Inc., 1969.

MCFARLAND, DALTON E., *Management Principles and Practices,* Chaps. 4, 5, and 8. New York: The Macmillan Company, 1958.

PETERSEN, ELMORE, E. GROSVENOR PLOWMAN, and JOSEPH M. TRICKETT, *Business Organization and Management* (5th ed.), Chap. 1. Homewood, Ill.: Richard D. Irwin, Inc., 1962.

RICHARDS, MAX D., and WILLIAM A. NIELANDER, *Readings in Management* (3rd ed.), Chap. 7, Sec. 25. Cincinnati, Ohio: South-Western Publishing Company, 1969.

TERRY, GEORGE R., *Principles of Management* (4th ed.), Chaps. 1 and 5. Homewood, Ill.: Richard D. Irwin, Inc., 1966.

3

Organizations

Central to developing a frame of reference for carrying out the management process is gaining a fundamental understanding of organizations. It should be understood that an organization is formed when two or more people are brought together to achieve a common objective or goal. In management these organizations take three fundamental forms. First, there is the formal organization, which constitutes the framework in which the business of the enterprise is carried out. Second, there is an informal organization, in which individuals band together for various reasons within the framework of a formal organization. Finally, there are labor unions, in which the employees of a formal organization are further formally organized to meet some common objective. The first two forms of organizations, the formal and informal, are consistent in that they are common to all work activities; the labor union organization is a variable depending on whether or not the employees of the formal organization have been organized by a particular labor union. The primary emphasis of this chapter will be on discussing the structure of formal organizations, with the informal organization and the labor union organization being discussed only in sufficient detail to be understood when they are brought up again in other chapters. This chapter includes these major topics: (1) the basis of a formal organization, (2) formal organizational structure, (3) principles of organization, (4) informal organizations, and (5) organized labor.

THE BASIS OF A FORMAL ORGANIZATION

As indicated in the previous chapter, whenever two or more people begin to work together toward a common goal, the work must be organized in some way. This concept is as old as recorded history. It was evident in the advice Moses received from his father-in-law, Jethro. When Moses received this visit in the wilderness, he was staggering under the same problem that has all but killed many modern leaders. He was attempting to perform the entire job himself.

According to Exodus XVIII, Jethro observed Moses' methods and saw what was wrong.

> "What you are doing," he said, "is not good. You and the people with you will wear yourselves out; for the thing is too heavy for you; you are not able to perform it alone." So Moses gave heed to the voice of his father-in-law, and did all that he had said. Moses chose able men out of all Israel, and made them heads over the people, rulers of thousands, rulers of hundreds, rulers of fifties, and rulers of ten. And they judged the people at all seasons: the hard cases they brought to Moses, but any small matter they judged themselves.[1]

In short, Moses developed a formal organization.

Today, the modern organization is based on well-defined jobs, each bearing a definite measure of authority, responsibility, and accountability arranged in a prescribed pattern to form a structure by which formal channels of communications can be established and interaction developed among various elements of the group. Its purpose is to provide the framework for coordinating, directing, and controlling the planned activities of an organization. But like in the days of Moses, the principle is the same. Whenever any effort requires the joint services of two or more people, the activities must be divided in some way so that the work of one member of the group does not duplicate or overlap the efforts of others. The work of a formal organization can be divided in several ways depending on the size and nature of the organization.

FUNCTION. The most common way in which work or activities is divided is by function or major homogeneous activities such as personnel, finance, productions, sales, or other elements required in the operation of the organization. Many organizations are divided in this way and have the advantage of keeping like functions together.

PRODUCT. Work activities may be grouped by product. This grouping may be used by an organization making and/or marketing different product lines. For example, one plant of an organization may make only shoes and the other may make only automobile tires, and so on. Or within a small organization, one department may make a certain type of fishing line while

[1] *The Holy Bible,* Revised Standard version.

another department may make reels. In either case, it may be to the advantage of the organization to divide the work by type of product. The same could be true for retail organizations or governmental agencies. They may be divided along the line of the service they provide.

Location. When activities are divided according to location, territorial or geographical aspects of the work are taken into account. This may be done by bringing all activities of a particular area together under a single organization on a regional basis. This grouping is used for both service and manufacturing organizations and pertains to organizations that have wide geographical operations.

Process. When a product is produced by a series of operations such as spinning, weaving, bleaching, dyeing, inspecting, boxing, or shipping, the division of work by process may be used. Each process or sequence can be identified as a separate division within the organization.

Customers. In certain organizations, activities may be more appropriately divided according to the type of customer they serve. For example, if an organization can break its service down to certain types of customers or categories of customers, dividing the organization accordingly may be an advantage.

FORMAL ORGANIZATIONAL STRUCTURE

For an organization to achieve its objective, not only should the work be divided, but some form of structure must be developed so that the work of the organization can be carried out. The formal structure of an organization is formed by developing activities into functional components and arranging these components along managerial lines. It sets up the framework for developing a communications channel by which the manager can coordinate, direct, and control the activities of the operation.

Types of Formal Structures

The formal structure of an organization depends on the size of the operation, the nature of its activities, and a host of other factors. Nonetheless, there are two basic structures that can be modified and adapted to the variables of most organizations—the line and the line staff structures.

Line Structure. This is the simplest form of organization and is shown in Figure 4. As this figure indicates, the functions of the organization

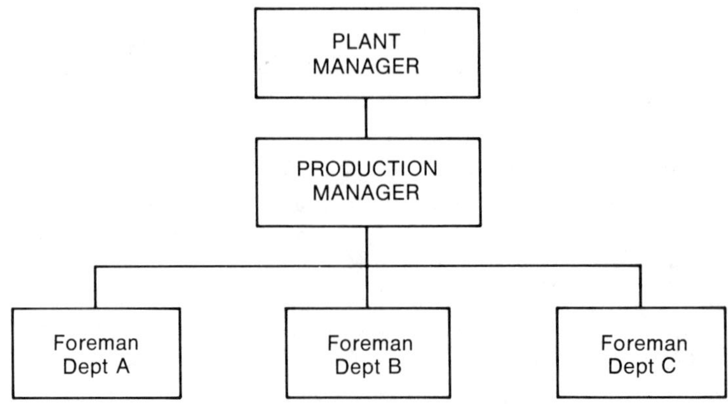

Figure 4 Line Organization Chart

are grouped in three levels coinciding with the three levels of management. At each level, the manager is responsible to the level immediately above him and for directing those immediately below, thus forming a vertical line of authority. This form of structure is used by most small operations and is the basic structure on which most organizations are developed.

LINE STAFF STRUCTURE. In large organizations, a need normally exists to add specialists to the organization to assist in certain areas. These specialists perform duties referred to as staff functions and may consist of a single individual or a major component of an organization, such as a division. The addition of staff functions of personnel and purchasing creates the line staff type of organization as shown in Figure 5.

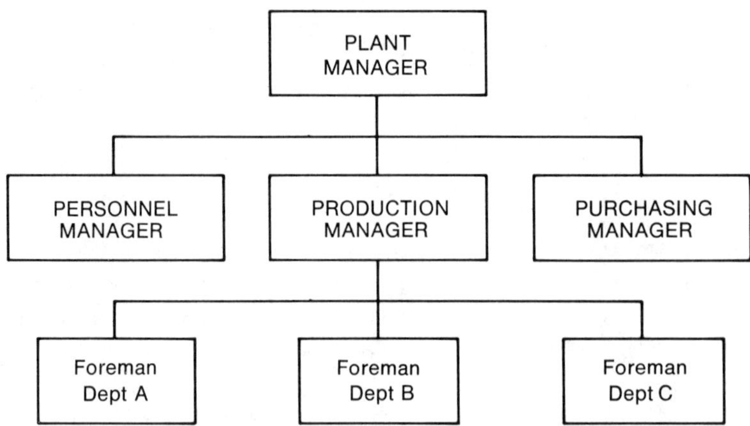

Figure 5 Line and Staff Organization Chart

Line and Staff Relationships

In the traditional sense, the role of the staff specialist is advisory and supplemental, freeing the line manager of technical, special, and detail duties. This means that the staff personnel of an organization are removed from the line of action in order that they may counsel, advise, and assist the line. Staff functions are responsible for getting the facts upon which decisions on appropriate actions may be based. The staff should be ready to provide technically competent advice. They continually audit and appraise line operations, thus determining the effectiveness of both policies and practices. The results of such appraisals, together with the best information obtainable from other organizations and from research, are then placed at the disposal of the line organization. The major responsibilities of a staff division include: (1) formulation of policy, (2) program planning, (3) constant review and appraisal (including the definition of criteria and controls), (4) consultation, and (5) service to the operating line.[2]

Although the role of the staff specialist has changed in recent years, giving him (or his function) more authority, the wise advice of the noted international management consultant, Ernest Dale, still applies:

> The staff specialist should get line managers to accept his ideas by using argument and negotiation rather than by forcing his authority upon them. His advice, therefore, must not only be sound; it must be tactfully presented as well. This requires much diplomacy on the part of the staff specialist. Suggestions should be integrated with line operations and with other staff proposals and should be carefully considered and tested. Informal checks might be made with the line before the ideas are formally presented to assure that they are practical and thus forestall any possible resentments. The ideas should be presented at the right time and in language understandable to the operators. There should be scope for amendments. Finally, the staff specialist's proposal should not be introduced until it is approved in its final form by the joint superior of the staff specialist and the line executives affected (many companies insist on the agreement of all line executives). Though credit for success often goes to the operators, staff specialists must remember that success is often as much dependent on them as upon the man on the line. Exceptions to the rule of staff consultation and coordination with the line should be made only under extenuating circumstances.[3]

[2] See Dale Yoder, *Personnel Principles and Policies—Modern Manpower Management* (Englewood Cliffs, N.J.: Prentice-Hall, Inc., © 1952), pp. 21-22.

[3] Ernest Dale, *Reconciling Staff Specialists and Line Operators in Planning and Developing the Company Organization Structure,* Research Report No. 20 (New York: American Management Association, 1952), pp. 76ff.

Departmentation

The functional configuration of most organizations is made up by grouping like functions together into departments. These departments evolve from operational experience that determines which functions of the organization should be grouped together. Departments can be either large or small, line or staff; but when they are logically organized, they develop the basis for the various people of an organization to work toward a common objective. The way in which departments are organized will, of course, depend on the functions and the type of organization. Typical ways in which departments are organized are shown in Figure 6 and Figure 7.

As the two figures indicate, departmentation allows the functions of an organization to be grouped in like clusters and provides a means by which the structure of the organization can be arranged in a logical pattern. For example, in Figure 6 the major functions of the organization have been divided into four departments: controller, merchandising, publicity, and store manager. This allows like functions of each department to be grouped into small units all the way down to the individual employee. The same concept is shown in Figure 7. By grouping the predominant functions under five major departments, marketing, industrial relations, and so on, a basic structure is formed for achieving the objective of the organization.

PRINCIPLES OF ORGANIZATION

Regardless of whether an organization is large or small, line or staff, to be effective in providing a basic structure for people to work together in achieving predetermined objectives, certain principles apply. The principles, which are discussed in this section, establish the fundamental basis for forming these relationships and are equally applicable to the organization as a whole as well as to its smallest element. Since these principles will be dealt with either directly or indirectly in other chapters, they are discussed here only in sufficient detail to form a frame of reference.

THE PRINCIPLE OF AUTHORITY. This means that for an organization to carry out its planned activities toward a predetermined objective, there must be some means by which the efforts of the members are directed. The authority to direct the members and activities of a formal organization is vested in its managers. Since the responsibility and hierarchy of the management group were discussed in previous chapters, they need not be repeated here. However, it is to be understood that the authority for carrying out the work of the organization is consistent with the three levels of man-

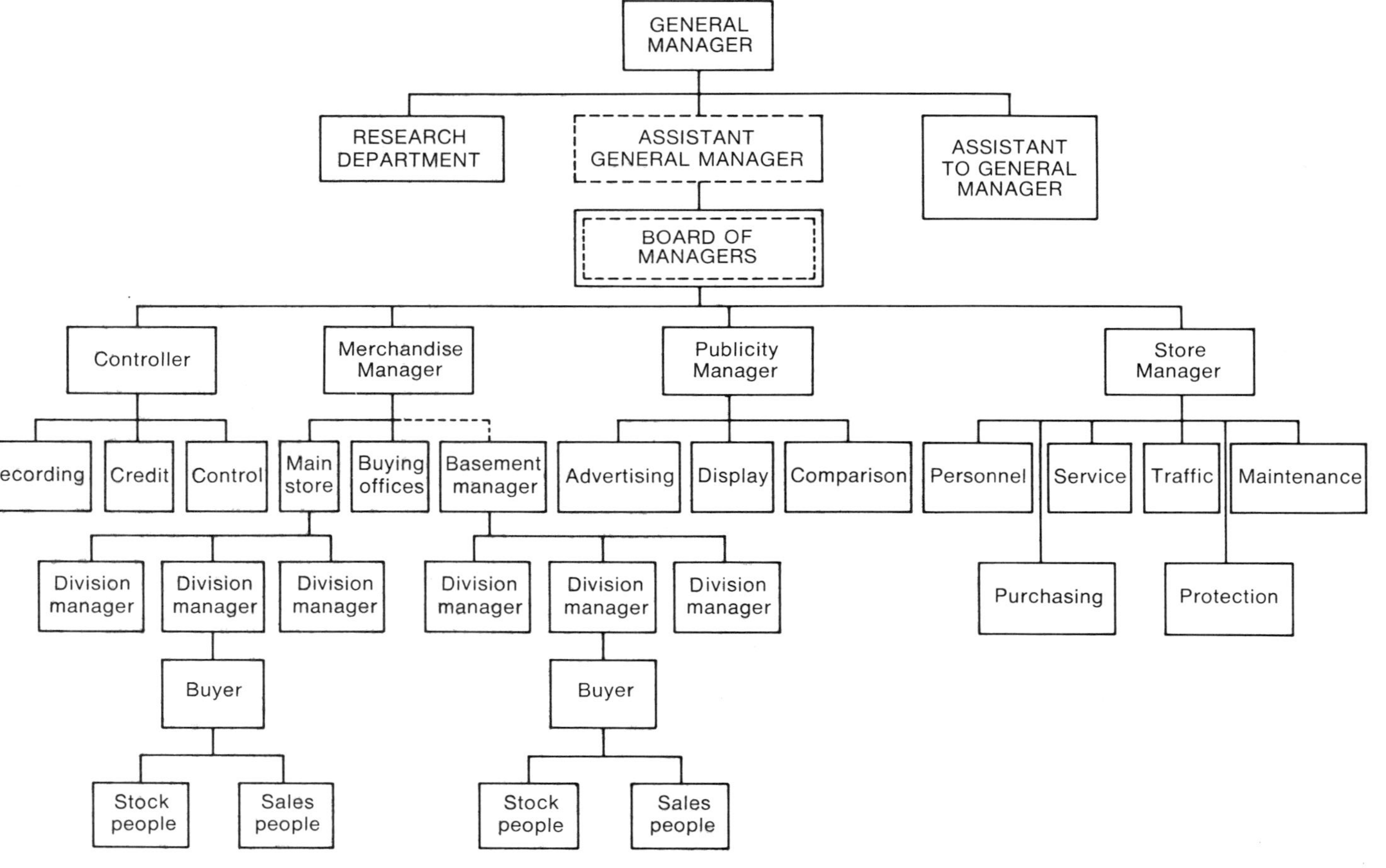

Figure 6 Typical Organization Chart for Large Department Store (Source: Gerald Pintel and Jay Diamond, *Retailing*, p. 78. © 1971, Prentice-Hall, Inc.)

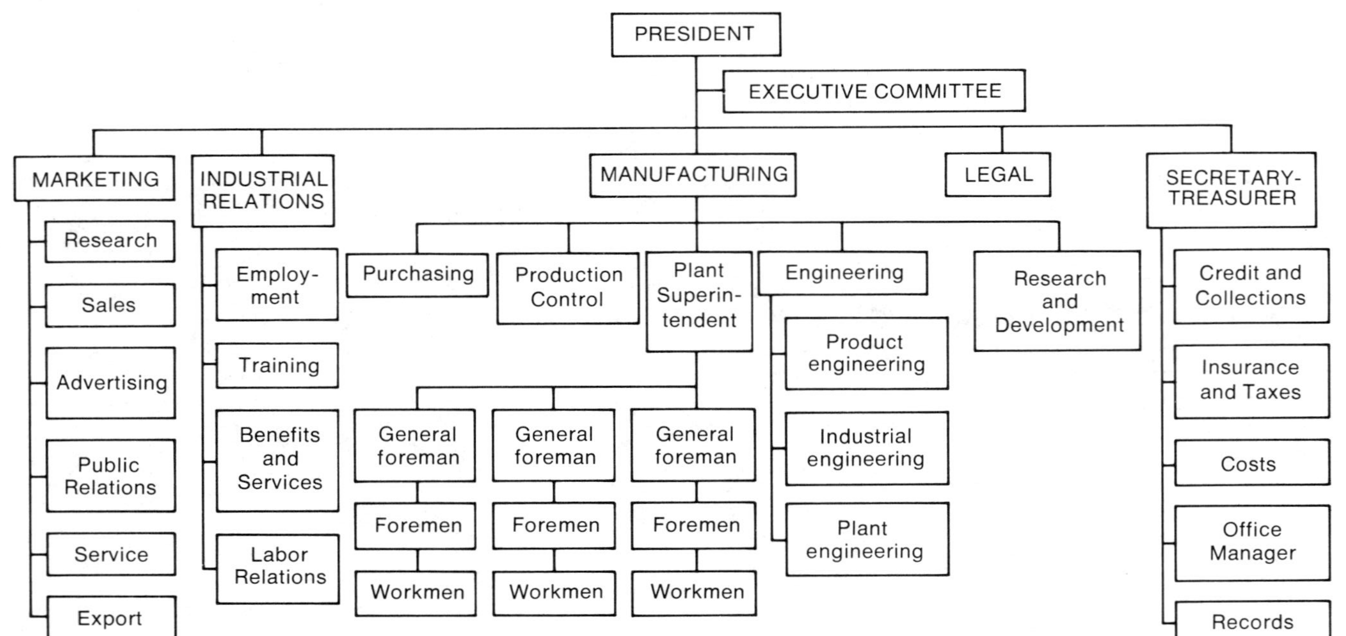

Figure 7 Typical Organization Chart for Medium-size Manufacturing Company (Source: Harold T. Amrine, John A. Ritchey, and Oliver S. Hulley, *Manufacturing Organization and Management*, 2nd Edition, p. 30. © 1966, Prentice-Hall, Inc.)

agement, and authority flows from top to bottom along the vertical line of the organizational structure. Also, it is to be remembered that authority is inherent in all managerial positions.

THE UNITY OF COMMAND PRINCIPLE. This simply means that one man should have one boss. This principle is illustrated in both Figures 4 and 5. The worker is responsible to the first-line manager; the first-line manager reports only to the middle manager; the middle manager reports only to the top manager. The staff functions in Figure 5 are not in the authority line; therefore, they have no direct authority over the functions below them. Also, this principle implies that the manager at each level is responsible for the operation he manages and the results of that operation.

THE SPAN OF CONTROL PRINCIPLE. This means that in order to control an operation, there must be a limit as to the number of individuals that a manager controls. The number of people that one manager can supervise depends on several factors. Among these are:

a. *The manager's ability.* The greater the manager's mental and physical ability, the more people he can manage.

b. *Kind of work.* If the work is routine, simple, or repetitive, it is obvious that the manager can control more people. On the other hand, if the work is highly skilled and complex, more attention is required by the manager.

c. *Work the manager must do himself.* If the manager has numerous and special tasks that cannot be delegated, or if he has many special projects, then his span of control is limited.

d. *Training requirements.* This will offset the manager's span of control if it is unduly high as a result of starting new assignments or turnover, for instance.

e. *Physical location.* If the workers are spread over a wide area, the manager cannot control them as easily as if they were grouped together.

These factors make it clear that there is no magic number that works in all cases.

THE PRINCIPLE OF HOMOGENEOUS ASSIGNMENTS. This means that like jobs should be grouped together, and like duties within a job should be similar in nature. This principle is applied when major functions of an organization are grouped together by departments as discussed earlier. At the operational level, this means that the manager should avoid the duplicating or overlapping of jobs and unclear and dissimilar work assignments. Not only will this help in training his employees, but permit the individual employee to be more productive. If work is not assigned homogeneously, the employee will be confused and poor work will result.

THE PRINCIPLE OF DELEGATION OF AUTHORITY. This means that whenever a person is given the responsibility for doing a job, he must also be given the authority necessary to accomplish it. It also requires that a responsibility be transferred to another person only when that person is prepared to assume it, and full authority must be given at the time of the responsibility. When authority is delegated, it should be remembered that the person delegating the authority is not relieved of accountability of the duties delegated. Delegation of authority is the essence of a formal organization. Unless each management level is willing and able to pass on to their subordinates the authority and responsibility for operating their departments, a formal organization is of little use. There could be no division of labor or functions or departments. Both organizational charts shown in Figures 6 and 7 illustrate this point. For example, the merchandising manager indicated in Figure 6 must delegate some of his authority and responsibility to the main store manager. The main store manager in turn must give each division manager the authority and responsibility for doing his job and so on down to the stock and sales people who must be given the authority and responsibility for doing their particular jobs.

As it will be amplified in other chapters, like other principles, the five principles of organization often overlap and merge together on the job. However, by keeping the basic points of each principle in mind, the manager can organize and plan his work more effectively.

INFORMAL ORGANIZATIONS

In forming a frame of reference for understanding and applying the principles and concepts pertaining to the formal organization, the manager should recognize that in addition to the formal organization there is also an informal organization that he must deal with. In any organization involving a large number of people, smaller groups, often appear in which the individuals are aware of some common bonds, making them feel closer to one another than to "outsiders." These groups may have as their core interest some specific aspect of the operation that is common to them, or some other experiences, such as proximity of work stations or neighborhoods, or social ties. Because members of such groups feel a certain amount of closeness to one another, they normally prefer to deal with one another. The members of the group talk things over among themselves; they prefer to help one another; they "promote" one another. This process tends to erect an "informal organization" within the prescribed formal organization reflected in the organizational chart with its definite lines of responsibility and authority. Since the informal organization will be discussed at various points throughout the book, it is mentioned here to keep the discussion in perspective. The manager should remember that the informal organization must never be allowed to set aside the responsibility pattern reflected in the formal organizational chart. The informal organization should never be allowed to become a major factor in competition with the formal organization. To allow it to do so is to divide responsibilities and loyalties and to confuse the personnel involved. Fortunate is the organization in which the formal and informal patterns coincide. Such organizations are "going places" and tend to become models of effectiveness.

Also, the manager will find it futile and frequently disruptive to attempt to stamp out informal organizations wherever they fail to coincide with formal patterns. A more positive approach is to recognize and to take into account their existence within his activity and to use them whenever feasible to foster the blending of people into a smoothly functioning operational system. This blending is called teamwork and will be treated as a separate chapter later in the book.

ORGANIZED LABOR

A third type of organization that the manager is often required to deal with is labor organizations. Historically, the purpose of organized labor has been to give employees more equal power to bargain collectively with their employers for such things as more pay and better working conditions. Through this process, many organizations have been formed. Although most of these organizations are affiliated with a single national organization (AFL-CIO), there is not one organization that represents all union members. Therefore, in any one organization, employees may belong to several different union organizations. For example, one union may represent the electrical workers of the organization, another the truckers, and still another the clerical employees. This does not mean that the majority of employees belong to some form of labor organization. In fact, the opposite is true. Of the approximately 80 million American workers, about one-third belong to organized labor. This may lead to the conclusion that labor management relationships are unimportant to the study of management. Although a manager may never be associated with an organization that has a union, the potential for his employees to join a union is always there. This is made clear in the law that provides the basic guidelines for management-labor relations. This law is the *National Labor Relations Act* or *Wagner Act,* as revised by the *Taft-Hartley Act.* This law is very complicated and difficult to understand. But three of its fundamental elements, which establish the framework for management-labor relations, should be understood by every manager.

Employee Rights

The Taft-Hartley Act guarantees employees the right to bargain collectively with their employers and to join unions. Part of the law reads as follows:

> Employees shall have the right to self-organization, to form, join, or assist labor organizations, to bargain collectively through representatives of their own choosing, and to engage in other concerted activities, for the purpose of collective bargaining or other mutual aid or protection, and shall have the right to refrain from any or all of such activities except to the extent that such right may be affected by an agreement requiring membership in a labor organization as a condition of employment. . . .

This means that an employee can join or not join a union with one exception. This exception is that when an organization is covered under a union shop contract, the employees must join the union in a specified period of time. This is a clause in the contract and according to the *Taft-Hartley Act,* the time can be no less than thirty days.

Employer Unfair Labor Practices

The *Taft-Hartley Act* establishes five unfair labor practices that an employer cannot use. These practices are of particular importance to the supervisor, for the law makes it clear that the employer (company) is responsible for the acts of his supervisors. The five practices are identified below:

1. Employers cannot interfere with employees in their right to bargain collectively with their own representatives. This means that a supervisor should be particularly careful not to discriminate between a union and a nonunion employee.

2. Employers cannot dominate or interfere with the formation or administration of labor organizations, financially or otherwise. This means that all unions should be given equal treatment. One union cannot be given preferential treatment over another. It also means that the supervisor should not interfere or become involved in the union activities of his employees.

3. Employers cannot discriminate against employees in hiring or in tenure of employment because of their union membership or activity. This simply means that a supervisor should be very cautious not to let an employee's membership in a union influence his decision to hire, fire, or lay off an employee. In cases where the organization has a union shop clause in its contract, an employee may be fired if he has not paid his dues.

4. Employers cannot discharge or discriminate against employees because they have filed charges against the company. This means that employees cannot be

penalized for bringing a legal charge against their company or for testifying in legal hearings.

5. Employers cannot refuse to bargain collectively with the employee representatives. The exception here is that the organization does not have to bargain with its supervisors or other management personnel. While supervisors may join unions, they cannot participate in collective bargaining with their employers.

Union Unfair Labor Practices

The *Taft-Hartley Act* also makes provision for unfair union practices.

1. Unions cannot force employees to join a union unless a legal union shop exists in the plant. They cannot interfere with the employer's selection of representatives for collective bargaining.

2. Unions cannot pressure employers to force employees to join a union or discriminate against employees who have been denied union membership or who have been let out of the union unless they have failed to pay their dues and initiation fees under a union shop agreement.

3. Unions cannot refuse to bargain collectively with employers if they are the legal representatives of the employees.

4. Unions cannot engage in secondary boycotts to force an employer or self-employed person to stop doing business with any other person or business. They cannot strike to force an employer to assign work to one union rather than another. Unions cannot strike to force an employer to recognize a union which is not certified as the legal representative of the employees.

5. Unions cannot charge excessive or discriminatory fees.

6. Unions cannot cause an employer to pay for services that are not performed or not to be performed.

Although the conflicts stemming from labor-management relations and their implications on such things as teamwork will be explored in another chapter, in concluding, one point should be remembered by the supervisor. Each manager, whether he is top, middle, or first-line, is part of management and as such he should stand firmly by his organization in all labor-management relations. This is an important point to remember in developing a management-minded philosophy.

KEY POINT SUMMARY

1. In developing a frame of reference for carrying out the management process, the manager should develop a basic understanding of three types of organizations:

a. The formal organization
b. The informal organization
c. Labor union organizations

2. The purpose of a formal organization is to provide a structure and framework for coordinating, directing, and controlling the planned activities of an organization necessary for the people working together to achieve its predetermined objectives.
3. When two or more people work together, work must be divided to preclude overlapping of duties and responsibilities. Some of the common ways in which work is divided in a formal organization include:
   a. Function
   b. Product
   c. Location
   d. Process
   e. Customers
4. To carry out the work in a formal organization, the activities of an organization must be structured along managerial lines. Two common organizational structures are:
   a. The line structure
   b. The line staff structure
5. The primary role of the staff specialist is to assist line personnel in carrying out the objectives of the organization. In performing this function, the staff member has no direct authority over the line. Therefore he must establish a sound relationship with the operational personnel to get his ideas and procedures across.
6. The functional configuration of most formal organizations is made up of grouping like functions together by departments, which in turn makes up the operational structure of the organization.
7. For an organization to be effective in reaching its objective, it must be organized around certain fundamental principles. The principles are:
   a. Authority
   b. Unity of command
   c. Span of control
   d. Homogeneous assignments
   e. Delegation of authority
8. Within the framework of a formal organization, people with like interests and goals tend to band together and form informal organizations. In dealing with informal organizations, the manager should remember two points.

   a. Never let the informal organization take over the responsibilities and authority of the formal organization.
   b. Try to blend the goals of the informal organization with those of the formal organization.

9. Other organizations that the manager should understand are labor union organizations. The basic rules for working with these organizations are covered in the *Taft-Hartley Act,* which includes three elements of which the manager should be aware:
   a. The right of employees to bargain collectively
   b. Employer unfair labor practices
   c. Union unfair labor practices
10. In working with the union, the manager should always remember that as part of management, he should support his organization's position.

DISCUSSION QUESTIONS

1. In developing a frame of reference for the management process, what three types of organizations must the manager take into account? What is the relationship among these organizations?
2. What is the basis of a formal organization? How can work in an organization be divided?
3. What are two common types of organizational structure? What is the basic difference between each type?
4. What is the responsibility of the staff specialist? What is his relationship with line personnel?
5. What should the staff specialist consider when working with line personnel?
6. What is meant by departmentation? How are departments formed? What is the relationship between departments and the formal organizational structure?
7. What is the relationship between the five fundamental principles of organization and the formal organization structure as follows:
   a. Authority and each level of management
   b. Unity of command and staff specialists
   c. Span of control and the division of work
   d. Delegation of authority and the organization achieving its predetermined objectives
8. What is an informal organization? What should the manager consider when dealing with an informal organization?
9. Why should the manager understand labor unions? With what essential information should the manager become familiar in each of the elements of the *Taft-Hartley Act:*
   a. Employee rights

b. Employer unfair labor practices
c. Union unfair labor practices

10. The statement was made that a manager should always support his organization in labor-management relations. Why? Is there a conflict between this position and developing a people-minded philosophy?

11. What principle or principles are involved in the following instances?
    a. The manager who finds that he is receiving instructions and orders from staff personnel as well as his own supervisors.
    b. The manager who finds it hard to organize his work and the work of his department due to his many diversified duties.
    c. The employees of a department who must clarify each assignment with their supervisor before they feel confident in carrying it out.
    d. The manager who goes along with his employees when the goals of the organization conflict with the goals of his employees.
    e. The employees of an organization who are pressured and harassed by management and a labor union to join or not to join a union.

CASE PROBLEM

Case 3–1

A small corporation consists of twelve divisions. Since the organization is decentralized, each division has its own general manager, research director, production manager, treasurer, and so on. In one of these divisions, Division *A*, the research director of that division, Al Smith, assigned a project to one of his department managers, Bill Jones. In his initial investigation, Jones discovered that research men in two of the other divisions were working on projects that duplicated his efforts. He suggested to the others that they join forces in a common research effort; the other two men agreed. In the beginning Smith, the research director, attended several of the joint meetings and made suggestions. Later he assigned specific areas for the group to investigate, and left them alone. After two months the research men from the other divisions told Jones they believed it would be better for each man to do his research independently. Some time later Smith reported to his general manager that the research project had not worked out. He implied that Jones had not organized the project very effectively.

Questions

1. *What principles are involved in this case?*
2. *Who had overall* responsibility *and* accountability *for the success or failure of the project?*
3. *Who failed to organize the project successfully, Jones or Smith?*
4. *Why did the project fail?*

SELECTED REFERENCES

ALLEN, LOUIS A., *Management and Organization,* Chap. 4. New York: McGraw-Hill Book Company, Inc., 1958.

AMRINE, HAROLD T., JOHN A. RITCHEY, and OLIVER S. HULLEY, *Manufacturing, Organization, and Management* (2nd ed.), Chap. 3. Englewood Cliffs, N.J.: Prentice-Hall, Inc., 1966.

DALE, ERNEST, *Planning and Developing the Company Organization Structure.* Research Report No. 20. New York: American Management Association, 1955.

DALE, ERNEST, and L. C. MICHELON, *Modern Management Methods,* Chap. 3. Cleveland, Ohio: The World Publishing Company, 1966.

JUCIUS, MICHAEL J., and WILLIAM E. SCHLENDER, *Elements of Management Action* (rev. ed.), Chap. 5. Homewood, Ill.: Richard D. Irwin, Inc., 1965.

MCFARLAND, DALTON E., *Management Principles and Practices,* Chap. 8. New York: The Macmillan Company, 1958.

PINTEL, GERALD, and JAY DIAMOND, *Retailing,* Chap. 4. Englewood Cliffs, N.J.: Prentice-Hall, Inc., 1970.

TERRY, GEORGE R., *Principles of Management* (4th ed.), Chaps. 15 and 20. Homewood, Ill.: Richard D. Irwin, Inc., 1966.

4

Communications in Management

Possibly the most vital and fundamental element in the management process is effective communications. The reason for this is readily apparent. Because the management process is based on working with people, which is done through some form of communication, the success of managerial actions depends to a large extent on the effective use of the communications process. This makes it apparent that communication is so fundamental that it is closely interrelated with other management elements. Consequently, although communications will be discussed in this chapter as a separate process, the principles and factors of effective communications become integrated parts of other processes and elements discussed elsewhere in this book. Therefore, understanding the communications process is not only useful for understanding the management process but also for the application of the management functions on the job. With this in mind, this chapter includes: (1) basis of effective communications, (2) formal communications patterns, (3) means of communications, (4) communications barriers, (5) guide to effective communications, and (6) informal communications.

BASIS OF EFFECTIVE COMMUNICATIONS

Communications can be judged effective if it produces the results for which it is intended. In management, communications serves both a functional and psychological purpose. Functionally, as a means of transmitting and receiving information, communications serves the essential purpose of linking the components of an organization together, thereby providing the vehicle by which the functions of management are executed. Psychologically, because most personal relationships are carried on through some form of communications, organization communications constitutes the primary means by which sound human relations are established and cultivated. Taken together, the result expected is positive employee action through modified attitudes and conditioned behavior.

Whether used to modify attitudes or condition behavior, communications can be viewed as a process that always includes four elements:

1. The *source* (a sender, writer, speaker, drawer, demanstrator, instructor, or encoder)
2. The *message,* (the meaning the source is attempting to transmit)
3. The *symbol* used to transmit the message (words, signs, symbols, gestures, music)
4. The *receiver* (a listener, reader, watcher, decoder)

These are the essentials of communications, and the process is complete if no specific results are intended by the communications, or if the results are unimportant. This is often the case in mass media communications such as radio, television, motion pictures, newspapers, and the like.

In management, however, communications is more than the one-way process of disseminating information. While dissemination of information is important, equally important is the response of the receiver. This places emphasis on determining if the message is understood and assessing the reaction of the receiver. Consequently, the process must provide means for an exchange of information between the sender and the receiver. This is called two-way communications and is the basis of an effective management communications process.

FORMAL COMMUNICATIONS PATTERNS

For two-way communications to be effective, channels for communicating must be open to all members of an organization. In formal organizations, communications channels closely approximate the vertical and horizontal pattern of the formal organizational structure. This permits communications to flow in three directions: upward, downward, and across.

Downward Communications

As the term implies, downward communications flow from the top elements of the organization to the bottom. This allows communications to be transmitted downward along vertical lines of the organization from manager to manager to employee. This form of communications is related to directing people, and management has been quick to recognize the problems of downward communications. The growth and complexity of modern industry and business have placed pressure upon management at all levels to develop effective means of transmitting to lower echelons information that is vital to the continuing efficient operation of the organization. The passing on of orders, policies, and plans is the backbone of efficient management.

Management recognizes, too, that misinformation and the resulting misunderstanding lessen work efficiency. Sharing information with subordinates at all levels of the organization tends to diminish the fears and suspicions that workers sometime have in their work and toward their employer. This sharing affords the security and feeling of belonging so necessary for efficiency. It recognizes and fosters the pride people want to have in their work and improves the morale and stature of the individual. Finally, effective downward communications helps subordinates in understanding, accepting, and cooperating with the frequent changes in materials, methods, and personnel that are part of modern organizations. In general, it may be said that downward communications is an integral part of the traditional organization and is readily accepted and made use of by management.[1]

Upward Communications

The flow of information and ideas up the organizational structure, from the employee at the bottom to management at the top, has not been as readily accepted as downward communications. Unfortunately, some managers tend to consider communications a one-way process. One manager expressed this attitude in saying,

> I am responsible for formulating plans and issuing directives that put these plans into effect. The people in my division are responsible for carrying out these directives. This is the only way a business can be operated efficiently. Someone is responsible for giving orders and making decisions; others must carry them out.

[1] Earl G. Planty and William Machaver, *Communications in Business and Industry* (Washington, D.C.: Office of Industrial Resources, International Cooperation Administration, October 1956), p. 34. The material for this manual was based on an extensive study made of the communications process of the Johnson and Johnson Corporation. Due to its classical nature, portions of this study have been used as a base for many articles and textbook discussions since the study was made in 1949 and revised in 1954. See, for example, *Effective Communications on the Job,* M. Joseph Dooher and Vivienne Marquis, eds. (New York: The American Management Association, 1956), pp. 141-57, and Dalton E. McFarland, *Management Principles and Practices* (New York: The Macmillan Company, 1958), pp. 445-46.

Many managers at all levels share this authoritarian point of view. They fail to see the value in encouraging employees to discuss fully the policies and plans of the organization; neither do they provide a clear channel for funneling information, opinions, and attitudes up through the organization. Managers should recognize, however, that there is much value in listening willingly and urging subordinates to talk freely and honestly. Upward communications reveals to them the degree to which ideas passed down are accepted. In addition, it stimulates employees to participate in the operation of their department or unit and therefore encourages them to defend the decisions and support the policies cooperatively developed with management. The opportunity for upward communications also encourages employees to contribute valuable ideas for improving departmental or company efficiency. Finally, it is through upward communications that managers learn in time to avert them, the many explosive situations that arise daily in an organization.[2]

Across Communications

Within formal organizations, across communications flow along the horizontal lines of the organizational structure. It involves lateral communications between those at equal levels of the management hierarchy and staff functions of the organization. It also concerns communications with others outside the organization. It permits managers of one department to communicate with those of other departments. It allows various departments to coordinate their activities: sales personnel can communicate with their customers, supervisors can communicate with union stewards, and the like. In short, it opens the communications channel for various elements to work together to solve problems and relate information of common interest and concern. It promotes teamwork.

MEANS OF COMMUNICATIONS

Achieving effective communications in an organization requires establishing means by which each member of the organization can participate, consistent with the established communications channels. Wherever possible, such a program should make provisions for upward, downward, and across communications. Ideally, a sound organizational communications system should provide a means to furnish managers and employees of each level with the information they need for their operation to function

2 See Planty and Machaver, *Communications in Business and Industry,* p. 34.

smoothly. Consequently, to achieve effectiveness, both the information and the media to communicate it should be taken into account.

Information to Communicate

There are no hard and fast rules for determining what information to communicate. However, knowing what each echelon of the organization needs or wants to know can serve as a useful guide in selecting, developing, or using the appropriate media for upward, downward, and across communications.[3]

WHAT MANAGEMENT NEEDS TO KNOW. Collectively, the management of an organization is concerned with those things that affect the overall operation of the organization. This includes:

1. Managers' and employees' attitudes toward the company
2. How well employees understand organizational rules, policies, and programs
3. How employees contribute to greater operational effectiveness
4. The gripes and complaints of individual employees and managers
5. Statistical facts and data on which sound decisions, policies, and objectives can be based

WHAT INDIVIDUAL MANAGERS NEED TO KNOW. Managers are concerned about things that affect their jobs and about the company in general. This includes:

1. Information about the job
    a. Opportunities for advancement
    b. Facts about wages
    c. Limits of supervisory authority
    d. Information bearing on job security
    e. Benefit programs
    f. Service programs
    g. Their functions in relation to higher management, other departments, and the total plant
    h. The end results of their department's work
    i. All matters concerning the performance of their jobs
2. Information about the company
    a. Company products, particularly new or proposed products
    b. Company research activities
    c. Public relations programs
    d. Advertising and publicity programs

[3] See I. I. Raines, *Better Communications in Small Business,* Small Business Management Series No. 7, 2d ed. (Washington, D.C.: Small Business Administration, 1962).

e. General policy
f. Stockholders as people
g. Company earnings and growth
h. Business trends affecting future operations
i. Employee benefits
j. Company history in human terms rather than cold statistics
k. Relations with union, including details of collective bargaining
l. Lines of authority and company organization
m. Shifts of management personnel
n. Financial matters, including problems concerning costs, in non-technical language

WHAT EMPLOYEES NEED TO KNOW. Often being less secure in their jobs than managers, employees are concerned about those things that affect them personally as well as facts about the organization. These are:

1. Facts about the company
   a. The history of the company
   b. Its position in the industry of which it is a part
   c. Its organizational structure
   d. The names of its top executives and something about them
   e. The financial position of the company
   f. Sales trends in unit volume
   g. What happens to each dollar of sales
2. Facts about company–employee relations
   a. Personnel policies
   b. Wage and job classifications
   c. Opportunities for advancement
   d. Opportunities for training
   e. Future employment prospects
3. Facts about future company plans
   a. Advertising campaigns
   b. Public and community relations programs
   c. Research programs
   d. New product development
   e. New equipment, production methods, or machine techniques
   f. Expansion of the business

Communications Media and Devices

Many media and devices can be used to gather and disseminate information. A large number of the media and devices used by organizations are multipurpose. They can be used to collect and disseminate information in the two-way process up, down, and across organizational lines. Others are single-purpose media that direct the flow of information only one way. Some of the principal formal media used for upward, downward, and across communications follows:

1. Downward communications media
    a. Direct personal contact between superior and subordinate to transmit orders, instructions, requests, and so on
    b. Employee orientation materials and programs
    c. Bulletin boards for posting schedules, written announcements, notices, and general information
    d. Organization handbooks, manuals, written policy, directives, and procedures
    e. Employee magazines and newspapers
    f. Financial statements and other information about the organization's progress
    g. Letters to employees
    h. Inserts in paycheck envelopes
    i. Various audio-visual media such as public address systems, motion pictures, slides, posters, signs, charts, and so on
2. Upward communications media
    a. Suggestion systems where employees can express their ideas, opinions, and criticism for improvements
    b. Formal grievance procedures
    c. Morale and communications surveys
    d. Open discussion group meetings between management and employees
    e. Union publications and union representation
    f. Letters to editor of organization newspaper
    g. Employee committees
3. Across communications media
    a. Conferences, meetings, and small group discussions
    b. Training programs
    c. Meetings with community leaders and other outside groups
    d. Collective bargaining between various levels of management and organized labor
    e. Daily coordination between managers of various departments and staff functions

COMMUNICATIONS BARRIERS

As stated earlier, the effectiveness of the two-way communications process is based on keeping the channels of communications open among all levels of management. When these channels are blocked, the process stops functioning properly. In discussing barriers in managerial communications, there is a common tendency to describe a list of specific items that impede the effective two-way process. Of course, there are many things that block effective communications, such as distance between managers and employees (span of control), semantics, acoustics, and a host of others. But the greatest obstruction to effective communications can be discussed under one topic: *attitude.*

Attitude can be defined as the position or posture taken toward various objects, topics, and events.[4] In communications, attitude can serve both as a bridge or a barrier and can apply to either the sender or the receiver. Whether the message is presented verbally, in writing, or visually, the communicator's attitude or feeling is transmitted with the message to the sender. On the other hand, the position or posture taken by the receiver toward the message or the communicator can be one of resistance, of willingness, or of passive neutrality. If the reaction to the message is positive, it is a bridge; if negative, it is a barrier. To serve as a bridge to effective communications, both the attitude of the sender (organization or individual manager) and the receiver (employee) must be considered in applying the two-way communications process. Attitude is particularly important in face-to-face two-way communications as shown in the summary below: [5]

> The manager's attitude and behavior will play a vital role in either encouraging or discouraging effective two-way communications. If the boss seems anxious to get the conversation over with or appears to be impatient with his subordinate, or annoyed or distressed by the subject being discussed, this attitude will place an insurmountable communications barrier between them in the future. Also, a manager may fall into the familiar error of thinking that he knows what subordinates think or feel, or he may have such an exaggerated sense of duty that he feels it is disloyal to listen to complaints. This attitude tends to discourage employees with justifiable complaints from approaching their superiors.
>
> Managers often resent and resist communications which indicate that their actions have been less than perfect. Where this attitude is evident, loyal workers who could be most helpful withhold information. In such cases, communicating is of necessity done by the less loyal workers and the maladjusted. In other words, unless managers are willing to hear criticism freely, much they learn about the operation will come from those who are the least loyal to it. Moreover, managers often resist becoming involved with the personal problems of their subordinates. This resistance also may affect the subordinates' willingness to communicate on other matters more directly related to the job. Since job problems and personal problems are often closely linked, it is difficult to discuss one without the other.
>
> One of the strongest deterrents to two-way communications is the attitude of managers to ignore undesirable conditions previously brought to their attention. The result is that the workers lose faith both in the sincerity of management in general and the value of communications in particular. Many managers feel that they are too involved with daily problems and responsibilities to provide adequate time for listening fully to their subordinates' ideas, reports, and criticisms. Neverthe-

[4] See James C. Coleman, *Personal Dynamics and Effective Behavior* (Fairlawn, N.J.: Scott, Foresman and Company, 1960), p. 58.

[5] Adapted from Planty and Machaver, *Communications in Business and Industry*, pp. 38-39.

less, many time-consuming problems could be minimized or eliminated if superiors were free to listen to their employees, for in listening they can discover solutions to present problems or anticipate causes for future ones.

A manager's philosophy of management determines the value he places upon communications and the time he gives to it. A manager who has built a people-minded philosophy, is engaged in building individual subordinates and developing teamwork in his group will rank communications high in priority and will allow time for it since it is the nerve center of such a leader's management. In contrast, the manager who acts alone, solves most of his department's problems himself, and lets the growth of subordinates take its own course may well be too busy to communicate.

Employees are also emotional and prejudiced. Their feelings mix freely with their facts creating further attitude barriers to two-way communications. Their observations and reports to management are prejudiced by their own personal habits and sentiments. Developing a people-minded attitude will help the manager understand and interpret what employees are trying to tell him. The manager, of course, must recognize and minimize his own prejudices and idiosyncrasies before he can do this.

GUIDE TO EFFECTIVE COMMUNICATIONS

To be effective, all people at the management level must know the value of two-way communications and must create the conditions within the organization for it to take place. This means that each manager must not only keep himself informed, but should develop the necessary communications skill and constructive attitude to assure the flow of information and ideas down as well as up the organizational structure. Due to their complexity, only general guides for effective two-way communications will be discussed here. However, since the following guides are basically universal, they can serve as a fundamental framework for using the communications process in its many managerial applications.

Guides for Downward Communications

The first requirement of effective two-way communications is for the sender to have his message understood. To have the message interpreted in the same context requires a meeting of minds between the sender and the receiver. While this can best be facilitated through the two-way exchange of ideas and information, in the initial process of disseminating information down, the responsibility for making the message understood is the responsibility of the sender.

The Receiver. A major reason for failures in communications is the lack of common background and experience between the sender of the message and the one who is to receive it. For a message to have the same meaning to the sender as it does to the receiver, the two must speak the same language. Symbols used to convey a message take on meaning in relation to people's backgrounds. Because the backgrounds of no two people are ever exactly the same, the symbols in the mind of the sender will never coincide perfectly with the meaning they have to the receiver. Therefore, such things as the education, experience, and general socioeconomic background of the receiver must be taken into account if the message is to be understood. Also, it is helpful to know the receiver's attitude, because attitude will determine the receiver's reaction to the message.

The Symbol. The second thing that must be considered in downward communications is the symbol to use in getting the message across. Whether the message is to be conveyed in writing, orally, or through the means of some visual presentation, all use some sort of symbol.

Because words are used in written and spoken communications, and words are inexact and mean different things to different people, the sender must select words that have meaning to the receiver. To do this, the following will prove helpful: 1) Use words that are within the receiver's experience. (2) Use concrete and specific words. This narrows and controls the meaning. (3) Define words that the receiver may not understand. This applies particularly to technical words and words that may have several meanings.

In visual communications, signs, gestures, pictures, demonstrations, and other nonverbal symbols are used to convey meaning. While generally less stressed than oral and written communications, visual symbols are more effective to convey the feeling, intent, and emotions of the sender than mere words. Like words, the symbol used should be based on the background of the receiver. Here, the use of symbols is discussed separately for convenience, but to have the message better understood, a combination of words and visual symbols is normally more effective. For example, written words are better understood if illustrated by a picture; a demonstration conveys more meaning if explained; a lecture is more effective if the speaker uses gestures.

The Presentation. In selecting a method of presentation, both the media and the method should be considered. The following general rules apply: (1) It is generally more effective if more than one medium is used, and if the context of the message is complex, repetition by using the same media or a different media is often necessary. (2) In selecting a method, as a general rule the higher the official making the presentation, the wider effect it will have. However, a message is more readily received by the employee's immediate supervisor. (3) Where persuasion is needed, oral face-to-face contact is more effective than other media since there is a better opportunity for the manager to observe reaction and to adapt the presentation to obtain the desired results.

THE TIMING. Timing is important in downward communications, and these rules apply: (1) Timing should be such that a supervisor always hears information before his subordinates. (2) If one person or a department is told about an event, all who equally need the information should be informed at the same time. (3) Communications should be timed so that the information will not appear to be in conflict with other information. (4) Factual information should be timely disseminated to avoid rumors, gossip, and conjecture.

Guides to Upward Communications

Communications upward must provide for continuity. Whenever possible, communications upward should move through the organization from level to level until it reaches the person or department responsible for taking action. On the part of the manager in relationship with employees, this implies both understanding and action.

Understanding requires the manager to listen to what a subordinate has to say. To be effective, listening must be both sensitive and objective. Listening is *sensitive* when the manager: (1) recognizes that individuals with different backgrounds get different meaning from the same communicator; (2) is aware that complaints that he hears are often not the real cause of the employee's criticism or irritation; (3) understands that much of the information he hears has been sifted, and only those things the employee wants heard are given; and (4) knows that subordinates are especially alert to all gestures, sighs, and nonverbal expressions.

Listening is *objective* when the manager: (1) shows a constructive and receptive attitude toward direct and implied criticism of himself and his department; (2) is attentive when what the employee is telling him is not to his direct advantage; (3) guards against listening only to those employees with whom he agrees; and (4) demonstrates a willingness to change when shown where he is wrong.

Upward communications implies action on the part of the manager. It is the responsibility of each manager at each level to either take action on the employee's communication or to pass the information on to the next level as accurately and as timely as possible. In taking action, the manager should use caution not to imply that action will be taken when none is intended. Sympathetic listening and encouraging remarks often lead the employee to believe that his proposal will receive action not contemplated by the manager. Of course this leads to resentment. To avoid this, the manager should be explicit as to his intentions.

INFORMAL COMMUNICATIONS

Up to this point, only the formal process of communications has been discussed. Before concluding the chapter on communications, mention should be made of the informal communications network that exists in all formal organizations. Whereas the communications network of a formal organization closely approximates the structure of the organization, informal communications networks follow no established pattern. They are normally centered on the natural leader of the informal organization and thrive in the absence of formal and factual official information. Informal communications take many forms, but two types warrant special attention: the *clique* and the *grapevine.*

The Clique

Human instinct prompts people with common interests to band together in groups. Up to a certain point, there is nothing wrong with this tendency. Informal communications, social gatherings, and other types of activities that permit casual conversations between members of an organization build teamwork and are good for morale. However, when the ties binding members of a group become more important than the objective of the organization, the group becomes a clique and tends to circumvent the formal patterns of communications and authority. Cliques exist in all organizations, but are harmful when a strong formal communications system is lacking.

The Grapevine

Another pattern of informal communications is the grapevine–so named because it has a way of winding its way through the formal organization. Like the clique, the grapevine exists in all organizations and thrives in the vacuum of inadequate and timely formal information. This type of informal communications consists of rumor, gossip, and conjecture. It is based partially on facts someone has heard, seen, or been led to believe, which become grossly distorted through retelling. Grapevine information is normally harmless unless it becomes the major source of information in an organization. Although it cannot be eliminated, organizations and managers can control grapevine information by developing and maintaining an effective, formal two-way communications system.

KEY POINT SUMMARY

1. Effective communications is a vital element in the management process, since it is through some form of communications that the activities of management are carried out.
2. Communications can be judged effective if it produces the results for which it is intended. In management, the intended results are positive employee behavior by modified attitudes and conditioned behavior.
3. As a process, communications must always consist of four elements: (1) the source, (2) the message, (3) the symbol, and (4) the receiver.
4. For communications to be effective in management, not only the source, the message, the symbol, and the receiver are important but the receiver's response to the message as well. This two-way feedback process between the sender and the receiver is called two-way communications.
5. For two-way communications to be effective, there must be channels open to all members of the organization. In formal organizations, these channels are:
   a. Downward communications: from top to bottom
   b. Upward communications: from bottom to top
   c. Across communications: from one level to another, and from any level to an outside source
6. To achieve effective communications, both what to communicate and how it is to be communicated should be taken into account.
   a. What to communicate should take into account what each echelon of an organization wants and needs to know.
   b. How information is to be communicated concerns selecting the medium or device appropriate to the purpose and level for which the communications is intended.
7. While there are many barriers to effective communications, the prevailing one is the attitude of the sender and receiver.
8. Effective two-way communications requires each manager to develop the necessary communications skills to assure three-directional flow of information.
9. General guides for effective downward communications should take into account:

   a. The receiver's background and experience
   b. The symbols most appropriate to get the message across
   c. The media and methods by which the communications are to be presented
   d. The timing of the communications

10. General guides for effective upward communications include:
    a. Understanding what is said through effective listening
    b. Taking action on the employee's communications
11. In addition to formal communications, an informal communications network exists in all organizations. The two most common types are:
    a. The clique
    b. The grapevine

DISCUSSION QUESTIONS

1. Why is effective communications important in the management process?
2. What is the basis for effective managerial communications? Explain the purpose of communications in management. What is meant by two-way communications?
3. What are the normal communications patterns of a formal organization? What is the relationship between these patterns and the functions of directing and coordinating?
4. In developing means of communications, what factors should be considered?
5. What are some of the things that management, managers, and employees want and need to know? Explain.
6. What are some of the media and devices used to gather and disseminate information:
   a. For downward communications
   b. For upward communications
   c. For across communications
7. Why is attitude a common barrier to effective communications?
8. As guides to effective downward communications, what factors should be considered? Explain.
9. What are two major factors to be considered in effective upward communications? Why?
10. In what way does informal communications differ from formal communications in an organizaion? Relate *clique* and *grapevine* to effective formal communications.

CASE PROBLEM

Case 4–1

Recognizing that two-way communications is a key factor in assessing employee attitudes, one major company conducted a survey to determine the effectiveness of its communications. To do this, 2,116 employees and 325 supervisors were asked to give their response to a set of statements regarding how they felt about some aspects of their jobs. The statements and the results are indicated below:

	Favorable Response	
	Company as a Whole	*All Supervisors*
1. You can say what you think around here.	57.3%	67.4%
2. My boss lets us know exactly what is expected of us.	68.7%	68.9%
3. Management fails to give clear-cut orders and instructions.	64.6%	72.0%
4. They encourage us to make suggestions for improvements here.	89.5%	93.5%
5. I know how my job fits in with other work in this organization.	84.3%	91.7%
6. Management tells employees about company plans and developments.	68.0%	74.5%
7. Management keeps us in the dark about things we ought to know.	60.9%	75.1%
8. My boss really tries to get our ideas about things.	64.3%	76.0%
9. You always know where you stand with this company.	45.8%	48.3%
10. I'm really doing something worthwhile in my job.	81.7%	93.8%
11. I really feel part of this organization.	75.9%	84.0%
12. If I have a complaint to make, I feel free to talk to someone up the line.	78.0%	83.4%
13. Management ignores our suggestions and complaints.	71.9%	88.3%
14. They have a poor way of handling employee complaints around here.	62.6%	80.0%
15. Sometimes I feel that my job counts for very little in this organization.	68.5%	77.8%

Questions

1. *Did this organization practice effective two-way communications?*
   a. *Identify and discuss each area that indicates that downward communications needs improving.*
   b. *Identify and discuss each area where upward communications needs improving.*
   c. *For each area identified, discuss how the organization in*

general and the supervisors in particular can improve their two-way communications procedures.

2. *What is the significance (if any) of the fact that supervisors' favorable responses were higher than the company as a whole?*

SELECTED REFERENCES

BOYD, BRADFORD, *Management-Minded Supervision,* Chap. 3. New York: McGraw-Hill Book Company, 1969.

DALE, ERNEST, and L. C. MICHELON, *Modern Management Methods,* Chap. 4. Cleveland, Ohio: The World Publishing Company, 1966.

HEPNER, HARRY W., *Psychology, Applied to Life and Work* (4th ed.), Chap. 22. Englewood Cliffs, N.J.: Prentice-Hall, Inc., 1966.

———, *Perceptive Management and Supervision,* Chap. 7. Englewood Cliffs, N.J.: Prentice-Hall, Inc., 1961.

KAZMIER, LEONARD J., *Principles of Management,* Unit 9. New York: McGraw-Hill Book Company, 1969.

PARKER, WILLARD E., ROBERT E. KLEEMEIR, and BEYER V. PARKER, *Front-Line Leadership,* Chap. 5. New York: McGraw-Hill Book Company, 1969.

TIFFIN, JOSEPH, and ERNEST J. MCCORMICK, *Industrial Psychology* (5th ed.), Chap. 13. Englewood Cliffs, N.J.: Prentice-Hall, Inc., 1965.

5

Economics in Management

Like management, economics concerns the organization and use of resources; also like management, it is both a science and an art. As a science, economics concerns the means and the manner used by a society to produce and distribute its goods and services. As an art, it concerns the study of factors and means governing the allocation and use of scarce resources in meeting the various objectives of a society. Taken together, they form the society's economic system. Since a society's economic system is created by and through management, economics establishes the fundamental base for the management process. Therefore, the final element the manager must consider in developing a basic frame of reference for understanding and carrying out the management process is the use of economic principles as they relate to management. From the manager's standpoint, this understanding is useful in two ways: First, it provides him with a basic guide for allocating and using his resources; second, it helps him understand the reason for developing a management-minded philosophy. With this dual purpose in mind, this chapter will discuss (1) forms of business ownership, (2) profit and cost, (3) profit and cost relationships, (4) cost budgeting, and (5) financial statements.

FORMS OF BUSINESS OWNERSHIP

To understand the relationship of management and economics, it is first necessary to discuss briefly the forms of business ownership. In our society, the economic system is one of free enterprise. A society is said to have a free enterprise or capitalistic economic system if its major means of production and distribution are owned and operated by private businessmen to make a profit. Under this system, industrial and business organizations are allowed to be formed to meet certain economic objectives. These objectives include: (1) providing the public with a quality product or service at the lowest possible cost, (2) providing jobs and paying workers an adequate and equitable wage, and (3) providing the owners of the organization a compensation for their investments. To meet these objectives, business organizations take several forms. The three most common ones are sole proprietorships, partnerships, and corporations. Since these three forms of organizations are the basic economic units by which management produces and distributes goods and services, their fundamentals should be understood.

Sole Proprietorships

As the title implies, a sole proprietorship is a business owned by one person. It is the simplest form in which a business can be conducted. The owner simply goes into business with the assets of the organization in his own name. This form of ownership has both advantages and disadvantages. From the economic standpoint, it has the advantage of the owner keeping all profits made from the business for himself. On the other hand, he must assume total responsibility for liabilities, including any monetary losses that the business may incur. From the management standpoint, a sole proprietor has the obvious advantage of being his own boss and being accountable for the behavior of no one except himself. Conversely, many individuals who go into business for themselves are ill-equipped managerially to meet the challenge of operating a modern business despite its small size. Also, small businessmen are normally handicapped by lack of resources. Studies show that lack of managerial know-how and insufficient capital (back-up money) are the reasons for most small business failures.

Partnerships

In a partnership, the business is conducted by a number of persons who have equal status and authority as owners. Setting up a partnership ordinarily involves the contribution from the partners of the property, money, credit, skills, or labor that will increase the organization's potential to meet its objectives. Like the sole proprietorship, partnerships are simple to form since no contract—written or oral—is required. A partnership can be created simply by several persons conducting a business for profit as co-owners. Although this form of organization has the obvious advantage of providing the business with more skills and possibly more capital, it has certain disadvantages. One is that each partner of the firm is liable for the debts and actions of the others. Another serious disadvantage is that partners sometime fail to work in harmony. Although this can be helped somewhat by a written agreement or articles of partnership spelling out the rights and duties of each partner, failing to get along is still a major disadvantage.

Corporations

The most sophisticated form of organization and the one that has the greatest economic significance is the corporation. Unlike the two other forms of ownership, the corporation stands on its own as a separate entity. It is recognized by the state as being apart from its owners as an "artificial" person.

After a corporation has been legally recognized by the state, it is owned by those who have money invested in the organization. These investors or shareholders expect a return on their investment in the form of dividends, and have voting rights that allow them some measure of control over the operation of the corporation. However, the declaring of dividends and the actual management of the corporation are normally vested with a board of directors elected by the shareholders.

There are several advantages to the corporation form of ownership. First, shareholders are not, as a rule, responsible for the corporation's obligations. Because the corporation is recognized as an "artificial" person, the corporation, not the shareholders, is held accountable for the transactions of the organization. Second, corporations are more enduring than the sole proprietorship or the partnership. Where the death of an owner or bankruptcy of the company may permanently end the existence of either of these forms of ownership, the legal and collective structure of a corporation makes this less likely. Finally, a corporation can usually borrow money more easily than a business operating in one of the other forms. Also, when additional capital is needed, investors prefer corporations since the shares are readily transferable and liability is limited.

Of course there are other types of ownerships and several variations of the three mentioned above. Because the purpose here is only to exemplify the role of private ownership in our economic system of free enterprise, this brief discussion will suffice. However, it is well to realize that while most of our means of production and distribution are privately owned, all goods and services are not provided by private organizations. There is a wide array of nonprofit organizations, which also provide both goods and services. They include foundations, church-related operations, charitable organizations, and government agencies and institutions at the local, state, and national levels. Although we are basically a free enterprise society, this makes it apparent that all economic means are not privately owned. The nonprofit organizations have basically the same economic goals as private businesses with the obvious exception that their motive is not profit.

PROFIT AND COST

In carrying out the management process, as the previous chapters clearly indicate, the use of resources is required. Since in most organizations the availability of resources is limited, factors governing the use of these limited resources among competing and often conflicting objectives become obviously apparent. Although the factors that influence the use of resources defy complete classification, two factors that underlie the economic foundation of business organizations are profit and cost. Taken together, they constitute the fundamental base by which the effectiveness of a business organization is judged and on which most management decisions are made. Therefore, these two factors—profit and cost—should be understood.

The Factor of Profit

As indicated earlier, under our economic system of free enterprise, most goods and services are produced and distributed by industrial plants and commercial outlets owned and operated by private individuals or groups of individuals for the purpose of receiving a monetary return or profit on the money and effort invested. This incentive or "profit motive" is fundamental to all industrial and commercial organizations, and is the underlying principle of the free enterprise system. Without the motive to make a profit, people simply would not invest their money in a business enterprise, nor would businessmen take the risk or exert the effort to establish new businesses or expand old ones. Therefore in a very real sense, without profits our free enterprise system simply could not exist. This makes it clear that despite the importance of other organizational goals there are some practical limits beyond which profit cannot be overridden. In carrying out the management process, this point should be kept uppermost in the manager's mind.

Although the need for the profit motive in our free enterprise system is generally recognized, profits are often misunderstood. This misunderstanding is due primarily to the lack of knowledge as to who receives profits and the amount of the return on investments.

First, most people fail to realize that numerically most businesses are small individually owned operations such as service stations, small stores, agencies, franchises, and other retail outlets. The return on these owners' investments for both time and money is comparatively small and the risk is great. Studies show that many small businesses fail during the first year.

Second, most people do not understand that major corporations, which produce and distribute most goods and services under our free enterprise system, are not owned by a few families as some suspect, nor do most large corporations realize an exceedingly high rate of return on the money invested. Millions of people from all walks of life own shares of stock in American corporations, and with some exceptions the average annual rate of return on investments (dividends) averages only 3 to 6 percent.

These misunderstandings often cause problems for the management of an organization. By not understanding the profit motive, customers want lower prices and employees want higher wages, thus placing an inequitable demand on the resources of the organization. Large corporations are also faced with the problem of middle and lower management thinking in terms of security and routine or personal ambitions that conflict with the company's profit-making objectives. These tendencies are often manifested by these managers in three common ways: (1) Energy spent in expanding sales volume and product lines rather than in raising profit, which is the valid company objective, (2) subordinates establishing perfectionist standards of quality that cost far more than they are worth, and (3) lower management tending to be too cautious and oversafe since they fail to see the direct rewards of increased profits of the organization.[1]

The Factor of Cost

The second factor underlying the economic foundation of a business enterprise is cost. Cost, expressed in dollars, is the expenditure made by the organization in reaching its objectives. Cost is an essential factor in a business or industrial organization. First, if in the long period of time costs exceed income, the organization cannot make a profit; therefore, it simply cannot exist. Second, only through the management of cost can an organization best achieve its economic objectives: (1) To pay higher dividends to the stockholders of the business, (2) to provide the customer with a better quality product or service at lower prices, and (3) to expand or create new business to provide more jobs and pay higher wages to workers and managers. Consequently, the factors of cost play an important role in a business enterprise, both as a reference point for judging the effectiveness of the organization and by the manager in making management decisions.

Business costs can be classified in two basic categories and further subdivided into several types. The two categories are *investment costs* and *operating costs.*

[1] See Joel Dean, "Managerial Economics" in *Handbook of Industrial Engineering and Management,* 3d ed., eds. William Grant Ireson and Eugene L. Grant (Englewood Cliffs, N.J.: Prentice-Hall, Inc., 1957), Sect. 2, pp. 61-62.

Investment Costs. These are the costs, called capital investment, necessary in establishing and operating a business. Capital investment includes expenditures for such things as land, buildings, machines, equipment, and other nonconsumable goods not used directly in the operation of the business. It also includes the money necessary to operate the business. Total capital investment per employee in manufacturing, for example, varies from about $6,000 to $20,000 depending on the type of industry. From their capital investment, owners (stockholders or individual operators) expect to receive a return on their money in the form of dividends, which, as discussed earlier, are derived from the profits of the organization. Not all profits, however, are used to pay dividends to the owners of the business. For a business to be successful, it necessarily has to expand its operation, meet competition by producing a quality product, and improve its production methods. Therefore, a portion of the company's profits are reinvested in business expansion, research and development, and work method improvement, and of course businesses pay taxes. Through these methods an organization indirectly shares some of the profit made on its capital investment with the customers, workers, and general public.

Operating Costs. This category of cost consists of the expenditure of money for those things used directly or indirectly in the production and distribution of the company's product or service. These costs are briefly discussed below and are of four common types.

Material costs are the expenditures for the materials that are used directly or indirectly in the production of the product or service. This cost includes such things as raw materials (wood, metal, cotton), or parts (screws, nuts, bolts), or subassemblies (carburetors, nozzles, hoses), and such other things as cleaning materials, oil, lubrication, and so on.

Labor costs are expenditures for the wages and benefits that are used in making the product or providing the service. In addition to the workers' salaries, labor costs may include such things as insurance and health plans and other benefit programs such as pension plans, worker's compensation, and social security, which the organization expends to attract and maintain a worker on the job. In most firms, the cost of employee wages and benefits is the single largest expenditure.

Selling costs are expenditures that are incurred by the company in marketing its product or service. Examples of this type of cost are commissions and salaries paid to salesmen, advertising and promotional costs, and marketing research expenditures.

Overhead costs include such expenditures as taxes, management costs, rent, lights, power, water, telephone, and other costs not included in the other three types of costs.

In the above discussion on profit and cost, it is apparent that these two factors must be considered in all managerial decisions in establishing priority of claim in the use of resources. When confronted with a choice between conflicting and competing alternatives, the factor of profit must be kept utmost in the manager's mind, and other things being equal, the factor of cost must be given priority. When, for example, a manager is confronted with a choice of either approving or disapproving an employee's suggestion to improve the way a certain task is being done, the cost of installing the new method should be weighed against its potential improvement. If in the manager's judgment, the installation cost would be excessive, the suggestion should be disapproved although the method suggested has considerable merit. This line of reasoning can be applied to the purchase of new machines or equipment, adding additional employees, recommending employees for a raise, and the many other decisions the manager is faced with involving cost. Whereas the factor of profit is obviously not a consideration in nonprofit organizations for the allocation of resources, the factor of cost applies to these organizations as well. In most activities such as schools, governmental agencies, and other tax-supported or nonprofit type organizations, resources allocated for the operations are normally limited, and like profit-making concerns many demands are vying for their use. Therefore, it can be said that as in profit-motivated organizations, other things being equal, cost should be the determining factor in the manager's decision.

PROFIT AND COST RELATIONSHIPS

As the above discussion implies, there is a close relationship between profit and cost. Since this relationship is the very basis for understanding economics in management, it should be further clarified. This can best be done by taking a brief look at a fundamental management tool called break-even analysis. Break-even analysis is a means of determining the cost-volume profit relationship. It provides management with a flexible set of projections under assumed conditions for planning and controlling profit and cost.

The term *break-even* refers to a point where sales income equals cost, and neither a profit nor a loss will be realized. To find the break-even point, the total fixed cost and the variable cost must be known for a given sales volume.

Fixed costs are those costs that do not change with the sales or production volume. These costs include such things as rent, insurance, lights and other utilities, and certain salaries of managers and office workers.

Variable costs are those costs that increase or decrease directly with the sales or production volume. They are basic materials, direct labor, commissions to salesmen, and the like.

In order not to complicate the discussion, so-called semivariable costs that do not vary in direct proportion to sales volume will not be considered here.

By knowing the sales volume, fixed, and variable costs, the break-even point can be determined either mathematically or graphically. Because the purpose here is to understand the relationship between profit and cost, not how to make a break-even analysis, only the graphic method will be discussed.

Figure 8 illustrates a break-even chart. In a break-even chart, the measure of volume is scaled on the horizontal axis of the graph. In this chart, percentage of plant capacity is used, but sales volume, units sold, direct labor hours, or some other measure can also be used as the base of the chart. Dollar sales, income, and cost are scaled on the vertical axis of

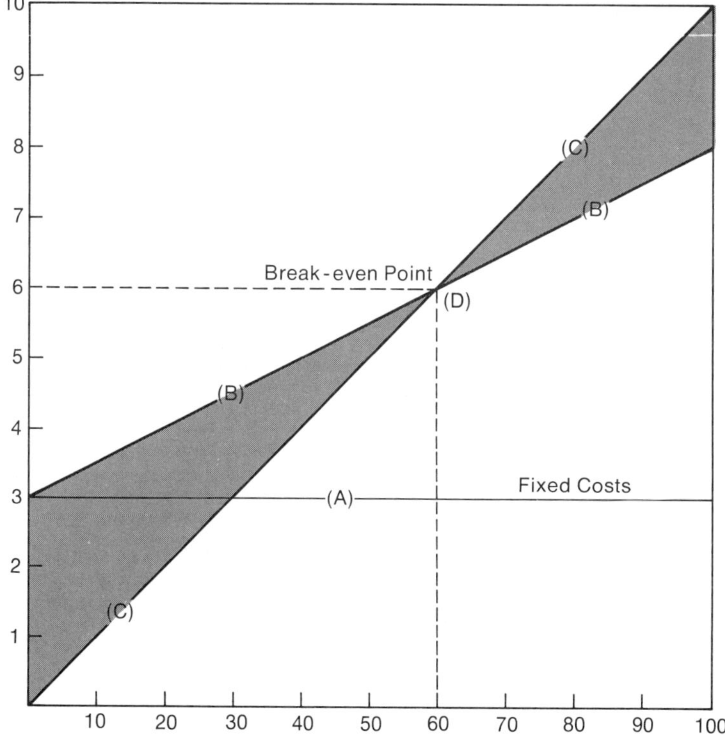

Figure 8 **Break-even Chart with Plant Capacity on Horizontal Line (Source: Adapted from Management Research Summary, *Management Planning for Small Firms*, Small Business Administration, Washington, D. C.)**

the chart. Then, fixed costs can be plotted (Line *A*), total costs (Line *B*), and sales (Line *C*). The point at which the cost line and the sales line cross (*D*) represents the break-even point. The shaded areas between the two lines indicate loss or profit, depending on whether it precedes or follows the break-even point. In the chart shown in Figure 8, when sales exceed $600,000 a profit is shown; when it is below that point, costs exceed income, and a loss is incurred.

There are a number of variations of the break-even chart, some giving additional information. But because all start with the basic chart design illustrated and discussed here and are based on the same principles, this chart is sufficient for understanding the graphic method of break-even analysis. However, it should be recognized that a single break-even chart of this type has the limitation and disadvantage of presenting information only under a single set of circumstances based on past experience and assumed conditions. Any change in these circumstances will change the break-even pattern, thus affecting its validity. Despite this, however, break-even analysis is a useful tool in planning, controlling, and making decisions concerning the allocation of resources. But more important for the purpose here, it shows the close relationship between profit and cost in a business organization.

COST BUDGETING

The importance of cost in a business organization makes it evident that this factor should be planned and controlled. A way this is done in both profit and nonprofit organizations is through cost budgeting. Cost budgeting is the systematic method of coordinating a series of estimates designed to forecast and project future costs and the process of comparing these estimates against actual results. The document produced as a result of this process is called a *budget*. Budgets may be prepared for the total business or a subdivision of the business and may be stated in time, materials, labor, sales volume, produce, or other measurable elements that can be converted to a monetary unit (dollars and cents). Standards are the most convenient basis for drawing up a budget, but in their absence the budget can be based on previous experience.

Budget Preparation

Budget preparation varies from business to business, but in most organizations it follows this general pattern.

1. Departmental managers prepare estimates of the expenditures for their departments for the coming fiscal or calendar year.

2. Each manager then coordinates his estimate with the managers of the other departments.

3. A budget committee, normally made up of the operating department managers and the financial managers, meet and make necessary revisions. This usually requires some "give and take" to bring the budget estimate in line with an established ceiling.

4. Finally, an operating budget is prepared indicating the estimated expenditures for various items for the coming year.

To be an effective controlling device, periodic reports are made comparing the estimates and actual expenditures for a specified period, normally by the month. These monthly projected figures may then be used as a tool for planning and controlling cost by all managers of an organization.

Advantages of a Budget

The major advantage of a budget is that it provides a device by which cost can be planned and controlled. It also sets goals toward which all members of an organization can work. By knowing limits of his expenditures, each manager can more realistically plan and control his operation toward its objective. The budget has many other advantages, ten of which are summarized below:

1. The budget assists in putting the responsibility for each function of the organization exactly where it belongs: with the operating manager.

2. Because of its coordinating character, the budget makes all the departments of the organization cooperate toward achieving the general goals set up by the budget.

3. The budget is a target for all departments in the organization; and like a target with its circles, the budget is a means of checking the efficiency of the results.

4. The budget prevents waste in that it limits expenditures to specific maximums.

5. The budget regulates planned expenditures within the limits of income or allocated funds.

6. The budget calls for the most economical use of the resources of the organization, since the plans drawn up before the budget are aimed at maximum efficiency.

7. The budget requires managers to study their operations and to search for the best means of obtaining maximum results from their resources.

8. The budget warns against any unreasonable optimism that might result in too large an expansion of certain functions or divisions.

9. The budget helps to determine the effect of operating policy, such as the production policy and the financial policy of the organization.

10. The budget makes it possible to analyze differences between estimates and results.

Controlling Cost

As indicated above, a major purpose of the budget is to control cost. Cost control is the major concern of most businesses and rightly so. As it has been pointed out, only through the control of cost can an organization best meet its economic goal. This makes it apparent that cost control is a prime responsibility of every manager. Of course there are many ways to control cost. Some organizations establish sophisticated programs involving all levels of the organization to reduce and control cost. However, on a day-to-day basis, cost control simply means making effective use of resources. Although this is the concern of all management personnel, the effective use of resources is particularly applicable at the lower management level. It is through the middle and first-line manager that manpower, machines, material, time, and space, which make up the cost of the organization, are brought together and used to produce or sell the product or provide the service. When resources are brought together in actual operation their effective use becomes integrated and interrelated.

In controlling cost, one resource over which the supervisor has direct control must be given particular attention. That resource is manpower. Not only does manpower make up the largest single cost factor in an organization's operating budget but it is through people that most of the other resources are used.[2] Therefore, a major factor in controlling cost is through the effective use of manpower. The measure of this effectiveness is called *productivity*—the value of output per man hour expended to produce a product or provide a service. The higher the output per man hour for the money invested, the lower the cost. Most economists, business leaders, and labor union officials agree that increased productivity is the key to a higher standard of living, a competitive edge in foreign markets, and economic growth. For example, a 1 percent national increase in our overall productivity would in turn increase our gross national product (total dollar value of goods and services produced) by $1 billion. At the operating level of a single department of an organization, increased productivity can mean the difference of the company making a profit or taking a loss.

Increased productivity depends on many factors such as modern machines and equipment, facilities, and the like, but on balance the effective use of manpower is brought about by supervisory effectiveness. Conse-

[2] Most studies show that in manufacturing a product, employee wages and benefits make up about 47 percent of the operational budget, with about 43 percent going for raw materials. Of course this percentage is higher in service organizations where no raw materials are involved.

quently, the ways and means of controlling cost are the ways and means of effective supervision.

FINANCIAL STATEMENTS

Financial statements serve two useful purposes in management. First, because they show the financial status of the business, they are useful to managers and investors for making decisions. Second, they serve as a means by which the organization can keep its investors, managers, employees, and in some cases the general public informed concerning the economic status of the business. Although first-line and middle managers seldom use financial statements to make decisions, it is their responsibility to not only keep themselves informed concerning their company's financial condition but to advise their employees as well. Therefore, two common financial statements should at least be recognized: the *balance sheet* and the *profit and loss statement*. The balance sheet presents a financial picture of the business on a given date. The profit and loss statement (also called *income statement*) measures costs and expenses against sales revenue over a definite period of time, such as a month or a year, to show the net profit or loss of the business for the entire period.

The Balance Sheet

A typical balance sheet is shown in Figure 9. As this figure indicates, the balance sheet has two main sections. The first section shows the assets. The second section shows the liabilities (or debts) and the owner's equity (or capital), which together represent the claims against the assets. The total assets always equal the total of the liabilities and the owner's equity; thus, the name—balance sheet. The two sections are briefly explained below:

Assets include anything the business owns of money value and are classified as current assets, fixed assets, and others. Current assets include cash and assets that are expected to be converted into cash during the normal operating cycle of the business, which is generally one year. On the other hand, fixed assets are those acquired for long-term use in the business and are not for resale, but for use. To offset the wear and tear on fixed assets, a depreciation allowance is shown on the balance sheet. Other assets include such things as patents, trademarks, and so on.

Liabilities are the claims creditors have against the business. Like assets, liabilities are classified as current (due within a year) and fixed (due in a longer period of time). On the other hand, *equity* is the investment of the owners plus or minus any profits that have been left to accumulate in the business.

XYZ Manufacturing Company

Balance Sheet
December 31, 19 __

Assets

Current assets:			
Cash		$40,000	
Accounts receivable........	$90,000		
Less allowance for doubtful accounts...........	10,000	80,000	
Inventories:			
Finished product.........	75,000		
Work in process	75,000		
Raw materials	20,000		
Supplies	10,000	180,000	
Prepaid expenses		10,000	
Total current assets			$310,000
Fixed assets:			
Furniture and fixtures	$10,000		
Less allowance for depreciation	5,000	$5,000	
Machinery and equipment ...	$30,000		
Less allowance for depreciation	16,000	14,000	
Buildings	$45,000		
Less allowance for depreciation	9,000	36,000	
Land		15,000	
Total fixed assets			70,000
Investments			20,000
Total assets			$400,000

Liabilities and Equity

Current liabilities:			
Accounts payable		$40,000	
Notes payable		80,000	
Accrued liabilities:			
Wages and salaries payable	$4,000		
Interest payable	1,000	5,000	
Allowance for taxes:			
Income tax	$16,000		
State taxes	4,000	20,000	
Total current liabilities			$145,000
Equity:			
Capital stock		$200,000	
Surplus		55,000	
Total equity			255,000
Total liabilities and equity.			$400,000

Figure 9 Balance Sheet (Adapted from Jack Zwick, *A Handbook of Small Business Finance,* Small Business Administration, Washington, D. C., 1965.)

Profit and Loss Statement

Figure 10 is a simplified profit and loss statement. To clarify the profit and loss statement, a brief explanation of each item is given below:

SALES. The item *sales* includes all sales of merchandise or services. The sales figure represents net sales computed by subtracting sales discount and sales return, and allowance for gross sale.

The XYZ Company

Profit and Loss Statement
For the Year Ended December 31, 19__

Sales		$120,000
Cost of goods sold		70,000
Gross margin		$50,000
Selling expenses:		
Salaries	$15,000	
Commission	5,000	
Advertising	5,000	
Total selling expenses		25,000
Selling margin		$25,000
Administrative expenses		10,000
Net profit		$15,000

Figure 10 **Profit and Loss Statement (Adapted from Jack Zwick, *A Handbook of Small Business Finance,* Small Business Administration, Washington, D. C., 1965.)**

Cost of Goods Sold. In retail operations, this item includes the total price paid for the product sold during the accounting period. Because manufacturers convert raw materials into finished products, to avoid a long and complicated profit and loss statement, the cost of goods sold is normally reported separately.

Selling Expenses. These are expenses directly or indirectly involved in making sales. This includes salaries of the sales force, commissions, advertising, and shipping, to name a few.

Administrative Expenses. These are the overhead expenses incurred in operating the business.

Net Profit. This is the profit made during the reporting period and represents the difference between gross margin of sales and the selling expenses minus the overhead or administrative expenses.

To aid managers and investors in interpreting financial statements to make them meaningful as decision-making tools, a number of indicators have been worked out. These indicators, too numerous and complicated to discuss here, are normally expressed in ratios and are useful for analyzing a business operation. When properly applied they provide clues for spotting trends in the direction of better or poorer performance, and allow the company's financial performance to be compared with the average performance of other similar businesses. On the other hand, as a means of interpreting and understanding the company's financial statements by lower management, stockholders, employees, and the general public, many companies simplify their financial statements and present them in a more attractive and understandable form. Through the use of illustrations, pictures, and graphs, the financial language of the accountant is not only easier to comprehend, but creates a feeling of intimacy and confidence toward the company.

KEY POINT SUMMARY

1. Like management, economics concerns the use of resources and is both a science and an art.
    a. As a science it concerns the means and manner in which a society produces and distributes its wealth.
    b. As an art it concerns the study of factors governing the allocation of resources.
2. Under our economic system of free enterprise, the production and distribution of goods and services are accomplished mostly through business and industrial organizations owned and operated by private citizens with the following objectives:
    a. To provide the public with a quality product or service at the lowest possible cost.
    b. Provide jobs and pay workers an adequate and equitable wage.
    c. Provide the owners of the organization a compensation for their investments.
3. There are several forms of business ownerships. Among the most common are:
    a. Sole proprietorships
    b. Partnerships
    c. Corporations
    d. Nonprofit organizations
4. In the allocation and use of scarce resources when carrying out the management process, two factors that influence a manager's decision are profit and cost.
    a. Because under the free enterprise economic system businesses could not exist without profit, profit takes first priority to the claim on resources.
    b. Because only through the management of cost can an organization best meet its objectives, cost is an overriding factor in making business decisions.

5. Whereas the necessity for the profit motives of business organizations is generally recognized, it is often misunderstood:
   a. As a general rule most organizations make only a small return on investments, and numerically most businesses are owned and operated by individual owners.
   b. Misunderstanding of the profit motive leads to unrealistic demands being placed on the organization by the customers for lower prices and by workers for higher wages.
6. The two categories of business costs are investment costs and operating costs.
   a. Investment costs include the expenditures for equipment, land, buildings, and capital needed to establish and sustain a business organization.
   b. Operating costs are those costs for items used directly or indirectly in the production or distribution of products or services and include:
      (1) Material costs
      (2) Labor costs
      (3) Selling costs
      (4) Overhead costs
7. Although the factor of profit is obviously not a factor in allocating resources in a nonprofit organization, like profit-oriented organizations, cost is a major factor in making managerial decisions.
8. Break-even analysis is a means of determining the point at which sales equal income and neither a profit nor loss will be realized, is useful in planning and controlling profit and cost, and shows the relationship between profit and costs.
9. Cost budgeting is the process of forecasting and projecting future costs and comparing estimates against actual results.
   a. The budget developed as a result of this process is used to make business decisions and to plan and control cost.
   b. Controlling cost can best be done through the effective use of manpower.
10. Financial statements are useful for showing the financial status of the business and for managers and investors in making business decisions. Two common types that the manager should understand and be able to explain to his employees are:
    a. Balance sheet—which presents the financial picture of the business at a given time.
    b. Profit and loss statement—which shows the profit or loss of the organization over a period of time.

DISCUSSION QUESTIONS

1. Why is economics like management? Explain.
2. Under our economic system of free enterprise, how are goods and services produced and distributed?
3. What are the economic objectives of a business organization, and what are their common forms of ownership? Who owns American businesses?
4. In allocating resources, what two factors should be considered? Explain.
5. What is the role of profit in our free enterprise system, and why is profit often misunderstood?
6. How does the misunderstanding of profits affect the management of a business organization? Explain.
7. What is the role of cost in business organizations? Relate cost to the three objectives of business organizations under the free enterprise system.
8. Why is the factor of cost important to nonprofit oriented organizations? Should cost be considered in allocating resources?
9. In business organizations, what are the two categories of costs? Explain each.
10. What is meant by *break-even analysis,* and how is this instrument used in making decisions? Using the break-even chart in Figure 8, page 77, what affect would the following have on profits:
    a. if fixed costs were increased?
    b. if sales were increased?
    c. if operation costs were decreased?
    d. if plant capacity were increased?
11. What is *cost budgeting?* Explain the process used in developing a budget. What are the advantages of a budget? What is the relationship between controlling cost and supervision?
12. What are two common forms of financial statements? How is each used?
    a. Using the balance sheet in Figure 9, page 82, answer the following questions:
        (1) What is the dollar value of the current assets?
        (2) What is the dollar value of fixed assets?
        (3) What is the dollar value of the equity of the company?
    b. Using the profit and loss statement in Figure 10, page 83, answer the following questions:
        (1) In dollar value, what was the net sales in the period ending January 1?
        (2) In dollar value, what was the total of cost of goods sold?
        (3) What was the gross profit of the organization?
        (4) What was the net profit of the organization?

CASE PROBLEM

Case 5–1

Seven years ago, John Tabor started a small store serving a relatively large neighborhood. Within two years, John's business had grown so that he asked his brother-in-law to join him as a partner. After another five years of steady growth in sales, John and his partner are considering expanding their operation to include three more stores in other parts of the city. They are thinking of asking one of their senior employees to serve as general manager with the responsibility of hiring the necessary people to operate the stores. To put the plan into effect, the store will have to raise prices slightly to take care of the additional overhead. This will mean that the customers of the original store will have to pay more, but at the same time approximately thirty people will be added to the payroll and a convenient service afforded people of other neighborhoods of the city. In their planning, the partners are also considering forming a corporation.

Questions

1. *What economic factors are involved in this case regarding the objectives of a business organization?*
2. *How could the following be used to assist the partners in making their decision to expand the business:*
   a. Break-even analysis
   b. Budget
   c. Balance sheet
   d. Profit and loss statement
3. *What economic guidelines should the general manager use in hiring people for the three new stores?*
4. *What would the pro and con arguments be for changing the business from a partnership to a corporation?*

SELECTED REFERENCES

AMRINE, HAROLD T., JOHN A. RITCHEY, and OLIVER S. HULLEY, *Manufacturing, Organization, and Management* (2nd ed.), Chaps. 23 and 24. Englewood Cliffs, N.J., Prentice-Hall, Inc., 1966.

DEAN, JOEL, "Managerial Economics" in *Handbook of Industrial Engineering and Management,* Sec. 2. Englewood Cliffs, N.J.: Prentice-Hall, Inc., 1955.

PFIFFNER, JOHN M., and MARSHALL FELS, *The Supervision of Personnel* (3rd ed.) Chap. 6. Englewood Cliffs, N.J.: Prentice-Hall, Inc., 1964.

TERRY, GEORGE R., *Principles of Management* (4th ed.), Chap. 28. Homewood, Ill.: Richard D. Irwin, Inc., 1966.

WOELFEL, B. LASALLE, *Guides for Profit Planning,* Small Business Management Series No. 25. Washington, D.C.: Small Business Administration, 1960.

ZWICK, JACK, *A Handbook of Small Business Finance,* Small Business Management Series No. 15 (7th ed.). Washington, D.C.: Small Business Administration, 1965.

II

Human Relations

Human relations from the impersonal point of view involves the integration of manpower resources into an effective work organization. In Part I, human resources were treated along with nonhuman resources in this matter. Although this detached viewpoint is useful in conceiving the working of the management process, it has very limited use in day-to-day operations. People are different from machines, money, material, space, and time, and must be treated differently both for ethical and for practical reasons. In short, the manager should become people-minded. Developing this people-minded philosophy includes acquiring a fundamental understanding of why people act and react as they do. Not only will this understanding serve the manager in developing his leadership style but it will provide a frame of reference for obtaining "results through the efforts of others," which as stated previously is the essential element that distinguishes a manager from a worker. To develop this understanding, human relations is discussed in this part under the following major topics:

Fundamental Factors in Effective Human Relations
Factors of Employee Adjustment
Factors that Influence Teamwork
Factors of Employee Performance
Factors of Employee Relations

6

Fundamental Factors of Effective Human Relations

Human relations, like most other subjects, can be defined in many ways. Some define it as the golden rule in action, others call it employee–employer relations, and still others define *human relations* as group interaction. Regardless of what it is called, the aim of human relations is the same: to obtain results through the better use of people. Of course, when related to a business organization, the results are called productivity. *Productivity,* as defined in a previous chapter, is the value of output per man hour expended to produce a product or provide a service.

The exact relationship between the factors of individual behavior and the effect they have on individual productivity is very complex and not fully understood. But it is generally agreed that people work more efficiently and effectively in an organization where management in general and the individual manager in particular have made a conscious effort to take into account the employees' desires and drives, and have made maximum ethical use of the principles of human relations. This simply means that because a manager must work with and through people to get results, the principles that cause people to act and react as they do should be understood and applied. Although it is the purpose of this part of the book to discuss the principles for the effective use of manpower, certain fundamental factors that provide the structure for effective human relations should first be understood. Therefore, this chapter will identify and describe some fundamental factors that can serve as a basic reference point for understanding the principles presented in the other chapters. This will include these major topics: (1) leadership styles, (2) individual differences, (3) attitudes and opinions, (4) pressure and stress, and (5) behavior patterns.

LEADERSHIP STYLES

Possibly the single most influential factor in effective human relations is the leadership style of the manager. The reason is basically simple. Because leadership is the process (act) of influencing the activities of a group of individuals toward certain goals, it can be readily seen that the style or pattern of the leader sets the pace for the group's behavior. This is not to say, however, that leadership involves only human relations. It was indicated in the previous chapters that to achieve a goal, people must be organized, their work planned, and their efforts coordinated, directed, and controlled. This is a part of leadership. However, to do this in such a way as to achieve results, the manager must apply the principles of human relations. Therefore, although the management process is involved, leadership boils down to getting results through people. This means that human relations is not only the key to effective leadership but effective leadership is a key to effective human relations. Unfortunately, the style of leadership that will produce sure-fire results has not been pinned down. Like the qualifications of a manager, an effective leadership style depends on a combination of peculiarities and circumstances that are always changing. A leadership style that may be effective under one set of conditions and with a certain group of employees or an individual may be weak in another situation. However, some insight can be gained as to what constitutes an effective leadership style by taking a look at the basic types of leaders. It is generally agreed that managers as leaders can be broadly classified into four basic types.

1. *Dictatorial leadership* is that type of leadership which gets work done through fear. The dictatorial leader—or negative leader as he is frequently called—holds over the heads of his subordinates the threat of penalties and punishments, such as discharge, demotion, poor ratings that may prevent promotions or wage increases, and so on. The theory is that the followers, in order not to lose the means of satisfying some of their needs and wants, are motivated to do what the leader tells them to do. Although this type of leadership apparently gets results, there is serious doubt that the quantity and the quality of the results achieved can remain high over the long run, particularly in view of the fact that the results obtained are frequently accompanied by the dissatisfaction of those led.

2. *Autocratic leadership* is characterized by centralization of authority and decision-making in the leader. Although this type of leader tends to emphasize neither negative nor positive leadership, he motivates his subordinates by forcing them to rely upon him for need satisfaction. As such, he takes full authority and responsibility for the work to be done. He permits no participation in the decision-making process

and tolerates no deviations from what he has told his followers to do. This type of leadership also gets results. But it suffers from the serious disadvantage that it can be only as good as the leader is. If the leader is weak and inefficient, the followers will be weak and inefficient.

3. *Democratic leadership*, unlike autocratic leadership, is based on decentralization of authority and decision-making. This type of leader is characterized by the degree to which he consults with his subordinates on problems, goals, and tasks that face him and the group as a whole. The theory behind this type of leadership is that it encourages the followers to function as a social unit and that it makes full use of the talents and abilities of the members of the group. As a result, the subordinates achieve a greater measure of belonging and recognition, which motivates them to higher levels of efficiency. Although some people do not agree with this, there is, nevertheless, general agreement that democratic leadership offers more promise than any other type of leadership. It suffers, however, from the disadvantage of requiring a better quality of leader.

4. *Laissez-faire leadership*, or *free-rein leadership* as it is popularly called, exists when the leader allows the group to establish its own goals and make its own decisions. Usually the only contact the leader has with the group occurs when he provides the information it needs to get the job done. As such, he makes little contribution to overall effort. The net result is frequently disorganization or chaos, primarily because this type of leadership permits different individuals to proceed in different directions.[1]

Although it is generally agreed that a democratic leadership style centered on a people-minded philosophy will on balance produce the best results, the other styles should not be ruled out. For as it will be amplified in other chapters, on a day-to-day basis the style of the manager will be influenced by many factors. But for present purposes it can be assumed that the democratic style is the most effective.

INDIVIDUAL DIFFERENCES

Fundamental to developing a frame of reference for effective human relations is recognizing that each individual is different. This means that behind every time card or slot on an organizational chart, there is a distinct and different human being. This is so obvious that at first glance it hardly seems worthy of special mention. But as obvious as it appears, too frequently this important factor is all but ignored. This is unfortunate, for not only is recognizing individual differences a basic requirement for developing a people-minded philosophy, but it serves as a base for almost everything a

[1] I. L. Heckmann, Jr., and S. G. Huneryager, *Human Relations in Management*, 3rd ed. (Cincinnati, Ohio: South-Western Publishing Co., 1960), pp. 48-49. Reproduced by special permission.

manager does. When executing such duties as giving orders, training employees, recommending an employee for promotion or demotion, and every other fundamental function where people are involved, individual differences must be taken into account. So it follows that effective human relations is predicated on the manager knowing the qualities and properties of people if he is to treat human resources in the proper perspective by taking individual differences into account.

Basis of Individual Differences

The basis of individual differences is influenced by heredity and environment. Heredity is normally referred to as those factors or individual processes that are endowed by nature, and include such things as skin and hair coloring, body shape and size, strength, and so on that form the structure for individual behavior. On the other hand, environment is the physical and social arena in which development and behavior take place. The degree to which each of these two factors influences behavior will be left to the argument of psychologists. For the purpose here, it is sufficient to state that both heredity and environment shape individual personalities, which in turn make up the variables that cause individual differences. Personality variables, whether caused by heredity or environment, are called *traits,* and when taken together constitute the individual potential for behavior. Therefore, by recognizing these traits, a manager is in a better position to understand his employees.

1. *Physical appearance* includes physique, hair color, eyes, facial features, and other characteristics of body equipment.
2. *Temperament* is the individual's prevailing mood pattern.
3. *Capacity* is the individual's potential for development in a given area.
4. *Ability* pertains to the actual skill of performing in an area.
5. *Interest* is the degree to which the individual is attracted toward an activity.
6. *Aptitude* is the individual's capability for doing well in a particular area.
7. *Attitude* is the individual's capability to react in a given way (for example, favorably, unfavorably, cautiously, recklessly), to a given object, or to a situation.
8. *Character* is the individual's moral and external dimensions of personality.
9. *Stress tolerance* is the individual's level of resistance to physical and psychological stress.
10. *Action pattern* is the individual's characteristic way of interacting with his environment (for example, extraverted or introverted, aggressive or submissive).

Although a detailed treatment of these traits and their specific relation to individual behavior will be left to the study of psychology, it is important to recognize that these traits are present in all people. True, they vary from person to person, which makes each individual different. But psychologists have found that traits are not either present or lacking in people, only distributed differently. In any large group selected at random, most traits, such as general intelligence, mechanical or artistic ability, height, and so on, follow a curve of normal distribution with about sixty-eight percent falling in a normal range with extremes at both ends. This distribution curve is shown in Figure 11.

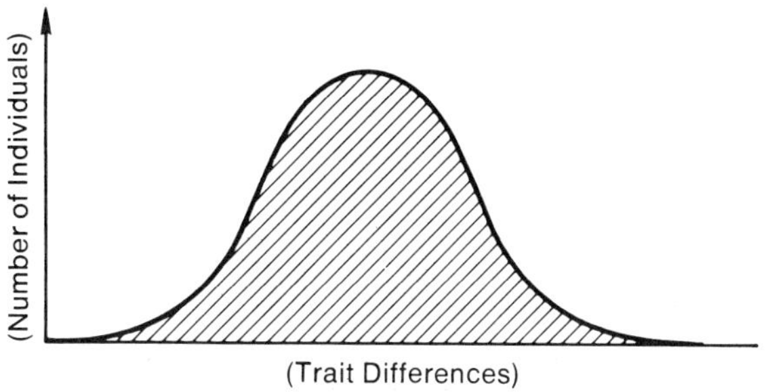

Figure 11 Distribution Chart

As this diagram shows, people are seldom "all-or-nothing" or "either-or," but that approximately two-thirds of all people have each of the commonly observed traits to a moderate degree, that is, they are close to the average in it, and that only a small percentage have markedly large or small degrees of any traits. Not "either-or" but "the degree to which" should be the guiding concept in studying people. This means that most employees can learn, can produce, can adapt, can follow instructions, and so on, but the degree to which they can do these things is the crux of individual differences. This is the factor that the manager must take into account.

Personality Types

Personality has been defined as the totality of habit. In other words, it is the individual's general pattern of behavior as influenced by his individual traits. Psychologists have found that people with certain personalities follow a general pattern of behavior and thinking that can be identified and classified into three basic types: (1) the *introvert,* who expresses his emotion inwardly; (2) the *extravert,* who expresses his emotion outwardly; and (3) the *ambivert,* who is a balance of the two extremes. The behavior and thinking pattern of the introvert and the extravert has been further clarified by Donald A. Laird, who developed a scale of signs by which these two personality types may be recognized. Because this scale can be of value to the manager in better understanding his employees, it is included below:

Personality Signs Revealed in Behavior and Actions

1. The introvert blushes easily; the extravert rarely blushes.
2. The extravert laughs more readily than the introvert.
3. The introvert is usually outspoken; the extravert is usually careful not to hurt the feelings of others.
4. The extravert is a fluent talker; the introvert can prepare a report in writing more easily than he can tell it in conversation.
5. The extravert lends money and possessions more readily than the introvert.
6. The extravert moves faster than the introvert in the routine actions of the day, such as walking, dressing, talking, etc.
7. The extravert does not take particular care of his personal property, such as watches, clothing, and so on; the introvert is found continually oiling, polishing, and tinkering.
8. Introverts are usually reluctant about making friends among those of opposite sex, while extraverts are attracted by them.
9. Introverts are easily embarrassed by having to be in front of a crowd.
10. The extravert is a more natural public speaker.
11. The introvert likes to argue.
12. The introvert is slow about making friends.
13. The introvert rewrites his letters, inserts interlineations, adds postscripts, and corrects every mistake of the typist.

Personality Signs Revealed in Thinking and Attitudes

1. The introvert worries; the extravert has scarcely a care in the world.
2. The feelings of the introvert are easily hurt; the extravert is not bothered by what is said to him.
3. The introvert deliberates in great detail about everything—what to wear, where to eat, etc., and usually tells one why he decided to do what he did.
4. The introvert rebels when ordered to do a thing; the extravert accepts orders as a matter of course.
5. The introvert is urged to his best efforts by praise; the extravert is not affected by praise.
6. The introvert is suspicious of the motives of others.
7. The introvert is usually radical in religion and politics; the extravert —if he entertains any opinions—is usually conservative.
8. The introvert would rather struggle along to solve a problem than to ask for help.

9. The introvert would rather work alone in a room than with others.
10. Extraverts follow athletics; introverts read books and "high-brow" magazines.
11. The introvert is a poor loser.
12. The introvert daydreams a great deal.
13. The introvert prefers fine, delicate work (die making, accounting), while the extravert prefers work in which details do not bother.
14. The introvert is inclined to be moody at times.
15. The introvert is very conscientious.[2]

By being able to recognize the various signs associated with individual behavior and thinking patterns, a manager can better determine how an employee will react to his work situation and better predict his behavior.

Barriers to Understanding People

Like everyone else, a manager is a creature of habit. He often falls into the habit of thinking of people in certain roles or stereotypes. Although habit is useful in many things, when applied to people it can create barriers that can prevent the manager from understanding his employees as individuals. Therefore, to help the manager in recognizing these barriers, some common habits are discussed below:[3]

THE DIE-CASTING HABIT. Too often, as we observe individuals, we try to sort them into types or to force them into imaginary molds, much as the die-caster squirts metal into different kinds of molds. They may be different shapes before they go in, but they are all alike when they come out.

We feel that we have completely cataloged Bill Jones when we say that he is a "good mixer," that we have defined Tom Smith when we put him down as a "tough customer." But we cannot do that with people, if we really wish to understand them. We must study each one from all sides, not pour them into molds or cast them into types.

THE "JUST LIKE" HABIT. "He reminds me for all the world of Bill Brown," we say, and thereafter we notice most easily the traits that are like Bill Brown's and ignore those that are different. Once we have made up our minds he is "like Bill Brown," we close our minds to the possibility of his having other characteristics that we may need to know. We stop studying

[2] Harry Walker Hepner, *Psychology Applied to Life and Work,* 4th ed. (Englewood Cliffs, N.J.: Prentice-Hall, Inc., © 1966), p. 186. From Donald Laird, "How Personalities Are Found in Industry," *Industrial Psychology,* October 1926, pp. 1-2.

[3] Adapted from the *Training Within Industry Report* (Washington, D.C.: War Manpower Commission, Bureau of Training, 1940–1945).

him, with the result that we never discover many of the interests and abilities that are a part of the man.

THE "GO, NO-GO" HABIT. "I can tell whether a man will make a good operator in this job as soon as I see how he follows directions," said a supervisor. "If he listens carefully to my directions for doing a job, and does it exactly as I tell him, he will make a good man. If he doesn't get the directions the first time, but tries to 'dope out' his own way of doing it, he seldom learns to do good work here." This supervisor, if he really does follow the way of thinking that he described, is classifying all employees into two classes: (1) those who follow directions to the letter, and (2) those who try to figure out methods of their own. His gauge of men is two-valued, "go" or "no-go." There are no "in-betweens." He is applying an inspection technique, not an understanding one.

THE "FORMULA" HABIT. Closely related to these "stereotype" ways of looking at people is the practice of dealing with each "type of person" in a certain set manner. It has been said that the way to get along with the "chronic kicker" is to "lay down the law"; that the way to teach the new worker is to "show him how" to do the job and "tell him what" the requirements are.

Of course, these methods work a good deal of the time with many of the people with whom supervisors have to deal. Otherwise, they would not be so commonly accepted. But they become a hindrance when they are used as excuses for lumping people together in groups or types and avoiding the responsibility of trying to understand each person as an individual.

In short, people cannot be handled like piece parts or apparatus. Each is an individual, different from every other. Stereotyping them, classifying them, standardizing them, or reducing them to formulas—habits of thinking that work well with inanimate things—often prove to be actual hindrances in handling people.

THE "STANDARDIZATION" HABIT. Supervisors may become so accustomed to thinking in terms of standards that they look only for common responses of "the worker" and pay little attention to the special interests, abilities, and peculiarities of individual employees. Yet it is these special characteristics that yield fruitful contacts upon which to base effective supervision. It is the ways in which a person is different, and especially the ways in which he is superior to the "mine run" of people, which furnish the key to his special interests, for he tends to develop strong interests in the fields in which he possesses ability. The supervisor has the problem of taking each of these unique and different personalities, finding out what he is like and to what he will respond, and fitting him into a job and into a working organization.[4]

OPINIONS AND ATTITUDES

The manager soon finds that a major factor that affects his relations with employees is their opinions and attitudes. As pointed out in a previous chapter, attitude is the position or posture taken toward various objects, topics, and events.

Although how attitudes affect employee performance and manager-employee relationships will be amplified in other chapters, in developing a frame of reference for effective human relations, the formation of attitudes should first be understood. Opinions and attitudes are drawn from an individual's background and experience, which form his frame of reference. They shape his behavior as he sees things in relation to his needs. Putting it another way, a person has certain opinions about topics, events, and situations based on information he has obtained from his total experience. In turn, he adopts attitudes based on his opinions. If his information is in error, his opinions will be distorted and his attitude will be equally distorted, thus influencing his behavior. The following examples will help clarify this point.

EXAMPLE 1

Information	*Opinion*	*Attitude*
Individual learns that Company X pays poor wages.	Company X does not give fair treatment to its employees.	Company X is a poor place to work.

EXAMPLE 2

Information	*Opinion*	*Attitude*
Woman employee learns that she is making less money than men doing the same work.	Women are discriminated against.	Why work as hard as men?

Employee attitudes have long been a concern of management and rightly so, for they are a major factor in influencing human behavior. Not

[4] See *Training Within Industry Report, op. cit.*

only is an employee's attitude important to effective communications, as discussed in Chapter 4, but if the employee's attitude is positive, chances are his action or behavior will be goal-directed and result-oriented. His positive behavior will be reflected in such things as high productivity, willingness to stay with the company longer, and a lowering of absenteeism from the job.

PRESSURE AND STRESS

In our pressure-cooker society, pressure and stress are a day-to-day occurrence. This is particularly true in business and industry. Demands made on management and employees come from all sides. Deadlines must be met, customers satisfied, quality maintained, production increased, and a host of other major and minor, large and small, important and trifling requirements demand attention. As a result, pressure and stress become a major factor in human relations. Therefore, to understand the personality and behavior of his employees, certain basic factors should be recognized.

Types of Pressure and Stress

Although pressure and stress take many forms, psychologists have divided them into three basic types.

Frustration is caused by the blocking of a path to a goal. It normally arouses hostility and is often expressed in anger. For example, if an employee thinks that his supervisor stands in the way of a possible promotion to a better job, he is likely to feel hostility toward him and be angry with the supervisor. Frustration is a common type of pressure experienced by everybody on and off the job.

Fear is caused by the threat of immediate danger to one's well-being. If it is perceived by the individual as something beyond his control, fear can cause actual physical or psychological flight or withdrawal. For example, if a worker knows that he is going to be transferred to a new job that he has not been trained for and feels totally inadequate to handle, his fear of failure may cause him to leave the company. Fear can cause severe pressure on the individual and can affect his behavior.

Anxiety is a warning signal of some sort of danger that may affect an individual's well-being. Unlike fear, it cannot be pinned down and defined. It tends to be more internal than external and so vague that the individual can sense danger, but he is not sure of its exact nature. For example, if an employee has suppressed his hostility against his boss, he may feel anxious whenever it attempts to break through because it would jeopardize his job. Being unaware of his repressed feelings, he will not know what makes him anxious.

Job Performance and Pressure

The relationship between pressure and stress to job performance and learning a skill has long been a study of psychologists. Some generalizations that the manager will find useful are discussed below.

JOB FEATURES AND STRESS. In general, there is little association between the incentive relation factors on the job and symptoms of psychological or physical stress. One major study found with respect to symptoms of stress that the greatest number of stress symptoms was shown by people in difficult jobs that have frequent time limits but who have low control over work methods and low feedback on performance.

> Where there are frequent time limits and work is difficult but employees have more control over work methods and more feedback on performance, anxiety and other symptoms of stress are much less frequent. Even lower in reported symptoms of stress are those who have fairly difficult jobs but have only infrequent time deadlines as well as high control over means and high feedback on performance. The implication appears to be that if one wants to reduce psychological and physical symptoms of stress among employees (which may affect efficiency as well as health), it is best to reduce time pressures as much as possible. If time deadlines are necessary, giving those who must meet them as much control over and information about the situation as possible may reduce their stressful effects.[5]

PRODUCTION AND STRESS. It has been found that slight anxiety causes an increase in the individual's ability for productive behavior, whereas severe anxiety causes the individual to disregard safe work habits. This would imply that anxiety is not altogether bad. For example, slight anxiety may be used by the manager to motivate an employee to greater effort by applying some pressure, but if the pressure is too great the employee's performance would diminish and safety habits would be ignored. The effect of slight anxiety on production is often shown when a plant is in the process of employee reduction. When a number of employees are laid off, the production rate of the remaining employees normally increases. Also, a wide variety of experimental investigations seem to support the generalization that stress increases the speed with which repetitious tasks are carried out, but that this increase is generally accompanied by a higher error rate.

[5] See Martin Patchen, *Participation, Achievement, and Involvement on the Job* (Englewood Cliffs, N.J.: Prentice-Hall, Inc., 1970), p. 237.

LEADERSHIP AND STRESS. Fear as a motivating factor used to increase production is less effective than other methods. This generalization is supported by the previous discussion on dictatorial leadership style. As stated, although fear can produce results, other methods of leadership are more effective.

As these generalizations seem to indicate, whereas stress and pressure as means of influencing employee behavior should not be ruled out, the manager should apply them with discretion. It should also be pointed out that some people, of course, can take more pressure than others and that some employees like a certain amount of force from above. Therefore, when applying pressure, individual differences must be taken into account.

Defense Mechanisms

When an individual is placed under stress, psychologists have found that he may unconsciously and automatically try to maintain his personal worth by resorting to behavior that guards some aspects of his personality from scrutiny by others or by himself. He resorts to using *defense mechanisms.* They are common to all human beings and unless used to extremes are not a sign of abnormal behavior. Understanding that these mechanisms do exist helps the manager to cope better with his and his employees' behavior on the job. Some of the more common defense mechanisms and examples of each are discussed below:

RATIONALIZATION. This is a common defense mechanism often used to ease hurt or disappointment when failing to meet a goal or to justify behavior to make it more acceptable. For example, a supervisor who failed to get a desired promotion may rationalize by saying he did not want the higher job. Or, a worker who stays out "sick" when actually he is not, justifies his action by saying that everybody does it. Rationalization takes many forms and is more easily recognized by others than by the one who is doing the rationalizing.

PROJECTION. This is another common mechanism and is characterized by placing the blame for one's failures and problems on others, or ascribing to others his own unacceptable behavior. For example, the supervisor who did not get promoted may blame it on his not playing politics, or the worker who is a bigot may accuse others of discriminating against those of a minority race. Projection is normally used to cover inferior feelings or to hide unethical or antisocial attitudes when rationalization fails to work.

COMPENSATION. This is a means by which the individual substitutes a rewarding trait or activity for one that makes him feel inferior or inadequate. It can be unconscious or conscious, positive or negative. For example, if a supervisor is an expert in a certain field such as welding, but is inept in English or mathematics, he may downgrade the paperwork side of his job as being unimportant and build up the technical side as being the only function that really counts. He may be totally unconscious of this attitude, and of course it is a very negative approach to his job. On the other hand, a craftsman with the same problem may fully recognize his lack of administrative ability and refuse to accept a supervisory position, instead concentrating his efforts on being a better welder. This too is compensation, but it is conscious and positive. Compensation is a common defense mechanism and is in constant use in everyday life, both at home and on the job.

Denial of Reality. Failure to face the situation if it is unpleasant is a denial of reality. A manager putting off making a hard decision, thinking that the problem will resolve itself, or the employee who has been fired not seeking new employment, thinking his old company will call him back, are examples. A host of activities such as keeping busy, being sick, saying we are not in the mood to do something, are often used to escape the necessity to face up to an unpleasant task.

Displacement. This defense mechanism is used to take action on one object or person when the real source of anger involves a risk. Typical examples are when an employee gets angry with his boss and goes home and takes it out on his wife, or when a manager gets angry at his wife and goes to work and gives his secretary a hard time. Kicking a chair, machine, or other objects instead of hitting a person, quitting a job, and so on, are other examples of displacement.

BEHAVIOR PATTERNS

Individual behavior patterns are either positive or negative. Behavior is considered positive if it is directed toward an objective or goal. It is considered negative if it is directed at protecting the individual's self-structure. If the individual feels adequate to meet the situation, he will attempt to meet the goal and his behavior will be positive. On the other hand, if he feels inadequate, his behavior will be self-centered and negative. Positive behavior is expressed in job satisfaction, high morale, and motivation, and when these are combined, maximize the employee's potential for production. Job satisfaction is the employee's individual attitude toward his job and work organization and his actions toward factors that make up his work environment. On the other hand, morale is the sum of the individual attitudes of a group toward the work situation and the factors that make up the structure of an organization. Motivation is the individual or group desire to perform well. Although these factors are basically different and will be discussed as major themes in other chapters, all three have as their common base the employee's desire and drive to meet his basic needs. This being so, the general nature of basic needs should first be understood.

These needs have been identified by the late A. H. Maslow of Brandeis University and are widely accepted by psychologists as a means by which basic needs can be studied. According to Maslow, basic needs of all human beings consist of five levels and can be arranged in the following order:[6] (See Figure 12.)

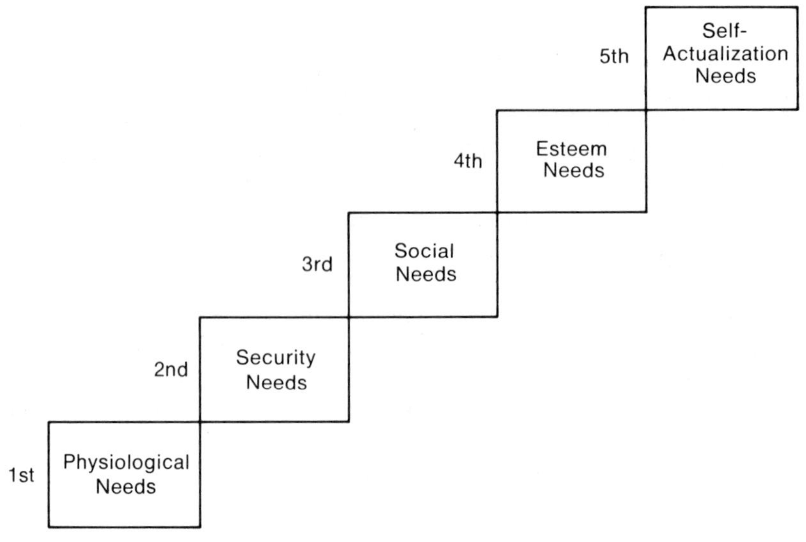

Figure 12 Levels of Man's Basic Needs

FIRST LEVEL NEEDS. At this level man is concerned with the physical needs necessary for his survival. They include such things as water, food, clothing, shelter, and other essentials.

SECOND LEVEL NEEDS. This level pertains to man's need for security and safety. It includes protection from danger, threat to his safety, loss of life, or anything that may take away the means of providing for his survival.

THIRD LEVEL NEEDS. This level relates to man's need for belonging.

[6] Adapted from A. H. Maslow, "A Theory of Human Motivation," *Psychological Review,* Vol. 50, 1943, pp. 370-96.

These are his needs to associate with others and to be accepted and approved by them.

FOURTH LEVEL NEEDS. This level is man's need to have satisfactory relationships with others. These needs include being valued as a person and being appreciated and respected.

FIFTH LEVEL NEEDS. At this level man is concerned about achievement and self-expression: the need to do things that are useful, to be of value to others, and self-fulfillment—becoming what he is capable of becoming.

There are several points that should be understood about basic needs. In the first place, they form the basic motivation or drive for human behavior. Most, if not all, of whatever we do is caused by one or more of our basic needs. The second point is that they are listed in the order of importance to the person. In other words, our basic need for food is more important than our need for being of value to others. Another point is that the five needs are overlapping. A higher need may be started before a lower need is completely satisfied, or a need may be skipped altogether. Finally, when related to the job, basic needs can be identified as economic, social, and psychological needs.

ECONOMIC NEEDS. These needs are related to the basic needs of survival and security. These include salary, insurance plans, retirement plans, and the security of a steady job.

SOCIAL NEEDS. These needs are related to a person belonging and being accepted as a member of the organization by his department and as a person by his supervisor and co-workers.

PSYCHOLOGICAL NEEDS. These needs are related to obtaining satisfactory relationships with others and to the need for achievement, self-expression, and recognition. They include the opportunity to learn the job, get promoted, use abilities, and be rewarded for a job well done.

To sum up, it is the job of the manager to keep his employees' behavior positive and result-oriented. In doing this, the manager will find that in actual operation the principles and practices of human relations, like the functions of management, become interrelated, overlapping, and practically indistiguishable. Nonetheless, the fundamental factors discussed here, taken with the other factors discussed in this book, will set the stage for assisting the manager in obtaining results on the job.

KEY POINT SUMMARY

1. Human relations can be defined in many ways, but the aim is the same: to obtain results through the better use of people by understanding the principles that make people act or react as they do.
2. An overriding factor in human relations is the leadership style of the manager. Leadership has been classified into four basic types:
   a. Dictatorial leadership
   b. Autocratic leadership
   c. Democratic leadership
   d. Laissez-faire or free-rein leadership
3. Whereas on a day-to-day basis a manager may have to adapt his leadership style to the situation, on balance, studies show that the democratic style is more effective.
4. Recognizing that each of his employees is different is a fundamental requirement for developing effective human relations.
   a. Although all individuals are different, certain traits are common to all. These traits are:
      (1) Physical appearance
      (2) Temperament
      (3) Capacity
      (4) Ability
      (5) Interest
      (6) Aptitude
      (7) Attitude
      (8) Character
      (9) Stress-tolerance
      (10) Action pattern
   b. In any large group selected at random, traits are distributed, with about sixty-eight percent being in a normal range.
5. In studying his employees, the manager should understand that psychologists have divided personalities into three basic types. These are:
   a. The introvert, who expresses his emotions inwardly
   b. The extravert, who expresses his emotions outwardly
   c. The ambivert, who is a balance of two extremes
6. In studying his employees, the manager should remember that habit is a hindrance to understanding people as individuals.

7. Attitudes are important in human relations because they affect the employee's behavior. Opinions and attitudes are drawn from an individual's background and experience, which form his frame of reference. They shape his behavior as he sees things in relation to his needs.
8. Pressure and stress have the following effects on job performance and learning skill:
   a. When the individual is given control of the work and told how he is doing, stress and pressure are less evident.
   b. Slight anxiety increases productivity, but fear causes a disregard for safety. Stress and pressure increase speed of repetitive tasks but increase the error rate.
   c. Fear as a motivating factor in increasing employee performance is less effective than other methods.
9. When placed under stress and pressure, the individual may use behavior patterns that guard his personal worth. These are called defense mechanisms and include:
   a. Rationalization
   b. Projection
   c. Compensation
   d. Denial of reality
   e. Displacement
10. Individual behavior is either positive or negative. Positive behavior is result-oriented and expressed as:
    a. Job satisfaction
    b. Morale
    c. Motivation
11. Behavior is caused by the employee attempting to satisfy his basic needs which have been divided into five levels. When related to the job, these needs can be reduced to:
    a. Economic needs
    b. Social needs
    c. Psychological needs

DISCUSSION QUESTIONS

1. What is the value of human relations in relation to management? How is human relations related to employee productivity?
2. What is the relationship of leadership to human relations? How are leaders classified? Relate the various leadership styles to developing a people-minded philosophy. Which leadership style is more effective?

3. What makes individuals different? Discuss personality traits and their relationship to the manager's position in the organization. Also, relate the introvert and extravert pattern of thinking and acting to the job. How does habit affect a manager understanding people as individuals?
4. How is an attitude formed? Discuss the relationship among attitudes and the work organization and the manager.
5. In which forms are pressure and stress manifested? Discuss the relationship between pressure and stress and performance on the job.
6. What is meant by defense mechanisms and what do they include? Discuss the relationship between each mechanism and the work organization.
7. How is positive behavior expressed as related to the job and work organization?
8. What are man's five levels of needs? What is the relationship of these five levels to factors on the job?
9. Which of the fundamental principles discussed in this chapter are involved in each of the following instances?
   a. An employee who quits a company because he feels that it does not treat its employees fairly.
   b. A manager who uses the threat of firing a person to increase production.
   c. An employee who quits his job because he feels that he has no opportunity for promotion.
   d. A manager who increases production by steadily increasing the workload of his employees.
   e. An employee who smokes in a "no smoking" area of the plant because he says others do it.
   f. A manager who blames the low production rate of his department on the low quality of people recruited by the personnel department.
   g. An employee who constantly talks about his perfect attendance record and downgrades the importance of his low production rate.
   h. A manager who takes a day of sick leave (when he is not sick), knowing that he should have a serious talk with a troublesome employee about his drinking on the job.

CASE PROBLEM

Case 6–1

Jack Gross is known as a perfectionist and is highly qualified in his field. He is very careful in planning the work of his department; when work assignments have been made, he provides detailed supervision over the work being performed and the manner in which it is being done. Jack says, "It is my job to get employees to stay on the job and get the work out. I size up each new man when he comes in and determine what he can do. My biggest headache is getting employees to do their best." Known for his good judgment, Jack makes practically all of the decisions himself and either orders or "sells" people on carrying out his wishes. He seldom admits making an error in front of an employee because he wants to preserve his position of authority.

When an employee does poor work, Gross gets the facts, assembles the whole group, and then makes his criticism sharp and to the point. On the other hand, when an employee does an exceptionally good job, Gross never mentions it since he feels that this is what the employee is getting paid for. He believes that what people do off the job is their own business unless he thinks such activities are interfering with their work. Then he talks with employees about their after-hours activities. Jack does not stand in a man's way when an opportunity for promotion arises, but he rarely initiates a recommendation. He will listen to employees' complaints if they are related to their work assignments, but otherwise he acts in accordance with his conviction that to employees "no news is good news."

Questions

1. *What fundamental human relations principles are involved in this case in relation to the following:*
   a. Recognizing individual differences
   b. Pressure and stress
   c. Basic needs
2. *What is the leadership style of this supervisor?*

SELECTED REFERENCES

COLEMAN, JAMES C., *Personality Dynamics and Effective Behavior,* Chaps. 5 and 6. Fair Lawn, N.J.: Scott, Foresman and Company, 1960.

GILMER, B. VON HALLER, *Industrial Psychology,* Chap. 5. New York: McGraw-Hill Book Company, Inc., 1961.

HECKMANN, I. L., JR., and S. G. HUNERYAGER, *Human Relations in Management,* Parts 1 and 2. Cincinnati, Ohio: South-Western Publishing Company, 1960.

HEPNER, HARRY WALKER, *Perceptive Management and Supervision,* Chap. 24. Englewood Cliffs, N.J.: Prentice-Hall, Inc., 1961.

———, *Psychology Applied to Life and Work* (4th ed.), Chaps. 3, 4, and 9. Englewood Cliffs, N.J.: Prentice-Hall, Inc., 1966.

PARKER, WILLARD E., ROBERT W. KLEEMEIR, and BEYER V. PARKER, *Front-Line Leadership,* Chap. 6. New York: McGraw-Hill Book Company, Inc., 1969.

PFIFFNER, JOHN M., and MARSHALL FELS, *The Supervision of Personnel* (3rd ed.), Chaps. 12 and 20. Englewood Cliffs, N.J.: Prentice-Hall, Inc., 1964.

7

Factors of Employee Adjustment

In the previous chapter, it was indicated that an employee's behavior was either positive or negative depending on whether the individual felt adequate to meet the situation. To feel adequate, the employee must first make the appropriate adjustment to the job and to the work organization. Studies show that the better this adjustment is made, the more positive the employee's behavior is apt to be. Job adjustment is a continuous process, not restricted to the first few days on the job; nor is it limited to a single level of management or to a particular department. Effective job adjustment is influenced by many factors involving each level of management and all facets of the organization, making it a very important element of human relations. It is the purpose of this chapter to discuss some factors that influence effective job adjustment and by so doing, provide the manager with a basic framework for making his employees more productive on their jobs. To do this, these major topics are covered: (1) basis of effective job adjustment, (2) factors of job adjustment, (3) individual variables in job adjustment, and (4) resistance to change.

BASIS OF EFFECTIVE JOB ADJUSTMENT

The basis of effective job adjustment is the value that employees place on various aspects of their work situations. This is expressed as job satisfaction, or dissatisfaction, as the case may be. Therefore, to obtain an understanding of the basis of effective job adjustment, it is necessary to examine what satisfaction an employee expects from his job. In our work-oriented and highly mobile society, the job and the work organization are looked to more and more by working adults as a source for satisfying their economic, social, and psychological needs. This was not always so. In the early stages of our history, work was seen by most people as a means of providing food, clothing, and shelter essential for survival. At that time, the church, family, and community furnished the source for many of their social and psychological needs. Now, sheer economic survival is less pressing for the majority of the people, and since many of them move from the neighborhood, town, city, or state in which they were born, ties with institutions they once depended on have lessened. Therefore, today the job is considered not only as a means of satisfying the economic needs for survival and security but as a major source of social realization and psychological fulfillment. This has been confirmed by numerous surveys seeking to find what employees want from their jobs. Whereas the results of these studies differed in the order in which job factors were listed, practically all showed seven factors considered important by most employees. These factors and their relationship to economic, social, and psychological needs are shown below:

Job Factor	*Need Factor*
Job security	Economic
Opportunity for advancement	Psychological
Opportunity to use ideas	Psychological
Adequate pay	Economic
Concerned supervision	Social and psychological
Opportunity to learn	Psychological
Coworkers	Social

Although there may be disagreement as to which job factor relates to which need, there can be little argument that most employees expect their jobs and work organization to furnish a source for satisfying their economic, social, and psychological wants.

Dr. Frederick Herzberg and his associates in their significant research and analysis have done much to clarify and give meaning to the job factors on which employees place value. According to Dr. Herzberg, employees can be divided into two basic types: "motivation seekers" and "maintenance seekers." Motivation seekers are those who are concerned with such job factors as achievement, opportunity, responsibility, recognition, and other factors associated with the job itself. Conversely, maintenance seekers are those people who are more concerned with such factors as supervision, working conditions, pay, and other physical, social, and economic aspects of the job and the work organization. This allows job factors to be designated as what Dr. Herzberg termed "motivators" and "satisfiers." Of course, motivators are such things as achievement, opportunity, responsibility, recognition, and other factors sought by the motivation seeker; and the satisfiers include factors like supervision, working conditions, and pay sought by the maintenance seekers.[1]

While space does not permit a complete discussion of Dr. Herzberg's motivational-maintenance theory, mention should at least be made of his job-enrichment theory. Simply defined, job enrichment is an approach in which the job is made more meaningful by redesigning the job to give the worker more control over his work and make the work more challenging. Motivational factors such as achievement, recognition, satisfaction from the work itself, and personal growth and achievement are also built into the job structure. Of course the job-enrichment concept does not work for all jobs or with all people. Assembly jobs on a production line can hardly be redesigned to allow the employee much control over the process, nor do the motivators mentioned above work with all people. Some processes and some people simply do not lend themselves to job enrichment. Moreover, to utilize low-skilled persons, some jobs must by necessity be de-skilled rather than upgraded. To keep cost down, retailers, for example, rely on low-skilled, low-paid employees to fill a large number of their jobs, thus making job enrichment more difficult. Despite these difficulties, job enrichment, so called or not, is being applied by more and more major corporations and is showing exceptional results. An electronics assembly plant has been quite successful in implementing this concept. For example, in one department employees assembled a number of different models of electronic apparatus called "hot plates," using a normal assembly line operation. Without making any other changes in the department or its personnel, jobs were redesigned so that each employee assembled an entire hot plate, rather than its individual parts. Marking a positive reaction to the change, employees made such comments as, "Now it's *my* hot plate." To further demonstrate the positive aspects of the change, controllable rejects dropped from 23 percent to 1 percent in the next six months, while absenteeism dropped from 8 percent to less than 1 percent during the same time, and productivity increased 84 percent in the second half of the year.[2]

FACTORS OF JOB ADJUSTMENT

In view of the above, it can be seen that the key to employee adjustment is management taking into account those factors that the employee values. These factors will be discussed in this section. However, before doing

[1] See Frederick Herzberg, *Work and the Nature of Man* (Cleveland, Ohio: The World Publishing Company, 1966), pp. 71ff.

[2] See Edgar F. Huse and Michael Beer, "Eclectic Approach to Organizational Development," *Harvard Business Review*, September–October 1971, pp. 103-7.

this, two points should be understood. First, the Herzberg research and the findings of others also indicate that while the job factors sought by the maintenance-seeking employee had no positive effect on behavior, in their absence the motivating factors were ineffective. This means that although job satisfaction is different from morale and motivation, it forms the base for group attitudes and the desire for individuals and groups to excel in performance. Therefore, job satisfaction, morale, and motivation become so interwoven that the factors that contribute to one can hardly be distinguished from another. This being so, the factors discussed here can serve as fundamental reference points for the study of morale and motivation when these topics are discussed in the next two chapters. Second, although some attention is given to presenting the factors in the order in which most employees see them in relation to value, it should be understood that when treated in a general way, as done here, factors tend to overlap, making an exact order all but impossible. In addition, since all factors influence employee adjustment, the order in which they are listed is really of little importance. These two points should be kept in mind when reviewing the factors below.

Security

As a factor of employee adjustment, security is possibly the most important. Not only is it rated high on most job-satisfaction surveys but it is a psychological fact that a person cannot adjust properly to a new or changing situation unless he feels a reasonable degree of security. Security concerns how the employee feels about his job. It involves more than the steadiness of the job and the employee's reasonable assurance of fair treatment by his organization. These things are important, but equally important is the employee's relationship with his immediate supervisor. First, it concerns the attitude of the employee's supervisor, since this establishes the condition or atmosphere of approval. In the absence of the attitude of approval, the employee feels threatened, fearful, and insecure. Second, to feel secure the employee needs a knowledge of his job, the work situation, and the company as a whole. He must feel adequate to meet the requirements expected of him. Finally, he needs guidance and direction and the assurance that he will be given firm support by his supervisor if needed.

Opportunity

Also ranked high as a factor of employee adjustment is opportunity. Opportunity can be expressed in many ways. It can be in the form of advancement on the job, or promotion; or it may be simply a chance to learn something new. Moreover, opportunity means different things to different people. For example, some people do not want additional responsibility, whereas others do. Therefore, the opportunity to advance to the management level may be seen as an opportunity by one employee and as a threat to another. Also, studies show that men place greater importance on opportunity for advancement than women do. The age and position of the employee may also have a bearing on how opportunity is viewed. To a young man just starting on the job, opportunity may be a strong factor in job satisfaction. On the other hand, to the employee who is reaching retirement age, opportunity may be less important. Despite this, however, opportunity is a very important factor in job adjustment. The "dead-end job," which provides no opportunity for advancement, is a major source of worker dissatisfaction.

Recognition

A third major factor in job satisfaction and employee adjustment is recognition. Like the other factors in job adjustment, recognition affects different people in different ways, but most people want to be identified in some way. One of the problems of modern business and industry is the loss of identity of the employee. Too frequently, he becomes so involved in a process that the process submerges his identity. As a result of this loss of identity, he loses interest in the job and becomes bored and generally dissatisfied. Because studies show that if an employee is treated as a mere cog in the machinery of production he will be a less desirable employee, major attention should be given to providing him with some recognition. This may be in the form of praise by his supervisor, company awards and suggestion programs, or by some other means that will make the employee feel that he is appreciated and respected, both as a human being and as a valuable employee.

Belonging

When applied to job satisfaction, belonging pertains to the employee identifying with the work organization. This includes (1) the sharing of common goals with other members of the organization, (2) the feeling of solidarity with the organization, and (3) support given to the organization.

As a factor in employee adjustment, belonging is more or less a summation of the employee's perception of how the organization is meeting his social and psychological needs. According to one major study, there is positive correlation between the following job factors and the employee's identification with his organization: (1) solidarity with coworkers, (2) satisfaction with his promotion, (3) participation in decisions, (4) promotion chances, and (5) chance to use ability.[3] Most studies show no positive correlation between an employee's loyalty to his company and his productivity on the job. However, job-satisfaction surveys indicate that the five factors listed above are considered very important to most employees and when considered separately, each of the five factors has a positive affect on employee behavior. This would indicate that despite studies to the contrary, belonging as a factor of employee adjustment is significant.

Economic Conditions

Economic conditions pertain to the financial rewards that the organization provides its employees. Financial rewards include such things as pay, bonuses, insurance plans, stock-sharing plans, and pensions. Although the economic conditions of a job situation are normally overstressed by management and labor unions, financial rewards are important. Overall, organizations that offer a well-rounded financial benefit package attract and hold the type of people they want in their organization. This would imply that financial rewards help prevent labor turnover. On most job-satisfaction surveys, pay is ranked lower in importance by employees than by managers and labor union officials. This indicates that the amount of pay is not too important as a factor of job satisfaction, but it becomes very important when compared by one individual with the pay of other individuals in the same organization. For example: If Joe is doing similar work to Tom's but Joe is receiving less pay, chances are that pay would be a major factor in Joe's attitude toward his job and work organization.

Working Conditions

This factor refers to the physical environmental structure of the organization. It includes such things as illumination, noise, atmospheric conditions, and other physical aspects of the work situation. On most job-satisfaction surveys, working conditions are rated low by employees in comparison to other factors. This lack of concern is generally supported by scientific studies showing no proof that working conditions have a direct bearing on such things as turnover, absenteeism, or errors. This does not mean to imply, however, that working conditions are not a factor in employee adjustment. Whereas it may not be measurable, working conditions establish a conducive atmosphere for employee adjustment. When an organization makes an honest attempt to provide its employees with a clean, well-lighted, attractive place to work, it shows it cares about the employees. This, in turn, is often reflected in the attitude of its employees toward the overall organization.

[3] See Martin Patchen, *Participation, Achievement, and Involvement on the Job* (Englewood Cliffs, N.J.: Prentice-Hall, Inc., © 1970), p. 268.

Psychological Climate

A factor that has a major effect on employee adjustment is the psychological climate of the organization. It pertains to the attitude of management toward the employees.

The management attitude of an organizaion is referred to as its management philosophy. This philosophy lays the groundwork for the organization's psychological climate. It is reflected in the policies, procedures, practices, and the attitude of the organization's managers, and forms the base for employee adjustment. The late Douglas M. McGregor classified management philosophy into two categories. He called one *Theory X,* and the other *Theory Y.*[4]

Reduced to the barest essentials, *Theory X* philosophy is based on the premise that the practice of being tough on people is the best way of getting things done. The *Theory X* philosophy contends that the average worker is basically lazy and therefore has to be coerced, directed, and controlled. The employee is hired to do as he is told and is not expected to initiate action.

On the other hand, the *Theory Y* philosophy regards the employee as an individual with needs and aptitudes of his own. This theory is based on the assumption that the worker will exert more energy if the right atmosphere is provided to stimulate his inner reserves of energy and talents; when left alone, the worker tends to perform far beyond what is expected.

The management philosophy of most organizations is neither purely *Theory X* nor *Theory Y* but a blend of the two with a tendency to lean more toward one theory than the other. As a general rule, employees in an organization leaning toward a *Theory Y* philosophy, by allowing the employee to have a degree of control over their work, tend to show higher job satisfaction.[5]

INDIVIDUAL VARIABLES IN JOB ADJUSTMENT

Because each person is different, no criteria have yet been developed that take into account all of the variables that affect job adjustment. There-

[4] From Douglas M. McGregor, "The Human Side of Enterprise," in *Human Relations in Management,* by I. L. Heckmann, Jr., and S. G. Huneryager (Cincinnati, Ohio: South-Western Publishing Co., 1960), Part 3, pp. 145ff.

[5] It should be recognized that the works of McGregor have made a significant contribution to management, and his total writings are worthy of full exploration in the advanced study of management. But for the purpose here, this brief treatment is all that is necessary.

fore, it should be recognized that each individual has a set of unique traits and a distinct personality that make him respond differently to his job. However, as the characteristics of most people fall within a general range of normal distribution, it can reasonably be assumed that, other things being equal, job adjustment of one employee is not totally different from another and that the application of sound human relations practices would facilitate their adjustment. This assumption is valid with some exceptions. It has been found that certain employees, due to their physical, psychological, or social makeup and background, possess certain characteristics that deviate from the norm sufficiently to warrant special consideration. These include: (1) women, (2) older workers, (3) the disadvantaged (hard-core) employee, and (4) the physically handicapped worker.

Women Employees

Since World War II, women have become a major factor in the work force of many organizations. Now, women make up about one-third of the total labor force. Because women have been traditionally treated differently in our society, have a different physical makeup, and are generally thought to be emotionally different from men, their adjustment to the job is often thought to be more complex than that of men. To a point, this is true. The results of studies show that it is the general opinion of most authorities that women face certain adjustment problems. Some factors that bear on the job adjustment of the woman employee are discussed below.

ATTITUDE. Research indicates that women often differ from men in their attitude toward work. Some women see work as a secondary role and their responsibilities as wife and mother as their primary duty; consequently work is often considered a temporary arrangement. This, of course, is a concern to most employers because a stable work force is a prime management factor in most businesses. This factor can also cause a conflict of interests between job and family that places a psychological as well as a physical strain on the woman employee, thus affecting job adjustment. But more and more women are taking jobs with a career in mind, which makes their attitude toward work equal to that of men. In addition to their attitude toward the job, women tend to place more emphasis on cleanliness, working conditions, and treatment by their supervisors than men do. They, too, place less importance on the economic factor of the job and are generally more sensitive than men. Possibly the greatest adjustment factor faced by the woman employee is the attitude of management toward her place in the world of work. Although changing, it is still the attitude of many management men that women are less capable, harder to supervise, and in general less desirable employees than men. Despite the efforts of the Women's Liberation Movement and equal opportunity laws, not only does the woman employee generally receive less pay for like work, but in many cases, she is not offered the same opportunities for advancement or the same consideration for such things as job training as men are. This attitude has tended to place restrictions on woman's role in industry and business and thereby appreciably affects her adjustment to the work situation.

LIMITATIONS. Because women are thought to have limitations, they are often treated as if they do. Some of this treatment is justified; some is not. There is no scientific proof that women are less intelligent than men. Test after test proves this to be true. But in the technical areas of acquired knowledge, men are generally more knowledgeable than women, which is due more to the role of the sexes in our society than to mental limitation. Men, expected to be more technical and to do things of a technical or mechanical nature, naturally acquire more scientific and technical know-how than women. Physically, however, studies indicate that women do have certain limitations. Obviously, if the work is heavy, a woman is limited due to size and physical makeup. But in certain areas of work, women are more physically apt than men. For example, it has been found that women have greater finger dexterity, are more adept at bending and stooping, and are generally more proficient in using circular arm motions in doing assembly work. In regard to supervision, it is possibly true that most men dislike working for a woman, but this does not indicate that women possess less administrative or supervisory abilities. In most cases, women have had less opportunity to develop their managerial abilities, but when given the opportunity, women with the proper background have proved to be equal to men in managerial positions. Of course, such things as facilities pose a problem in some organizations as well as the design and condition of the work situation. These and other variables should be taken into account in assisting the woman in adjusting to the job.

EFFECTIVENESS. There is a lack of scientific studies concerning women in regard to turnover, absenteeism, error rate, and accidents. In the absence of factual information, only some generalizations based on the opinions and experience of businessmen can be offered regarding effectiveness: (1) In general, the turnover of women is higher than men, (2) Absenteeism of women is somewhat higher, (3) On certain jobs, women make fewer errors than men, and (4) Accidents are more the result of general factors than innate differences between the sexes.

Older Workers

The term *older worker* is normally applied to those forty-five years of age and over. Whether age is a factor in job adjustment depends on the individual, the job, and the general makeup of the work situation. It has been found, for example, that older workers may be more set in their ways than younger ones and therefore resist change more. Also, the older worker in general is less agile, and in many cases has less strength than the younger person. These factors obviously place some limitations on the adjustment of the older worker to the job. Despite these limitations, however, the older worker has many assets. Some of these assets as related to job adjustment are listed below:

1. He normally has greater versatility and can handle more jobs.
2. He has fewer accidents.
3. He is less likely to change jobs; therefore, his group has fewer turnovers.
4. In sustained performance, he is often more productive on similar jobs.
5. He has less absenteeism.
6. He has fewer grievances.

As pointed out earlier, the older worker is less concerned with opportunity for advancement (to a point) and is more concerned with security. Therefore, if placed under stress he may resort to some defense mechanism if he feels his security is threatened.

Disadvantaged Employees

The term *disadvantaged employee* (also called *hard-core*) is applied to those who by reason of personal characteristics, background, education, economic conditions, and other factors, are different from the average employee. For years these people were all but excluded from the job market. Now, an attempt is made to afford the hard-core worker an opportunity to become a full member of the work force. Often thought to include only the ghetto Negro, actually only about 25 percent of the hard-core are black.[6] The poor whites, Puerto Ricans, Mexican-Americans, and American Indians also fall into this classification. Due to their socioeconomic background, they have special adjustment problems to the job and the work organization. No attempt will be made here to psychoanalyze the inherent and environmental causes for these problems, but some of the more common problems resulting from the hard-core background that affect job adjustment are identified below: [7]

The initial entry of the hard-core employee to the job is especially difficult. The surroundings are completely new to him, and the complexity of the business or industrial atmosphere is completely foreign. His back-

[6] See Leon H. Keyserling, *Progress or Poverty,* Conference on Economic Progress, (Washington, D. C., December 1964), pp. 50ff.

[7] For a more complete discussion of the hard-core, see *Effectively Employing the Hard-Core* (New York: National Association of Manufacturers, 1968).

ground makes him feel that he is different and apart. His behavior is often different, and his frame of reference is totally inadequate to understand his surroundings. This often causes him to act with surliness, indifference, and toughness.

Communication is often another problem in his adjustment to the job. The cultural background of the hard-core not only gives him a unique vocabulary that some find difficult to understand, but with his previous background of rejection, he is often reluctant to communicate his doubts to his supervisor, or to ask instructions about things he does not understand. This may cause him to start without understanding how to do a task, thus subjecting him to errors or accidents.

Past failures and the lack of opportunity affect his ability to do the job. Normally having little or no experience, a low educational achievement level, and possibly a police record, he may have a feeling of complete worthlessness and inadequacy. This feeling of hopelessness may cause the disadvantaged worker to rationalize to the extent that he may not try, or he may quit the job the very first day.

Time is another factor that the hard-core finds difficult to cope with. Having had to keep no regular schedule, often time is of little relevance to him. Therefore, concern for promptness often puzzles him. Consequently, the rate of absenteeism and tardiness is exceptionally high for the hard-core.

To assist the hard-core employee in adjusting to the job, some companies have designed and developed special programs to include special employee job training and sensitivity training to help supervisors and other workers deal more effectively with the disadvantaged employee. This is a step in the right direction; by recognizing that only through special assistance can those who have lived in poverty and deprivation adjust sufficiently to the world of work to achieve their potential as productive human beings.

Physically Handicapped Employees

The handicapped worker also faces problems not normally encountered by the average employee. First, since his handicap is often visible, he may feel conspicuous and self-conscious and will be less likely to adapt to the work situation. Second, because he is handicapped he often feels a sense of insecurity. Third, due to his handicap his potential to perform a variety of jobs is limited, which in turn limits his opportunity for advancement. But numerous studies show that when assigned jobs within the limits of their capabilities, as a group people with physical handicaps produce at a rate equal to or higher than the nonhandicapped worker. Also, their turnover rate and absenteeism are frequently lower and their safety records are better.

RESISTANCE TO CHANGE

An overriding factor in employee adjustment to the job and work organization is the human tendency to resist change. In work organizations, resistance to change is normally reflected in higher rates in turnover, absenteeism, and errors and accidents. Why people resist change has not been fully defined. It is the general belief of most psychologists that this resistance stems primarily from a threat to the individual's security, that it is a form of fear of the unknown. Resistance to change could be better understood if it applied only when the change affected an individual's security. But people (employees and managers alike) tend to resist change even when the change is to their advantage. Regardless of the reasons, resistance to change is a major factor in employee adjustment, and management must make every effort possible to cope with it.

To cope with resistance to change, many organizations have orientation programs for new employees. These programs, which are discussed in other chapters, are designed to lessen the impact of change and make job adjustment easier. On a day-to-day basis, resistance to change can be partially overcome by applying the following three general principles:

Prepare the Employees for the Change

Possibly the most important factor in making a change is preparation. People simply do not like sudden changes. Therefore when a manager is anticipating a change, he should let his employees know about it as far in advance as possible. When possible, a change should be included as a part of an existing procedure and phased in over a period of time. This way, the change will not be entirely new, and the shock will be taken out of it. Also, it has been shown that employees accept change more readily if they know the reason for the change. By explaining why, even if the change is disagreeable to the employees, most of them will go along with less reluctance. In this connection, the manager should where possible show where and how the change will benefit the employees individually or as a group. People in general like to know what benefits they will get from a change. In other words the manager should answer the question: "What's in it for me?" In short, employees should be "sold" on the change. This may be done better by someone other than the manager. For example, if one of his employees is enthusiastic about the change, he may be asked by the manager to sell the change to the other employees.

Allow the Employees to Participate in the Change

When effecting a change, employee participation is very important. The reason is simply this. If the employee is allowed to contribute to making the change, part of it becomes his. Therefore, the new idea is not "their" idea, but to the employee it is then "our" idea. For participation to be effective, the manager should listen to his employees' suggestions and make an honest attempt to understand the employees' point of view. Besides, the employees may make a contribution that the manager can use.

Give Support to Change

This third and final principle for effecting change is very important, for unless the change is given wide support, the chances of it being accepted by the affected employees are indeed remote. For a change to be accepted, this support must come from two levels. First and most important, the manager making the change must give it his unqualified support. He must support it before he can sell it to his employees. If the manager even remotely shows a sign in his attitude that he does not believe in the change being made, his attitude can only be interpreted by his employees to mean that the change is unimportant. This point is extremely important since a manager is often required to implement changes that he may not fully accept himself. These may be policy and procedure changes developed by staff members, or changes instigated by higher management, which the lower manager had no say in developing. But even though he does not particularly like the change, once the policy or procedure has been made, the supervisor as a part of management must give the change his support. Second and conversely, the change should be supported by top management. As it was pointed out in Chapter 4, employees like to be informed by those in a higher position of authority. This is also true in the case of change. Therefore obtaining the participation and visual support of top management will make the change more acceptable to the employees and make the change more effective.

In conclusion, it should be added that these three principles should be kept in mind when the manager is executing many supervisory skills and management techniques. In a very real sense, overcoming resistance to change is an underlying factor that must be considered when the manager is performing most of his supervisory duties. Therefore, these principles will be used as a frequent point of reference in other chapters in the book.

KEY POINT SUMMARY

1. Employment adjustment is how an individual adapts to his job and work situation and is expressed as job satisfaction.
2. Job satisfaction is the employee's attitude toward his job and work organization and is based on factors on which employees place value.
3. According to Dr. Frederick Herzberg, employees can be divided into two basic types, motivation seekers and maintenance seekers.
    a. Motivation seekers are concerned with such factors as achievement, opportunity, responsibility, recognition, and other "motivators."
    b. Maintenance seekers are concerned with factors such as supervision, pay, working conditions, and the "satisfiers."
4. The major factors that influence job adjustment are:
    a. Security
    b. Opportunity
    c. Recognition
    d. Belonging
    e. Working conditions
    f. Economic conditions
    g. Psychological climate
5. Due to their physical and psychological makeup or social background, some employees have special problems in job adjustment and therefore require special attention. These people include:
    a. Women employees
    b. The older worker
    c. The disadvantaged or hard-core employee
    d. The physically handicapped
6. In regard to women employees, it should be remembered that:
    a. She often has a different attitude toward work than men.
    b. She has both limitations and assets.
    c. She is not inherently inferior to men either as a person or as an employee.
    d. Her effectiveness is superior to men in some areas and less in others.
7. In regard to the older worker, it should be remembered that:
    a. Age as a factor of adjustment is relevant to the job.

b. He has more assets than limitations.
c. He is more concerned with job security.

8. In regard to the disadvantaged or hard-core employee, it should be remembered that:
    a. His social background restricts his ability to adapt to his job and work organization.
    b. To overcome these restrictions, he needs special assistance.
9. In regard to the physically handicapped employee, it should be remembered that when given work within his capabilities, he can adapt to the job and become an effective employee.
10. In employee adjustment the human tendency to resist change is a major factor. Why people resist change is not fully understood, but resistance to change can be partially overcome by applying these general principles:
    a. Preparing the employees for change
    b. Allowing employees to participate in making the change
    c. Giving support to the change

DISCUSSION QUESTIONS

1. What is meant by *job adjustment?* How is it expressed? Relate job satisfaction to morale and motivation.
2. What is the basis of job satisfaction? Discuss Dr. Herzberg's research concerning job factors on which employees place value.
3. What is the relationship of the following factors to job adjustment?
    a. Security
    b. Opportunity
    c. Recognition
    d. Belonging
    e. Economic conditions
    f. Working conditions
    g. Psychological climate
4. Why do certain employees warrant special consideration in their adjustment to the job? Explain.
5. What are some significant factors concerning women employees?
6. What are assets and limitations of the older employee?
7. What are some of the factors that the hard-core employee must overcome in adjusting to the job?
8. Why does the physically handicapped employee require special consideration?
9. Why do people resist change?
10. What are some principles that can be applied in overcoming resistance to change?

11. What job satisfaction factor or factors are involved in the following descriptions?
    a. The older worker who brings his boss small gifts and also agrees with what his supervisor has to say.
    b. The employee who feels she was not promoted because she is a woman.
    c. The arrogant hard-core employee who feels that his menial job affords him no opportunity for advancement.
    d. The management of an organization that believes that the employees are basically lazy but affords them some control over their work.
    e. The handicapped, hard-core older woman worker who complains about her pay being less than others in her department.
    f. The manager who argues vigorously with his supervisor and his employees to win a point and get his own way.
    g. A manager who believes in the old adage that a "new broom sweeps clean."

CASE PROBLEM

Case 7–1

Marjorie Smith, the only woman in a large department, had worked there for a year. It was known that she was the best and most experienced worker there. However, Miss Smith was rather quiet and very rarely contacted her supervisor, Mr. Dennet. Also, even after a year she was not fully accepted by the other members of the department. Mr. Dennet was satisfied with Marjorie's work and tended to ignore her. Mr. Jackson had just come in recently. His work was average. But he brought himself to the attention of Mr. Dennet by asking questions and making suggestions. When an assistant supervisor had to be appointed, Mr. Dennet chose Mr. Jackson for the job. A week later Marjorie requested a transfer to another department explaining that she desired a change from the work she was doing because it was too monotonous. Her supervisor said he would consider it. Upon investigation, Mr. Dennet found that if he granted Miss Smith a transfer she would have to take a reduction in salary. Moreover, he felt she was more valuable where she was. Three weeks later, Marjorie stopped him:

"How about that transfer, Mr. Dennet?"

"Oh, didn't I tell you? I have decided that it would be better for you to stay here."

Being busy, he then dismissed the instance from his mind. Next day Miss Smith resigned.

Questions

1. *What are the principles in this case?*
2. *What is the possible real reason for Marjorie asking for a transfer?*
3. *In your opinion, why did Marjorie resign?*

SELECTED REFERENCES

Effectively Employing the Hard Core. New York: National Association of Manufacturers, 1968.

GILMER, B. VON HALLER, *Industrial Psychology* Chaps. 10, 11, and 13. New York: McGraw-Hill Book Company, Inc., 1961.

HERZBERG, FREDERICK, *Work and Nature of Man,* pp. 71–167. Cleveland, Ohio: The World Publishing Company, 1966.

JUCIUS, MICHAEL J., *Personnel Management* (6th ed.), Chap. 24. Homewood, Illinois: Richard D. Irwin, Inc., 1967.

LINDGREN, HENRY CLAY, *Psychology of Personal and Social Adjustment,* Chap. 12. New York: American Book Company, 1953.

PARKER, WILLARD E., ROBERT W. KLEEMIER, BEYER V. PARKER, *Front-Line Leadership,* Chap. 7. New York: McGraw-Hill Book Company, Inc., 1969.

PFIFFNER, JOHN M., and MARSHALL FELS, *The Supervision of Personnel* (3rd ed.), Chaps. 7, 9, and 23. Englewood Cliffs, N.J.: Prentice-Hall, Inc., 1964.

TIFFIN, JOSEPH, and ERNEST J. MCCORMICK, *Industrial Psychology,* Chap. 12. Englewood Cliffs, N.J.: Prentice-Hall, Inc., 1965.

8

Factors that Influence Teamwork

In work organizations, people are brought together to do certain tasks and performing these tasks requires interaction among the various members of the organization. Through this interaction, various groups are formed as social counterparts of the tasks being performed. These tasks or work groups establish the social and functional structure of an organization. Like individual behavior, the behavior of these groups can be positive or negative. Group behavior is positive when it is directed toward the goals of the organization. This goal-directed behavior is called *teamwork.*

However, it is to be understood that for the various groups to become teams, they must have more in common than social interaction. A team implies common motivation, common attitudes, and common goals. In management, a team has as its common characteristic the mutual dependency of its members to accomplish the predetermined objectives of the organization or elements of the organization (department, branch, or unit). For a group to become a team, its accomplishments must be greater than the sum of the accomplishments of its individual members. Each employee must not only do his task, but contribute to the overall effectiveness and efficiency of the group. This extra contribution is more psychological and social than physical. It is a feeling, a feeling stemming from the employee seeing the goal of the group as being greater than his own and his willingness to lose part of his personal identity by adjusting to the general pattern of behavior of the group. This feeling is the psychosociological essence that distinguishes a team from a group. It is called morale. Because it is the job of every manager to build his work group into a goal-directed team, it is the purpose of this chapter to discuss some of the factors that influence a group in becoming a team. The following major topics are discussed: (1) supervision and teamwork, (2) social factors and teamwork, (3) labor unions and teamwork, and (4) morale and teamwork.

SUPERVISION AND TEAMWORK

Study after study shows that the single most influencing factor in building a group into a goal-directed, highly motivated team is the behavior of the group's supervisor. These studies show that the supervisor's behavior not only influences the group's ability to produce more, which will be amplified in the next chapter, but has a profound effect on the group's morale. Consequently, the logical place to start a discussion of factors that influence teamwork is by examining the various types of supervisors and finding out which type produces the most effective teamwork.

Supervisors and supervision can be typed in many ways. Supervisors can be typed by leadership styles as discussed in Chapter 6, or as production-centered or employee-centered supervisors, which will be discussed in the next chapter. When applied to teamwork, supervision has further been typed according to the characteristics of the supervisor. While this method of typing is cross-sectional and interrelated to the two other methods, it is useful here since it allows supervision to be related to teamwork and group behavior. When related to developing teamwork, supervisors have been divided into four basic types that produce a certain pattern related to group behavior.

THE DEPENDENT TYPE. This type of supervisor is concerned primarily with his own security. He is normally afraid to take chances. He follows rules and regulations to the letter. He has infrequent and impersonal contact with his employees. He avoids communication with his employees if at all possible. The climate of his group is one of apathy.

THE DRIVER TYPE. This supervisor seeks power and responsibility primarily for himself. He is critical and detailed in supervising his employees. He practices one-way communications. He gets the work done but without regard to employee attitude. Antagonism is normally the prevailing climate of his group.

THE DIPLOMATIC TYPE. This type of supervisor gets along well with top management and his employees. He knows how to manage people. His motivation is primarily personal advancement and security. He has frequent contact with his employees but it is often superficial. The prevailing atmosphere is competitive, and his people are interested in their own selfish goals.

The Quarterback Type. This type of supervisor is aimed at building a real work team. He is motivated by group interests. He seeks recognition, advancement, and security for those with whom he works as well as himself. His personal contact with his work group is one of give and take. There is sincere two-way communication, and an atmosphere of teamwork exists.

The patterns of these four types of leaders are summarized in the chart in Figure 13.

	Dependent	Driver	Diplomat	Quarterback
1. Frame of reference	"They"	"I"	"You"	"We"
2. Method	Interpreting	Telling	Selling	Discussing
3. Motivation of Supervisor	Strengthen systems	Maintain control	Overcome resistance	Strengthen relationship
4. Basis of decisions	Rules and regulations	Authority of supervisor	Judgment of supervisor	Mutual agreement
5. Communi-cations	Routine Supv. ↓ Man	One-way Supv. ↓ Man	Two-way Man ↑ ↓ Supv.	Two-way ← Supv. Man →
6. Relies on man's . . .	Loyalty	Obedience	Ambition	Cooperation
7. Employee reaction	Apathy	Antagonism	Competition	Teamwork

Figure 13 Four Leadership Styles (Adapted from *The Role of the Supervisor*, Study Guide, Educational Resources Foundation, Columbia, S. C.)

As the above discussion and this chart indicate, not only is the quarterback type of supervisor more effective, but his primary method of supervision is through two-way lateral communications. The effectiveness of using two-way communications in building teamwork is strongly supported by most studies, which show that participation is a prime factor in achieving high group morale. These studies indicate that the group's attitude toward the company, the supervisor, and their work in general is highest among those groups where their supervisors frequently hold group meetings to get their views. On the other hand, it has been further found that if the supervisor seldom holds group meetings, or fails to listen sincerely to their ideas, it will have a reverse effect on morale. This means that although (as shown above) the diplomatic type of leader practices two-way communications, it is less effective because it is less sincere. Therefore, it can be concluded that a key factor in developing teamwork is not only the supervisor practicing two-way communications, but his motives and his attitude toward people.

SOCIAL FACTORS AND TEAMWORK

It has been found that an organization with high morale and high productivity consists of a tightly knit, effectively functioning social system.

> This social system is made up of interlocking work groups with a high degree of group loyalty among the members and favorable attitudes and trust between superiors and subordinates. Sensitivity to others and relatively high levels of skill in personal interaction and the functioning of groups are also present. These skills permit effective participation in decisions on common problems. Participation is used, for example, to establish organizational objectives (by management by objective) which are a satisfactory integration of the needs and desires of all members of the organization and of persons functionally related to it. High levels of reciprocal influence occur, and high levels of total coordinated influence are achieved in the organization. Communication is efficient and effective. There is a flow from one part of the organization to another of all the relevant information important for each decision and action. The leadership in the organization has developed what might well be called a highly effective social system for interaction and mutual influence.[1]

This makes it apparent that the social aspect of an organization is important. However, in welding a group into a team, a manager is often confronted with social factors that may run counter to developing teamwork. These factors can be identified and discussed as aggregates and in-groups and out-groups.

[1] See Rensis Likert, *New Patterns of Management* (New York: McGraw-Hill Book Company, 1961), p. 99.

Aggregates

People who are classified together because they show some common characteristics are called aggregates. For example, it was indicated in the previous chapter that women, older workers, hard-core employees, and physically handicapped workers had different adjustment problems since they possessed certain physical, psychological, or social characteristics that made them different. All of these groups are aggregates since they possess certain common characteristics. Other examples are racial groups, language groups, hippies, or all women with red hair. If members of a group feel that certain individuals possess certain qualities that are inconsistent with the group, these people will be made to feel unwanted and may therefore preclude the group from becoming a team. For example, because some people believe that women have less administrative ability, are more emotional, and as an aggregate possess other behavior patterns that are less desirable than those of men in certain work situations, women members of a group may not be assimilated as full members and share the full feeling of the group as a team. The same concept applies to race. While there is no scientific evidence that there are differences among races, some people insist that such differences exist. Because they believe that is true, they act as if it were. This can alter the attitude of a group toward minority aggregates, which in turn can directly preclude the group from being a team.

Although many of the social barriers that have been raised over the years have been torn down, many still exist. Therefore, the manager should make every effort to assist representatives of aggregates in becoming fully integrated members of their work groups. Of course the logical question is—*How?* Unfortunately, there is no concrete answer to this question. If the question could be answered, it would not only help solve the problem of the manager in developing his group into a team, but help solve many of the social problems confronting our society today. However, since a work group often patterns its behavior by the example set by the manager, he can do much to influence the group's attitude by his own attitude and action toward aggregates. If, for example, a manager's attitude or action in dealing with a certain aggregate is either negative or positive, chances are it will influence the group's attitude in either accepting or rejecting an aggregate member as a part of the team. So it follows that a manager should take a hard look at his prejudices in regard to the aggregate members of his department.

In-Groups and Out-Groups

Another factor that can affect teamwork either positively or negatively is what sociologists call in-groups and out-groups. The in-group is an association or subgroup toward which its members feel a sense of solidarity, loyalty, friendliness, and cooperation. It is characterized by the expression "we." Its members feel a keen sense of belonging and develop a protective attitude toward other members of the group. They see the group as meeting and satisfying some of their needs and interests. On the other hand, the out-group consists of those persons toward whom the group feels a sense of indifference, avoidance, disgust, competition, or outright hostility. In other words, the group feels no closeness to those outside the group, who are referred to as "they." The "we group"–"they group" is found to some extent in all organizations. Obviously, the "we group" concept is the essence of a team. But when seen from a total organizational point of view, there is some danger in creating within the same organization competing groups that may be to the disadvantage of the total organization. If, for example, one department develops a "we group" attitude to the extent that it sees people in the other departments of the organization as "they," the efficiency of the organization can only suffer from lack of cooperation. In developing a team, it is the job of the manager to not only attempt to develop the "we group" concept for his department, but for the total organization. Lucky is the organization when employees and managers alike refer to people in its various elements as "we" instead of "they."

In previous chapters it was pointed out that in every organization there exists an informal organization centered around a natural leader. Often these groups form cliques with a strong "we" group attitude. Since these groups occasionally have objectives that differ from the goals of the organization and exclude certain employees from becoming members, cliques are counter-productive in building a team. Therefore, when strong informal "we" groups develop that fail to coincide with the formal pattern of the organization, they should be recognized and the manager should make an honest effort to reconcile the goals of the informal group with the goals of the organization.

LABOR UNIONS AND TEAMWORK

Another factor in some organizations that may affect teamwork is labor unions. The primary role of labor unions, as indicated in Chapter 3, is to improve the wages, hours, and working conditions of its members. No attempt need or will be made here to discuss all aspects of union-management relations. But since the objectives of the union often conflict with the objectives of the organization, thus affecting group behavior, some understanding of management-employee-union relations is needed.

Common Union-Management Conflicts

Before discussing areas of disagreement between management and labor, it is well to recognize that there are several areas in which they cooperate to their mutual advantage. For example, both union and management generally agree on increasing the size of the industry or firm, but for different reasons: Management from the standpoint of increasing profits, and unions from the standpoint of increasing job possibilities. A similar situation exists in the case of health and safety. From a purely business sense, management is interested in these areas because, according to law, the employer is responsible for health hazards and on-the-job accidents. Also, poor health and accidents affect production by causing employee absenteeism. On the other hand, the union is interested in health and safety for the employee's welfare. Another area in which management and the union normally agree, again for different reasons, is the goal of maintaining a stable work force. Management wants a stable work force for efficiency's sake, while unions are interested in employee job security.[2]

Despite these areas of mutual agreement, the two groups have areas of disagreement that cause conflict. The two most common ones are wages and benefits, and work hours.

In the case of wages and benefits, the conflict normally concerns cost versus income. As pointed out in the chapter on economics, one of the largest costs in operating a business is wages paid to employees. This being so, wages must be controlled by management in relation to production. To make a profit (or in the case of nonprofit organizations, the restrictions imposed by fund allocation), there is a point beyond which management cannot raise wages without an increase in production or service. Conversely, labor sees wages not in terms of cost of production but as income. Like management, labor sets a limit based on the employee's standard of living which it will not lower regardless of production. From these over-simplified examples, it can be seen why wages are a major source of conflict.

In the case of work hours, the conflict concerns the interest of the company versus the welfare of the employee. Management is primarily concerned with obtaining maximum production from its employees during the time they spend on the job. This may cause establishing shifts, prescribing work methods, and establishing pay systems that employees consider contrary to their welfare. Obviously, when this occurs a conflict develops between union and management.

Regardless of their nature, union-management conflicts are a major factor in developing teamwork, and when the conflict is carried to extremes, it can destroy teamwork altogether, or at least temporarily, especially if the union calls its members out on strike. For clarification, a strike is the term used to describe the action of employees when they refuse to perform their jobs. A strike is normally—but not always—initiated by the union. It is labor's ultimate weapon in obtaining what it wants from management.

[2] See Merle E. Strong, *Industrial, Labor, and Community Relations* (Albany, New York: Delmar Publishers, 1969), pp. 100ff.

Strikes are often harmful to both the company and to the employees. To the company, besides the damage it does to teamwork, a strike causes a loss in production or sales that can severely affect its financial position. In the case of a long strike, the employees seldom recover the money lost from the lack of wages incurred during the strike.

Employee-Union-Management Loyalty Conflict

Because according to the old adage, "one man cannot serve two masters," it would appear that there would have to be a conflict between the employee's loyalty to his union on the one hand and the company on the other. But according to one of the few major studies on this subject, this may not be so. The result of Theodore Purcell's study of a unionized Swift plant showed that seventy-three percent of the employees felt that they could be loyal to both the union and the company.[3] Of course whether or not a loyalty conflict exists depends on many factors. If, for example, the employee feels that his needs are being met by the company, that his job is secure, his pay adequate, and his supervisor is interested in him as a person, and he feels that he is truly a part of the organization, chances are that he will show his loyalty to the company as well as to the union. Conversely, if he has to look to the union to extract these things from the company, his loyalty may be substantially swayed toward the union.

Reconciling Union-Management Conflict

As pointed out earlier, it is normally to the advantage of both the company and the union to avoid a strike. This makes it apparent that union-management conflicts shoud be reconciled if at all possible. The basis for resolving union-management conflict is to establish an agreement regarding the conditions under which employees render their service to the employer. This agreement is usually in the form of a written contract between the company and the union, which can be used as an instrument for resolving grievances.

THE UNION-MANAGEMENT CONTRACT. Although the agreement may vary in content, most union-management contracts include the following major topics:

1. Management prerogatives
2. Union recognition
3. Hours of work
4. Wages

[3] See "Dual Alliance to Company and Union Workers. A Swift-UPWA Study in a Crisis Situation, 1949–1952," *Personnel Psychology*, Spring 1954.

5. Seniority
6. Working conditions
7. Lay-off and hiring
8. Vacations and holidays
9. Adjustment of grievances

Before being made part of a contract, topics such as these are negotiated by management and labor. By making concessions, conditions that can be condoned by both sides are established. This process is called *collective bargaining.*

GRIEVANCES. In union-management relations, a grievance is an official complaint filed by an employee or a union against management. It can concern some managerial action or interpretation of the union contract. In either case, the grievance procedure is an orderly way for resolving union-management conflict. It allows the complaint to be reviewed and discussed at each level of the union-management hierarchy until it is finally resolved. Very basically, here are the steps in the grievance procedure:

1. The employee having the grievance or the union steward or both discuss the grievance with the employee's immediate manager. (A union steward is an employee who has been elected or appointed to represent the union in addition to his other duties.)

2. The chief steward discusses the grievance with the manager at the next level, normally the superintendent or department head.

3. A grievance committee discusses the complaint with the manager of the business organization.

4. National union representatives take the complaint up with the president, or chairman of the board, or the highest officials of the company.

5. Finally, if the complaint is not resolved *at any one of the above levels,* it can be placed in arbitration. Arbitration is when union and management agree to abide by the decision of an impartial individual or a board of individuals for handling the grievance.

Of course, it is the responsibility of management at each level to resolve the grievance at that level and to preclude a complaint from becoming a formal grievance. It is to the advantage of all concerned that the conflict be resolved as quickly and as satisfactorily as possible.[4]

MORALE AND TEAMWORK

It should be recognized that whereas morale is the measure of teamwork, morale involves more than individual interaction in the group. As

[4] The supervisor's role in precluding a problem from becoming a grievance is discussed in Chapter 14.

pointed out earlier, morale is the sum of individual attitudes of a group toward the work situation and the factors that make up the structure of the organization. The individual's attitude toward his job was expressed in the last chapter as job satisfaction and included such factors as security, opportunity, recognition, belonging, and so on. This means that both job satisfaction and good group interaction constitute the structure of a team and the measure of teamwork. In other words, for a group to have high morale, most employees of the group must be reasonably satisfied with their jobs as well as with their interaction (working together) with their work group. This concept is important for it clearly indicates that when the manager is building a team, each individual of the group must be considered. In addition, this concept lays the groundwork for discussing two significant topics concerning morale: (1) Measuring morale, and (2) Improving morale.

Measuring Morale

It should first be understood that morale cannot be weighed like cheese or measured like cloth. It must be assessed by trying to determine the employees' opinions and feelings as indicated by their attitudes. As a result, measuring morale is inexact and at best only an indication of how employees actually feel. Nonetheless, much attention has been given to measuring morale, and two common methods are used.

OBSERVATION. On a day-to-day basis, informal observation is the best method for assessing morale. This is particularly true at the lower management level. The manager as a supervisor in his day-to-day, face-to-face contact with his employees can gain insight into the morale of his work group by observing the feelings and behavior of each employee. But to use observation as a means of assessing morale, the manager should develop a system for observing. First, he should realize that employees' feelings are normally manifested by their behavior. Any sudden change in an employee's behavior should alert the manager to a possible change in attitude. This means that the manager should pay particular attention to such minute behavior patterns as a shrug of the shoulders, the raise of an eyebrow, or a change in tone of voice, as well as more obvious behavior such as sullenness, open hostility, outbursts of anger, or excessive aggressiveness. All these signs tell the manager something about his employees' feelings. Second, morale can be assessed by listening to his employees talk. This includes tuning in on the "grapevine." As pointed out, the "grapevine" is a group's informal communications system. Since employees are often reluctant to express their true feelings to their supervisors, the "grapevine" is often a more reliable source for assessing morale than formal means. Third and finally, the manager should assess his own attitudes as well as his employees', for to be meaningful as a measure of morale, information gathered by observation must be interpreted and evaluated. This interpretation can only be as accurate as it is free from prejudice and bias of the interpreter. Before concluding, it may be well to point out that assessing morale, like any other process, is to determine areas that require attention. Therefore, it goes without saying that when a situation is detected that requires attention, corrective action is implied.

QUESTIONNAIRES. A more formal method of measuring morale is by having a group of employees fill out a questionnaire concerning their feelings about certain aspects of their jobs. These questionnaires or opinion surveys can be constructed to measure employees' feelings and attitudes about the organization as a whole or certain specific areas such as training, orientation, personnel policy, communications, and the like. Some typical statements included on an opinion survey to determine employees' overall attitudes toward an organization are shown in Figure 14.

STATEMENT
1. I think this company treats its employees better than any other company does.
2. If I had to do it over again, I'd still work for this company.
3. They don't play favorites in this company.
4. A man can get ahead in this company if he tries.
5. I never understood what the company's policy was.
6. The company is sincere in wanting to know what its employees think about it.
7. A wage incentive plan offers a just reward for the faster worker.
8. On the whole, the company treats us about as well as we deserve.
9. I can never find out how I stand with my boss.
10. In my job I don't get a chance to use my experience.

Figure 14 Typical Statements for Morale Survey

From these questionnaires, management makes an assessment of the morale of the employees involved. Many organizations have outside management consultants conduct these surveys, whereas others perform their own. In either case, this method has at least two advantages. First, because the employee is not identified as an individual, he is more apt to give his true feelings. Second, this method provides a permanent record that can be used to develop trends when compared with other surveys. Despite these advantages, morale surveys have to be used with caution. When an organization makes a survey of its employees' opinions, employees expect that positive action will be taken on any unsatisfactory condition. Therefore, if no follow-up action is contemplated, it is better not to make the survey in the first place. Also, when the sampling technique is used, the danger of drawing conclusions from too few opinions always exists.

Improving Morale

The reason for making a morale survey is to determine areas where morale needs to be improved. If, for example, a survey indicates that a majority of the employees in an organization feel that their pay is not consistent with other like organizations in their area, the company may by improving its pay system in turn improve employee morale. Or, when a survey indicates that employees of a certain department are dissatisfied with the behavior of their supervisor, the supervisor may improve morale by improving his leadership style. But improving morale is a day-in day-out job, not predicated on the results of a morale survey nor the pay and personnel policy of the organization. Improving morale, when boiled down to its basic substance, is a basic supervisory responsibility. For as it has been said before, *in the mind's eye of the employee, his supervisor is the company*. What then, can the supervisor do to improve morale? This question can best be answered by taking a brief look at some of the characteristics displayed by the supervisors of high morale groups.

Study after study shows that the supervisors with the most favorable and cooperative attitudes in work groups treat their employees as unique human beings. They treat individuals as important members of the team and take individual differences into account in all phases of their supervision. The supervisors of high morale groups assure that each individual is trained to do his job, coach and assist those who are below standard, and generally try to assist their employees in achieving their highest potential. They endeavor to serve the best interests of the individual employees, the work group, and their organization.

Also, studies show that in work groups with high morale, the supervisors' behavior is characterized by planning and scheduling work, supplying their employees with adequate materials, tools, and equipment, and directing the work firmly but fairly. They further provide employees with technical assistance when required. An area frequently overlooked when improving morale is the flow of materials and information. Many studies show that employees' attitudes (morale) are directly affected by this factor. Most psychologists believe that this factor stems from the feelings of employees that lack of information and materials to do the job indicates that the supervisor (or management in general) is not concerned with their problems.

Studies also show that managers of high morale groups develop their employees into a work team by using the quarterback style of supervision as discussed in this chapter.

Consequently, it can be seen that developing teamwork, as measured by morale, is an important factor in creating the conditions for positive employee behavior.

KEY POINT SUMMARY

1. Organizing the various work groups of an organization so that their behavior is positive and goal-directed is called teamwork.
2. In management, a group is a team when its members see the goals of the work unit and the organization as greater than their own, are willing to contribute more than required by their individual tasks, and when they develop a feeling of solidarity with the group. This feeling is called morale.
3. The leadership style of the manager has a major effect on building a group into a team. As related to teamwork, four common leadership styles are:
    a. The dependent type, who is concerned with his own security
    b. The driver type, who seeks power and responsibility for himself
    c. The diplomatic type, who is concerned with personal advancement and security
    d. The quarterback type, who is concerned with building a real work team
4. To develop a group into a team, the manager should take certain social forces into account. These include:
    a. Aggregates—those who have certain common characteristics and may be socially defined as having innate behavior patterns incompatible with other members of a work group.
    b. In-groups and Out-groups—subgroups within an organization that include or exclude other members.
    c. Informal groups—groups within an organization that may have goals that are counter-productive to building teamwork.

5. Since the goals of labor unions often conflict with the goals of an organization, union-management relations are important in developing teamwork.
6. Common union-management conflicts are caused by disagreements concerning wages and benefits, and work hours.
    a. The union is interested in increased income for its members, whereas management is concerned with cost in relation to production.
    b. The union is interested in work hours in relation to the employee's welfare. Conversely, management is concerned with the amount of production in relation to the time spent on the job.
7. In case of employees being loyal to the company or to the union, a conflict is likely to exist when employees feel that only through the union can they achieve their objectives.
8. To avoid a strike, union-management conflicts should be resolved as effectively and quickly as possible by:
    a. Solving an employee's problem before it becomes a formal grievance
    b. Negotiating a satisfactory union-management contract through collective bargaining
    c. Resolving the conflict through moral grievance procedures
9. Teamwork can be measured by obtaining the attitudes and opinions of employees through two common methods: observation and questionnaires. In using morale surveys, two points should be kept in mind:
    a. For observation to be effective in measuring morale, the manager must develop a system of observing.
    b. The questionnaire has the advantage of allowing the employee to be anonymous and affords a permanent record.
10. The purpose of measuring morale is to detect areas where morale needs to be improved. On a day-to-day basis, the manager should consider these three points to improve morale:
    a. Treat each employee as a distinct individual
    b. Plan and schedule his employees' work
    c. Develop his employees into integrated work teams

DISCUSSION QUESTIONS

1. What is the difference between a group and a team? Explain the characteristics that make a group a team.

2. What are four common leadership styles and what are the behavior patterns of each? Relate each style to teamwork and group behavior.
3. What are some social forces that influence teamwork? Relate the "we-group"—"they group" concept to teamwork. Why are cliques counter-productive to teamwork?
4. Why are union–management relations important in the study of group behavior?
5. What are some common areas in which management and union agree? Disagree? Explain.
6. Under what circumstances is there likely to be a conflict between the loyalty of an employee to his work organization and his union?
7. What are some major means of reconciling union–management conflicts? What is meant by collective bargaining? What is a grievance? Relate human relations to resolving union–management conflict.
8. What is the relationship between morale and job satisfaction and social interaction?
9. What are two common means of measuring morale? What are the significant factors in each method?
10. How can morale be improved? Relate improving morale to understanding individual differences.
11. What principles are there involved in the following instances and what effect would they have on teamwork?
    a. The supervisor who relies entirely on his own judgment, makes all the decisions himself, and tells his employees exactly what to do and how to do it.
    b. The supervisor who has the opinion that all members of a certain minority group are socially inferior.
    c. The supervisor who, after listening to a union steward concerning a complaint of an employee, asks that the problem be presented in writing as a formal grievance.
    d. The supervisor who fails to invite one of his employees to a party he is giving for his department.

CASE PROBLEM

Case 8–1

Jack Rawlings, manager of a small department, can be relied upon to get the job done. He plans his work carefully but once he assigns work to employees, is inclined to let them alone. However, he believes in strict enforcement of rules. When an employee is seen violating an established procedure, he calls the employee aside and tells him in a forceful way that rules are made to be followed without exception. Jack is known for making decisions slowly but accurately. When confronted with a problem, he discusses the situation with his employees, but after obtaining the facts, he thinks them over carefully and makes a judgment concerning the best course to follow. When a change in work procedures is necessary, he sells the new method to those who will be affected by pointing out how it will improve their production and make their work less demanding. He maintains a friendly and cordial relationship with his employees on and off the job, but on the job there is no doubt in anyone's mind as to who is boss.

Questions

1. *What is the leadership style of this manager?*
2. *Would the morale of the employees of this department more likely be high or low? Why?*

SELECTED REFERENCES

HEPNER, HARRY WALKER, *Perceptive Management and Supervision,* Chap. 5. Englewood Cliffs, N.J.: Prentice-Hall, Inc., 1961.

———, *Psychology Applied to Life and Work* (4th ed.), Chaps. 20 and 24. Englewood Cliffs, N.J.: Prentice-Hall, Inc., 1965.

LIKERT, RENSIS, *New Patterns in Management,* Chap. 8. New York: McGraw-Hill Book Company, 1961.

LUNDBERG, GEORGE A., CLARENCE C. SCHRAG, and OTTO N. LARSEN, *Sociology* (3rd ed.), Chap. 4. New York: Harper and Row, Publishers, 1963.

STRONG, MERLE E., *Industrial, Labor, and Community Relations,* Sec. 4. Albany, N.Y.: Delmar Publishers, Inc., 1969.

TIFFIN, JOSEPH, and ERNEST J. MCCORMICK, *Industrial Psychology* (5th ed.), Chap. 11. Englewood Cliffs, N.J.: Prentice-Hall, Inc., 1965.

YOUNG, KIMBALL, and RAYMOND W. MACK, *Systematic Sociology* (2nd ed.), Chap. 2. New York: American Book Company, 1962.

9

Factors of Employee Performance

In the past chapters, primary attention has been given to establishing conditions for positive employee behavior. But does creating these conditions produce results as measured by productivity on the job? Some think that it does, others disagree. Putting it more explicitly, what motivational factors make people produce? It all depends on the manager's (or management's) assumption of why people work. It was pointed out that the employee's desire to perform well is called motivation. Consequently, this has created two opposing motivational assumptions about getting people to produce. One assumption is that a person will produce more if management attempts to integrate the goals of the individual with the goals of the organization by treating him as an individual, developing integrated work teams, and allowing him to have some control over his work through participation in decision making. This assumption is based on McGregor's *Theory Y* philosophy of management. On the other hand, the opposing motivational assumption is based on the *Theory X* concept with strong emphasis on the economic motives of "buying" a man's time and telling him precisely "what to do and how to do it." So far in this book, the position leans toward the *Theory Y* motivational assumption. However, when related to performance, the two assumptions should be put into perspective. This can best be done by discussing the relationship of attitudes, supervision, and participation to performance. But it should be understood also that although psychologists generally agree that motivation is the innate drive, urge, or force that causes people to behave as they do, when applied to work and the worker, motivation is not the sole determining factor of employee performance. This means that although motivation is stimulated by the employee's attempt to satisfy his economic, social, and psychological needs, other individual and situational variables come into play. Keeping these things in mind, factors of employee performance will be discussed under these major headings: (1) attitudes and performance, (2) supervision and performance, (3) participation and performance, (4) developing a motivational assumption, and (5) individual and situational variables.

ATTITUDES AND PERFORMANCE

Over the years, much research has been done concerning the relationship between employee attitudes and performance as measured by productivity. Whereas it is not the intent of this book to cite the results of research but to discuss principles, two projects are of such significance that an exception is made here. These are the Hawthorne Study and the continuing studies being conducted by the Institute of Social Research, University of Michigan. The results of these studies are briefly described below:

The Hawthorne Study [1]

One of the most significant studies regarding the relationship between attitudes and performance is the classical and now famous Hawthorne Plant studies conducted in cooperation with the Western Electric Company by Professors Elton Mayo and Fritz Rorthlisberger. Three studies were made, starting in 1924 and spanning a fifteen-year period, to test the effect of illumination on production. In the first two experiments, using a control group and a test group, it was found that not only increased lighting raised production in the control group and the test group, but decreased lighting produced an increase in production still further. This led to the conclusion that although the illumination study was a failure, other factors besides working conditions had an effect on productivity. Therefore, a third study was conducted in which other work factors were included and the results recorded.

In the third experiment, which covered a five-year period, a test room was used and five women assemblers participated. In this experiment, work factors other than illumination were interjected. But like the first two experiments, the elimination of the work factor incentive produced an increase rather than a decrease in productivity. This led to two important conclusions: (1) That work factors as previously thought were not an incentive

[1] See Harry W. Hepner, *Perceptive Management and Supervision*, 2nd ed. (Englewood, N.J.: Prentice-Hall, Inc., 1954), p. 33; Henry Clay Lindgren, *Psychology of Personal and Social Adjustment* (New York: American Book Company, 1953), pp. 275ff.; and B. von Haller Gilmer, *Industrial Psychology* (New York: McGraw-Hill Book Company, Inc., 1961), pp. 32ff.

for an employee to increase productivity, and (2) that what really produced the increased performance were the attitudes of the five women employees.

It was found that in the process of the experiment, the women had established a close interpersonal relationship, which gave them a feeling of solidarity, and the attention given them by the company had made them feel important. This improvement of attitudes had been the cause of the increase in productivity, not the work factors, as such. Even though the clinical methods used in the Hawthorne study have been criticized by some, it still remains one of the most important projects undertaken in relation to attitudes and employee productivity.

The Michigan University Continuing Studies [2]

The close interrelationship of job satisfaction, morale, and productivity has been found in many studies other than the Hawthorne experiment. The most comprehensive of these is the systematic research conducted by the Institute for Social Research, University of Michigan. In analyzing a variety of organizations of many types, and varied types of work, this organization has found some significant factors related to employee attitude and productivity. Pertinent findings and inferences of this group are summarized as follows:

1. Very little relationship within a company has been found between employees' attitudes toward the company and their productivity.
2. The less productive groups (sections of the company) participate more often in company sponsored activities than do more productive groups.
3. For blue collar and white collar workers, there is a marked relationship between worker morale and how much employees feel that their boss is interested in discussing work problems with the work group. Work groups with high group pride and loyalty are more productive. The workers in high production work groups not only have greater group loyalty and pride, but help one another more and give this help on their own initiative.

These studies seem to support the motivational assumption based on the *Theory Y* philosophy. When employees are treated as individuals by their supervisors and developed into teams with close social interaction, higher productivity will result. However, before drawing an absolute conclusion, two factors should be understood. First, some studies show no relationship between job satisfaction, morale, and productivity. Therefore, it is erroneous to assume that high morale will automatically and solely produce high productivity. But it is reasonable to assume that taken with other variables, high morale will substantially influence productivity for the bet-

[2] See Rensis Likert, *Motivation: The Core of Management,* Personnel Series No. 155 (New York: American Management Association, 1953).

ter. Second, it is to be further noted that it has been found that closely integrated groups exert pressure on their members to conform to the groups' norms. Although this may add to high morale, it sometimes has an effect on an employee's productivity. Studies support the contentions of some managers that pressure in closely integrated groups is a restrictive factor on employee productivity. Despite these two factors, and also recognizing that morale is only one of many variables that influence employee performance, attitudes are still a significant influencing factor in positive behavior.

SUPERVISION AND PERFORMANCE

Another important factor that influences employee performance is supervision. There is evidence that supervision and the leadership styles of the immediate manager not only contribute to or detract from teamwork but have a significant influence on individual and team productivity. This was found evident in both the Hawthorne experiment and the Michigan University studies cited above. In the Hawthorne study it was discovered that the employees' attitudes toward their supervisors could be associated with the workers' productivity. In the Michigan University studies, a more definite relationship was established.

In one long-range study by the Michigan University researchers, supervisors were classified in two types. One was called *employee-centered,* and the other *production-centered.* The employee-centered supervisors were those primarily concerned with workers as people. In their leadership style, the employee-centered supervisors took into account the employee's feelings, his desires, and his opinions. On the other hand, the production-centered supervisors were those that thought of people merely as cogs in the machinery of production. The production-centered supervisor's style was patterned toward the output of his department with little thought given to the feelings of the employee. When the leadership styles were compared between seventeen high-production sections and twenty-one low-production sections, it was found that (1) in high-production sections, thirteen of the leaders were employee-centered and four were production-centered, and (2) in the low-production sections, only seven of the supervisors were employee-centered.

From this and other studies, the following conclusions were drawn: (1) When a worker or a person at any level in a hierarchy feels that his boss sees him only as an instrument of production, as merely a cog in a machine, he is likely to be a poor producer. However, when he feels that his boss is genuinely interested in him, he is more likely to be a high producer; (2) Groups having employee-centered supervisors are higher producers than groups with production-centered supervisors; (3) Close supervision tends to be associated with lower productivity, and more general supervision with higher productivity; (4) In using his supervisory skills in supervising his employees as a group (by using group methods), the greater is the productivity and job satisfaction of the work group.[3]

Factors that Influence Supervision

These and other findings tend to support the *Theory Y* motivational assumption that the democratic leadership style is more effective not only in promoting teamwork, but in increasing employee production. Used as a general pattern of leadership, the democratic approach is without question the most productive, but when applied on a day-to-day basis, several factors should be considered. In any given situation, the effectiveness of supervision is influenced to a large extent by four factors: (1) the manager, (2) the employee, (3) the type of work, and (4) the psychological climate of the organization.

THE MANAGER. The personality of the manager has a very definite effect on employee behavior and can affect his performance. All people being different, the personality of one supervisor may elicit a totally different response from the employee under similar circumstances than another would. This attraction involves the total makeup of the manager's personality, and it may possibly account for the fact that in some cases, production-centered supervisors obtain maximum performance from their workers, whereas the employee-centered supervisor experiences low productivity.

THE EMPLOYEE. Employees respond in different ways to supervision. The style that works well with one employee may not be best for another. For example, if the employee is the dependent type or unskilled, he may be more effective if his decisions are made for him and therefore would be more effective under a production-centered supervisor. Conversely, if the employee is independent or competent, he would possibly be more productive under employee-centered or democratic leadership. There are other examples that could be cited, but the point is that individual differences are an important factor in the manner in which employees respond to leadership styles, and individual traits and personality should be taken into account when directing the efforts of others.

Also, the occupational makeup of the work group may influence the appropriateness of the leadership style used by the manager. In work groups made up of professional people (scientists, engineers, lawyers) or in groups where the employees are highly skilled, the democratic or employee-centered

[3] See Likert, *Motivation: The Core of Management, op. cit.*

leadership style is often more effective. But in groups where the employees are unskilled or when their socioeconomic background has not taught them to act independently, the production-centered approach may produce greater results.

TYPE OF WORK. The type of work also has a bearing on whether the employee-centered or the production-centered approach would produce the greater results. If the work is repetitious, once trained, the employee may be left on his own without close supervision. But if the work is hazardous, close supervision may be required. (This applies more to accident and error rate than to production; but as these two factors affect production, it is included here). Another work factor that should be considered in the effectiveness of close or loose supervision is the complexity of the work. If the work is a process—one step following another—normally close supervision within each step tends to disrupt the process and cause a lowering of production. Of course this and the other factors given will depend to a large degree on the competency of the worker.

THE ORGANIZATION. The psychological climate of the organization as manifested by its management philosophy has an overriding effect on the leadership style of the manager of an organization. If the overall management philosophy of an organization tends to lean toward either the *Theory X* or *Theory Y* approach, chances are that its managers will by necessity and self-preservation have to adapt their individual styles accordingly. Therefore, a production-centered supervisor in a *Theory Y* organization may have to modify his style to be more employee-oriented. Or, an employee-centered supervisor in a *Theory X* firm may be required to adapt his style to a more production-centered pattern. In most larger organizations, the management philosophy is broad enough to tolerate some variance in styles of leadership. However, the variance between the philosophy of the company and the leadership style of the individual manager must be reasonably compatible. Otherwise, the conflict will affect his overall effectiveness as a leader, which may result in lower production.

PARTICIPATION AND PERFORMANCE

There can be little argument concerning the motivational assumption that when an employee is allowed to participate in the decision-making process, he will perform better. Most studies show a close association between the amount of control the employee has over his work and positive job performance. These studies indicate that when employees are encouraged and provided the proper setting to decide for themselves or in combination with others how their work should be done, their motivation to do the work is likely to be considerably enhanced.[4] Although control over work through employee participation is closely associated with other management factors such as communications, since it is considered by some as the single most influential factor in employee performance, participation deserves special attention.

Influencing Factors

Participation may be thought of as the giving and receiving of information, advice, and suggestions, and the sharing of experience among members of an organization. In management, it particularly applies to allowing the employee to have a voice in shaping policy, procedures, and processes that directly or indirectly affect him. The effectiveness of participation will depend on *the organization, the manager,* and *the employee.*

THE ORGANIZATION. For participation to be effective, the organizational psychological climate must be conducive to encouraging and providing the means for the employee's participation. First, for participation to take place, the organization must provide and encourage two-way communications. Obviously, if information is directed only one way—down—then no exchange between management and the employee can take place. Therefore, two-way communication is the first requirements for employee participation. Secondly, the organization's attitude toward its employees has a direct bearing on employee participation. To encourage employees to participate effectively, the employee must be made to feel that his opinions and ideas mean something, that he is valued both as a person and an employee. As a general rule, *Theory X* management philosophy tends to stifle participation, whereas the *Theory Y* approach encourages it. Next, the organization's effort to encourage participation must be sincere. If employee participation programs are used as a gimmick to improve "morale," with little intent of using the employee's opinion's or suggestions to influence decisions, it becomes meaningless and often does more harm than good. Finally, the organization needs to establish guidelines as to the freedom managers can allow employees in making decisions concerning work in their departments.

THE MANAGER. The factors that apply to the organization are equally applicable to the manager. He must practice two-way communications, treat the employee's opinions and suggestions with respect, and be sincere in his attempt to encourage employee participation. In addition, the manager

[4] Martin Patchen, *Participation, Achievement, and Involvement on the Job* (Englewood Cliffs, N.J.: Prentice-Hall, Inc., 1970), p. 234.

should take at least two other factors into account. First, he must remember that participation does not relieve him of authority or his responsibility for making decisions. This means that although the employee's opinions and suggestions should be taken into account, the last word rests with the manager. Second, the manager must remember that he has a dual responsibility: One to his organization and one to his employees. Therefore, the desires and wishes of the employees must be measured against the goals and objectives of the organization. Where possible, the desires and wishes of the employee must always be considered, but when a conflict exists, the manager is obligated to support the goals of the organization.

The Employee. The degree to which an employee is allowed to participate depends to a great extent on the employee's background and training. If the employee has no background on the subject being discussed, then his opinions and suggestions would have little value. This does not mean that all employee advice and opinion should not be sought. If the employee has no background and training, his advice can be used to identify areas of concern and to collect information. On the other hand, if the employee has considerable experience and training, his advice may prove beneficial in making decisions. By allowing the experienced and inexperienced to participate, both will feel that they have some control over their work.

Methods of Encouraging Participation

Within the framework of the above guidelines for effective participation, there are several methods by which employees can be encouragd to participate in executing some degree of control over their work. Methods can be formal or informal, and include employee committees, suggestion programs, group discussions, and individual contact.

Employee Production Committees. These are formal groups, consisting of representatives from both workers and managers, formed to discuss work problems. Although these committees appear to have great potential, indications are that they have seldom worked well. This is due to several factors. First, management of the organization is reluctant to cede to the committee the authority to make decisions. This possibly stems from the fear that employees (especially in unionized organizations) will exercise too much control on usual management prerogatives in running the firm. Another factor is that union members are sometimes reluctant to participate in management decisions. Also, poor human relations, getting bogged down in red tape, and the failure to hold frequent meetings often render production committees ineffective. As a result of these drawbacks, production committees seldom prove effective as a method of employee participation.

Suggestion Programs. These programs are designed to afford employees a formal method of making suggestions concerning their work and work place. Suggestion systems have proven effective in some organizations and ineffective in others. To be effective the program must be properly administered and the employee made to feel that his suggestions will be considered. Also, employees must be encouraged to submit suggestions by providing some assurance taht their ideas will not cause more work or cause other employees to lose their jobs. Often management, especially first-line supervisors and staff personnel, see employee suggestions as a form of criticism, in which case, suggestion programs are only reluctantly supported. Despite this, suggestion systems or programs are a common and can be a useful method for encouraging employee participation.

Group Discussion. Another widely used method for encouraging employee participation is the group discussion method.[5] This method is useful to: (1) gather information, (2) give information, (3) praise or commend workers, (4) develop understanding of common work goals, work requirements, and production standards, and (5) solve problems and assist in decision making, using the creative problem-solving method. But for the group discussion method to be effective in encouraging employee participation, there must be a free exchange of information between employees and the discussion leader, and among the employees involved. Used in this way, the group discussion is a most effective means of encouraging employees to take part in exercising control over their work.

Individual Contact. The most effective method of encouraging employee participation is the day-to-day, face-to-face exchange of information, opinions, and experience between the manager and his employees on an individual basis. Closely associated with the employee-centered or democratic style of leadership, individual contact has the advantage over the other methods in several ways. First, it requires no formal preparation because there are no formalities imposed. Second, it allows each employee to be treated as an individual, thereby making the employee feel that he is valued as an employee and as a person. It also permits the manager to encourage employee participation in the absence of other more formal systems.

Despite these advantages, some managers are reluctant to encourage employees to express themselves concerning their jobs. This is possibly due to the fear of the manager of losing control of the group and work situation, and the opinion of some managers that asking the advice of employees shows weakness in his leadership ability. With few exceptions, this leadership trait is considered by most as a strength instead of a weakness, and if it is made

[5] How to lead group discussions is discussed in Chapter 18.

clearly understood that the manager reserves the right to make the final decision, there is little danger of his losing control of his employees or of his operation.

DEVELOPING A MOTIVATIONAL ASSUMPTION

What logical assumption should the manager draw concerning his attitude and behavior as it pertains to motivation and employee productivity? In other words, what style and method should he use to get the work out? It can be seen from the above discussion that the answer to this question is still not clear. The discussion above supports the statement at the onset, that the exact relationship between the factors of individual behavior and the effect they have on individual productivity are very complex and not fully understood. This is true. No general principles that apply across the board can yet be stated with any degree of accuracy. However, the preponderance of research findings as projected and clarified by the significant writings of Rensis Likert support these basic generalizations for work groups with high productivity.[6]

> 1. A preponderance of favorable attitudes of members of the organization toward all aspects of the job (toward other members, supervisors, the work, the organization); the favorable attitudes toward the organization and work are attitudes of identification with the organization and its objectives.
> 2. The highly motivated, cooperative orientation is achieved by harnessing effectively all the major motivational forces which can exercise significant influence in an organizational setting (the ego, security, curiosity, and economic motives).
> 3. The organization consists of a tightly knit, effectively functioning social system of interlocking work groups.
> 4. Measurement of organizational performance is used primarily for self-guidance rather than for superimposed control.
> 5. Widespread use of participation is employed in various aspects of the job and work.
> 6. Full advantage is taken of the technical resources of the classical theories of management, such as work simplification, budgeting, and financial controls, but these are used in different ways than by the low-producing managers; in particular these techniques are used in such a way as to bring into play some of the motives mentioned above (such as

[6] For a complete discussion of these generalizations as well as supporting research findings, see Rensis Likert, *New Patterns of Management* (New York: McGraw-Hill Book Company, Inc., 1961). Also see Joseph Tiffin and Ernest J. McCormick, *Industrial Psychology,* 5th ed. (Englewood Cliffs, N.J.: Prentice-Hall, Inc., 1965).

through participation) as opposed to being used to exercise control through authority.[7]

Also, Likert points out that research findings do not show that all high producing managers follow this pattern. He states that technically competent, job-centered, insensitive, and tough management can achieve relatively high productivity. The evidence clearly indicates that if this kind of supervision is coupled with the use of tight controls on the part of the line organization, impressive productivity can be achieved. Members of units whose supervisors use these high-pressure methods, however, are more likely to be among those that have the least favorable attitudes toward their work and their supervisors and are likely to display excessive waste, scrap loss, and turnover. In general, these are work groups that show the greatest hostility and resentment toward management, the least confidence and trust in their supervisors, the largest number of grievances that go to arbitration, and the greatest frequency of slowdowns, work stoppages, and similar difficulties.[8]

INDIVIDUAL AND SITUATIONAL VARIABLES

It was stated that whereas motivation is a key factor in employee performance, it is not the only factor that influences employee productivity. This means that on any job, productivity is determined by many individual and situational variables not directly related to motivation. Individual variables include such things as traits (aptitudes, intelligence, and so on), sex, education, experience and the like. On the other hand, situational variables that influence performance are things like work design, work space and arrangement, method of work, and other factors such as training, organizational personnel policies and procedures. Although these factors are present in all work situations, their influence on individual productivity will vary according to a specific individual, job, department, or organization. Therefore, these factors will be treated, either directly or indirectly, as general topics in other parts of the book. However, there is one nonmotivational variable that influences individual productivity in all work situations: fatigue.

Work Curve

Work curves are useful in understanding fatigue. A typical day work curve for an employee performing a motor-task is shown in Figure 15.

[7] See Tiffin and McCormick, *Industrial Psychology,* p. 375.

[8] See Likert, *New Patterns of Management,* p. 59.

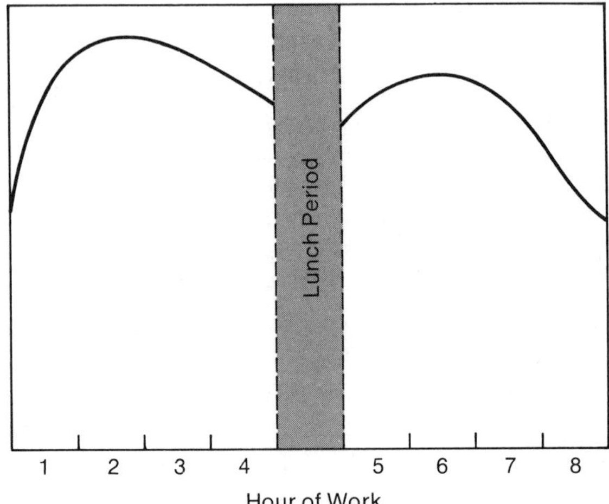

Figure 15 Typical Work Curve (Source: *Technical Aids for Small Manufacturers,* Small Business Administration, Washington, D. C., Jan.-Feb. 1960.)

As this figure indicates, after the worker starts in the morning, he tends to increase his productivity. He starts out cold and warms up to the task. This warm-up period is part physical and part psychological. Physically, the ability of the muscles to function increases as the body adjusts to the activity. Psychologically, warming up involves a change in attitude and attention. It takes time for him to focus his thoughts away from other things and onto the work. As the worker becomes more absorbed in his work, an increase in productivity results. There is a similar warm-up period following the lunch break.

The initial warm-up period is followed by a period of high productivity. But as the work continues, the performance will begin to fall off and will continue decreasing to the end of the work period. In addition to this general downward trend, the performance also shows an increased variability with continued work. The worker alternately speeds up and slows down.

The morning and afternoon work curves for most activities have the same general shape. There are important differences, however: (1) The morning's maximum productivity is usually higher than that reached in the afternoon. (2) The afternoon warm-up period starts at a higher performance level than the worker's initial efforts in the morning. (3) The impairment in productivity is more marked in the afternoon than in the morning. (4) The downward trend frequently begins earlier and the productivity usually falls to a much lower level by the end of the afternoon.[9]

[9] I. L. M. Bosticco, Ernest L. Loen, and Robert B. Andrews, "Is Worker Fatigue Costing You Dollars?" in *Technical Aids for Small Manufacturers* (Washington, D.C.: Small Business Administration, January–February 1960).

Physical and Psychological Fatigue

The general downward trend in employee productivity as indicated in Figure 15 is generally attributed to the worker becoming physically tired. Physical fatigue is naturally a factor in employee performance. Scientists have proven that if a person exceeds his energy level of about five calories per minute over a sustained period of eight hours per day without a rest, his performance will suffer. However, in all tasks (the majority of which have an energy expenditure rate well below the five-calorie level) people often show marked increase in feeling tired as the work day continues. This applies to jobs requiring motor skills as well as clerical tasks and is illustrated in Figure 16.

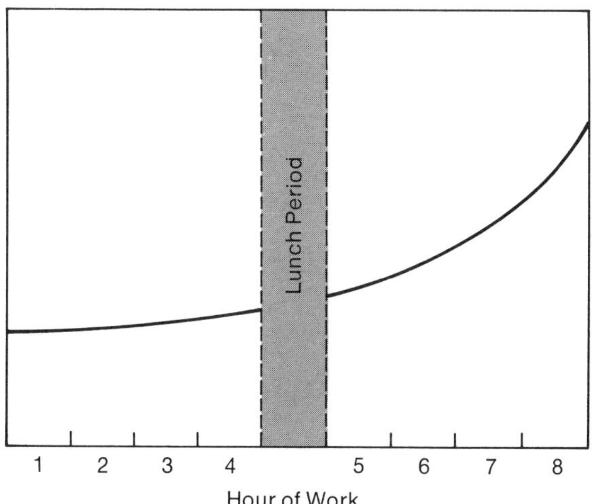

Figure 16 **Feelings of Tiredness for Typical Motor-skill and Clerical Tasks (Source: *Technical Aids for Small Manufacturers,* Small Business Administration, Washington, D. C., Jan. Feb. 1960.)**

This has led to the belief that the decrease in employee productivity is due to frustration, boredom, or monotony rather than the physical aspect of the work. This is supported by studies indicating that there are consistent downward trends in performance in relation to time worked for both heavy and light duties. Also, giving support to the psychological aspect of fatigue is the fact that: (1) People, at times, can feel tired without having exerted themselves. (2) They can go all day without feeling tired, if their activities are varied and interesting. (3) They can awaken after a full night's sleep feeling more tired than when they went to bed. (4) In emergencies, they can expend large amounts of energy without feeling tired. This makes it clear that both the physical and the psychological factors of fatigue should be taken into account when related to employee performance.

Rest Periods

One means by which physical and psychological fatigue can be taken into account is providing rest periods.

Physically, to work at a level above his capacity, a person must draw from his energy reserve. The energy reserve for the average person is only about 25 calories. Once this energy reserve has been exhausted, it must be replenished by a rest period for the employee to continue a sustained level of performance. The length of the rest period necessary to restore the energy reserve expended depends on the activity being performed by the individual. For example, scientists have found that for such jobs as light and medium assembly work, general laboratory duties, washing dishes, and bricklaying, the average person does not exceed the 5 calories per minute. This means that physically a person could perform these tasks for an eight-hour day with only a lunch break. On the other hand, drilling in a coal mine requires the use of 5.8 calories and a fifteen-second rest is necessary for each minute worked. To maintain his level of performance, this would mean that for each hour on the job, forty-eight minutes should be spent working and twelve minutes resting. Other examples could be cited, but the point is that planned rest breaks are necessary when an employee is doing heavy physical work. In scheduling rest periods, several factors must be considered. First, the 5-calorie per minute expenditure limit is only an average and will vary from person to person. Also, this limit could be affected by other conditions such as heat, humidity, and the type of body movement involved in the job. The length and frequency of the break is also a factor. As a general rule, where possible, many short breaks are more effective than a few long ones.

Psychologically, it has been found that rest periods improve employee performance even when the task does not exceed the five-calorie limit. A typical work curve for a motor skill task with rest pauses is shown in Figure 17.

When this work curve is compared to the one shown in Figure 15, the effect of rest periods on productivity is readily apparent. This would mean that rest periods are not only necessary to restore a person from physical exertion, but also from the psychological strain of the work involved. In scheduling rest periods to restore a person from psychological fatigue, two break periods per day is normally adequate. However, for tasks requiring high concentration, such as inspection work, four breaks per day may be necessary. Also, attention should be given to activity during the break

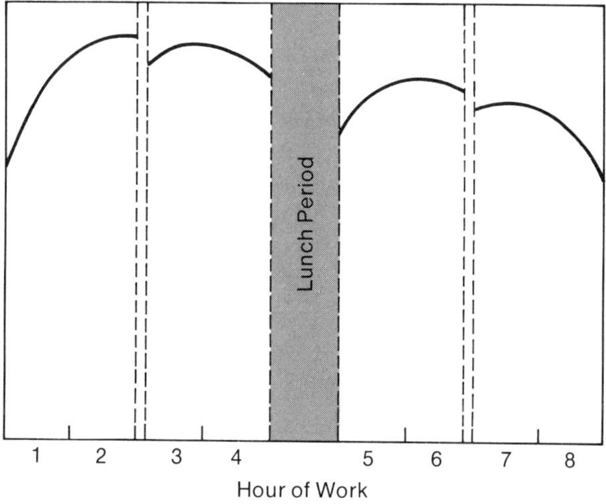

Figure 17 Typical Work Curve with Rest Pauses (Source: *Technical Aids for Small Manufacturers,* Small Business Administration, Washington, D. C., Jan.Feb. 1960.)

period. Where possible, activity during the break should be different in tempo from that being performed on the job. For example, if the employee's job is highly physical, just relaxing may be the best break activity. Conversely, if the work is monotonous, some sort of physical exercise may be best.

KEY POINT SUMMARY

1. A central point in employee performance is determining the answer to the question: "Why do people work?"
2. There are two opposing views on this question depending on the manager's motivational assumptions:
    a. One motivational assumption is based on McGregor's *Theory Y* philosophy and is people-centered.
    b. The other is based on McGregor's *Theory X* philosophy and is economic- or production-centered.
3. Two significant research projects that help to establish the relationship between employee attitudes and performance are the Hawthorne Study and the continuing studies of the Institute of Social Research, University of Michigan.

   a. The Hawthorne Study found that employee attitudes, not work factors as such, are a factor in increased production.
   b. The Michigan University studies found that although the employee's attitude toward his organization does not influence his production, his attitude concerning his supervisor and his work group influences his performance.

4. A close relationship has been found between what is called employee-centered and production-centered supervision and employee productivity.
   a. Employee-centered supervisors are concerned with the worker as an individual. This style normally produces higher results.
   b. Production-centered supervisors are concerned more with the output of their department, and they treat people as mere cogs in the machinery of production. This style normally results in lower production.
5. When used as a general pattern of leadership, the employee-centered or democratic style is usually more effective, but when applied day-by-day, supervisory effectiveness is influenced by:
   a. The manager's personality
   b. The employee's response to a particular style of supervision, and the occupational makeup of the group
   c. The organization's psychological climate
6. Control over work by allowing employees to participate in shaping the policies, procedures, and processes that directly or indirectly affect them is considered by some authorities as the single most influencing factor in achieving positive behavior.
7. For participation to be effective:
   a. The organization must establish the psychological climate that will encourage the employee to participate.
   b. The manager must encourage employee participation and assume responsibility for making decisions.
   c. The employee's background and experience must be considered.
8. Methods of encouraging participation include:
   a. Employee production committees
   b. Group discussions
   c. Individual contact
9. Although there is no absolute answer to the question of which motivational assumption produces the best results, research seems

to support the *Theory Y* people-oriented assumption as best overall.

10. There are many nonmotivational factors that influence employee performance. A common one is physical and psychological fatigue.
    a. Physical fatigue is caused by the expenditure of calories in excess of the individual's energy reserve.
    b. Psychological fatigue is caused by the employee becoming bored and disinterested in his work.
11. Both physical and psychological fatigue can be remedied by rest periods.

DISCUSSION QUESTIONS

1. What are the two opposing motivational assumptions regarding employee performance?
2. What significant contribution did the Hawthorne Study make toward relating employee attitudes and performance? What motivational assumption did this study support?
3. What were the findings of the University of Michigan research projects regarding employee attitudes and performance? Relate performance to employee morale and conformity. What motivational assumption did these studies support?
4. What are the major differences between the employee-centered and the production-centered styles of supervision? Relate each style to employee performance.
5. In day-to-day application, which style normally produces better results? Relate the following to supervision:
    a. The manager's personality
    b. The employee's background and the occupational makeup of the work group
    c. Type of work
    d. The psychological climate of the organization
6. How does control over work relate to performance?
7. What influence does each of the following factors have on effective employee participation?
    a. The organization
    b. The manager
    c. The employee
8. What are some methods by which employees can be encouraged to participate? Explain the advantage of each.
9. Which motivational assumption does research tend to support? How is this assumption manifested in the supervisor's attitude and behavior? What is the contrast between the assumption as related to the supervisor and employee performance?

10. At what time during the day does the average employee reach his highest peak of performance? His lowest?
11. Why is fatigue both physical and psychological?
12. How do rest periods relate to employee performance? Discuss the relationship of rest periods to physical and psychological fatigue.
13. What principles are involved in the following instances, and what effect would they have on employee performance?
    a. A highly effective employee in a closely integrated work group with overall low productivity.
    b. An employee-centered supervisor of a low skilled work group in a strictly *Theory X* or production-centered organization.
    c. The management of an organization that practices as well as pays lip service to employee participation.
    d. The supervisor of a high production work group who uses the *Theory X* motivational assumption.
    e. The supervisor who sees no need for work breaks since the work of his employees is routine and physically easy.

CASE PROBLEM

Case 9–1

In a small department that packed and sealed small vials, the supervisor, Miss X, was very strict and set close schedules on her work. There were seven girls in the department: four worked on packing; one worked on glassware washing; one ran a sealing machine; and one who was a technician acted as the supervisor's assistant. The girls' schedule on the packing line was set so close that they had to work at top speed in order to make the schedule. If one girl fell behind, she was immediately told about it by the supervisor in front of the other girls. The sealing machine operator was in constant trouble with the supervisor. That machine seemed to be the supervisor's pet peeve. The flame was too high or too low, and the sealing was rarely done to her satisfaction, although the material continuously passed inspection by the inspection department. The girl at the sink was constantly in trouble, for the supervisor was dissatisfied most of the time with the washing and sterilizing of the vials and with any breakage that might occur. Miss X had trouble keeping girls in her department, and she had the reputation throughout the plant as being a very hard supervisor. The supervisor's methods caused continuous bad feelings toward her in the department although the production rate in the department was very high.

Questions

1. What principles are involved in this case in relation to:
   a. The supervisor's motivational assumption about people
   b. Production-centered and people-centered supervision
   c. Participation
   d. Fatigue

2. *What could possibly account for the unit's production being high?*
3. *If you were Miss X's supervisor, would you attempt to alter her supervisory style? Why?*

SELECTED REFERENCES

CLARK, JAMES V., "Motivation in Work Groups," in *Readings in Management* (3rd ed.), Sec. D, Chap. 13, Article 49. Cincinnati, Ohio: South-Western Publishing Company, 1969.

HEPNER, HARRY WALKER, *Psychology Applied to Work and Life* (4th ed.), Chap. 21. Englewood Cliffs, N.J.: Prentice-Hall, Inc., 1966.

———, *Perceptive Management and Supervision* (2nd ed.), Chaps. 3 and 24. Englewood Cliffs, N.J.: Prentice-Hall, Inc., 1954.

LIKERT, RENSIS, *New Patterns in Management,* Chaps. 2 and 3. New York: McGraw-Hill Book Company, 1961.

PATCHEN, MARTIN, *Participation, Achievement, and Involvement on the Job,* Appendix *M*. Englewood Cliffs, N.J.: Prentice-Hall, Inc., 1970.

SIEGEL, LAURENCE, *Industrial Psychology,* Chaps. 9 and 15. Homewood, Ill.: Richard D. Irwin, Inc., 1962.

TIFFIN, JOSEPH, and ERNEST J. MCCORMICK, *Industrial Psychology* (5th ed.), Chaps. 2, 12, 13, and 15. Englewood Cliffs, N.J.: Prentice-Hall, Inc., 1965.

10

Factors of Employee Relations

Employee relations refers to the means and manner used by an organization in procuring and maintaining a stable and qualified labor force. In most organizations, employee relations is a staff function administered by the personnel or industrial relations manager. However, since this function depends on the support of operating personnel for its success and is closely tied to human relations, factors that affect employee relations should be understood by all managers at all levels. It is not the purpose of this chapter to include all aspects of personnel management, but only to discuss those factors that have a more direct bearing on human relations. This will include: (1) staffing, (2) wages and salary, (3) benefits, (4) services, and (5) turnover.

STAFFING

Fundamental to the effective operation of an organization is the acquiring of an adequate work force, both in quantity and quality. This process is referred to as *staffing*. From the human relations standpoint, staffing is important because it assists the organization in fitting the right man to the right job, and facilitates his adjustment to the job and work organization.

Job Analysis

To effectively staff an organization, some criteria are needed to serve as a guide for personnel recruitment and selection. The usual procedure for developing these criteria is through job analysis.

Job analysis is the process of determining, by observation and study, and reporting, pertinent information relating to the nature of a specific job. This includes determining the task that comprises the job, the skill, knowledge, ability, and responsibility required of a worker for successful performance, and factors that differentiate the job from all others. It may be added that job analysis is concerned with the demands and requirements of the job, not with the ability of the person who is doing the work.

JOB REQUIREMENTS. The essence of job analysis is identifying job requirements (also referred to as job specifications). A job is a collection of tasks to be accomplished. Each of these tasks is normally different in that each consists of a different set of requirements. Therefore, to be useful as staffing criteria, these requirements must be identified. Some of the requirements to be considered follow: [1]

1. *Qualifications or Job Prerequisites* are the factors required of the worker before he can qualify for the job, and they include:
    a. Mental development or education.
    b. Pre-job experience and training.
    c. Analytical ability or mental skill.
    d. Dexterity, accuracy, and manual skill.
2. *Job Deterrents* are the factors which affect a job applicant's willingness to accept the job and they include:
    a. The physical effort required of the job.
    b. Working conditions.
    c. Mental effort.
    d. Job hazards.
3. *Job Responsibility* includes factors which have a direct bearing on the effect the job has on the overall operation, such as:
    a. Supervision of others.
    b. Use of materials.
    c. Use of equipment.
    d. Involvement in production.
    e. Access to confidential information.

The data concerning job requirements can be collected by one or a combination of three ways: (1) Having the holder of the job fill out a questionnaire, (2) Interviewing the employee holding the job, and the supervisor of the department where the job is located, and (3) Observation and audit by a trained job analyst. Whichever method is used, the aim is

[1] See *Personnel Management,* Training Manual No. 127 (Washington, D.C.: Office of Industrial Resources, International Cooperation Administration, 1957).

to collect information to develop a summation of the total requirements of the job.

JOB DESCRIPTION. The summation of the total requirements of a job is called a *job description*. A typical job description is shown in Figure 18.

Job Title: SENIOR OFFICE MACHINE REPAIRMAN

Job Description:

1. Under direction, repairs, maintains, and tests all types of office machines, such as typewriters, adding machines, calculating machines, comptometers, duplicating machines, postage machines, etc., of various makes, operated either manually or electrically.

2. Performs routine servicing of all office machines and inspects office machines referred to him for repair, adjustment, or maintenance.

3. Performs repairs on the spot if defects are minor in nature. Overhauls machines in the shop when machines need overhauling and reconditioning. Dismantles machines in the shop for general cleaning, adjusting, paint retouching, and repairs.

4. Prepares a schedule of jobs, reports on jobs performed, noting type of machine, serial number, and company number.

5. Prepares material requisitions and time sheets of Office Machine Repairmen of lower grade.

Job Requirements:

1. Must be at least a high school graduate.

2. Must have at least 2 years' experience as office machine repairman or its equivalent.

Figure 18 Sample Job Description (Source: Training Manual No. 127, *Personnel Management, Job Evaluation,* Office of Industrial Resources, International Cooperation Administration, Washington, D. C.)

The primary purpose of a job description is to provide criteria for personnel recruitment and selection, but the job description is also useful for such things as: (1) Ranking jobs for establishing salary and wage scales, (2) Orienting a new employee to the job, (3) The transfer and promotion of employees, and (4) As a standard the manager can use in making employee appraisals.

STAFFING SCHEDULE. Job analysis also serves as a basis for developing a staffing schedule or manning document (also called manning table). By combining the job titles of the job description with the total number of jobs, an overall summary of the manpower requirements of the organization can be developed. In addition to its use as a staffing guide, it is a valuable tool for personnel planning and budgetary control. The role of the supervisor and other departmental managers in manpower planning, although an important one in some organizations, is so varied that it defies standardization, thus making its discussion in a book such as this impractical.

Recruitment

In staffing, *recruitment* is the process of attracting personnel to apply for existing or projected job vacancies. Since this is a function performed almost exclusively by the personnel department, it is mentioned here only to keep the discussion in perspective. Therefore, it is sufficient to say that normally, the objective of recruitment is to obtain as many applicants for a given job as possible since the number of applicants will increase or decrease the probability of selecting the best man for the job.

Selection

The purpose of the selection process is to choose the best possible candidate for the job. Whereas the employee selection process varies by organization, and according to the applicant and type of job being filled, most organizations follow a general pattern that includes the following steps:

1. They must be sold on the basic principles.
2. Participating in a preliminary interview
3. Taking a test or series of tests
4. Participating in a job interview
5. Investigating the applicant's personal background and work history
6. The personnel department making a tentative selection
7. The supervisor of the department having the vacancy, making the final selection [2]

Though not perfect, this process has proved to be the best means of fitting "the right man to the right job."

Orientation and Placement

After an applicant has been selected for the job, the next step in the staffing process is to assist the new employee in adjusting to his new surroundings. As indicated earlier, the better this adjustment is made, the more positive the employee's attitude toward his organization is apt to be. Recognizing this, in recent years more and more organizations have developed standard job orientation programs.

[2] The supervisor's role in the selection process is discussed in Chapter 15.

Orientation programs are not only important for employees who have no previous work experience but beneficial to more experienced workers. Typical orientation programs include a tour of the organization, and if the organization is unionized the new employee is introduced to the union representative, who can give the employee information about the organization's history, general sales position, wages and benefits, and safety policy. Some companies include a talk by the president or other management representative as part of the orientation program.

Following or in connection with the general orientation program, the employee is assigned to his department for further job orientation and job placement by his immediate supervisor.[3]

Training

Seldom is the staffing process so adequate that the skills of the employee match the requirements of the job. This, plus the ever-changing conditions and circumstances within an organization, and the technological advances of equipment, make the need for training readily apparent. Although the need for training is generally recognized, unfortunately too few organizations are willing or able to expend the effort and cost that are necessary to develop meaningful training programs for their employees. For an organizational training program to be meaningful, it should be planned and organized with both the human element and the job factors in mind, and should include the assessment of training needs, the formulation of adequate training programs, the administration of these programs, and appraisal of their results. The personnel departments of some organizations have a director to coordinate the overall training program, but it is a basic responsibility of the manager at each level to train his employees. This being so, training is included here to keep the discussion in perspective, leaving the full treatment of this important topic to a later chapter.[4]

WAGES AND SALARY

A major problem concerning most organizations is determining and establishing a satisfactory wage and salary system. As implied in previous chapters, this problem is two-fold. First, since wages and salaries paid employees represent a substantial part of the total cost of operation, they must be kept consistent with profit and production. On the other hand, wages and salaries have a definite effect on human relations. Employees are not only concerned with their actual pay but with the relation of their pay

[3] The supervisor's role in job orientation is discussed in Chapter 12.

[4] The supervisor's role in training is discussed in Chapters 12 and 17.

to coworkers' and the community for comparable work. Therefore, pay inequalities, real or imagined, can cause employee dissatisfaction. If employees are unionized, this dissatisfaction is often expressed in employee grievances. If the employees are not members of a union and if individual protests are ineffective, their dissatisfaction may be expressed by lower production and higher turnover.

How Wages and Salaries Are Determined

In determining wages and salaries, organizations are normally influenced by several factors. These include: (1) The rate paid for comparable work by other organizations, especially in organizations in its particular field, (2) The supply of labor, (3) The type of work and the skill level of the work, (4) The prevailing pay rates of the community, and (5) Other factors such as negotiated wages by unions and the organization's economic position. As this indicates, wage and salary determination is quite arbitrary at best. But in recent years, many organizations have attempted to establish a systematic means of determining wages through job evaluation.

Job Evaluation

Job evaluation is a systematic approach used to measure the relative value of jobs. It is a method of determining the requirements of a particular job in relation to all other jobs in the organization. It is based on the job analysis discussed earlier, and it is possibly the best means of determining wages from the human relations standpoint. First, it permits the job to be perceived according to its value. This means equal pay for equal work and reduces the possibility of discrimination in pay between employees doing the same type of job. Second, by rating the job—not the employee—such variables as personality favoritism is less likely to be a factor. Also, job evaluation takes into account working conditions that allow the employee to be compensated for undesirable and hazardous work factors that may exist.

METHODS. Using the information accumulated through job analysis, there are four methods that can be applied in job evaluation. These methods are identified and briefly discussed below.

The ranking method involves a committee being asked to rank each job in the organization according to its importance, considering the job as a whole. After each committee member has arranged the jobs in rank order, the results are averaged and a final ranking recorded. This method has the advantage of simplicity and convenience. It is best used in evaluating salaried employees, and when only a few jobs are involved.

The grading method also makes use of a committee, and jobs are considered as a whole. Functions are first developed and defined, and then the jobs are classified into grades, levels, or groups. The evaluating committee considers each job, compares its description with the definition of various grades, and classifies the job in the appropriate grade. Like the ranking method, this method has the advantage of being simple and convenient; and, it is best used for salaried employees and when a small number of jobs are being evaluated.

The factor comparison method is similar to the rank method except that jobs are broken down into factors, and each factor is ranked separately. This has the advantage over the two previous methods since it considers the job in more detail.

The point plan method takes into account the various factors of the job such as experience, education, physical factors, and responsibility and assigns points to each factor. The points are then totaled and the total compared, and a point rating is assigned to each job. This method is more complex but has the advantage of considering jobs in greater depth and provides a more accurate and complete criteria for classifying jobs according to their value. It is the method most widely used, especially in organizations that have trained job analysts.

To be meaningful, after jobs have been classified the monetary equivalent of the job has to be determined. This is done either by negotiation or by a wage survey. If the wage scale has previously been established by collective bargaining, that existing wage scale is commonly used in applying money values to the estimated job worth. If the wage scale has not been negotiated, a wage survey is normally used to determine what other organizations are paying for similar jobs. For a wage survey to be valid in pricing jobs, both the organization and the jobs included on the survey must be comparable to the organization and the job being analyzed.

EMPLOYEE RESISTANCE. Like any change, employees often resist job evaluation. To overcome this resistance, the employee must be prepared for the change by proper instruction and indoctrination, which can be done best by the employee's immediate supervisor. If employees are to accept job evaluation with little resistance, the supervisor should remember that: [5]

1. They must be sold on the basic principles.
2. They must be convinced of the competency of the evaluation committee.
3. They must be informed that a job evaluation program is not a remedy for all wage ills. At the very start, they must be told that some

[5] See P. W. Jones, "Salesmanship in Job Evaluation," in *Personnel Management*, Training Manual No. 127.

individuals will not benefit financially. It is better to meet this issue in the beginning than to be confronted with it later.

4. They must be told that this type of adjustment is one of the few possible under a stabilization program.

5. They must be convinced that they will have a part to play in the program, either directly or through their duly authorized representatives.

6. They must know that those in charge will keep them informed on the progress of the program.

7. They must be promised that the resulting evaluation will be of such a nature that all can understand it.

8. They must be assured that they are not merely the subject of an experiment.

9. They must be assured that no individual will suffer a loss of salary or wage as a result of the program.

10. They must be convinced that upon completion of the job description and classifications, compensation is to be determined by a uniform measurement of jobs. They must be told that it is the job that counts; and that former methods of bargaining for services, which resulted in considerable amounts of highly skilled pretense on both sides and corresponding amounts of suspicion and ill-will, are a thing of the past.

11. Employees must be assured of a reasonable completion date for the program.

Types of Pay Systems

The method or system that an organization uses to compensate its employees for services rendered is called its *pay system*. Basically, pay systems are of two types: one is based on some measure of time; the other is based on some measure of output. An organization may elect to use either system or a combination of the two, depending on which system is best for its particular operation. From the standpoint of human relations, the method used and the manner in which pay is computed should be understood by each employee of an organization.

TIME-PAY SYSTEM. This system is based on some measure of time such as hour, day, week, month, or year. Which of these units is used is normally based on the kind of work and type of job. For example, skilled labor, craftsmen, assembly or production workers, and some clerical personnel are normally paid by the hour or at an hourly rate. For most clerical and office workers pay is figured by the week or the month, as is the pay of supervisors. On the other hand, the salaries of technicians, mid- and higher managers, and professional personnel are usually computed and expressed as so much per year or as an annual salary. The day rate is not as widely used as it once was and now applies primarily to work of short duration and to certain unskilled occupations.

The time-unit system has the advantage of being easy to compute once the rate is established for a particular job. It has the disadvantage of providing little or no incentive to increase production. Therefore, the time-pay system works best when jobs require individual concentration and thought, when quality is more important than quantity, and when an organization does not have qualified personnel to develop exacting standards for its jobs.

OUTPUT UNIT SYSTEM. Under this system, a person is paid according to his production rate or output. It can be used separately or in connection with the other system. It may be complex or simple, and it may be applied to a number of different jobs. For example, salesmen may be paid a base salary plus a commission on their output of sales or by commission only. Executives may be paid a bonus for their performance in addition to their annual salary. Workers may be paid according to a certain minimum day or hourly rate with additional pay for each piece of work produced above an established minimum; or, the worker may be paid strictly by his output. This system provides an additional motivational factor and when applied to production workers is referred to as "an incentive wage system" or "piece-work."

There are a number of different "incentive wage plans" designed to increase employee performance, but to increase output and to preclude employee dissatisfaction, these common principles apply: [6]

1. The unit of output should be measurable and readily distinguishable.
2. A clear relationship must exist between output and worker's efforts.
3. A steady flow of material should be maintained, and machines and equipment must be in proper condition, preventing breakdown.
4. The worker must be able to detect the results of his output in direct relation to his pay. Otherwise, the incentive will be lost.
5. A competent system must be used for inspecting, counting, and recording employee output, so the employee will know precisely what he has produced.
6. A close check must be kept on quality because employees in their haste to increase quantity may ignore this factor.

A major cause of employee dissatisfaction with the incentive system is the fear that when they acquire greater skill and speed in increasing production, the established rate will be cut. Therefore, employees should be

[6] See Ernest L. Loen, *Personnel Management Guide for Small Business,* Small Business Management Series No. 26 (Washington, D.C.: Small Business Administration), pp. 24-25.

assured that rates will be recomputed only when there is a change in production methods, not as a result of increased efficiency.

BENEFITS

The term *benefits* covers indirect compensations, which most organizations provide their employees. Due to their close interrelation with other factors, the exact relationship between good human relations and the benefits an organization provides its employees are indistinguishable. However, it is generally agreed that benefits do have a positive effect on the employee's attitude toward the organization, and an organization's benefit programs serve as a factor in attracting and retaining better qualified personnel.

Time Off With Pay

Most organizations provide in their benefit program provisions for allowing employees time off with pay. The three most common types are sick leave, holidays, and vacations. Of course, the policy of providing time off with pay varies by organization.

Sick leave is normally granted on the basis of time with the organization. For example, many organizations grant one day of sick leave for each month of employment after one year. Some organizations grant time off for local holidays, but as a whole, time off for national holidays is a common practice. Therefore, most organizations grant six holidays per year—New Year's Day, Memorial Day, Independence Day, Labor Day, Thanksgiving Day, and Christmas. To provide employees longer time off, Monday following the day on which these holidays actually fall has been declared the official holiday for leave purposes. Vacations also vary widely among organizations, but most grant an employee a vacation after a certain period of service.

Insurance Plans

This category of benefits falls within two general types: Private and government sponsored.

PRIVATE INSURANCE PLANS. Employee insurance plans for which the organization pays a portion or all of the cost is a standard procedure in most organizations. These are group insurance plans and include various combinations of benefits including hospitalization payments for basic surgery, life insurance, accidents, or sickness benefits, and the like. The current trend is for the organization to bear the total cost. But even when the employee is required to pay a portion of the premium, it is still a benefit in that group insurance plans are less expensive than individual coverage.

GOVERNMENT INSURANCE PLANS. There are several insurance plans of this type, but the one organizations are required to administer and make monetary contribution to is Social Security. The Social Security Act of 1935, and its later revisions, provides workers in industry and commerce certain retirement benefits under a federal system of unemployment and medical insurance. Since programs under this act vary according to a complexity of circumstances, they will not be discussed here. It should be noted, however, that despite the fact that Social Security is government sponsored, the organization and the employee make equal contributions. Therefore, Social Security can be considered a benefit.

Pension Plans

In addition to the pension plan provided employees under the Social Security Act, many large organizations and some of the smaller ones have developed employee pension plans of their own accord. Pension plans vary among organizations, but their common purpose is to reward employees for their long service to the organization. Some indications are that most employees never realize the benefits of a pension plan. Nevertheless, employees consider pensions as a form of security and they are therefore important to employee morale.

Another benefit, furnished by some companies, that is closely associated with pension plans is profit sharing. (It is also associated with wages and salaries.) When this benefit is applied, several methods can be used. Some companies use a specified term of service with the organization. Other organizations allocate an amount according to a percentage of the employee's income, and still others make distribution according to merit or performance. Whichever method is used, from the human relations aspect, profit sharing is one means of allowing employees to feel that, at least in part, they are working for themselves. Also, profit sharing may foster a closer employee-organization identity.

SERVICES

Like benefits, the services an organization provides its employees vary considerably. Although studies show that the services an organization provides its employees have no direct effect on employee productivity, they do afford a means by which employees can become more closely identified with their organization. Therefore, many organizations consider employee services an important part of their employee relations program. Services are of three general types: educational, recreational, and financial.

Educational Services

The policy of organizations encouraging their employees to participate in off-duty educational programs is becoming more widespread. Also, some companies encourage their employees to participate in educational programs at colleges or universities, or in industrial training programs on company time. Usually, the organization pays part or all of the cost, with some doing so only after the prescribed training has been successfully completed. Programs that are more effective and have the fewest dropouts are those that allow the individual some freedom of choice and provide some incentive that the employee can relate to his personal goals.

Recreational Activities

These activities range from the customary Christmas party to year-round programs including recreational parks and special facilities. Often recreational activities serve two purposes. The first is to provide employees with a means of participating jointly in company-sponsored affairs, which may establish a closer employee-employer relationship. The other is that directly or indirectly, intentionally or unintentionally, company-sponsored recreational programs, such as bowling teams, can gain favorable publicity for the organization, which may well amount to free advertisement and serve to promote the organization's public image. To be effective, a recreational program should be something that the employees want to do and one that they will support voluntarily.

Financial Assistance

A common means by which larger organizations furnish their employees with financial assistance is through credit unions. Credit unions provide both an investment service and a credit program. As members, employees can invest their money, often at a relatively high rate of interest, and also obtain loans when they need them. Because credit unions are employee operated, they have the advantage of promoting group solidarity and self-reliance. Of course in very small organizations, the method of financial assistance through advance pay and direct loans is still sometimes practiced. Also, an organization may on occasion assist its employees in securing a loan from a commercial financial institution such as a bank. However, the most common method of financial assistance is the credit union.

TURNOVER

The opposing factor in maintaining a stable labor force is employee turnover. The term *turnover* applies to those employees who voluntarily or involuntarily leave their organizations. Excessive turnover is not only expensive, but the continual process of hiring and training new people has its effect on organizational efficiency.

The cost of employee turnover will differ from organization to organization and job to job. The average cost is estimated to range from a low of $200 to as high as $2,000 per man, depending on the job. Like cost, the average turnover rate varies widely. Some organizations experience the very low turnover rate of less than one percent per month, but others show a rate of well over 200 percent. Also, there is a wide variance in the rate of turnover among jobs within an organization. Some jobs experience no turnover year after year; on others there is continuous change. Overall, a 2 to 3 percent per month rate can be used as a watch point for determining excessive turnover. However, a more accurate guide can be obtained by comparing the average turnover rate with like organizations or with similar jobs within the same geographical area.

The reasons that employees quit their jobs are so varied that they defy complete identification and normally involve a combination of circumstances rather than a single cause. Some companies conduct exit interviews to determine why people leave their jobs.[7] Because most people are seldom willing to give the real reason for their behavior, information obtained by asking the employee why he is quitting is less than absolute. But most studies show that the reasons people quit involve the human relations aspect of the job rather than physical or economic conditions, with poor supervision being given as the major cause.

Another inexacting area is the control of turnover. There are no absolute methods to preclude an employee from leaving an organization. But a first step in controlling turnover is identifying the area of greatest turnover. This can be done by maintaining accurate records of the turnover rate for the organization as a whole and by each department, unit, and job. To determine the turnover rate the following formula applies:

$$\text{Turnover Rate} = \frac{\text{Number of Employees Separated}}{\text{Total Number of Employees Involved}}$$

[7] The supervisor's role in the exit interview is discussed in Chapter 15.

For control purposes, turnover rates are more meaningful if a rate is obtained for each of the following categories: (1) Quits—those who leave the organization of their own initiative for any reason; (2) Discharges—those who are fired; (3) Layoffs—those who are required to leave without prejudice; (4) Miscellaneous—those who leave for reasons not included in the other categories. By recording the turnover rate for each category in a way that they can easily be compared (graph, chart, or columniation) with the rates for each department or job category, trouble areas can be more easily identified.

KEY POINT SUMMARY

1. Employee relations refers to the means and manner an organization uses to acquire and maintain a stable labor force.
2. The process of acquiring a labor force and fitting the right man to the right job is called staffing, which includes:
   a. Determining the quality and quantity of people needed by the organization to meet its objective
   b. Attracting prospective employees to apply for job vacancies
   c. Selecting the best employee for the job
   d. Helping the employee to adjust to the job through proper placement, orientation, and training
3. The method normally used to determine personnel requirements is by job analysis. Job analysis includes:
   a. Determining job requirements
   b. Developing job descriptions
   c. Developing staffing schedules
4. The process of attracting people to apply for jobs is called recruitment and involves developing a program to attract job applicants through advertisement and direct contact.
5. To select the "right man for the right job," most organizations use an established pattern that includes:
   a. The applicant filling out an application form
   b. A preliminary interview
   c. Tests
   d. The job interview
   e. Background investigation
   f. Tentative selection by the personnel department
   g. Final selection by the supervisor

6. To assist the employee in adjusting to the job, many companies have employee orientation programs, followed by job placement and training.
7. Since wages and salaries affect an organization both from the aspect of economics and human relations, determining a satisfactory pay system for its employees is very important.
8. One of the most satisfactory methods of determining wages and salaries is through job evaluation since it:
   a. Determines job requirements in relation to all other jobs.
   b. Reduces the possibility of paying different wages for like work, and the showing of favoritism.
   c. Allows compensation for undesirable or hazardous work.
9. Pay systems are of two basic types:
   a. The time system, based on some measure of time (hour, day, week, month), has the advantage of being simple to compute, but provides no incentive for increased production.
   b. The output system (also called incentive or piecework) has the advantage of providing a motivational factor since the employee is paid more if he produces more.
10. Benefits are a means of employee compensation, and include time off with pay and insurance plans.
11. Services are another form of compensation and normally are of three basic types: educational, recreational, and financial.
12. Turnover applies to those employees who leave their jobs for any reason. Excessive turnover is expensive and affects an organization's efficiency. Therefore, excessive turnover should be controlled.

DISCUSSION QUESTIONS

1. What is *employee relations?*
2. Why is proper staffing important to an organization?
3. What does job analysis include? How are job requirements determined? What is the purpose of job descriptions? How are staffing schedules used? Relate job analysis to human relations.
4. What is the importance of recruitment?
5. What is the purpose of the selection process and what steps are commonly used to select the best man for the job?
6. Why do more and more organizations include employee orientation as a part of their staffing process?
7. Who is responsible for employee training?

8. How are wages and salaries determined? What are the two basic types of pay systems and what are the advantages of each? Relate wages and salaries to human relations.
9. Why are benefits important in maintaining a stable labor force and what do they include? Relate benefits to human relations.
10. Why are services important in maintaining a stable labor force? Relate services to human relations.
11. What effect does turnover have on an organization? How can turnover best be controlled?
12. What employee relations factors are involved in the following statements?
    a. The employee whose ability and skills are not suited to his job.
    b. The employee who is dissatisfied because he is receiving less pay than a coworker for like work.
    c. The job applicant who selects one company over another after studying the benefits offered by each organization.
    d. The organization that rejects the idea of developing an employee services program, since no direct relationship can be shown between services provided by a company and employee efficiency.
    e. The organization that has difficulty in retaining employees, but keeps no records of its turnover rate.

CASE PROBLEM

Case 10–1

The Midlands Steel Company, employing some 300 people, was founded in 1920 and is located in a fast growing city of approximately 40,000. Initially, being the major employer in the area, the company experienced no labor shortage by using the "drop-in" or "hire at the gate" method of selection. But in recent years, with the addition of more progressive companies to the city, Midlands finds this method less and less effective and is constantly in need of personnel. The company starts all new employees at the minimum hourly rate prescribed by law and grants raises based on the recommendations made by the foremen of the various departments. The organization sponsors an annual Christmas party for its employees and grants them the six customary holidays with pay. It is the custom of the management to allow employees time off with pay in certain emergencies and to advance pay if justified. Some employees take courses at the local vocational training center to obtain a better job in another company. Through dictatorial leadership, employee production is fairly high. However, the organization is plagued with the high employee turnover, above average absenteeism, and low morale. A labor union, which the company has managed to keep out for years, is being discussed more and more by the employees.

Questions

1. *What employee relations factors are involved in this case?*
2. *What action can the management of this organization take to update its employee relations policies?*

3. *What effect would the present personnel policies have on supervisor-employee relations?*

SELECTED REFERENCES

AMRINE, HAROLD T., JOHN A. RITCHEY, and OLIVER S. HULLEY, *Manufacturing, Organization, and Management* (2nd ed.), Chap. 18. Englewood Cliffs, N.J.: Prentice-Hall, Inc., 1966.

Job Analysis, Training Manual No. 84. Washington, D.C.: Office of Industrial Resources, International Cooperation Administration, 1956.

LOEN, ERNEST L., "Personnel Management Guides for Small Businesses," Small Business Series No. 26. Washington, D.C.: Small Business Administration, 1961.

McFARLAND, DALTON E., *Management Principles and Practices,* Chap. 19. New York: The Macmillan Company, 1958.

Personnel Management, Training Manual No. 127. Washington, D.C.: Office of Industrial Resources, International Cooperative Administration, 1957.

TERRY, GEORGE R., *Principles of Management* (4th ed.), Chap. 34 Homewood, Ill.: Richard D. Irwin, Inc., 1964.

III

Supervisory Skills

Effective management is judged by visual and tangible proof of productivity. Although developing a management-minded and people-oriented philosophy is essential to effective management, this alone will not produce results. A manager's philosophy only provides the frame of reference for effective management. To produce results, the actual merging of resources must take place. This means that the manager must deal directly with his employees face-to-face, on-the-spot, day-to-day, and through them provide an end product or service consistent with the objectives of his organization. In short, to produce results, principles and processes must be put into practice. This was discussed in Chapter 2 as the supervisory process, and to be effective it is centered on the manager developing certain supervisory skills. The skills required of most managers are covered in this part and discussed as:

11

How to Allocate and Schedule Work

The primary and ultimate goal of supervisory management is to attain maximum output at the least possible cost. Essentially, this means that the manager as a supervisor must demand and get optimum production for the salaries and wages paid his workers and for the cost of other resources used in reaching the objectives of his department. The major means of production, whether it is manufacturing or selling a product or providing a service, is done with, through, or by people, suggesting that the sum of supervisory management is the effective use of manpower. Basically, this is true, but unless work is allocated and scheduled to assure that each employee is fully used on essential tasks, that his skills are used to maximum advantage, that he is given a full workload so he can use resources properly, it is doubtful that the employee can produce a quality product in the prescribed quantity within a certain time-frame. Therefore, although the effective use of manpower is predicated on the manager using the sum of his managerial know-how, a basic requirement in meeting this goal is that the manager develop the skill of allocating and scheduling the work of his department. Although this skill is cross-sectional, involving most of the management functions, it is primarily a planning and organizing activity. This means that even though this chapter outlines a specific procedure, in actual practice the manager should apply the essential principles of planning and organizing as well. With this in mind, the procedure for allocating and scheduling work can best be understood by examining these topics: (1) analyzing the organization, (2) evaluating the work situation, (3) the manager and his time, and (4) work plans.

ANALYZING THE ORGANIZATION

In order for the manager to allocate and schedule the work of his department to attain the best utilization of his manpower, he must first become aware of the factors and forces that influence the work of his operation. The first factor that influences the work of any department is its objective. Because the objective is the reason for the department existing and the work being done, it must be clearly stated and thoroughly understood. To do this the manager may want to state briefly in writing what he thinks his objectives are and review his statements with his immediate supervisor. Not only will this assist him in allocating and scheduling work consistent with the overall goals of his organization but it will also allow him to come to a meeting of minds with his boss concerning the priority in which his manpower is to be used in meeting these objectives. Both are important, for unless the manager and his supervisor have the same understanding concerning goals and priorities, mass confusion can only be the result. Work will be allocated and reallocated and schedules will be in a constant state of change, with little work actually being done. So clarifying his objective is a major first step in allocating and scheduling work.

After the manager has clarified his objective, he should analyze other aspects of his organization to determine what other factors and forces influence his work. There is no single, standard method for analyzing an organization. However, since factors and forces that influence the work of a department involve both the organizational structure and physical conditions, the manager can best analyze his operation by taking a close look at these two areas.

Structure

The purpose of analyzing the structure of an organization is to determine if the existing organizational chart is built on the basic principles of sound organization. Obviously, the principle of unity of command (one man–one boss), span of control (too many, too few), logical assignment (jobs and tasks, specific and similar), and delegation of authority (authority with responsibility) are major influencing factors on the effective use of manpower and should be examined closely.

Although the organizational chart is a useful guide in analyzing the structure of an organization, it should not be relied on exclusively. To get a true picture the manager should "go behind the scenes" of his organization by seeking impartial answers to these questions:

1. Is there an up-to-date job description for each position in my department? Does it depict the actual work to be done?
2. Does each employee of my department report to and receive directions from only one supervisor?
3. Does each employee know specifically to whom he reports and is responsible?
4. Are personnel homogeneously assigned?
5. Are related operations and tasks grouped together?
6. Is authority delegated commensurate with responsibility?
7. Do I have more people reporting to me than I can effectively coordinate and direct?
8. Are responsibilities decentralized to the lowest possible level?
9. Is span of control considered for: (1) time, (2) distance, and (3) numbers?
10. Does each employee understand the organizational structure and the relationship of his particular segment to all parts of the organization?

As the above questions imply, seeking impartial answers will not only pinpoint those factors that directly influence allocating and scheduling work but will suggest changes that will influence the effective use of manpower in the directing and controlling process as well.

Physical Conditions

Because the major aim of allocating and scheduling work is to attain the maximum production through the effective use of manpower, the physical conditions where the work takes place should be analyzed. Good physical conditions include such things as proper work space, adequate lighting, heating, and ventilation, and the least possible distraction by noise. However, the single most influencing factor bearing on the effective use of manpower is safe working conditions. Not only are disabling injuries resulting from unsafe working conditions costly from the standpoint of worker's compensation and the loss of production, but they directly and profoundly affect the process of allocating and scheduling work. This is especially true in operations where work is closely interrelated, such as assembly operations where much of the total work process must be reallocated and rescheduled when one worker is missing. This makes it apparent that in analyzing the physical conditions of his operation, particular attention should be given to the factor of safety. By keeping this in mind, the manager may use the checklist shown in Figure 19 to analyze the physical conditions of his organization. In reviewing this list, it should be understood that these items are not conclusive nor will all items pertain to each operation. However the list is general enough to apply to most situations and specific enough to serve as a guide for pointing out conditions that warrant corrective action.

OPERATIONAL CHECKLIST

1. Are lighting, heating, and ventilation adequate?
2. Are visual distractions reduced to a minimum?
3. Are acoustical distractions reduced to a minimum?
4. Is sufficient working space afforded each worker?
5. Are work areas kept orderly and free from obstructions?
6. Is space allotted on the following factors:
   a. number of workers?
   b. type of operations?
   c. amount and type of equipment?
7. Does physical layout make possible the maximum utilization of space for essential work?
8. Is adequate storage and shelving space provided?
9. Are furniture and equipment arranged in a neat and orderly manner?
10. Are work areas free of superfluous equipment and furniture?
11. Are trash baskets for papers, candy wrappers, and the like, placed at convenient locations?
12. Are floors vacuum-cleaned or swept daily; or if necessary, more than once a day?
13. Are oil and grease removed immediately?
14. Do you schedule work carefully so that there is no need for unusually large amounts of work-in-progress or finished items in work areas at any one time?
15. Have you instructed workers in drawing the correct amounts of needed materials and supplies in order to avoid cluttering up work areas?
16. Are restroom and washroom facilities adequate?
17. Are convenient, cold water drinking fountains available for all employees?
18. Are the facilities kept clean, sanitary, and well-lighted?
19. Do workers have a suitable, clean place, away from their work, in which to eat?
20. Are lockers provided for workers' clothing and other belongings? (when applicable)

Figure 19 Operational Checklist

EVALUATING THE WORK SITUATION

In addition to analyzing his organization, the manager should take a close look at his specific work situation. This step involves more than detecting the factors and forces that directly or indirectly influence the overall work of the manager's operation. It requires a systematic evaluation of the skills of his employees, the volume of work involved, and the way in which work is distributed. There are three basic tools which the manager can use to evaluate these specific areas: (1) The skills inventory, (2) The work count, and (3) The work distribution study.

Skills Inventory

Because the manager has to depend on the people of his department to get the work out, he should first look at the skill level of his employees. A systematic way to do this is to make a "skills" inventory. The format of a skills inventory is shown in Figure 20. This very simple exercise is outlined below:

1. First, take a sheet of paper and list the names of all employees vertically down the left margin, leaving about four inches at the top of the page.
2. Next, list all of the jobs in the department horizontally in the space provided at the top of the page.
3. Finally, go down the list, name by name, and determine which jobs can be performed by each employee. If the individual can perform the job, place a check or "X" in the space corresponding to that skill.

The skills inventory will furnish the manager with an invaluable tool in allocating and scheduling work. It can be used for such things as determining training needs of workers, shifting employees to fill temporary vacancies, and reassignment of workers to meet peak workloads.

Work Count

Another valuable tool in allocating and scheduling work is the work count. The work count is a technique for determining the impact of the volume of work of an operation. The basic step in making a work count is determining significant work to be counted. This should be an end product or an indication of work related to the individual or group making the effort. The work count can be applied to both office and sales work, and shop or assembly operations. In office or clerical situations, letters, phone calls, checks, vouchers, files, and inquiries may be identified as sound work units

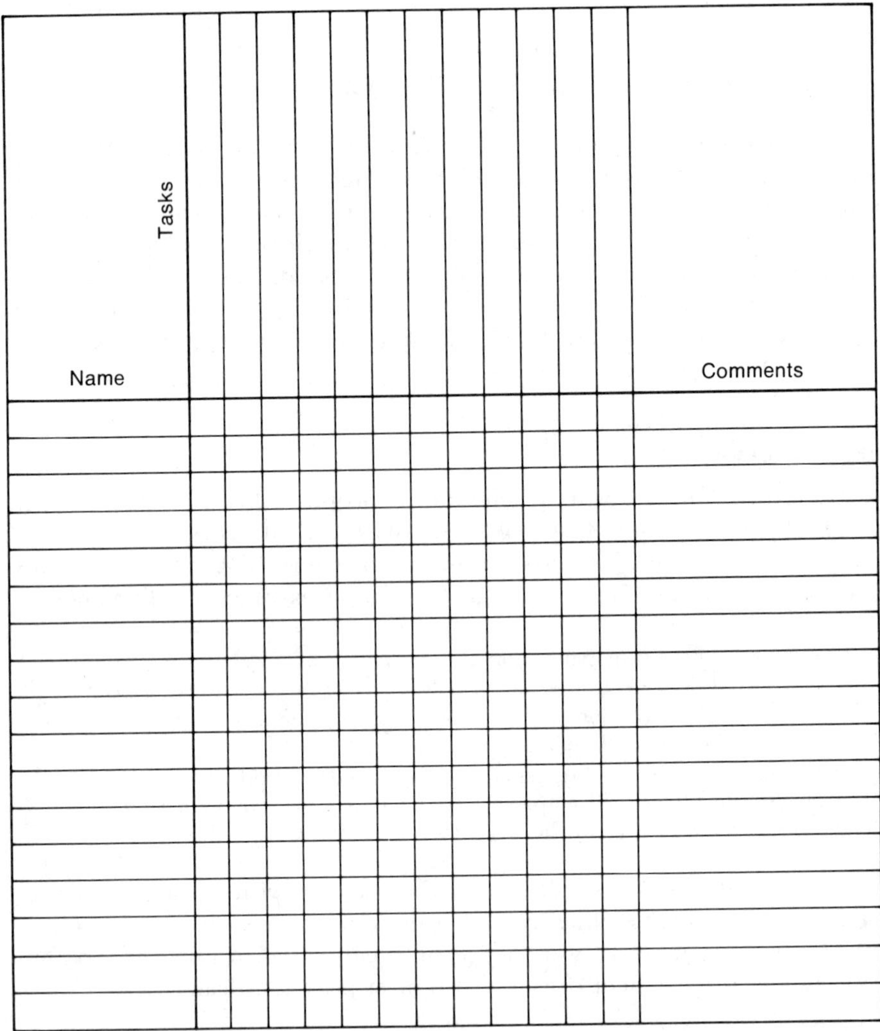

Figure 20 Skills Inventory Chart

to be counted. In sales, dollar volume can be used as indicators. In shop or assembly type operations, the number of units produced is a valid measure. In all cases, only those things considered significant should be counted. Also, although the method used to make the count will depend on the type of operation, as many automatic methods such as cash registers, adding machines, and so on as possible should be considered. When this is not possible, weight counts, tally, or manual counts are appropriate to use.

Once completed, the work count can assist the manager in the following ways:

1. *To schedule work.* The work volume can assist in determining the time required for each step of a process so that a valid schedule can be made.

2. *To relate tasks.* If several people in work places are performing unrelated tasks, the work count can assist the manager in analyzing these tasks to determine whether or not they can be combined into a more harmonious effort.

3. *To divide work.* A work count may be used to identify the type of action required by various kinds of work and to separate exceptions for special treatment. Thus, idle time can be put to effective use.

4. *To locate bottlenecks.* The number of units being processed or passing through a critical point may give the manager a clue to needed adjustment for improved operation.

Work Distribution Study

As the title implies, the work distribution study is a method of determining the way in which work is distributed. Without this knowledge, the manager cannot possibly allocate and schedule work equitably and fairly. Despite this, work distribution is overlooked by most managers. The reasons for this are many, but primarily most managers think the process is too complicated and time consuming. This is not the case if a basic, systematic approach is used. The approach used by the Armed Forces for years consists of four fundamental steps. Information for a work distribution study may be recorded on preprinted forms or the manager may construct his own form using the format shown here.

The first step is to have each person in the department, including the manager, prepare a task list of individual jobs that are done during a week. The list should be a clear and complete description of what each worker actually does. Figure 21 shows a task list.

The second step is to prepare an operation list. This list should contain the basic functions accomplished by the department. It should be prepared by the manager and should include the major jobs that are performed to fulfill the assignment or objective. Figure 22 shows an operation list.

The third step is to prepare a work distribution chart using the individual task lists and the operation lists. To make this chart, first list the major jobs of the department in order of importance using the operation list as a guide. Next, summarize the tasks of each individual and list them under "tasks." One column should be completed for each person in the department. Each task listed must be related to the operations indicated in the left column. Hours per week and work count should be recorded in the appropriate columns. Columns should be totaled and entered in the

TASK LIST OF INDIVIDUAL JOBS (For work distribution chart)			
Name	Working Title		
Opr No.	Description of Operation	Work Unit Volume	Hours Per Week
Total Hours of Work			
Date	Function	Certified by	

Figure 21 Task List of Individual Jobs

appropriate space. A portion of a work distribution chart is shown in Figure 23. This chart can be continued to show each position in a department.

The fourth step is to systematically analyze the work distribution chart. This can be done best by examining the completed chart and asking questions concerning it. The following questions are suggested as a guide:

What operations and tasks take the most time? Are they the ones that should take the most time? Normally, the largest total time should be spent on what are considered major operations directly related to the objective

OPERATION LIST (For work distribution chart)		Date
Opr No.	Description of Operation	Weekly Volume
Function		Certified by

Figure 22 Operation List

of the department. Operations that take the most time may require further study such as method analysis, which will be covered in another chapter.

Is there misdirected effort? Is too much time being spent on relatively unimportant operations or unnecessary tasks? Instances of misdirected efforts are frequently found in "miscellaneous" or "administrative" categories. Therefore, attention should be given to these areas.

Are skills being used properly? Is everyone being used in the best possible manner or are special skills and abilities being wasted? Highly skilled

WORK DISTRIBUTION CHART				Function Charted ADMINISTRATIVE SECTION		
Distribution ☐ Present ☐ Proposed				Name		
Charted by				Position		
Opr/ Process No.	Operation/Process	Work Count	Hours Per Week	Task	Work Count	Hours Per Week
Total (Man-hours)						

Figure 23 Work Distribution Chart

employees should not perform tasks that could be performed by less-skilled employees. Also, to have a person working too far below his ability is wasteful.

Are individuals doing too many unrelated tasks? The principles of homogeneous assignment apply here. When a worker continually goes from one type of work to another, time and manpower are wasted. Greater efficiency results if workers are assigned related tasks.

Are tasks spread too thinly? Usually, one person working steadily can accomplish a task more effectively than many workers doing a small part of the same task.

Is work distributed evenly and equitably? Do the tasks of some workers look thin compared to others? Overloading or underloading workers will get poor results and may lower morale. Aim for a balanced workload among workers.

Once the work distribution chart has been analyzed, a new chart can be made showing the new work distribution.

THE MANAGER AND HIS TIME

The most essential resource the manager must consider in allocating and scheduling work is time. Unlike other resources, time is fixed. With only twenty-four hours in a day, if time is squandered more cannot be bought, built, added, or recalled and reworked. It must be used effectively the first time or it is lost. The manager must not only consider the time of his subordinates but be keenly aware of his own. Unless he plans and organizes his time wisely and productively, his total operation will suffer. Therefore, in allocating and scheduling work the manager should not overlook himself.

Time Analysis

To plan and organize his time effectively, a manager must first analyze his work and determine how his time is used. This can be done by taking a sheet of paper and listing his duties under the following headings:

ROUTINE WORK. These are minor duties done daily. They include such things as answering the telephone, cleaning up, putting files away, and various other routine tasks that require little or no skill and do not contribute directly to the objective of the department.

REGULAR WORK. These are duties that make up the major tasks directly related to the department objective. Such things as meetings, personal contacts, scheduling and assigning work, inspecting, and essential paperwork are included in this category.

SPECIAL WORK. This is emergency or rush work not directly related to the department, or work that due to its special nature cannot be handled in the regular manner.

CREATIVE WORK. This is incentive work, such as developing better methods, improving morale, and encouraging initiative.

Once duties have been listed under the four major headings, each category should be analyzed. A particularly close look should be taken at routine work. It is generally agreed that no more than 10 percent of the manager's time should be spent doing this type of work. Another area warranting close attention is special work. If this type of work requires more than 15 percent of the manager's time, there is a good chance that it is interfering with regular work and may indicate that priorities need to be established. Regular work should consume about 65 percent of the manager's time, leaving 10 percent for creative work. Creative work is the type most often overlooked. The average manager seldom finds time to systematically and deliberately concentrate on ways to improve his department. This is unfortunate, for it is in this area where problems can be solved, employees' ideas sought, new methods developed, training given, and changes affected to increase effectiveness and efficiency. Of course the percentages established here are only approximate. But the 10, 65, 15, 10 percent ratio for routine, regular, special, and creative work is a useful guide for analyzing a manager's time.

Delegating Work

One way in which a manager may manage his time better is by delegating some of his work to others. In doing this, some fundamental principles and practices should be followed. First, the manager should consider delegating to others as many routine and special duties as possible, thus freeing his time to concentrate on regular and creative work. However, this must be done with discretion. If the work is undesirable, it may be considered "buck passing" and cause resentment. Also, the person to whom the work is delegated should be capable of assuming the responsibility for performing the work. Secondly, the assignment should be specific and clearly defined and necessary authority should be given commensurate with the responsibility. The old adage "Everybody's work is nobody's work" applies here. Failure to delegate a specific task to a specific individual, or not giving authority sufficient to carry out the assignment, is a frequent example of poor delegation. Finally, the manager should remember that delegating work does not relieve him of his responsibility and that he is still inherently accountable for work of his department.

Allocating and Scheduling Time

Because the manager works in units of months, weeks, and days, his time should be scheduled and budgeted in these same units. The manager will find the following pattern helpful:

1. Start by planning and organizing his time one month in advance:
    a. In the last week of the month, list all things that should have been done in the present month and were not done.
    b. List all things that need to be done in the next month as far as they can be determined.
    c. List all things that have to be done for which he has no control (meetings, reports, and so on).
2. Look over the list and determine those items that must be done by him and those that can be delegated.
    a. Delegate those things that can be delegated.
    b. Determine the approximate time required to accomplish the things that must be done by the manager.
3. Using a desk calendar, notebook, or index cards, schedule the work to be done for each day of the month. Consider this sequence:
    a. First, schedule the work for which the manager has no control.
    b. Next, schedule regular work so that, where possible, each task is done during certain hours each day or day each week.
    c. Finally, list the remaining tasks according to priority and schedule this work consistent with its urgency.
4. In addition to the above sequence, the manager should consider these factors:
    a. Learn at what time of day he does taxing mental work best, and schedule work of this type accordingly.
    b. Plan difficult or most disliked tasks first.
    c. Alternate hard and easy tasks.
    d. Keep on hand short routine jobs to be done in spare moments.
    e. Allow time for some disruptions and pause points.
5. Review the schedule and make necessary adjustments.
    a. At the end of each day, check off work that has been accomplished.
    b. At the end of each week, review the schedule and eliminate, reschedule, or delegate work that was not accomplished.
    c. At the end of the month, repeat the above cycle.

WORK PLAN

Basic to effective allocating and scheduling work is a work plan. The purpose of a work plan is to reduce repetitious tasks and activities of a department to routine standard practices and to establish the flow and time sequence of the work. Consequently, work plans normally consist of a procedure or set of procedures and a schedule or set of schedules for the department.

Procedures

As indicated in Chapter 2, procedures prescribe the method or manner in which work is to be performed. A standard procedure may be developed for the overall work of the department and others developed for each task or activity. Procedures allow the work to be delegated to employees with specialized skills. They permit the operation to run smoothly without constant interruptions by having to explain each task or activity. Also, they conserve the manager's time for the important task of managing his operation. Procedures may be a simple set of instructions or they may be a part of a complete system interrelated to other departments for getting a certain project completed.

Schedules

Schedules establish the time sequence in which work is to be done. They provide the manager with the tool to determine the flow of work in his department and to establish the time-frame for getting the work done. Like procedures, schedules may pertain to only one activity in a department or be a part of a total schedule for a larger operation. They may be simply a statement of sequences of events, or charts, graphs, and so on, which show the flow and lead time for a complete project involving several departments.

Although it is obvious that no standard format can be used for all plans, in developing any work plan, the manager should consider the following factors:

WORKLOAD. Decide on the assignment of tasks to men and where applicable to machines. Determine the flow of work. Determine the sequence in which each task for man and/or machine must be done.

TIME-FRAME. Plan the work with respect to time. Establish deadlines for starting and finishing the tasks. Plan the use of available time of men and machines individually and by groups.

SET UP AND PUT AWAY. Consider the time and procedure for setting up a task and what is required to put it away. Consider such things as clean-up, routine maintenance of property and equipment, removing and returning records, reports, and letters to the files.

VARIABLE FACTORS. Take into account variable factors that may affect the plan. Consider holidays, training time, leaves, vacations, shifts, rest periods, turnover, meal times, and so on.

CONTROLS. Consider the factors and devices to be used to determine the effectiveness of the plan. Where possible, use built-in controls. Use work counts, standard times, and past average performances. Compare these with what is performed.

COORDINATION. Check the plan with those who will be affected by it. Consider the plan's relationship to other departments and the overall operation. Assure that each is aware of his involvement. Discuss the plan with the workers who will be asked to implement the plan and get their support and cooperation. Clear the plan with your immediate supervisor. Obtain his approval. Assure that your plan is consistent with company policy and other related procedures.

Before concluding the discussion on work plans, a few words should be said about making the plan work. The old adage "Plan your work and work your plan" points up the fact that a plan is of little value unless it is followed. This simply means that it is one thing to allocate and schedule well, but the more difficult task is seeing that schedules are met. Waste and scrap, errors and mistakes, absenteeism and tardiness, poor performance and unsatisfactory conduct, training new employees and up-grading the ones on board are some of the many problems that the manager must deal with on a day-to-day basis. Although the expertise in handling these and other problems can only be attained through experience, the skills and techniques discussed in the remainder of this book should assist the manager in making his plan work.

KEY POINT SUMMARY

1. The purpose of allocating and scheduling work is to assure that each employee is fully used on essential tasks, that his skills are used to maximum advantage, and that he is given a full workload so he can produce a quality product or service in a prescribed quantity and within an established time-frame.
2. While allocating and scheduling work is essentially a planning and organizing activity, a prescribed procedure can be used. The procedure the manager can use involves:
    a. Analyzing his organization
    b. Evaluating his work situation
    c. Planning and organizing his time
    d. Making a work plan
3. In analyzing his organization, the manager should:
    a. Clarify the objectives of his department
    b. Question the structure of his organization
    c. Determine the physical conditions under which the work will take place, paying particular attention to the factor of safety

4. To evaluate the work situation, the manager should take a close look at his employees' skills, his workload, and how this work is distributed. To do this he can use:
    a. A skills inventory
    b. A work count
    c. A work distribution study
5. The skills inventory determines the skills of the employees of his department. It can be used to:
    a. Determine training needs
    b. Shift workers to fill temporary vacancies and to meet peak workloads
6. The work count determines the impact of the volume of work on an operation. It can be used to:
    a. Schedule work
    b. Relate work
    c. Divide work
    d. Locate bottlenecks
7. A work distribution study determines if work in a department is distributed equably and evenly. The study contains four steps:
    a. Preparing individual task sheets
    b. Preparing an operation list
    c. Preparing a work distribution chart
    d. Analyzing the work distribution chart
8. A work distribution study helps the manager determine if:
    a. Effort is misdirected
    b. Skills are being used properly
    c. Individuals are doing too many unrelated tasks
    d. Tasks are spread too thinly
    e. Work is distributed evenly and equitably.
9. The purpose of a work plan is to reduce repetitive tasks and activities to routine standard practices and establish the flow and time sequence of work, and may consist of procedures and/or schedules.
    a. Procedures prescribe the method and manner in which work is to be done.
    b. Schedules establish the time sequence in which work is to be done.
10. In developing a work plan the manager should consider the following:
    a. Workload
    b. Time-frame
    c. Set up and put away

d. Variable factors
e. Controls
f. Coordination

DISCUSSION QUESTIONS

1. What is the relationship between allocating and scheduling work and the management functions of planning, organizing, coordinating, directing, and controlling? Specifically consider the following:
   a. Objectives and making the assignment understood
   b. The principles of organizing: unity of authority, span of control, homogeneous assignment, and delegation of authority
   c. Working with other departments
   d. Directing the operation to make the plan work
   e. Methods and type of controls
2. What is the relationship between the effective use of manpower and allocating and scheduling work? Discuss the cost factors that should be considered in allocating resources.
3. Within the framework of the relationship established by Question 1, discuss the significance of each of the questions on page 182.
4. What is the relationship between the physical working conditions discussed in Chapter 7 and the questions listed in Figure 18?
5. Why is it important to evaluate the work situation?
6. In evaluating the work situation, why is it necessary to make a skills inventory? Discuss.
7. What are some of the purposes of a work count? Discuss.
8. What are the advantages of a work distribution study? Discuss.
9. How can the manager use his time more effectively? Discuss.
10. What is the purpose of a work plan? Discuss.
11. What is the difference between a procedure and a schedule?
12. What is the interrelation between a schedule and a procedure?
13. What type of controls can a manager build in his plan to determine if it is getting the job done?
14. Why should a work plan be coordinated?
15. What is the meaning of the adage "Plan the work and work the plan?"

CASE PROBLEMS

Case 11–1

John Milburn, after a year on the job as manager of a fairly large department, was continuously confronted with numerous problems during his day-to-day operation. Recognizing that these problems were seriously affecting the efficiency of his department, despite his busy schedule, John decided to take a close look at his *past* and *present* operation to isolate those instances and situations that should be corrected to make his department more effective. Here is what John's analysis revealed:

1. He had been reprimanded for failure to follow through with an important assignment for which he was unaware that his department was responsible.

2. On several occasions, he could not meet a critical deadline because one of his workers was on sick leave and he did not know who could do his job.

3. He needed information to justify additional people for his department.

4. He received numerous complaints from his workers about the inequality of their individual workloads.

5. Some of his workers have time on their hands, while others never seem to get caught up.

6. Work output is being reduced by a pile-up at one part in the operation.

7. He has to do much of the routine work himself.

8. His workers leave their jobs without putting their work away.

9. He is constantly disturbed by employees asking questions about their work.

10. He has no time for creative work.

11. Sometimes he is caught shorthanded during the summer vacation period.

12. He is criticized by the maintenance department for dirty and uncovered machines and equipment.

13. His employees are slow to start their work day.

14. He has a relatively low production rate, but his employees are always busy.

Questions

1. *What factors are involved in each of the instances or situations revealed by the analysis?*
2. *What specific action can John take to correct his current problems and preclude his past problems from happening again?*

Case 11–2

Carl Bowman was a hard-working manager. He had enough personnel in his department to accomplish the workload. In spite of this, his work was rarely done on time. One day, Carl excused himself from a meeting with his boss stating that he just had to get back to the job. The boss decided to spend the next morning with him. Next morning when the boss arrived, Carl was talking on the phone; at the same time he was signing forms. He interrupted the phone conversation to greet the boss and still holding the phone called to his secretary, "Mary, the forms are signed." Carl, talking again on the same phone call, thrust the signed forms toward Mary as she entered. His movement pushed a disorderly pile of papers off of the corner of his desk. The papers were scattered on the floor by a breeze from an open window, and

Mary started picking them up. Carl shouted, "I'll think about it and call you back, Oliver." Then he said to Mary, "Don't pick them up, you'll just mix them worse." He scooped up a paper that was on his desk and handed it to the boss. "There's Don Pitts' idea of how to save about half the time we spend on processing. Wish we had time to try it out. What do you think of it?"

Mary came to Carl's desk. "Bill Evans wants to know if he can start on that priority job right now," said Mary.

"Tell him to wait," said Carl, "I haven't time to finish training him, and I just can't trust him to start a job that important without checking it myself."

"Oh! another thing," said Mary, "Bill would like to know who you want to do Bob Klien's job since he has called in sick."

Carl looked at his boss and shook his head, then turned back to Mary.

"Tell him that Bob's job will have to go undone, since I don't know who can do it except Bob, and I am too busy to do his job myself."

While Carl was picking up and sorting the papers, Mary brought in some forms. "Mr. Bowman, you just signed the reports on the line for the Personnel Manager's signature, so I typed them over."

"Too much to do," muttered Carl, glancing at his boss as he signed.

"If you sign them now, I'll take them to Personnel right away," Mary said, reaching.

"I'll take them," said Carl, "They might want to ask me about them."

Carl explained to the boss, "Don and Bill can't do a thing until I run through these. I'll be right back." He dashed out. In a minute, he stuck his head in the door. "I forgot to tell you, Mary, don't type that other report until I read it. We can get the due date backed up a day. See if the boss wants some coffee. I won't have time for any." And, he dashed away again, but before he went, he said to the boss, "No use Mary typing that report twice. Anybody as busy as I am knows you can't waste a second."

Questions

1. *What factors are involved in this case?*
2. *What procedures could Carl use to help him allocate and schedule his work more effectively?*
3. *Assume you are Carl's boss and prepare the basic outline of a work plan that you would recommend Carl to follow.*

SELECTED REFERENCES

BOYD, BRADFORD B., *Management Minded Supervision,* Chap. 10. New York: McGraw-Hill Book Company, 1969.

BROWN, MILON, *Effective Work Management,* Part 5. New York: The Macmillan Company, 1960.

ECKER, PAUL, JOHN MACRAE, VERNON OUELLETTE, and CHARLES TELFORD, *Handbook for Supervisors,* Chap. 1. Englewood Cliffs, N.J.: Prentice-Hall, Inc., 1959.

PARKER, WILLARD E., ROBERT W. KLEEMEIER, and BEYER V. PARKER, *Front-Line Leadership,* pp. 275–78. New York: McGraw-Hill Book Company, 1969.

12

How to Induct the New Employee

When a new or transfer employee comes into a department, it is the manager's responsibility to see that the employee is fully informed and started right on his new job. This process is called induction. As indicated when the staffing process was outlined in Chapter 10, in case of the new employee the induction process is normally the final phase of the organization's orientation program with the specific purpose of assisting the employee in adjusting to the job and his work place. Although this chapter will discuss the principles and skills necessary to induct a new employee, with slight modification they can be used to induct the transfer employee also. This chapter includes these major topics: (1) the importance of proper induction, (2) plan for proper induction, (3) job instruction, and (4) evaluation.

THE IMPORTANCE OF PROPER INDUCTION

Possibly, there is no function or supervisory skill that is more poorly handled than the induction of a new employee. This is unfortunate, because no function is more important in getting the new employee off to a good start on the job. Too often the manager is just too busy to stop and induct the employee properly. Consider this two-part instance, for example, of a busy manager and a nineteen-year-old clerk starting her first job:

First the manager:

> The office manager is right in the middle of a rush job! Pressure is on from all sides to get out production. The paperwork is piling up. The

> phone has been ringing constantly. He is wondering why he ever became a manager in the first place. Then, right in the middle of all this, someone from personnel brings in a new employee! During the introduction he mentally "curses" his hard luck at having this new girl come in right now when everything else is breaking. His whole tendency is to shove this girl off onto someone else as soon as possible, or to get her off in a corner, or to send her right out to work on some simple job—anything to get her out of his hair so that he can get back to the more "urgent" things.

Next, the girl as she told what happened later:

> The office manager was coldly polite and formal. I had the feeling that he didn't like me and that I'd better watch my step with him. I felt ill at ease. However, he took me almost immediately to my woman supervisor, who without further ado took me to one of the many high tables on which long rows of cabinets containing trays of stack cards were lined up. Trays were being pulled out noisily by the closely packed clerks, who would make entries on the cards and then slam the trays back. The noise and confusion were terrible. Stacks of papers were piled everywhere. I wondered how I could survive working for eight hours a day here! The supervisor introduced me to a rat-faced lady clerk who was told to get me started. She took a huge stack of papers, of all colors and descriptions, and spent the rest of the day plying me with endless details, innumerable exceptions. Most of it went in one ear and out the other. Loud bells would clang at certain hours, and a large group of clerks would jump up and disappear. I was afraid to leave, and I did not eat lunch because no one told me that there was a cafeteria nearby—besides, I did not know about the lunch hour. I do not know to this day how I ever survived those first few days on the job!

Scenes similar to the one indicated above are repeated day in and day out by managers in businesses, large and small. But unlike the girl indicated here, many new employees do not survive the first few days or months; they quit. This is supported by many studies that show that turnover is exceptionally high during the first ninety days of employment. For example, one study made by Scott and Clothier of fifty-five companies showed the turnover to be 1,026 percent (100 percent being the turnover rate for all employees) of less than one month of service; but for employees with one to three months of service, the turnover rate dropped to 226 percent.

In a survey conducted by the Hamilton Watch Company over an eighteen-month period, 40 percent of the employees who quit did so during this period.

In a study of American Air Lines, Inc., turnover showed that although only 13.4 percent of its employees had under one year of service, this group contributed to nearly one-half of all turnover. Over 70 percent of those quitting had under two years of service. Moreover, turnover is costly. Estimates for replacing workers who quit run from several hundred dollars for simple unskilled jobs to several thousand dollars for highly specialized personnel.

In addition to reducing high turnover, proper induction saves the manager time and the organization money in other ways. First, it gives the manager the opportunity to explain his position and that of the company before the employee is misinformed by others. It takes advantage of the principle of first impression, which is usually a lasting one. Second, it reduces ill-will, disciplinary action, and dismissals caused by the employee not knowing rules and the consequences of not following them. Next, it reduces wasted time on the part of the employee. If he knows the what, why, where, and how of his job and work place from the beginning, he will less likely need to ask questions later. It also helps him overcome the fear of the unknown, which is inherent in the worker's first few days on the job, thereby helping overcome the employee's resistance to change.

PLAN FOR PROPER INDUCTION

From the above discussion, it becomes obvious that ultimate value of the new employee to his organization depends to a large extent upon how well and how quickly he adjusts to his new and unfamiliar surroundings. This makes it equally obvious that a well-planned program to assure that the new employee is fully informed and properly and timely placed on the job is an important function of applied supervision. To be effective, the manager should have a plan ready to go into operation the minute a new employee comes into his department. Although each plan will vary as to details, the overall design is basically the same. Such a plan consists of ten steps arranged in an order to assure that each new employee is systematically inducted into his new department and started right on the job. The ten steps and the major factors to be considered in each step are listed below:

1. *Get ready to receive the new employee.*
    a. Have an updated description of his job and/or a list of duties and responsibilities to discuss with him.
    b. Have his working area, tools, equipment, and supplies ready.
2. *Welcome the new employee.*
    a. Put him at ease.
    b. Explain your relationship to him.
3. *Show sincere interest in the employee.*
    a. Discuss his background and interests.
    b. Inquire about his family, friends, clubs, and so on.
    c. Inquire about his transportation to and from work.
4. *Determine if he knows about the organization and its personnel policies.* (Note: If the organization has an orientation program, the information

required here is normally included. But it is the responsibility of the manager to assure that the new employee understands these factors.)

   a. The organization's history, background, and product or service.
   b. Method of calculating pay: how his pay is figured, where he gets paid, incentive plan, overtime, and payroll deductions.
   c. Group and individual benefits: Insurance plans, hospital and sickness benefits, pension and stock-sharing plans, and vacation and leave policy.
   d. Union contract and method of handling grievances.

5. *Explain the work of the unit or department.*
   a. Describe the function of the unit and how it relates to the other functions of the organization.
   b. Outline the organization.
   c. Tell him to whom he reports and, if applicable, who reports to him.
6. *Explain rules, policies, and procedures.*
   a. Hours of work
   b. Need for punctuality and good attendance
   c. Lunch periods
   d. Rest periods
   e. Use of telephone
   f. In-out procedures
   g. Other shop or office procedures—smoking, safety, special clothing, fire regulations, housekeeping
7. *Introduce him to his co-workers.*
   a. Indicate to each the new worker's duties.
   b. Explain duties of each person to whom introduced.
   c. Arrange for co-worker to go to lunch with him the first day.
8. *Show him the layout and available facilities.*
   a. Explain layout of shop, office, or store.
   b. Show him the elevator, washrooms, water fountain, and other facilities.
   c. Show him where he can obtain first-aid or medical treatment, if needed.
9. *Start him on the job or in a training program.*
   a. Assign him to work place or training area.
   b. Assure that he is given proper instructions.
10. *Follow-up.*
   a. Check on his progress.
   b. Encourage him to ask questions.
   c. Give him encouragement.
   d. Remember his name.

JOB INSTRUCTION

Whereas all steps outlined in the plan above are important and none should be slighted, the step requiring special emphasis is job instruction. Unless the new employee is given proper instruction on how to do his job, even if the other steps are diligently applied, much of his value will be lost. The reason is simply this: Since the measure of the employee's worth to the organization is productivity, he must know how to do the job before he is able to produce. This makes it clear that as soon as the new employee has been oriented, he should be thoroughly instructed concerning how to do his job.

A time-tested method for teaching an employee a new job or task is the job instruction method. This method was developed during World War II and used by supervisors to train millions of new employees as a result of the growing complexity of production and distribution spurred by the war. Since the war, this method, which consists of four basic steps and eighteen fundamental points, has been universally accepted as a means of teaching a new employee his job. This method is outlined in Figure 24.

However, it should be pointed out here that this method is not restricted only to the induction of new employees. The job instruction method can be used in modified ways in the process of giving orders and as a part of a formal training program. But since job instruction is particularly ap-

STEPS

I. Preparation of the Worker

- Put learner at ease.
- Find out what he already knows about the job.
- Get him interested and willing to learn.
- Place him in correct position.

II. Presentation

- Make proper use of telling.
- Make proper use of showing.
- Make proper use of demonstrating.
- Take one step at a time.
- Stress key points.

III. Performance—Tryout

- Learner performs the operation.
- Have learner explain key points.
- Question worker (why, what, when, who, where, how).
- Correct his errors.
- Repeat instructions when it is necessary.

IV. Follow-up, Evaluation

- Put learner on his own.
- Encourage questions.
- Check frequently.
- Taper off assistance.

Figure 24 Job Instruction Method

plicable in instructing a new employee and is normally given informally, it is appropriate that it be included here. It should be further understood that although the manager may not always give the instruction himself, the four-step method of instruction should be a fundamental supervisory skill of every manager, and the method can be used to instruct an employee on any job. For the clerk filling out a form, the cashier operating a cash register, or the short-order cook being told how to fry an egg, to the operation of complex machines, the method will apply; only the contents and time will vary.

Preparation

Before discussing the four steps indicated in Figure 24, it is first necessary to stress the importance of the manager getting ready to instruct the job. Unless this preliminary step is taken, much of the effectiveness of the four-step method will be lost. In getting ready to instruct the job, several factors should be considered.

If the job is long and complex, a time schedule may be necessary. This can simply be done by making an estimate of how long the instruction will take and making a mental or a recorded note of the time factor. Knowing the time will be beneficial to both the manager and the employee. It will permit the manager to arrange his work schedule to allow time for the instruction, and it will give the employee some idea as to the length of time he will be in a trainee status.

The second factor to consider is the breakdown of the operation. Again, the detail will depend on the complexity of the operation or task being taught. Figure 25 shows a breakdown of a fairly simple task of folding a paper into a cup. As this figure indicates, the breakdown is in two parts.

The *steps in the operation* should include major units of the task arranged in a sequence, as they are to be learned. Although all elements of the operation need not be listed, the elements should be small enough to be taught at one time and be performed by the employee immediately after the step has been learned. Some jobs are so simple that a detailed breakdown is unnecessary, but the major steps and the proper sequence should be kept in mind for even the simplest operations.

The *key points,* as the term implies, are the major factors of the job to be stressed. This includes special knowledge, knacks, or any particular information that will make the job easier and safer to perform. Key points are important in teaching the most simple skill since they give the new employee the benefit of the manager's experience.

The third factor to consider in getting ready to instruct the employee is having the material ready. Of course the material will vary according to the type of job. Material may consist of only a set of forms or it may include patterns and examples of completed work. The point to remember is that whatever material is needed to instruct the job should be assembled and in place before the instructor begins. There is nothing more discouraging than to discover that important material is not available when it is needed. In the first place, lack of material will preclude the manager from instructing the job properly, and secondly, it discourages the employee if he is not shown by example what he is supposed to do.

WORKSHEET 16c

OPERATION BREAKDOWN FOR TRAINING

STEPS IN THE OPERATION Step: A logical segment of the operation in which something is done to advance the work.	KEY POINTS Key point: Any directions or bits of information that helps to perform the step correctly, safely, and easily.
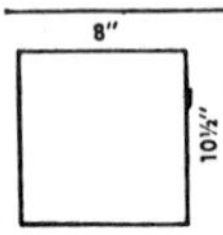 8" 10½" Place 8" x 10½" sheet of paper in front of you on flat surface.	1. Be sure surface is flat free of interfering objects.
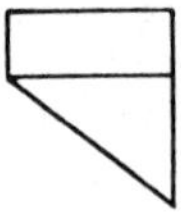 Fold lower left hand corner up.	2a. Line up the right hand edges. b. Make a sharp crease.
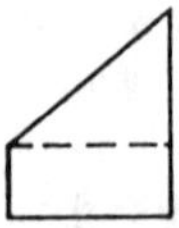 Turn paper over.	3a. Pick up lower right hand corner with right hand and place it at the top. b. Folded flap should not be underneath.
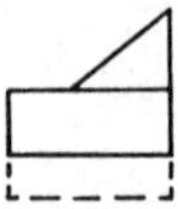 Fold excess lower edge up.	4a. Line up right hand edges. b. Fold should line up with bottom edge. c. Make sharp crease.
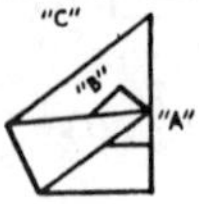 "C" "B" "A" Fold lower left hand corner flush with edge "A".	5a. Keep edges "B" and "C" parallel. b. Hold bottom edge in the center with finger while making fold.

Figure 25 Operation Breakdown for Training (Courtesy of U.S. Air Force Department.)

STEPS IN THE OPERATION	KEY POINTS
 Fold upper corner to point "D".	6a. Hold cup firmly with left hand. b. Bring upper corner down with right hand.
 Separate lower right corner and fold back.	7a. Hold cup with left hand. b. Fold back with right hand. c. Make sharp creases.
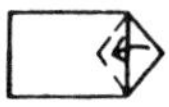 Turn cup over and fold remaining flap back.	8. Make sharp creases.
 Check cup to be sure it will hold water.	9. Open cup and look inside.

Figure 25 (cont'd.)

Fourth and finally, the manager should arrange the work place. This includes arranging tools, equipment, desk, chairs, or whatever is involved as nearly as possible as they should be in actual operation. Proper arrangement taken in this preliminary step will allow the manager to place the employee properly when instructions are given, and help discourage bad work habits that a poorly arranged work area often creates.

How to Instruct the Job

Having taken these four preliminary steps into account, the manager is then ready to use the four-step method of job instruction to teach the new employee how to do his job.

STEP 1: PREPARE THE WORKER. The preparatory step in job instruction involves getting the employee in the proper frame of mind, arousing his interest and curiosity about the job, and getting him physically situated to learn the job.

Putting him at ease. Although some of the fear of the unknown inherent in undertaking a new experience should have been partly overcome through the initial phase of induction, when placed in a situation where he is expected to perform, the new employee's security is threatened for the first time. "Will I look stupid?, Can I make a good impression?, Will I be given enough time to learn the job?," are possible questions the new employee is asking himself. To help overcome these fears, the manager should do his best to put the employee at ease. Since this involves feelings and emotions, how this can be done is no easy matter. Being friendly and cordial, discussing some common interests, telling him what is expected, and the time it normally takes to learn the job will help alleviate some of his fears. But more important, do not down-play the job. Making the job sound simple is a common fallacy in most cases where a job is being taught. Although this may have a temporary advantage, in the long run it may only lead to more stress by the employee thinking that he is not performing according to expectation. Rather than attempting to make the job sound easy, a better way to instill confidence is to assure the employee that he will be given sufficient time to learn the job and that accuracy and quality are more important than speed.

Finding out what the employee knows. After putting the employee at ease, the manager should next find out if the employee has some previously acquired knowledge of the job. This may be done by asking the employee what he knows, by reviewing his previous work record, and by having him perform as much of the operation as he can. While this information is helpful when the manager is instructing the employee in that it provides a common frame of reference, it may lead the manager into making another common mistake in instruction: assuming the employee knows. The rule here is that despite what the employee says he knows, never assume that he does. This means that the manager should cover all points of the job even though they may be known by the employee.

Arousing the employee's interest. This can be done by stressing the importance of the job and showing how it fits in with other jobs of the whole operation. For example, if the employee's job is a part of an assembly operation, the manager may show the completed product, how the product is marketed, and why the employee's job is important in making the product more attractive to the customer. Or if the job involves a service, the relationship between the employee's job and the reaction of the customer should be stressed. This will not only arouse the employee's interest but will establish the groundwork for stressing the key points when the operation is presented.

Placing him correctly. When teaching a skill that involves the use of tools and equipment, there are some important points which the manager should consider in placing or positioning the employee in relation to the work. First, he should be placed where he can see every motion made by the manager. For example, if a demonstration is to be a part of the instruction, the employee should be able to see the total operation. The employee also should be placed in such a way that he can see the operation as it will look when he performs it. This means that since an operation would be in reverse if presented with the manager and the employee face-to-face, a side-by-side position is best when most demonstrations are shown.

STEP 2: PRESENT THE OPERATION. Having properly prepared the employee, the manager can then present the operation. In taking this step, the job breakdown can be used as a guide. This step involves telling the employee how to do the job, showing him how the job is to be performed, explaining it to him, and demonstrating or illustrating how the operation is performed correctly. These four methods may be done simultaneously or separately depending on the job. But where possible all methods should be used, for to instruct a job effectively one method alone is seldom adequate. This can be illustrated by taking a look at the operation breakdown shown in Figure 25 and asking some questions about it: Could this simple operation be taught by words alone? Or would it be better understood if the employee is also shown by the diagrams how the paper is folded to make the cup? Going a step further, would explaining each step of the operation and stressing the key points make the operation easier to learn? The obvious answers to these questions make it clear that although this simple operation could possibly be learned through trial and error or by using one method, the four methods used together would without a doubt make learning the operation much easier and more effective.

STEP 3: LET THE EMPLOYEE PERFORM. How well the new employee learns the job can only be determined by having him perform the operation under supervision. This allows the employee to gain confidence and the manager to correct the employee's mistakes. The degree of supervision will depend on the difficulty of the job. For long tasks, this step may be interspersed in a sequence where the manager first does the more difficult task and the employee accomplishes the easier ones following a progression where the employee is finally allowed to do all tasks in the operation. This method is shown in Figure 26. For short tasks, the employee may be allowed to do all the tasks himself. As the employee performs the operation, the manager should have the employee explain the key points. This will not only help the employee fix the operation in his mind but will further assist the manager in determining if the operation is understood. Also, the manager should correct any mistake the employee may make and give additional instruction where required. Mistakes should be corrected tactfully, and the additional instruction should be given in such a way that the employee will not be made to appear stupid.

STEP 4: FOLLOW-UP. After the employee has demonstrated that he understands what he is supposed to do by successfully performing the task several times, he should be left to himself. This does not mean, however,

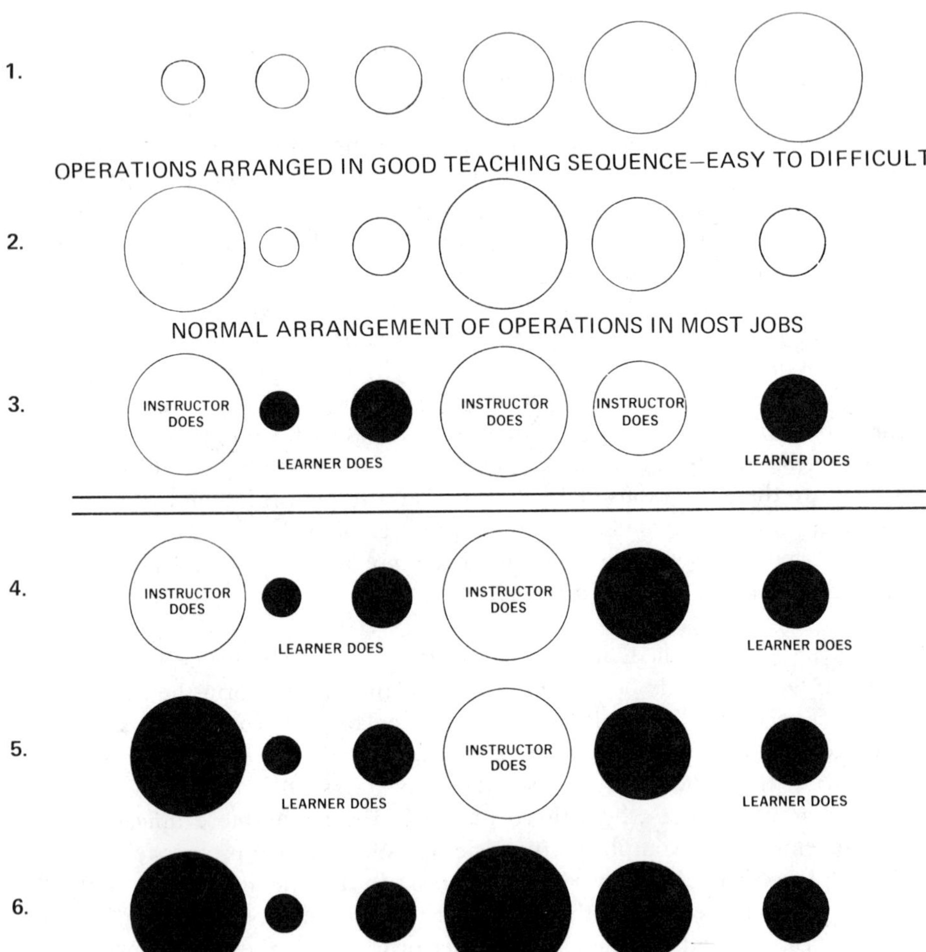

If a job can be taught by proceeding from the easy steps to the difficult, teaching becomes easier. Few jobs, however, have their working sequence arranged in an order of increasing difficulty as shown at the top of the chart. Instead, the difficult parts of the job are usually mixed in with the easy ones, like the second line on the chart. These steps have to be done on the job in the correct order, and therefore, they should be learned in that order. What can the supervisor-instructor do? He can keep the job in proper sequence and still teach the easier parts first by setting up his teaching plan as shown by the dark spots in each row of the chart. The instructor does the difficult or white spots while the worker does the easy or black spots, thus maintaining a learning sequence even in a difficult or long operation.

Figure 26 Sequence for Instructing the Complex Job (Courtesy of U.S. Air Force Department.)

that the employee should be left stranded with no one to consult in case he has questions. Where possible, a skilled employee should be designated to answer the new employee's questions and both the new employee and the one who is designated be advised accordingly. Also, the manager should make frequent checks and encourage the new employee to ask questions. This will allow the manager to determine if the new employee has grasped the fundamentals of the new job and at the same time make the employee feel that his manager is interested in him. When the manager feels that the employee has developed the fundamental skill to perform efficiently, and when he has gained more experience, this procedure can be tapered off by treating the employee as a regular member of the team.

EVALUATION

In many organizations, the new employee's immediate supervisor is required to make a formal evaluation concerning the employee's behavior and performance after a specified period of time. This is especially true of organizations with a probationary period, where a new employee is allowed a specific number of days to meet minimum organizational requirements. Normally, the factors to be judged are included on a preprinted form as discussed in Chapter 15. Whether an evaluation is specifically required or not, it is a good practice for the manager to be especially alert to any behavioral patterns the new employee has developed, which if left uncorrected may establish a bad precedence for the future. This includes such things as absenteeism, tardiness, infraction of safety and housekeeping rules, and other inappropriate practices and attitudes that may become habits.

KEY POINT SUMMARY

1. Learning how to induct a new worker properly is one of the first and most important skills that a manager should develop. Some reasons for this are:
    a. Proper induction helps reduce turnover.
    b. It gives the manager the opportunity to explain his position and that of the company before the employee is misinformed by others.
    c. Proper induction assures that the employee knows the rules; therefore, ill-will, disciplinary action, and dismissals

that may be a result of the employee not knowing or following the rules will be reduced.

d. It reduces wasted time.

e. It helps the employee overcome fear of the unknown and reduces resistance to change.

2. To induct an employee properly, the manager should have a plan. A typical effective plan includes ten steps as follows:
    a. Get ready
    b. Welcome the new worker
    c. Show sincere interest in him
    d. Assure that he understands the organization's personnel policy
    e. Explain the work of his department
    f. Explain rules, policies, and procedures
    g. Introduce him to co-workers
    h. Show him the layout and available facilities
    i. Start him on the job or in a training program
    j. Follow-up
3. During the induction process it is the duty and prime responsibility of the manager to assure that the employee is instructed on his new job. To do this, the manager must first make preparations by:
    a. Developing a time schedule
    b. Making a job breakdown
    c. Arranging the work place
4. A time-tested method of instructing an employee on a new job is the job instruction method (JIM), which involves four steps:
    a. Prepare the worker
    b. Present the operation
    c. Let the employee perform
    d. Follow-up
5. After a reasonable period of time (depending on the job), even if it is not specifically required by organizational policy, it is a good practice for the manager to evaluate the employee's performance and conduct and correct the new employee's mistakes before they become habit.

DISCUSSION QUESTIONS

1. Why is the induction of a new worker important?
2. What are the possible bad effects if an employee is not properly inducted to the job?

3. In your own words, what are the ten steps to follow in inducting a new worker?
4. Why is instructing the new worker on how he should do his job a major step in the induction process?
5. What are the four major steps involved in instructing the job? Discuss what the manager should do prior to giving job instructions.
6. What should you consider when taking Step 1?
7. What should you consider when taking Step 2?
8. What should you consider when taking Step 3?
9. What should you consider when taking Step 4?
10. Assume that you were the office manager discussed in the chapter, page 199. How would you have handled the new clerk coming into your department?

CASE PROBLEMS

Case 12–1

A visitor who is going through a large organization has asked permission to speak with one of the new employees. After the new employee was pointed out to him, he asked this simple question: "How do you like your job?" This was the response: "Well, I have been here two weeks and you are the first person who has asked me anything about it. My supervisor started me off the first day and told me to run this machine, but I haven't really talked to him much since. He introduced me to the man who was supposed to teach me the job, but I didn't catch his name. He's the short, gray haired man in the dark suit. And another thing, I was 'bawled out' for smoking on the job. I don't think that was fair since I wasn't told about the smoking rules. The other people in the department seem to be O.K., but I still don't know who most of them are and what they do. Frankly, I am thinking about quitting."

Questions

1. *What steps in the induction process seem to have been omitted here?*
2. *Who is responsible for the employee's dissatisfaction, the man in the dark suit or the supervisor?*

Case 12–2

Mary Smith, eighteen, was hired at the beginning of the summer by the purchasing department of a large department store. Her supervisor greeted her, introduced her to fellow employees and assigned her to an experienced worker for instruction. Mary was taught the necessary procedure for filling out purchase orders. This she did satisfactorily for the next three months. When her work had been checked by her instructor, it was turned over to the buyers. That was the last she saw or knew about it. After three months of working in this unit, Mary asked for a transfer to any other type of work.

Questions

1. *What principle is involved in this case?*
2. *What steps in the induction process were apparently omitted?*

Case 12–3

An experienced and capable supervisor found himself face-to-face with a sudden increase in work. Always before, he had been able to get over such a hump by skillful planning and by hiring some experienced help. But this was different. Problems came at him faster than he could handle them. Schedule changes. A new staff setup to get used to. A drive for better quality. And no letup on the push for more output. To make matters worse, no experienced help was available. And he didn't have the time to break in the new man he had hired. So, he decided to ask the most capable man he had to do the breaking in. The supervisor hardly gave the new man a thought for about a week. Then he was notified that the new employee had been hurt on the job. The employee claimed he had been doing the job exactly as he had been told.

Questions

1. *What principle is involved in this case?*
2. *What should the supervisor have done to prevent the accident?*

SELECTED REFERENCES

BOYD, BRADFORD B., *Management Minded Supervision,* Chap. 7. New York: McGraw-Hill Book Company, 1968.

ECKER, PAUL, JOHN MACRAE, VERNON OUELLETTE, and CHARLES TELFORD, *Handbook for Supervisors,* Chap. 8. Englewood Cliffs, N.J.: Prentice-Hall, Inc., 1959.

PARKER, WILLARD E., ROBERT W. KLEEMEIER, and BEYER V. PARKER, *Front-Line Leadership,* Chaps. 9 and 10. New York: McGraw-Hill Book Company, 1969.

PFIFFNER, JOHN M., and MARSHALL FELS, *The Supervision of Personnel* (3rd ed.), Chap. 15. Englewood Cliffs, N.J.: Prentice-Hall, Inc., 1964.

13

How to Give Orders

As indicated earlier, a vital and major part of the manager's job is directing the employees of his operation toward achieving established objectives. When applied on a day-to-day basis, this function is accomplished by the manager conveying to the employees what they are to do and how and when they are to do it. This means giving orders. In fact, giving orders is a major part of the manager's daily job. This being so, this skill should be thoroughly understood. Therefore, the purpose of this chapter is to discuss ways in which orders may be used effectively. This will be done by examining the following topics: (1) making orders acceptable, (2) the verbal order, (3) using orders to create initiative, (4) using orders to praise, and (5) written orders.

MAKING ORDERS ACCEPTABLE

Before discussing giving orders as such, the manager should first recognize that the effectiveness of the orders will depend in a large measure on how well they are accepted by his employees. Of course orders do not have to be accepted for them to be carried out. Consider this instance for example:

> He stood there just muttering and staring at me after I told him what to do. So I hit him on the jaw. He knew who was boss now. He picked himself up and walked back to his job laying tracks. Just then a fellow I'd never seen before tapped me on the shoulder. "Pretty handy with your fists, aren't you?" he said.
>
> "Sure, why? Want to make something of it?"

"Plenty, but not what you think. I like the way you manage your men. I saw how you got that fellow back to his work. My company can use a man like you as a foreman. How about coming across the street to my office and talking it over?"[1]

This story was told by the president of a major corporation, and it happened many years ago. This is not to say that today some managers do not resort to force short of violence or that force should be ruled out altogether. But a far better way is for the employee to accept the order willingly and carry it out with enthusiasm. Human nature being what it is, no rules have yet been devised that will assure that the manager's orders will be accepted by each of his employees with no questions asked. However, the acceptability of orders will depend in a large measure on the psychological climate in which the order is given and the personality of the employee receiving the order. This in essence means that the manager should in his day-to-day relations with the employees develop a psychological climate based on mutual respect and always be perceptive to the individual differences of the employees. This can be done by developing rapport with the employees and making an honest attempt to identify what makes each employee different.

Developing Rapport

The word *rapport* simply means harmonious relationships. If the manager's relationship with the employees is harmonious, chances are the psychological climate of his department will convey a feeling of warmth, sincerity, and confidence, which sets the stage for having his orders accepted. Ideally, the psychological climate should be such that the situation should give the order. Stated simply, this means that instead of resorting to authority, the manager need only to point out the requirements and the factors that make the task necessary, and the employee should under his own initiative carry out the assignment to meet the situation. The ideal may never be attained, but it should be the goal of every manager, and the better the rapport the more likely is this goal to become a reality.

There is always the chance that relationships can become "too harmonious," and the old adage that familiarity breeds contempt should be kept in mind. But on balance, as studies previously cited show, rapport is a key factor in result-oriented supervision. This makes it apparent that the effectiveness of the manager's actions, including giving orders, will depend in a large measure on the rapport he develops with the employees.

To develop rapport, the manager should take into account the em-

[1] See Willard E. Parker, Robert W. Kleemeier, and Beyer V. Parker, *Front-Line Leadership* (New York: McGraw-Hill Book Company, 1969), p. 1.

ployees' basic needs for security, belonging, recognition, and opportunity, and show through his actions and attitude that he is concerned about them as individuals. Although each manager should develop his own style for developing rapport with the employees, ten practical ways that have proved effective over the years for developing rapport are listed below. Since these factors are well grounded in the fundamentals of human relations discussed in previous chapters, they are essentially self-explanatory and require only minimum discussion:

1. The manager should know the employees personally. Find out about their interests, hobbies, family backgrounds, and ambitions.

2. The manager should greet each employee daily. Let the employee know that he is appreciated and that he belongs to the team. Encourage the employee to come to him with his problems.

3. The manager should let each employee know how he stands. Answer his burning question: "How am I doing?" Explain why something should be done.

4. The manager should encourage the employees to participate in plans that affect them, listen to their ideas, show that he has confidence in them.

5. He should give credit where credit is due.

6. He should inform employees in advance of change. He should not surprise them.

7. He should let the employees participate in setting goals. Help them to identify their goals and their relationship with the goals of the department. Show each employee the importance of his job and its place in the organization. Make the goal realistic.

8. The manager should settle all grievances promptly. Criticize constructively by talking about the act, not the employee.

9. He should establish a consistent leadership style. Never keep the employee guessing. Admit mistakes. Set an example that the employees should follow.

10. He should back up his employees. Gain their confidence by earning their loyalty and trust. He should support the organization, for the manager is "the company" to the employee.

The above list is not inclusive, nor does it represent fixed principles that will not change under the impact of actual practice. But when taken with the background and understanding acquired in previous chapters, these factors will not only create the psychological climate for giving orders, but can be used as a fundamental guide and reference points for other areas of applied supervision.

Identifying Individual Differences

As previously indicated, organizations are composed of groups of individuals with different makeups and hangups that make them respond uniquely and individually. This means that employees will respond differently to orders. In other words, an order that may be accepted and get a favorable response from John or Mary may not be acceptable and draw a negative response from Bob or Thelma. This being so, when giving orders or taking other personnel action, the manager must take individual differences into account. To do this, the manager should make an honest attempt to know his employees and identify as far as possible their individual differences. This is no easy matter and will never be close to perfection. Even the skilled psychologist will readily admit that personality variables are so inexact that even they cannot pin them down precisely. However, by taking a systematic look at each of his employees and questioning those areas that have a bearing on their response to orders, many individual variables can be identified. To do this, the following areas and questions are suggested:

1. The employee's limitations and strong points. Is he a fast or slow learner? Is he capable or incapable? Skilled or unskilled? Is he a fast or slow worker? What is his educational and experience background? Is he a natural leader?

2. The employee's emotional touchy points. What are his prejudices? Can he be rushed? Does he have a "chip on his shoulder?" Does he rub people the wrong way? How does he see himself: Capable? Incapable? Sociable? Antisocial?

3. The employee's motivational drives. Does he respond to praise? Increased responsibility? Competition? A more or less difficult job? What is he after? More money? Security? Recognition? Belonging? Opportunity? Does he have a goal?

4. The employee's response to supervision. Will he respond best to loose or close supervision? Does he resist authority? Does he resent being told? How does he see the manager as his boss: As a leader or as a driver?

5. The employee's attitude toward the organization. Does he see it as a good place to work or as a stopover while he is looking for something else? Does he willingly support policies and procedures? Would he quit tomorrow for a little more money? More opportunity? More security? Better working hours and conditions?

Getting answers to the questions posed under the five areas listed above cannot be done overnight, nor can their application be stated in a one, two, three order. This can be acquired only through observation and experience over a period of time. Despite this, by recognizing these areas and questions the manager is better prepared to recognize individual differences and in doing so make his orders more acceptable.

THE VERBAL ORDER

One of the most effective and frequently used tools the manager has in applied supervision is the verbal order. As opposed to the written order, which is discussed at the conclusion of the chapter, the verbal order has the advantage of being given in a face-to-face situation where two-way communications can be practiced and the reaction of the employee determined, thus allowing the manager to adapt his order to the employee and the situation. But to be effective, the use of the verbal order should be understood. Like most management tools, giving the verbal order involves a process.

Planning the Order

Essentially, planning a verbal order involves determining what is to be done, who is to do it, and what kind of order is the most suitable to obtain the desired results. On a day-to-day basis, the steps mentioned above should evolve naturally from the situation along these lines. What is to be done will require an assessment of the situation and will of course depend on the particular task. After this has been decided, who is to do it should evolve naturally from the nature of the task, which in turn should suggest the type of order which would work best with the tasks and the particular employee involved. It should be understood at this point that this process is based on the premise that the manager has acquired thorough knowledge of the duties of his department and has obtained an equally thorough knowledge of each of the employees. If this is not the case, his orders will be ineffective regardless of the system he uses. With this understood, the manager can select one of the four types of orders which can be adapted to fit most employees and situations.

THE REQUEST. By the nature of his job, when a manager asks or requests a subordinate to do something it becomes an order. If this fundamental principle is clearly understood by the employee, the request is the most effective type of order under most circumstances. There are several reasons for this. First, since most people resent being told, the request helps overcome this resentment. Second, if phrased properly the request can imply that the employee's opinion is sought and valued. It can facilitate two-way communications and employee participation. Third and finally, the request can establish a closer manager-employee relationship by breaking down the boss-employee barrier that exists between the manager and the subordinate. Therefore, the manager should use the request order when possible and phrase the order in such a way that it not only gets results in terms of what is specifically sought but the human relation by-product as well. Here are a few examples of such orders: "Bill, you did such a good job on the last project, I would like you to do this one too." Or: "Mary, would you look over this report and type me a draft for the meeting tomorrow." Or: "Jack, what do you think about arranging your schedule so you can cover some of Frank's work until he returns from the hospital?" It should be understood, however, that the requests phrased in the above manner will not work under all circumstances and with all employees. This type of order works especially well when manager-employee relations have been firmly established, with employees who are interested in their work, most older workers, sensitive workers, or women employees.

THE DIRECT ORDER. Whereas the request provides for employee feedback, the direct order is given in the form of a command leaving the employee with no suggested alternative. "I want this done now," "Come here," "I want it this way" are examples of the direct order. Although the request is appropriate under most conditions and works best with most employees, in some cases the direct order is more effective. For example, in case of danger or when haste is involved, the direct order is almost always appropriate. Also, as shown earlier, some employees by nature prefer the direct "no nonsense" approach and expect and often demand to be told exactly what is expected of them in no uncertain terms. Other times when the direct order is appropriate is with the careless, lazy, or indifferent employee, and the employee who refuses to obey established rules and procedures. Despite this, however, the direct order should be used as sparingly as possible and never made an established pattern.

THE IMPLIED ORDER. A third type of order the manager can use is the implied order. It is normally stated in the form of a suggestion or wish such as: "I wish that this job could be made more productive," or: "If only we could overcome our high error rate, the effectiveness of our department would be greatly improved." To the experienced employee with initiative and ambition, these statements imply an order for action. But to the inexperienced and the less motivated the statements would imply no such thing. Therefore, the manager should use the implied order only when he is thoroughly familiar with the individuals and should never rely on the implied order to get his employees to carry out instructions. However, under certain controlled conditions which will be discussed later in the chapter, the implied order can be used effectively to improve methods and develop initiative.

CALL FOR VOLUNTEERS. Under certain circumstances it is better not to give any order at all, but call for volunteers. Despite its military connotation, this method may work better than an order when a job is unusual and not a specific requirement of employees' jobs. Dangerous work, emergency work, disagreeable or extra heavy work are examples. Also, the manager may call for volunteers when overtime is required or when something needs to be done that calls for less skill than required by the employees' regular duties. Employees will usually volunteer more readily if the manager volunteers his services first.

Giving the Order

Once the manager has planned the order, he may then consider the best way it is to be given. Like planning, this phase, too, should follow a logical sequence.

Preparing the Recipient. An important step in giving an order is preparing the employee for the order. This is the motivational phase, and how this is done will affect the way in which the order is carried out. The amount of preparation required will depend on the work and the employee. If the work is simple and routine and the employee is skilled, little preparation is needed. Conversely, if the work is complex or is a new experience, thorough preparation may be required. Also, the amount of preparation will depend on the attitude of the employee. If rapport has been established between the employee and the manager, attitude should not be a problem. But if this has not been done (rapport established), the employee's attitude must be determined and taken into account. If the order constitutes a change, rules for effecting change apply here. Variables such as these must be considered and handled as the situation warrants. But under all circumstances, certain principles apply.

1. The employee must be told the reason for the order. Its importance. Why it is necessary. How it relates to the assignment of the department, and any unusual circumstances surrounding the order. Tell the employee the whole story.

2. The employee must be told when the order is to be carried out. When to start. When the assignment should be finished. The importance of meeting the deadline if one is involved. Alert the employee to any possible difficulties.

3. Finally, the manager must show enthusiasm. He must convey to the employee his interest in seeing that the order is carried out. He must convey to the employee that the order has his complete support. Give the order life.

Presenting the Order. This phase may involve both showing and telling. If the order involves instructions that are complex, it may involve complete job instruction, or if the job is simple, a few words may be sufficient.[2] But the point to remember is: *Take the necessary time and use whatever method necessary to get the order and instructions across.* Again, understanding individual differences is important. Is he a slow or a fast learner? Is he a slow or fast worker? Is he impulsive? Is he indecisive? Is he decisive? Is he talkative? Is he the silent type? Is he suspicious? Answers to these questions will determine how the order is to be presented.

[2] How to give job instructions is discussed in detail in Chapter 12.

Verifying the Order. The best way to determine if the order is understood is to have the employee repeat the order. If the order is complex, this is not possible. But when it is possible, having the employee "tell back" in his own words is the most effective way to assure that the order is understood. Also, the manager should encourage two-way communications. He should encourage questions from the employee. Not only will this assist the manager in verifying his order, but it will make the order more acceptable to the employee. It should be remembered, too, that employees have good ideas. They may suggest ways in which the order can be carried out more effectively. Therefore, the manager should ask questions if none is asked by the employee. Questions such as these, which ask the employee how he feels, sees, or thinks, are more effective: How do you feel about combining the two jobs into one? Or: Do you see any trouble in meeting the October 1 deadline? Or: Can you think of anything we left out? Questions like these will help get two-way communications flowing to verify the order.

Before leaving the discussion of giving orders, the importance of the manager's attitude should be stressed. For the order to be effective the manager's attitude must be positive, even if he disagrees with the order himself. Any hint that the manager thinks that the task is unimportant will be detected by the employee and interpreted to mean: "I am only doing this to satisfy the boss, but you and I both know we have better things to do." This, and similar negative attitudes by the manager can take the meaning out of an order and nullify its effectiveness.

Follow-up

The final step in the order-giving process is follow-up. Like other methods of control, this phase is to check up on results. It is to determine if the order was carried out as given or to see whether unforeseen circumstances are interfering with the order being executed. Also, it gives the manager an opportunity to assess the efficiency of the employee. In taking this step, the manager should be particularly observant of certain things. These include: (1) The quality and quantity of the work, (2) Whether the deadline was or is being met, (3) The attitude of the employee, (4) If initiative was used, (5) Whether new orders or redirection is needed, and (6) If instructions are being followed. The manager should remember that he is also checking up on himself as well as the employee. The results of the follow-up may point out that his order-giving techniques may need improving.

USING ORDERS TO CREATE INITIATIVE

If a person sees and does more than his job requires, he is said to possess initiative. Orders may serve as the basis for developing initiative.

To illustrate this point, examine first a simple order such as "Erase the board." Hearing that order, the person might ask himself several questions: "Should I also clean out the chalk tray? Should the eraser be dusted? The board can be erased in a horizontal or vertical manner but vertical strokes will make the board look much neater. Which method should I use?" To comply with such a commonplace order, the worker has a chance to see and do more than a strict interpretation of the order would imply. Such orders, then, can be a basis for judging whether or not the worker has initiative. One could carry the idea further by considering the following orders or assignments, examining them for all their possibilities and implications: (1) "Turn out the lights before you leave." (2) "Type this letter to the chief of the division." (3) "Place the chairs on the table." The manager can observe through his orders whether or not certain employees have initiative. He can also notice those employees who must be told every detail about a job, a necessity that is not only exasperating but also time-consuming.

Leave Out the Obvious

Immediately one is likely to think that it is unpardonable to leave an obvious item out of an order. Most studies will show, however, that many managers do it inadvertently and rather frequently. Leaving out an obvious item should not mean disaster when it is omitted consciously, because the person giving the order accepts the responsibility to keep the job under control. As an example, consider this order: "Arrange a display for all the charts used in the management course." When and where will they be displayed? How much space will be required for the display? How many charts are there? These are questions that the employee must answer in his own way. There are many possibilities in such an order. The employee would need to determine the size and quantity of the charts needed. He would need to look about for an appropriate room or building in which they could be displayed. There would be the matter of obtaining material, such as racks, tape, and thumb tacks. All these things could have been included in the original order, and in some instances probably would have been.

When checking for initiative, the manager should carefully observe what the employee did with the order. He should correct the employee if his actions were unreasonable, commend him if they were good. In instances where the employee displayed no initiative, the manager should work with him, pointing out the obvious mistakes.

This step may have to be repeated several times, checking each time in order to control the situation. Tact must be applied in this procedure, and the employee must be given credit when due in order to stimulate his initiative.

Omit the Less Obvious

A stenographer typing a paper found this statement: "A meeting of all employees was held on *October 9* to discuss absenteeism." On another page of the paper was this statement: "In the *October 10* meeting, it was discovered that the cause of the high absenteeism rate was due to colds." The manager having the paper typed should check to see whether or not she caught the error. If the stenographer showed initiative by taking appropriate action, then credit should be given. If she showed no initiative, then the manager should work with her, explaining the points that should have been observed. It is obvious that employees having several experiences like these and who show improvement are responding to the technique. They begin to look for "extra things" to do, no matter how small, and begin to develop initiative under guidance.

The technique of developing initiative is that of giving the worker problems to solve that become progressively harder. Although the samples listed here seem easy on the surface, they are more difficult when adapted to a particular work situation.

Give Idea Only

In an assignment where only the idea is given, the employee begins to fill in details of his own and has a wider latitude of freedom in which to operate. Suppose an employee was told to devise a procedure for checking attendance. In this case the employee is free to fill in the details as he sees them. An important part of the technique is tactfully checking on the employee. The employee can regard the manager's actions as traps or snares and may become resentful, or he can develop pride and enthusiasm for his work.

Suggest Only

The manager might say, "I wish something could be done about the backlog in the receiving unit." Notice that an order was not given, but there was a rather vague implication that the employee should devise some ways to decrease the backlog of work.

The employee might set a standard, improve the method, rearrange the personnel and their desks within the office, reroute the flow of work, or reassign some of the employees temporarily. Any system or plan he might put into execution for the purpose of decreasing the backlog of work would demonstrate initiative.

When the technique reaches this stage, the manager should have a thorough knowledge of his employee. He must gauge his suggestions according to the confidence he has in the employee, since some suggestions might easily disrupt an organization if acted upon too hastily or upon too large a scale. Moreover, careful follow-up is necessary in order to judge the quality of initiative being displayed by the employee.

Look for Initiative

This last step is one actual test of the preceding four steps. If the technique has received response, the employee will display initiative without the aid of carefully planned assignments and orders to guide him. It is always possible, and certainly desirable, to observe spontaneous activity before the four steps have been completed. Therefore, it is important that the manager be alert for such manifestations among employees at any time after he has started the procedure. He should remember, too, that a check on employees who show signs of too much enthusiasm is never out of order.

USING ORDERS TO PRAISE

It was mentioned in a previous discussion that, when phrased properly, an order could be used to praise an employee for commendable performance. Before discussing this further, this question should be answered: Is praise good or bad? Or putting it another way, is praise an effective motivator? Up until recent years, the answer to the question was an implicit "yes." Although many current management books strongly support the contention that praise should be used by the manager as a prime motivator, many psychologists use studies to support their claim that praise as such not only is *not* a motivator, but is sometimes a demotivator. For example:

> Richard E. Farson, a California psychologist, reports in the *Harvard Business Review* that findings of scientific experiments on praise do not clearly demonstrate its value. Most of the studies done on the subject compare praise with reproof or blame as motivational techniques. The results of the studies are mixed. In some instances, praise was slightly more effective than reproof. In other cases, the results were the opposite. Farson concludes: "After considerable observation I have come to the conclusion that praise usually does not reward."[3]

Does this mean that managers should not use praise? No, it does not mean that. Praise works well as a motivator for some. The extreme extravert, for example, not only enjoys praise but makes a conscious effort to seek it. But it does mean that the manager should use praise with discretion. To use praise effectively, he should know his employees and their responses.

[3] See John S. Morgan, *Getting Across to Employees* (New York: McGraw-Hill Book Company, 1964), pp. 131ff.

He should be sincere and let his employees know that when he says "a job well done," he means it. He should always give credit when credit is due. Getting back to orders, it has been found that praise is best given when connected with some other activity, and the order is a logical and an appropriate activity where the connection can be made.

WRITTEN ORDERS

On a day-to-day basis, the manager will use the verbal order more frequently. However, on occasion he will find that the written order is more appropriate. While no attempt will be made here to identify and discuss all the circumstances in which the written order should be used, before concluding the chapter on how to give orders, four of the more common ones will be mentioned and briefly discussed.

When it is necessary to hold the employee strictly accountable or a record is needed. This is sometimes required when the employee has disobeyed previous orders or rules or when all methods to improve his performance have failed. This category of order is useful in justifying action that may result later, such as showing cause for discharging an employee or giving reasons why an employee was not promoted.

When an order is of a general nature and applies to employees as a group. This includes routine work schedules, work assignments, vacation plans, shift changes, or other general information such as orders from higher authority that require no explanation and can be disseminated in mass or posted.

When orders involve instructions that have to be passed on or to transmit orders to another location. The span of control principle is involved here. The manager who relies on "word of mouth" to pass on information or gives verbal orders that have to go some distance risks the possibility of the order not being understood and thereby losing his span of control.

When precise figures and detailed information are involved that require exact interaction and application. A host of examples could be cited here, but it simply means what it says and requires no further explanation.

KEY POINT SUMMARY

1. A vital part of applied supervision is giving orders, the process of conveying to the employee what he is supposed to do and how and when he is supposed to do it.

2. In giving orders the manager should first create the climate for making his orders acceptable. This can be done by:
   a. Developing rapport (harmonious relationships) with his employees by applying good human relations practices.
   b. Identifying individual differences so he can determine the type of order that will be more acceptable to each of his employees.
3. Although orders can be either verbal or written, the verbal order is used more frequently on a day-to-day basis and has the advantage of facilitating two-way communications where the manager can "read" the reaction of the employee to the order.
4. The verbal order is more effective if used in a process that consists of three steps:
   a. Planning the order
   b. Giving the order
   c. Follow-up
5. Basically, planning the order involves an assessment of the situation and deciding on the best type of order to use. Types of orders are:
   a. The request
   b. The direct order
   c. The implied order
   d. The call for volunteers
6. Giving the order includes:
   a. Preparing the recipient
   b. Presenting the order
   c. Verifying that the order is understood
7. Follow-up is to determine if the order was carried out and to see if redirection and new orders are needed.
8. In addition to giving an employee direction, the order can be used to create initiative. This can be done by following this procedure:
   a. Leaving out the obvious
   b. Omitting the less obvious
   c. Giving idea only
   d. Suggesting only
   e. Looking for initiative
9. In using the order to praise, the manager should know the possible reaction of the employee, since everyone does not react favorably to praise.
10. On occasion the written order is more effective than the verbal order under certain conditions. Four common conditions are:
    a. When holding the employee strictly accountable

b. When the order is general and applies to employees as a group
c. When orders are to be passed on from one employee or group to another
d. When precise figures are involved

DISCUSSION QUESTIONS

1. What is the relationship between giving orders as discussed in this chapter and the directing process discussed in Chapter 2?
2. Why is developing rapport with his employees important to the manager in giving orders? Relate developing rapport with the basic needs of the employee.
3. Why is identifying individual differences important to giving orders? Relate the specific factors discussed in this chapter with individual variables discussed previously.
4. What is the major advantage of a verbal order, and what are the steps for giving this order effectively?
5. Which type of order (request, direct, and so on) would possibly work best with each of these employees?
    a. The experienced worker who is eager to please
    b. The sensitive and emotional worker
    c. The lazy and hostile worker
    d. The slow and methodical worker
6. When giving the verbal order, what steps should be considered, and what is the significance of each step?
7. In reference to presenting the order, why is it necessary to:
    a. Give reasons for the order
    b. Tell the employee when the order is to be carried out
    c. Show enthusiasm
8. Why is it necessary to understand individual differences in presenting the order?
9. In verifying the order, why is "tell back" necessary?
10. Why should attitude be considered in giving an order?
11. Why is follow-up on the order necessary? From the standpoint of the employee? From the standpoint of the manager?
12. With what type of employee and under what circumstances should the order be used to create initiative? Discuss the steps in this process.
13. In using an order to create initiative, what are some of the danger points that must be considered.
14. In looking for initiative in an employee, what basic factors should be observed?
15. Under what circumstances, and with what type of employee, should an order be used to praise?
16. When should the written order be given?

CASE PROBLEMS

Case 13–1

For four years, George Thomas had been manager of a small department consisting of seven highly skilled employees who worked well as a team requiring only a minimum of instructions and direction. Due to a reorganization, another small and similar department was abolished, and its six employees reassigned to work with George. Because the six transferred employees were also highly skilled and had been with the organization for a long time, George saw no reason why he should not treat them the same as other workers of his department. After a brief stand-up group meeting, George assigned the employees to their jobs and continued his regular method of giving orders.

However, George shortly found that the new employees were not responding to his suggestions and requests, and when an unsatisfactory situation was brought to their attention they tended to be resentful and argumentative. Thinking that the situation would straighten itself out, George continued treating them the same as his old employees. But after thirty days when the situation had not improved, George discussed the new employees' unsatisfactory behavior and performance with his supervisor.

Questions

1. *What principles are involved in this case?*
2. *Why was the method of giving orders used by George successful with his old employees but not effective with his new employees?*
3. *Based on the facts indicated, if you were George's boss what action would you recommend?*

Case 13–2

Bill Smith is manager of a department responsible for assembling orders of various material and subassemblies, which his company furnishes subcontractors working on national defense projects. On Friday, two hours before quitting time, Bill receives a call from his boss informing him that the order his department is assembling is urgently needed within forty-eight hours by the subcontractor to prevent a work stoppage that could conceivably cause the subcontractor to be penalized for a delay in completing the project. Bill was told that the company's agreement with the subcontractor called for delivery within forty-eight hours upon demand and therefore the order must be filled. After briefly analyzing the situation, Bill found that:

1. He was not fully convinced that the requirement for filling the order was as urgent as the customer made it seem.
2. He knew that the two men who were working on the order had plans for the weekend and would be reluctant to work overtime.
3. The two men who would volunteer to do the job were inexperienced and would require detailed instructions or close supervision.
4. He had an important out-of town meeting which he could not possibly cancel.

Despite these facts and circumstances, Bill knew that he had to get the order assembled.

Questions

1. *What are the options open to Bill?*
2. *From the standpoint of giving orders, what are the advantages and disadvantages of each option?*
3. *Discuss the best means of executing each option by considering each step in giving the verbal order, the use of initiative and praise, as well as the written order.*

SELECTED REFERENCES

BOYD, BRADFORD B., *Management-Minded Supervision,* Chap. 11. New York: McGraw-Hill Book Company, 1968.

BROWN, MILON, *Effective Work Management,* Chap. 7. New York: The Macmillan Company, 1960.

MORGAN, JOHN S., *Getting Across to Employees,* Chap. 7. New York: McGraw-Hill Book Company, 1964.

PARKER, WILLARD E., ROBERT W. KLEEMEIER, and BEYER V. PARKER, *Front-Line Leadership,* Chap. 11. New York: McGraw-Hill Book Company, 1969.

14

How to Control Employee Behavior

In the process of using his manpower, the manager soon finds that a sound plan for allocating and scheduling work, proper induction of new employees, and giving acceptable orders do not necessarily assure that his manpower will be used effectively. Unlike other resources, employees cannot and should not be manipulated according to any established pattern, but in order for manpower to be used effectively the employees' behavior must nevertheless be controlled. However, when used in regard to employee behavior, the word *control* takes on a broader meaning than controlling as discussed as a function of management. In its broadest sense, *control* is often used to describe functional responsibilities pertaining to certain operational areas such as personnel control, financial control, sales control, maintenance control, quality control, production control, and the like. In these instances, the word *control* is given the same meaning as applied supervision: The manager is responsible for seeing that each worker does the right thing at the right time, at the right place, with the right resources, for a particular area of operation. In this chapter, *control* is not given this broad meaning. Here it is used to mean the process of measuring and regulating employee behavior according to an established standard or norm. Employee behavior includes both performance and conduct, and on a day-to-day basis the process of evaluating and correcting employee behavior is a normal function of applied supervision, which is a form of control. With this in mind, the chapter will cover the following topics: (1) using standards effectively, (2) identifying and solving employee problems, and (3) taking disciplinary action.

USING STANDARDS EFFECTIVELY

Because both measuring and regulating employee behavior are based on standards, the first step in controlling employee performance and conduct is for the manager to learn how to use standards effectively. When applied to behavior, standards take many forms. They can be job descriptions or job specifications, policies or procedures, rules or regulations, written or verbal orders, or any form that establishes requirements that can be used as a base to measure and regulate employee behavior. Regardless of their form, to be used effectively to control behavior, certain steps must be taken and certain principles understood.

Making Requirements Understood

Because a basic purpose of a standard is to serve as a yardstick by which unacceptable or unsatisfactory behavior is detected and corrected, it is imperative that the requirements that constitute acceptable behavior be understood. This simply means that for a standard to be effective, there should be no doubt in the minds of the manager or the employee what performance or conduct is expected. This is further clarified by the separate discussion of performance and conduct requirements below.

PERFORMANCE REQUIREMENTS. These requirements are a determination of the acceptable behavior directly related to the employee's performance on his job or operation. Whereas the general requirements of most jobs may be stated in the form of job descriptions or job specifications, and procedures or work methods, their interpretation and application are normally left to the manager. Therefore, in making performance requirements understood, the manager should translate the requirements of the job into meaningful and, where possible, measurable *objectives*. Ideally, performance requirements when translated into objectives should be in measurable terms such as *quantity* (how much or many), *quality* (how well), and *time* (how long). But since this is only possible on jobs where tangible results are produced, some other means for other jobs, such as manner or other intangible measures, must be used. In any event, what constitutes acceptable performance must be understood by both the manager and the employee. This understanding may be obtained during the performance interview discussed in Chapter 15 or through other less formal means. In either case, since one of the major advantages of translating performance requirements into objectives is that objectives become a motivational tool or target for achievement, where possible the employee should be allowed to participate in setting acceptable performance requirements. Employee involvement in setting performance standards does not imply that the manager tells the employees to set their own standards and then withdraws. He must, of course, provide all necessary assistance. In other words, employee participation in setting standards must operate within a predetermined framework in which management sets the limits of reality and defines and communicates the department's objectives.[1] Moreover, while requirements set in this manner may not achieve the exact objective, it is obvious that when standards are defined and set through employee participation, it is hard for the employee to plead ignorance, forgetfulness, or misunderstanding. In addition, it has been found that when employees are allowed to participate, they set higher standards for themselves than when established by the manager alone.

Conduct Requirements. These are requirements that place limits or boundaries on the employees' behavior. They are normally in the form of written or posted rules and regulations, but they may be in the form of oral or written orders. Whichever form they take, these standards provide the necessary structure for acceptable employee conduct. Even without written or formal standards, it is doubtful that any successful manager would permit his work group to operate in a totally unstructured manner. On the other hand, it has been found that individuals are more comfortable and behave better within a framework of known rules, and if boundaries are not set for them, groups will establish some type of informal structure to govern their behavior. Therefore, conduct standards are not foreign to human behavior, and most employees look to their immediate supervisor to establish or interpret the requirements that constitute acceptable conduct. In doing this, the manager should take these factors into account: (1) First, he should allow for as much tolerance as permitted by the standard to offset the natural tendency for human error or for situations beyond the employee's control. Of course this is not always possible. For example, some rules are preestablished, leaving the manager little or no room for interpretation; and standards establishing requirements involving such things as health and safety must be followed exactly for the welfare of the employee concerned. But where possible, a certain degree of tolerance should be built into the standards establishing requirements for employee conduct. (2) The second factor to be taken into account is that the employee should be allowed to participate in establishing the requirements governing his conduct. Like performance requirements, standards set by the employee are usually higher than those established totally by someone else. Also, it is to be remembered that once rules are established they must be enforced, and if the

[1] See Charles L. Hughes, "Goal Setting: Key to Individual and Organizational Effectiveness," in Raymond F. Valentine, "Laying the Groundwork for Goal Setting," *Personnel* (New York: American Management Association), January-February 1966, p. 39.

employee has a say in interpreting the standards in the first place, he will be more likely to follow them in the future. (3) The third factor in making conduct requirements understood is that the reason for the rule must be understood by the employee. This means that the rule must be valid in the first place; therefore, before a rule is interpreted for the employee, the manager should be convinced himself that the rule is necessary. Why was the rule set? What do we expect to accomplish by the rule? Can the rule be logically enforced? These are some questions the manager should ask himself. If the answer to any one of these questions is negative, the manager should attempt to have the rule changed before it is imposed on the employee. Otherwise, if the reason for the rule is not clearly established, it is doubtful that it will be an effective tool for controlling employee conduct. (4) Fourth and finally, the manager should not blame "higher-ups" for the rules. The poor supervisor hides behind the old dodge: "Don't blame me for the rules—I didn't make 'em!" The average employee has greater respect for the man who stands on his own two feet than for the supervisor who passes the buck to someone else in management.

Comparing the Worker's Behavior with the Requirements

Once behavior requirements are understood, the next step in using standards effectively is for the manager to periodically compare the employee's behavior with the established and understood standards. As pointed out earlier (Chapter 2), this can be done by reviewing records or by personal observation. There are a host of records that the manager may construct and use as tools for comparing either performance or conduct requirements with the behavior of the employee. Some of the common ones are sales records, attendance records, work curves, quality control reports, accident reports, and many others depending on the type of operation the manager is supervising. Using records in comparing employee behavior against requirements has the advantage of objectivity. Although records are subject to interpretation, if the information is recorded accurately it is less likely to be misinterpreted than what the manager obtains through observation. Therefore, recorded information should be used wherever possible. But since all forms of employee behavior cannot be recorded statistically, the manager must rely on his power of observation in making comparisons. To be valid as a method of comparison, the manager must make his observation as objective as possible. Since means by which the manager may make his observation more objective will be covered in the chapter on interviewing, they will not be belabored here. However, one basic principle that applies to both records and observation should be understood. The principle is this: *When making comparisons, the employee's behavior, not the employee him-*

self, is to be weighed against the requirements. This means that what the employee does, not what he is capable of doing, should be considered. The difference is significant, and it is imperative that this concept be grasped. For example, it is possible that an employee may be fully capable of meeting the requirements, but his behavior is not up to the established norm. On the other hand, a less capable employee may far exceed the established requirements. In either case, by comparing the employee's behavior, not the employee, against the requirements established by the standards, a more objective assessment of the employee's behavior can be obtained.

Detecting Deviations from the Norm

As in all controlling processes, the reason for comparing the worker's behavior with the established requirements is to assist the manager in detecting any deviations of the employee's behavior from the established norms. The scale pictured in Figure 27 is a symbolic presentation of this concept.

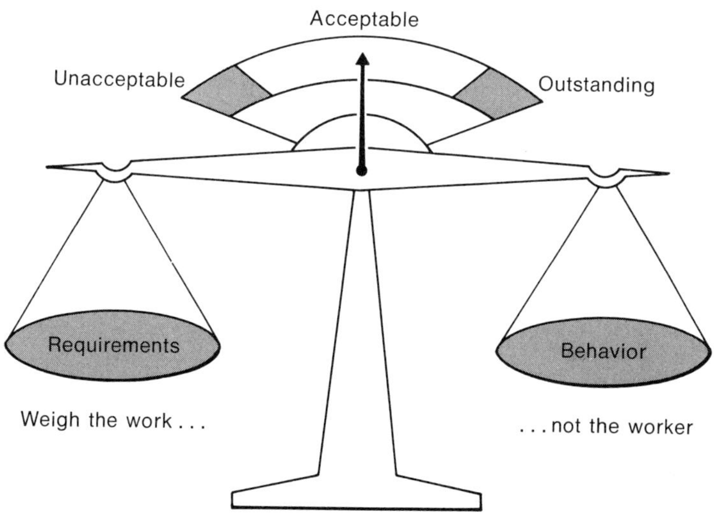

Figure 27 Behavior Requirements (Courtesy of U.S. Air Force Department.)

As this figure indicates, when the employee's behavior is compared or weighed against the established standards, one of three possible conditions is revealed: (1) If the employee's behavior far outweighs the requirements, it falls within the range of outstanding, (2) If the behavior weighs considerably less than the requirements, it falls within the range of unacceptable, and (3) If the behavior is about equal to the requirements, it falls within the range of acceptable behavior. In a well managed department, as the scale indicates, the behavior of most employees will fall within the range of acceptable behavior. However, consistent with the principle of normal distribution some will fall within the range of the two extremes. If the employee's behavior is so far above the norm that it is considered outstanding, recognition should be given. This may be in the form of promotions, pay raises, praise, or some other form of recognition to show the employee that his accomplishments are appreciated. On the other hand, if the employee's behavior is unacceptable, it is a joint responsibility of the manager and the worker to adjust the employee's behavior so it will fall within the range of the acceptable norm established by the standard. In short, the employee's behavior must be regulated to meet the established standard. This can be done by identifying and correcting employee problems or by taking disciplinary action. These are discussed separately in the remainder of this chapter.

IDENTIFYING AND SOLVING EMPLOYEE PROBLEMS

Unacceptable behavior is manifested in many ways. In the area of performance, it may include poor work quality, low productivity, or such things as not getting the work out on time. Unacceptable conduct often involves such things as tardiness, absenteeism, and "goldbricking," or it may include insubordination, a "don't care" or "I could care less" attitude, and serious infractions of rules and procedures. But regardless of how it is manifested, unacceptable behavior normally just does not happen without reason. More often it is caused by some problem the employee may be having that is interfering with his performance or conduct on the job. Therefore, as soon as unacceptable behavior is detected, the manager should attempt to identify the problem that is causing the employee to act or perform in an unacceptable manner. Of course this should be done as soon as possible, preferably before the employee's behavior becomes unacceptable, by the manager being constantly alert to signs indicating that an employee has a problem. A careful worker becoming careless, a punctual worker coming to work late, a conscientious worker leaving work early, or a congenial worker suddenly becoming quarrelsome, or any other sudden change in the employee's normal behavior are examples the manager should look for. Excessive use of alcohol or the use of drugs in any form are more serious indications of employee problems. Whether observed earlier or after the worker's behavior has deteriorated to an unacceptable level, before taking disciplinary action the manager should talk with the employee to determine the reason for the employee's behavior and assist the employee in solving the problem where possible. There are any number of reasons why an employee may have a problem that can influence his behavior. Because most problems are cross-sectional, interrelated and overlapping, often they can only be determined through in-depth counseling in an interview, which is discussed in Chapter 15. However, by recognizing the reasons for employee problems, the manager will be in a better position to assist the employee in adjusting his behavior to the acceptable norm. Some common reasons for employee problems are listed and discussed below.

Lack of Job Skills

A common reason for an employee's unacceptable behavior is lack of job skills. Although he may have had the necessary skills when hired, through his own or the organization's fault, he may have failed to grow with the job, or he may not have been given proper training to start with. In any case, lack of skills may not only be the reason for unacceptable performance but may be the cause of unsatisfactory conduct as well. To justify his lack of skills, the employee may rationalize or resort to some other defense mechanism to cover up his lack of knowledge of the job. Or he may become argumentative and quarrelsome and develop a negative attitude. The point is that lack of skills should be a major factor the manager should look for in identifying an employee's problem, and providing the employee an opportunity for additional training may be a solution to the employee's unacceptable behavior.

Misplacement

Closely associated with lack of skills is misplacement. Being in the wrong job is often the reason for the employee's unsatisfactory behavior. Obviously, if the person dislikes what he is doing, he may not do it well and again his dislikes may be reflected in other areas, such as absenteeism, tardiness, poor attitude, or some other form of inappropriate conduct. When misplacement is identified as a cause of unacceptable behavior, if the employee cannot be reassigned to a job within the organization more to his liking, it may be advisable for the manager to suggest that the employee take a job with another firm.

Lack of Job Structure

This topic refers to the employee being given detailed and clear instructions as to what he is to do and being provided with a set of standards that establishes known boundaries for his behavior. Because giving instruction was discussed in Chapter 12 and the need for standards was previously discussed in this chapter, it is sufficient to state here only that lack of job structure is often a reason for unacceptable behavior and a major cause of low group morale.

Incompatibility

Often called *personality clash,* incompatibility is when two people, for various reasons, fail to get along. This condition may exist between the manager and an employee or between two employees in the same department. In either case, it can become a major reason for unsatisfactory or unacceptable behavior, the seriousness of which will depend of course on how badly one person "bugs" the other. Although incompatibility should be recognized, it should also be understood that short of removing one of the parties involved, little can be done to correct this type of situation. Rearranging work schedules and avoiding direct personal contact may be possible under certain conditions, but by and large only tolerance on the part of those concerned can make the situation bearable.

Unsafe or Inadequate Workload

The reasons for many employee problems are due to unsafe or inadequate workloads. Both overload and underload can cause employee dissatisfaction. Obviously if the employee is assigned more than he can possibly do, or given a deadline that is all but impossible to make, the results can only be less than satisfactory and will probably be reflected in such things as accidents, errors, excessive physical and psychological fatigue, high turnover (he may quit), resentment, and slowdown (what's the use). On the other hand, underload has equally bad effects. When a worker does not have enough to do, results are usually michief, horseplay, excessive cost of operation, grievances and complaints, absenteeism, and tardiness. When this situation is identified, it can be corrected through proper work scheduling and allocation as discussed in Chapter 11.

Personal Problems

The most difficult types of problems to identify and correct are those in the catchall category called *personal problems.* The range of these problems is so broad that it defies complete identification. Family troubles, money troubles, and problems with the law are some examples. Nevertheless, they are a major source of unsatisfactory behavior on the job. If Sally is having problems with her son Johnny in school, it may be the reason for her coming to work late or the increase in her typing errors. Or if Joe's creditors are threatening to attach his pay, that may be the reason that he is careless about safety rules or account for his leaving work early so he can get to his moonlighting job on time. Moreover, personal problems may be interrelated with all the other reasons discussed above. Consequently, personal problems should be identified and corrected where possible. This can only be done if the manager has developed rapport with his workers and has their confidence.

Employee Grievances

Another overlapping and often overriding reason for an employee's unacceptable behavior is employee grievances. These are dissatisfactions that a worker has against management. Like personal problems, they come in many forms. But roughly, grievances can be divided into two categories: (1) Those resulting from working conditions, and (2) Those relating to interpretations of collective bargaining contracts or personnel policy statements. The first category includes problems concerning job satisfaction, discipline, change in work schedules, use of tools, equipment, standards (both performance and conduct), shifts and working hours, physical working conditions, and relationships with the manager or coworkers. As this indicates, grievances concerning working conditions are interrelated with many of the separate reasons discussed above. On the other hand, grievances of the interpretative nature usually involve seniority, overtime, transfer, promotion, demotion, discharge, pay, job rates, and the like. It should be added that the basis of many grievances on the job are also aggravated by off-the-job problems. The employee who is having problems at home may come to work "looking for trouble." Despite its nature, a grievance, either real or imaginary, can be the source and the reason for unacceptable behavior.

When a formal grievance is presented, the manager should take fair and impartial action to settle the grievance as quickly as possible. But more importantly, it is the primary role of the supervisor to preclude an employee from having a grievance in the first place. To do this, in addition to applying the principles of good management on a day-to-day basis, he should pay particular attention and question himself in the following four areas:

1. *Settling employee complaints.* Major grievances sometimes are the underlying cause of minor complaints. Each complaint should be carefully explored to find the actual source of the gripe.
   a. Are minor complaints handled fairly and quickly?
   b. Do your employees feel that they can trust you and get a fair and impartial hearing?
   c. Do your employees feel that they can turn to you to get things off their chest or blow off steam?
   d. Are you a good listener?

2. *Lines of communication.* Information channels must be clear to lessen the activity of grapevine misinformation.

   a. Are your employees "getting the word"?
   b. Are your employees able to talk freely, without fear?
   c. Are your employees encouraged to make suggestions?
   d. Are the employee suggestions being passed upward?

3. *Collective bargaining contract or personnel policy interpretation.* The basis of many misunderstandings is caused by faulty interpretation of the collective bargaining contract or personnel policy statements.

   a. Do you and your employees fully understand the contract or the policy?
   b. Are you passing information upward about areas of misunderstanding, if they exist?
   c. Do you recommend review or changes if areas of misunderstanding are noted?

4. *Improving human relationships.* Are you and your employees improving your methods of handling human relationships through grievance discussions?

   a. Are you and your employees learning to look at complaints impersonally, find the source of the complaint, look at both sides of the issue, and reach a point of settlement? [2]

Problem Employees

Before concluding the discussion on identifying and solving employee problems, a distinction should be made between the *employee with a problem* and the *problem employee.* In the first case, by identifying and solving his problem the manager can logically expect that the employee will adjust his behavior consistent with the established standards. The problem employee belongs in an entirely different category. This individual is one who either deliberately or unintentionally not only causes trouble for himself, but through this action or lack of action may disrupt others who are attempting to do a good job. Since studies show that only twenty percent of a manager's employees cause eighty percent of his control problems, the problem employee should be identified as soon as possible. Although these employees include both sexes, all racial extractions, and come from all economic and social levels, the manager will soon learn who his problem employees are. They may be the ones who require the most attention, can never be satisfied, chronically make excuses for their mistakes, spread malicious and damaging rumors, and make themselves look good at the expense of others; or they may be the ones who always show up late at a meeting, try to undermine the supervisor's authority and make him look bad in front of others; or the problem employee may lie, steal, cheat, take advantage of every situation, and do only enough work to get by. The list could go on and on, but the point is, once these individuals are identified they must be dealt with

[2] See Paul Ecker, John MacRae, Vernon Ouellette, and Charles Telford, *Handbook for Supervisors* (Englewood Cliffs, N.J.: Prentice-Hall, Inc., 1959), p. 206.

promptly. Like all employees, the problem individual must be handled individually and the principles and practices that apply to other employees can be used with this group as well. However, the manager should recognize that in some cases correcting this type of individual may be beyond his capability. In that case, the manager may seek professional assistance, or when everything else fails, the problem employee should be discharged without hesitation.

TAKING DISCIPLINARY ACTION

On occasions when the identification and correction of employee problems will not correct the employee's unacceptable behavior, the manager may be forced to take disciplinary action. As implied, the term *disciplinary action* stems from the word *discipline,* which is in itself the cornerstone of behavior control. Consequently, before discussing taking disciplinary action as such, *discipline* should be defined. When used as a control, discipline has two meanings. First, in its broadest sense, *discipline* means training that develops self-control, character, orderliness, and effectiveness. Used in this way, discipline implies that employees are expected to act voluntarily without immediate supervision within the framework of established standards. Building discipline of this type should be the aim of every manager, and if most of his employees do not apply this sort of discipline to themselves, the job of controlling behavior will be all but impossible. However, because in management utopias simply do not exist, occasionally the manager is confronted with situations where a more restricted meaning of *discipline* is required: treatment that corrects or punishes. This simply means that there are situations where disciplinary action is the only course open to the manager for correcting his employees' behavior or in restoring and maintaining control of his department. It may be added here that many managers are reluctant to use disciplinary action even when they realize that it is the only thing to do. But as distasteful as it may be, recognizing that each exception to a standard extends its limits and tends to lessen its effectiveness on others makes it clear that administering discipline fairly and firmly is a supervisory responsibility that should not be shunned. While the face-to-face method of administering discipline will be covered when the disciplinary interview is discussed in the next chapter, the process to follow in taking disciplinary action is examined below.

The Disciplinary Action Process

In many organizations, especially those with union contracts, the disciplinary process is outlined in an organizational policy or procedure. Although the process will vary by organization, and some organizations have no such policy or procedure, viewing disciplinary action as a process has the advantage of providing the manager with an orderly means of correcting an employee's unacceptable behavior. In addition, it has the advantage of insuring that the employee is treated fairly. Therefore, the steps the manager may use in administering discipline should be understood by all managers. It is to be recognized that before these steps are taken, the unacceptable behavior must first be identified and an attempt made to resolve the problem that caused the unacceptable behavior. With these points in mind, the steps in the process include: [3]

Oral Warning or Reprimand. The first type of disciplinary action is the oral warning or reprimand. The difference in the two is only a matter of approach. The oral warning is approached from the assumption that the employee does not fully understand the significance of his behavior; that by emphasizing the importance of his unsatisfactory action and warning him that further such behavior will make stronger action necessary, the employee will mend his ways. On the other hand, the reprimand is approached from the other point of view; that the employee has full knowledge or significance of his action and should be told explicitly and firmly that his behavior will not be condoned and any repetition of his undesirable behavior will warrant harsher treatment. The first approach is disciplinary action without censure, while the second method places blame. In either approach, the purpose is to correct the employee's behavior to preclude repetition of the offense. The approach that works best will depend on the employee involved. With some employees a warning is sufficient; with others a reprimand is necessary. The manager should make this judgment based on his knowledge of his people. Also, the manager should make a written record of the time, place, and circumstances for further reference.

Written Warning. If the employee repeats the same offense or commits another breach of the established standard, the employee should be warned in writing that his performance or conduct is in violation of a specific rule, policy, procedure, and so on, and that another infraction will result in whatever punishment that the particular standard prescribes or implies. A copy of the warning should be given to the employee, a copy put in his personnel file, and a copy given to the superior of the supervisor issuing the warning. If a union exists, the steward and/or the union should get a copy.

Administering Penalty. After an employee has been talked with in a counseling interview, warned during a disciplinary interview, and given

[3] These steps as well as some of this material were suggested by: Bradford B. Boyd, *Management-Minded Supervision* (New York: McGraw-Hill Book Company, 1968), p. 174.

a warning in writing, some sort of action other than verbiage is required. The type and severity of the penalty will depend on the nature of the offense and the policy of the organization. For example, some organizations have a policy that if an employee is late for work a third time, his pay is "docked," whereas the policy of other organizations may be to use the disciplinary lay-off, where an employee is suspended from his job without pay for a certain number of days. Still other organizations may discharge the employee on his third offense. In the absence of any policy, the manager should use his judgment based on the seriousness of the offense. In any case, after a third offense is committed, it is generally agreed that to maintain discipline and control, the employee should be penalized, and where possible it should be less than discharging or firing the employee.

DISCHARGE ACTION. It goes without saying that discharging an employee is the most serious form of disciplinary action, and this step should be taken only when the employee fails to respond to all efforts taken to assist him in correcting his behavior. This is not to say that all steps in the process must be taken before an employee is fired, or that they are to follow in order. Some infractions are so serious that an employee should be fired on the first offense. In other cases, the nature of the employee's behavior may require that certain steps be skipped. However, in all cases, discharging an employee should be used as a last resort.

KEY POINT SUMMARY

1. To use his manpower effectively, employee behavior, whether performance or conduct, must be controlled. When applied in this way, control is defined to mean the process of measuring and regulating employee behavior according to an established standard.
2. Since standards form the base for employee control, the use of standards should be understood. This involves three steps:
    a. Making requirements understood
    b. Comparing the worker's behavior with the requirement
    c. Detecting deviations from the norm
3. When making performance requirements understood, the manager should:
    a. Translate the requirements into meaningful and, where possible, measurable objectives.
    b. Allow the employee to participate in setting the objectives.

4. When making conduct requirements understood, the manager should:
    a. Allow tolerance
    b. Allow employee to participate in interpreting rules
    c. Give reason for the standard
    d. Assume responsibility for the rule and not "pass the buck"
5. When comparing the worker's behavior with the requirement, the manager should:
    a. Make his comparison as objective as possible
    b. Compare the behavior, not the employee (the work, not the worker)
6. The purpose of comparing the employee's behavior with the requirements of the standard is to detect deviations from the norm. When unacceptable behavior is discovered, corrective action should be taken by the manager to regulate the behavior with the norm by:
    a. Identifying and correcting the employee's problem causing the unacceptable behavior.
    b. Taking disciplinary action to correct the employee's behavior.
7. Since in many cases unacceptable behavior is due to an employee's problem, the manager should attempt to detect and correct the problem before taking disciplinary action. Common causes for an employee's unacceptable behavior include:
    a. Lack of job skills
    b. Misplacement
    c. Lack of job structure
    d. Incompatibility
    e. Unsafe or inadequate workload
    f. Personal problems
    g. Employee grievances
8. In addition to identifying and solving employees' problems, the manager should identify his problem employees. The difference is this:
    a. The employee with a problem is one who wants and will accept help.
    b. The problem employee is one who may not want or accept help.
9. If the employee's unacceptable behavior is not corrected by identifying and solving the employee's problem, disciplinary action is required. Discipline has two meanings:

a. Training that develops self-control
b. Action that corrects and punishes

10. The manager should strive to build self-discipline in his employees, but when disciplinary action to correct the employee is necessary he should follow this pattern:
    a. Give oral warning or reprimand
    b. Give written warning
    c. Administer penalty
    d. Take discharge action when all else fails

DISCUSSION QUESTIONS

1. When applied to controlling employee behavior, what does the word *control* mean?
2. What is the basic purpose of standards? What steps are required in using standards effectively? Relate these steps to the controlling-by-exception concepts discussed in Chapter 2.
3. Why is it necessary that the requirements of a standard be understood? In relation to: (a) Performance? (b) Conduct?
4. What is the advantage of the manager interpreting performance requirements in the form of objectives?
5. Why should the employee be allowed to participate in developing or interpreting: (a) Performance standards? (b) Conduct standards?
6. In interpreting conduct requirements, what factors should the manager consider? Relate these factors to the principles of resistance to change and employee participation.
7. Why is comparing what the employee does, not what he can do, important? How does the principle of individual differences relate to this concept?
8. When unacceptable behavior is detected, why is it a joint responsibility of the manager and the employee to correct the unsatisfactory condition? What are the two means by which an employee's unacceptable behavior can be regulated?
9. What are some of the types of unacceptable behavior? Relate these conditions to the possible effect that they may have on employee productivity.
10. Why is it necessary that the manager attempt to identify and solve employee problems?
11. What are the seven common causes of employees' unacceptable behavior? Relate each cause to a possible course of action.
12. What is the difference between an "employee with a problem" and a "problem employee"? How would your treatment of each differ?
13. What are the two meanings of the word *discipline?* Relate discipline to leadership styles.

14. What is the purpose of the manager taking disciplinary action? Relate taking disciplinary action to rapport.
15. Why should discipline be administered acording to a process? Relate each step of the process to taking discharge action.

CASE PROBLEMS

Case 14–1

Joe Cones was a friendly manager, indeed. He was a "regular guy," joking with the employees, letting them talk all they wanted at their jobs. He never seemed to take things too seriously. Occasionally he would indulge in a bit of harmless horseplay just to show the gang that he was "one of the boys."

Alma Martin was an employee in his department, just recently transferred from another unit. Her quality of work was okay, but she was very slow. Some of the other girls had to help her and give her additional instruction in order to help her meet the standard. Cones, after putting up with her low output for awhile, gave her a warning slip, and when she didn't improve, he fired her.

Questions

1. *What principles apply in this case?*
2. *Are any of the seven common problems that often cause unsatisfactory behavior involved here?*
3. *What action could Joe have taken to assist Alma in meeting the standard?*
4. *Was Joe's disciplinary action appropriate? Why?*
5. *What bearing does Joe's behavior as a supervisor have on the case?*

Case 14–2

A union representative came to Bill, a department manager, and told him about a grievance that had been passed on to him by another employee in the department. The representative claimed that the employee had been promised a better job by the previous supervisor. He wanted to know what was being done about it.

After thinking it over, Bill decided that he had five options: (1) Refuse to talk with the representative until a formal grievance was presented, (2) Seek out the employee with the complaint and talk with him, (3) Ask the union representative and the employee to meet with him to discuss the complaint, (4) Ask the union representative to take the complaint up with his (Bill's) supervisor, and (5) Ignore the complaint.

Questions

1. *What is the pro and con argument for each option?*
2. *If you were Bill, which option would you choose?*

SELECTED REFERENCES

EMERY, DAVID A., *The Complete Manager,* Chaps. 4 and 8. New York: McGraw-Hill Book Company, 1970.

McMURRY, ROBERT N., "Handling the Problem Employee," in *Small Marketers Aids,* Annual No. 7. Washington, D.C.: Small Business Administration, 1965.

SHULL, FREMONT A. JR., and L. L. CUMMINGS, "Enforcing the Rules: How do Managers Differ?" in *Personnel.* New York: American Management Association, March–April, 1966.

VALENTINE, RAYMOND F., "Laying the Groundwork for Goal Setting," in *Personnel.* New York: American Management Association, January–February, 1966.

15

How to Use the Interview

The final skill the manager should acquire in carrying out his role as a supervisor is using the interview. An interview is defined as a face-to-face discussion by two people for the purpose of exchanging information or solving a problem. Within the framework of this definition, the interview can be used by the manager as one of his most effective and versatile skills in applied supervision. In its relation with the function of management, the interview is cross-sectional in that it can be used as a means of seeking information to plan, organize, and coordinate, and in taking action to direct and control. It also can be informal or formal. Informal interviews include coordinating with other managers of other departments, chats between the manager and his employees, or the manager and his superior, and a host of other situations. Conversely, the formal interview can be structured and designed to handle many special situations. On a day-to-day basis, these situations may include such things as hiring an employee, evaluating and appraising employee performance, solving employee problems, taking disciplinary action, and talking with a departing employee. How to use the interview to handle these situations is covered by these major headings: (1) the basis of an effective interview, (2) the preemployment interview, (3) the performance interview, (4) the counseling interview, (5) the disciplinary interview, and (6) the exit interview.

THE BASIS OF AN EFFECTIVE INTERVIEW

Before discussing the five types of interviews to handle specific situations, it is first necessary for the manager to understand the factors that constitute an effective interview. Detailed factors that will influence effectiveness of a particular interview will depend on the type of interview. However, there are three factors that should be understood: The approach, the plan, and the technique.

The Approach

The manager should first understand that the effectiveness of the interview will depend on the approach he uses. In conducting an interview, two extreme approaches and one middle approach are available that can be adapted to the five interview situations.

The Direct Approach. This approach is characterized by the control that the manager exercises over the interview. He asks the questions and directs the interchange between the employee and himself. The manager assumes a large part of the responsibility for the solution or results. However, as much as possible, he should encourage the employee to understand and accept the solution. This technique allows the manager to obtain a mass of information in a short period of time and to get his views across rapidly. This approach is used when the employee's opinion is unimportant or when the solution to the problem or the course of action is the exclusive responsibility of the manager.

The Indirect Approach. The main feature of this approach is that it is the job of the manager to keep the employee active in the discussion and have him solve his own problems. The manager asks only guiding questions, encourages the employee to do most of the talking, and assists in developing a pattern for the solution to the problem that the employee attempts to solve. This approach has the advantage of the employee not knowing how to slant his answers to questions. This is based on the theory that the employee is more likely to reveal his true feelings and facts about himself or a situation than if asked direct questions. It has the obvious disadvantage of being time-consuming, and despite the theory, it permits the employee to hide facts that he does not wish to reveal.

The Patterned Approach. The patterned approach, also called the coanalysis approach, is a combination of the two approaches described above. In this approach, the interview is guided by the manager, and the employee is encouraged to speak freely about himself or the situation. To conduct this type of interview, questions to be asked are worked out in advance to pattern the interview along the lines the manager wants it to follow. These questions can be developed from the information gathered in the planning stage discussed elsewhere, and they are used to draw the employee out so he will discuss the relevant topics. In this approach, the manager maintains control of the interview, but at the same time the employee is allowed to have some degree of control over the outcome of the discussion. If the interview is for the purpose of solving a problem, the solution is sought jointly by the manager and the employee. This approach is applicable to most situations.

It is to be understood that although the patterned approach is best under most situations and with most individuals, in actual practice, normally, no single approach is followed exclusively. In one interview, the approach may be somewhere between the two extremes, and the manager may find himself moving in one direction, then in another. Therefore, in planning the interview, the manager should allow his approach to be flexible.

The Plan

Like all management action, for an interview to be effective it should be planned. In planning an interview two steps should be considered: (1) Obtaining background information, and (2) Setting up the situation.

OBTAINING BACKGROUND INFORMATION. The first step in planning an interview is obtaining information. This information should include both background on the problem or situation to be discussed and the employee involved. Gathering information cannot be overstressed, for the success of most interviews will depend in a large measure on this step. First, background information on the problem or situation provides the manager with the base on which he can pattern the interview to obtain the desired results. Also, it can provide him with the necessary background by which he can interpret the information provided by the employee during the interview. While the type of background information needed will vary according to the interview, it should include the specific facts concerning the particular situation and the standards or norms that apply in that particular case. Where applicable, the specific information needed in a particular interview will be included in the discussion of types of interviews later in the chapter. Secondly, by knowing the employee's (or job applicant's) background, the manager can determine how to phrase his questions and is in a better position to anticipate the reaction of the employee to the interview situation. Taken together, background information can assist the manager in setting up the situation for conducting the interview.

Before leaving planning, it should be pointed out that occasionally situations requiring an interview develop spontaneously, leaving little or no time for planning. When this occurs, where possible, the manager should listen but delay the actual interview until things are more normal. For example, if an employee contacts the manager at an inopportune time or in a place or circumstance where an interview would be awkward, or if the employee is exceptionally emotional, it is best that the employee be given an appointment so the interview can be properly planned. This should be done as tactfully as possible, and if the employee does not keep the appointment, the manager should contact the employee.

SETTING UP THE SITUATION. In this step the manager attempts to establish the best possible situation for conducting the interview. This includes both the mental and physical aspects of the interview.

The mental aspect involves determining what questions the manager should ask the employee and anticipating the employee's response to the questions and the situation. One way to do this is to try to visualize the interview as it will actually take place. Then with the objective of the interview and the particular employee clearly in mind, mentally role-play the entire scene. While the mental role-play may not exactly match the actual interview, it will at least help clarify the major points to be covered and assist the manager in anticipating the response of the employee. Further, in developing questions either mentally or on paper, they should be kept flexible to meet unexpected situations.

The physical aspect involves setting up the situation and arranging the time and place for the interview. In taking this step, the manager should consider these factors: (1) It should be planned for a time that is convenient to both persons involved. (2) It should be arranged in a place that is private and free from interruptions. (3) The other person should be notified in advance and told the purpose of the interview.

The Technique

The third and final phase of the effective interview is the technique. This is the manner or pattern in which the interview is to be conducted. The skills necessary to develop the techniques required of the professional interviewer may never be fully realized by the average manager, and the discussion of these skills is certainly beyond the scope of this chapter. Despite this, by following a systematic pattern and by recognizing certain basic factors, the manager can develop techniques that will make his interview more effective.

DEVELOPING RAPPORT. Even in the case of the disciplinary interview, it is important that the manager try to develop rapport with the employee. Time spent in establishing or restoring the employee's confidence gives him a feeling of well being, and showing interest in him as an individual will not only pay dividends later in the interview but will have an overall beneficial effect as well. Developing rapport will of course depend on the mood of the individual. If the employee is hostile or in an emotional state, it may be best that the manager let him speak his piece and get the emotional charge out of his system. In this case the manager should let him talk, never argue, and under any circumstances never lose his temper or show his emotions. Normally, the emotional or hostile employee will soon settle down and through talking lose much of his hostile feeling. If this is not the case, the manager should only listen and schedule the interview at a later time. After the employee has spent most of his emotional energy, or if the employee is calm in the first place, the manager may begin by discussing items of common interest, such as the employee's likes or dislikes, his strong points, or some other subject that will establish a relationship with the employee. At this point, the manager should be particularly careful not to indicate any bias or prejudice he may have (everybody has some) or reveal his own feelings, attitudes, or opinions about the subject or situation. To do so might influence the employee's response throughout the interview.

GATHERING AND INTERPRETING INFORMATION. After rapport has been established, or when the employee is in the proper frame of mind to be responsive, the manager can begin to gather and interpret information. The early part of the interview should be devoted to seeking facts. The manager can get more of the information needed if he avoids these types of questions: (1) Questions that can be answered by "yes" or "no," (2) Questions that will elicit an obvious answer ("Are you a hard worker?" "You want to make good, don't you?" "Do you normally come to work on time?"), (3) Embarrassing questions that will force the employee to defend a statement or admit a previous mistake, (4) Leading questions such as: "Was that you I saw leaving early last week?" "Why is your work not as good as the other employees?" Or: "You did finish high school, didn't you?" Of course these questions are only representative and will vary according to the type of interview that should have been worked out in advance. But the point is that questions should be phrased so the employee will talk and participate freely and make extended responses to the manager's questions without feeling threatened. Through these responses, the manager gains insight into the employee's personality, attitudes, and reactions, or obtains the information he is seeking. Responses also furnish the manager with clues to the individual's behavior pattern, which can be used to interpret the information the manager gets. Interpreting information is an art that can be acquired only through long experience and training, and due to personality traits, attitude, and so on, it may be beyond the reach of some managers. In any case, the manager should make his observation as objective as possible. In doing this, the employee's behavior during the interview should be measured against the individual's prior observed or recorded behavior and work patterns, tempered with a realistic appraisal of the manager's own prejudices. This, plus experience, should serve as an adequate guide in interpreting information in most interview situations.

Deciding Upon a Course of Action. Obviously, this step will depend on the type of interview. In the exit interview, for example, the course of action has been predetermined, the employee is quitting, being laid off, or has been fired. In other types of interviews, the course of action may be reserved exclusively for the manager, and the interview serves only to provide him with additional information on which to make a decision. But where possible, the course of action should be decided jointly by the manager and the employee involved. In all cases the solution or course of action should be made as acceptable to the employee as possible. This is a key factor in effective interviewing. Unless the course of action is made acceptable to the employee, the results of the interview remain in doubt.

Closing the Interview. The key factor in closing an interview is actually a continuation of the step above. After a course of action has been determined, the manager should, where possible, assure that the employee leaves the interview with a feeling of accomplishment. If the situation or problem has been resolved during the interview, and the employee is satisfied with the results, periodic follow-up after the interview may be all that is needed. Conversely, if the situation or problem has not been resolved or a decision is still pending, before the interview is closed, the manager should inform the employee of his anticipated action. This may require scheduling another interview, referring the matter to another department or to an outside agency, or simply giving the manager more time to make up his mind. In any event, the employee should be advised accordingly.

With this review of the factors that make up the basis of an effective interview in mind, the manager can use the interview to solve or handle many of his day-to-day, face-to-face problems and situations. This can be done by using one of the five interviews discussed in the remainder of this chapter.

THE PREEMPLOYMENT INTERVIEW

In the staffing process after a job applicant has been screened by the personnel department, the applicant is normally referred to the applicant's potential supervisor for an interview prior to final selection. The advantage of this interview is twofold. First, it gives the applicant an opportunity to size up the work situation and the person for whom he might be working. This assists him in determining if he wants the job. Secondly, it allows the manager to have a say in selecting the person who he feels can best do the job.

In conducting the preemployment interview the manager should seek answers to three fundamental questions. The first question is: *Can the applicant do the job?* This question concerns the applicant's technical or administrative qualifications and abilities and is largely determined by education and experience. The second question is: *Will he do the job?* This is determined to a large extent by the individual's initiative, ambitions, drive, and motivation. The third and final question is: *Will he "fit in"?* Because studies show that failing to get along with others is the major cause of disciplinary action, getting an answer to this question is important. But since it involves human nature, it is often the most difficult one to answer. As stated, it is the purpose of the interview to get answers to these questions, and a patterned interview using good interviewing techniques will no doubt help. But most authorities agree that the interview is the least effective method of selecting an applicant. A more reliable method is forming a thorough understanding of the requirements and comparing the applicant's background and experience against these requirements with the interview serving to supplement the findings and to obtain a general impression of the applicant. Therefore, major emphasis should be placed on determining job requirements and obtaining the background of the applicant as well as the interview itself.

Job Requirements

General job requirements can be obtained from an up-to-date job or position description, but to be meaningful the requirements of the job to be filled should be analyzed against the three questions the manager is attempting to answer. Not only will this serve in his evaluation of the background information but it will form the base to answer the applicant's questions about the job and help the manager evaluate the applicant during the interview. In determining job requirements, getting answers to questions such as these will help:

In regard to technical qualifications: What special skills should the person who is to fill the job have? What experience is needed? What education level is needed? Should the person who fills the job have advance qualifications or would entry level skills be sufficient? Does the job require broad or specific knowledge? Is there a training period allowed or is the person required to perform the first day, week, and so on? Is detailed work required?

In regard to motivation and drive: What are the opportunities for advancement in the job, or is it a dead-end? What is the pay range? What opportunities are there to use creative ideas? Is the position in good shape or does it need improvement? What type of person would be content and happy in this job: the slow methodical type or a person with "get up and go?"

In regard to relationships: Where does it fit in with other jobs of the organization? What relationship does the position require with others? What inside contacts? Outside contacts? What qualities of personality and temperament should the individual who fills the job have? What are the temperaments of the other employees in the department? What emotional stress does the job entail?

Applicant's Background

The best source of background information is the applicant's application form. This form is filled out by the applicant during the screening process, and a typical form is shown in Figure 28. This form is a valuable tool in selecting an applicant for a job. First, as this form indicates when properly filled out, it gives a wide array of information concerning the applicant's education, work record, and general personal data. This information can be used to plan the questions during the interview. By knowing this information, the manager can ask questions to obtain specific information. Questions such as: "What did you do on your last job?" and "How was it done?" are examples. Also, when asking questions such as these the manager should weigh the applicant's responses against other questions of his own: Does he seem to know what he is talking about? Are there gaps in his story? Does he seem evasive? Secondly, the application form is a written record of certain facts concerning education, experience, names of former employers, and other references that can be verified. If this information has not been verified by the personnel department, insist that this be done. This especially applies to the applicant's former work record. The reason is simply this: Study after study shows that the best indication to the applicant's future performance is what he has done in the past. Therefore, the manager should pay particular attention to the comments of the applicant's former employers. When an applicant has a good work record, other references are not very important. However, if he has had little or no work experience, other references such as those of school officials or others who are in a position to give an objective evaluation are of some value. But personal references of the "any one who knows you" variety are rarely worth anything and should be all but ignored. This information used within the framework of the basis of an effective interview, plus the prescreening process conducted by the personnel department, should go a long way in selecting the right man for the right job.

In conclusion, it should be noted that while it is not a good practice to make notes during the interview, after the interview is over, the manager

APPLICATION FOR EMPLOYMENT

Print Name ____________________

Address ____________________

City-State ____________ Phone No. ____________

In case of injury notify: Name ____________________
Address ____________________

Marital Status ________ No. of Dependent Children ________ Other Dependents ________

Physical Defects (explain) ____________________

Date ________

Position Desired ________

Earnings Expected ________

Date Available ________

Soc. Sec. No. ___ | ___ | ___

Height ________ Weight ________

Sex ________ Birth Date ________

Citizen of U.S.: Yes ____ No ____

Have You Ever Been Discharged from a Position ________

EDUCATION

School	Name and Location	Dates From	Dates To	Years Completed	Dipl./Degree Yes	Dipl./Degree No	Major Course (Subject/Degree)
Grade							
High School							
College							
Graduate School							
Business or Trade							
Other							

Extracurricular School Activities ____________________

Current Hobbies ____________________

ARMED SERVICES RECORD: Have you served in the U.S. Armed Forces? Yes ____ No ____

Dates: From ________ To ________ Branch ________ Final Rank ________

Type of Discharge ________ Current Draft Status ________

PERSONAL REFERENCES

Name	Address	Occupation

EXPERIENCE (in chronological order)

Present Employer | Address | Kind of Business

Starting Date | Salaries: Starting | Present | Reason for Leaving

Job Title | Supervisor's Name | May We Contact?

Description of Work ____________________

Figure 28 Typical Application Form

EXPERIENCE (continued in chronological order)

Next to last Employer	Address	Kind of Business

Starting Date	Leaving Date	Salaries Starting	Salaries Leaving	Reason for Leaving

Job Title	Supervisor's Name	May We Contact?

Description of Work ______________________________

____

Employer	Address	Kind of Business

Starting Date	Leaving Date	Salaries Starting	Salaries Leaving	Reason for Leaving

Job Title	Supervisor's Name	May We Contact?

Description of Work ______________________________

____

Employer	Address	Kind of Business

Starting Date	Leaving Date	Salaries Starting	Salaries Leaving	Reason for Leaving

Job Title	Supervisor's Name	May We Contact?

Description of Work ______________________________

____

Employer	Address	Kind of Business

Starting Date	Leaving Date	Salaries Starting	Salaries Leaving	Reason for Leaving

Job Title	Supervisor's Name	May We Contact?

Description of Work ______________________________

____

ADDITIONAL EXPERIENCE AND INFORMATION (licenses, special machines, etc.) ______________________________

____

____

____

____

____

____

INTERVIEWER'S COMMENTS ______________________________

____

____

Date of Interview ______________________________ Interviewed By ______________________________

Figure 28 (cont'd.)

should note his impressions so these notes can be compared with others involved in the selection process.

THE PERFORMANCE INTERVIEW

This type of interview, also called the performance review, is a systematic way to evaluate an employee's performance. This is a valuable tool in applied supervision. It allows the manager and his employee to sit down in private and discuss the employee and his job. This allows the manager to let the employee know how he stands, and it affords the manager with the opportunity to point out where the employee can improve. It also permits the employee and the manager to reassess job requirements and establish goals.

In many organizations, the performance interview is preceded by the manager rating his employee in certain areas of his performance. This is normally done by the manager filling out a rating form. Rating systems and rating forms vary, but most forms include such things as quality and quantity of work, cooperation, dependability, initiative, adaptability, and the like, and are prepared annually for all employees and at shorter intervals for new workers. A typical rating form is shown in Figure 29. It may be added that some organizations have no rating system at all. But when an organization does have a rating system, the manager is normally given some instructions on how the form is to be filled out and factors on which he should base his rating. Despite this, since the rating relies on the manager's judgment, which is influenced by such things as opinions, attitude, likes, and dislikes, a fair and impartial rating is hard to come by. On the other hand, it is the responsibility of the manager to make this rating as fair and impartial as possible. There is no foolproof method for achieving this end and no attempt will be made here to go into the various theories about the subject, but there are eight practical ways or rules that the manager can use in making his rating less subjective. The rules, which are self-explanatory, are as follows: (1) Rate employees by groups according to their level; carefully consider who is to be rated and when the rating is to be made. (2) Base the rating on the employee's actual performance on the one hand, and on his estimated potential on the other hand. (3) Observe workers over a period of time before making the ratings. (4) Collect information before the rating. (5) Guard against the common tendency to rate too high and against the less common tendency to rate too low. (6) Do not allow personal likes or dislikes to enter into the rating. (7) Rate the trouble-makers in the department honestly. Do not rate them higher than they deserve just to avoid trouble with them. (8) Do not allow the individual's

PERFORMANCE EVALUATION

Hire Date ______________

Name ______________ Clock # ______________ Department ______________

30 Days (________)	No. Days Late (________)	Absence (________)
50 Days (________)	No. Days Late (________)	Absence (________)
Annual (________)	No. Days Late (________)	Absence (________)

	Unsatisfactory			Satisfactory			Better Than Satisfactory			Highly Satisfactory		
Work Record ________	30 Days	50 Days	Annual	30 Days	50 Days	Annual	30 Days	50 Days	Annual	30 Days	50 Days	Annual
Quality & Quantity												
Cooperativeness												
Dependability												
Initiative												
Adaptability												

Comments: ______________

Comments: ______________

Supervisor's Signature: ______________ Date: ______________

Supervisor's Signature: ______________ Date: ______________

Employee's Comments: ______________

Employee's Comments: ______________

☐ Request Discussion with Area Manager Employee's Signature: ______________

☐ Request Discussion with Area Manager Employee's Signature: ______________

Comments: ______________

OD 70-11

____
Area Manager

Figure 29 Typical Employee-Rating Form

good or bad performance on one trait or instance to influence the rating of his performance on other traits.

After the manager has rated an employee, it is the policy of most organizations that the rating be discussed with the employee concerned. If this is not the policy, or even if the organization has no formal rating system, *it is important that the manager conduct a performance interview at least on an annual basis.* Although this interview may take many forms, in recent years the result-oriented or management by objective approach has been widely used. This approach, which involves four basic steps, is an effective means for conducting the performance interview by any manager at any level, with all types of employees in all types of organizations with or without a rating system. The four steps are briefly discussed below and a combination of the three approaches to interviewing may be used in conducting the interview.

STEP 1: At the beginning of the interview, the employee and the manager discuss the employee's duties and responsibilities and agree on the work that the employee is getting paid to do. Then they jointly agree on areas of the job that are most important. In this step the employee's job description can be used as a guide.

STEP 2: In this step, the employee and the manager discuss the employee's past performance. How well he is doing, what problems he is having, and where the manager can assist are things to consider. The rating should be shown to the employee, and any questions concerning the rating should be clarified. In this case, the manager should attempt to obtain agreement, or if agreement is not reached, the employee should be given the opportunity to appeal. Then the objectives for the next rating period are discussed. Again, the objectives should be agreed upon through a give-and-take discussion.

STEP 3: After the objectives have been agreed upon, the manager and the employee discuss how performance is to be measured. Where possible, the results expected should be in measurable terms: so much, so many, in this quality, over this time. This will help overcome the subjective rating disadvantage.

STEP 4: In this step, commitments are made to obtain the desired results. This again calls for a give-and-take discussion as to what each party will do in order to meet the objectives. Concession may be necessary, but this commitment must be made if the results expected are to be achieved.

As this four-step cycle is repeated, results should begin to show. The employee will have a definite target, and the manager will have criteria to measure results.

THE COUNSELING INTERVIEW

In this type of interview, the manager attempts, through an interchange of information, to assist the employee in solving a problem that is affecting employee-manager relationships. Problems that affect the harmonious relations between the employee and his manager vary widely, but they can be classified in two general types: Employee-oriented or manager-oriented. The first concerns those where the employee has a complaint or grievance about some aspect of his work, whereas the latter involves some dissatisfaction the manager has with the employee's behavior. In either case, the purpose of the interview is to identify the problem and work out a course of action that will resolve the grievance or complaint, or effect a change in the employee's behavior so normal relations can be restored. Although each interview is unique, most problems of both types can be resolved within the framework of the effective interview if two special factors are recognized by the manager when conducting the interview.

First, it should be recognized that employee complaints and grievances and unsatisfactory behavior are often only symptoms of the problem, not the real problem to be solved. For example, the employee who complains about his pay may really feel that he is not appreciated, or the employee whose work is unsatisfactory may have a personal problem. Other examples could be cited, but the point is that the real reasons for most problems are often hidden from the employee as well as the manager. This makes it clear that by assisting the employee in analyzing all aspects of the situation both the manager and the employee can better understand the real problem to be solved. To determine the actual cause of the problem, the manager should encourage the employee to talk freely during the interview. Only if the employee speaks up and reveals his true feelings can the cause of the problem be determined. Since emotions are normally involved here, the employee's attitudes and opinions should be taken into account. This is especially important if the problem is personal. Listening sympathetically, being patient, and trying to understand the employee's point of view will help the employee express himself freely. Also it is important to recognize that although some problems will seem more imaginary than real, to the employee all problems are significant. It is also important that the manager get all the facts and avoid jumping to conclusions or making premature judgments.

The second factor the manager should recognize is his own limitations. This simply means that he should be aware of when he should do the counseling or assist the employee in obtaining a solution to a problem and when this should be referred to someone else. This does not mean that he should never counsel an employee or prescribe a course of action. Whenever possible the manager should solve the problems and never "pass the buck" when he can do the job himself. But he should recognize that there are some problems that the average manager does not have the training and experience to handle. Drugs, alcoholism, sex, family problems, and problems involving psychological disorders are examples. When these are identified or suspected as being the cause of the employee's problems, the assistance of a professional person or agency is normally required. Also, it may be best that certain problems be handled by the appropriate staff agency within the organization. If the problem involves pay, for instance, the employee should be referred to the personnel department, or if the problem is medical or highly personal (offensive odors or unclean habits), the organizational medical doctor or health nurse should handle the problem. Not only can these professional persons or agencies handle the problem better than the manager, but the employee will be more likely to accept the advice of an authority with less embarrassment. If no medical personnel are on the staff, the Public Health Service may be asked to help. Moreover, if the problem is a formal grievance, the organization's procedure for handling a grievance should be followed.

THE DISCIPLINARY INTERVIEW

This interview is used when the counseling interview fails to correct the employee's behavior. It includes punishing the employee in some way for his undesirable behavior. Punishment can range anywhere from a mild reprimand to discharging the employee from his job. Although this type of interview is disagreeable to most managers, it is a necessary part of applied supervision. Whereas all that is possible should be done to preclude a situation from deteriorating to the point that disciplinary action is required, it happens in most departments, and disciplinary action is necessary when everything else fails. Like the other types of interviews, the nature of the disciplinary interview will depend on the facts of the situation and the employee involved. But when a disciplinary interview is necessary, the following general principles apply.

The manager should always discipline in private and keep what goes on between him and the employee from other members of the department. The interview should be conducted when both the manager and the employee are calm.

Discipline should be administered promptly, fairly, and consistently. This means that the action should follow as closely to the act as possible, and if one employee is disciplined for a certain act, other employees that commit that act under similar circumstances should also be brought to account. However, this must be tempered in individual cases because some employees will respond to different treatment. The manager should know what works best with each employee.

The punishment should be matched to the severity of the offense. In some instances where a specific rule has been violated, the punishment is prescribed by the organization. In other cases it is left to the discretion of the manager. While this will vary among managers, the rule to apply here is that in all cases where there is a choice, the least amount of punishment should be used.

Finally and most important, since the purpose of the action should be to correct the employee's behavior, not punish him for his mistake, the action should be made as acceptable to the employee as possible. At best, this is no easy matter to achieve. But by stressing the importance of the mistake and how it can be corrected, and by criticizing the work or act, not the worker, most people will accept discipline more willingly.

THE EXIT INTERVIEW

The exit interview is used when an employee either quits his job, is being laid-off by his organization, or has been fired. In some organizations the exit interview is the function of the personnel department. In others it is the job of the first-line manager, or it may be done by both the manager and the personnel department in separate interviews. Regardless of the policy, it is a good supervisory practice for the employee's immediate supervisor to conduct an exit interview prior to the departure. Although all these are exit interviews, the rules for conducting each type are different. Therefore, each is discussed briefly below.

When an employee *quits* his job and is leaving the organization, the purpose of the exit interview is primarily to determine why the employee is quitting. In some cases the reasons are obvious. A woman employee leaving to have a baby, husband being transferred, or retirements are examples. In these cases, the purpose of the interview is to let the employee know that his services were appreciated and that the manager is willing to assist him where possible in the future. On the other hand, if the reasons are not obvious, the manager should ask the employee for his reasons. Since most employees who quit seldom give the real reason voluntarily, using the techniques of the direct approach is important here. The manager should ask specific questions such as: How does the employee feel about the company? His supervisor? His fellow employees? His pay and working conditions? During the interview, the manager should also try to determine the employee's feelings, since more is often told by attitude than by what is said. It may be added that some managers do not want to know how the employee feels since it may be a reflection on them. Therefore, the manager should assess his own attitude as well. Finally, because the employee is an ambassador for the company, he should be encouraged to feel as congenial toward the organization as possible.

When an employee is being *laid off*, the exit interview is particularly important. First, most lay-offs are temporary, which means that the employee may return to the organization. Secondly, since the action is not the fault of the employee, except in disciplinary cases, he may feel that the organization is treating him unfairly. This is especially true if the lay-off was subjective rather than objective. In either case, whether the employee is being laid off according to seniority or some other objective system, or by the "pick and choose" method, the lay-off interview is difficult to conduct. But the interview may be somewhat easier if these rules are followed: (1) The lay-off should be announced as far in advance as possible. This will allow the employee to make plans and lessen the impact of sudden change. (2) A detailed explanation of the reasons for the lay-off should be given. This applies to all employees. Those who are affected deserve to know the reason why, and those who are not affected are interested since it concerns their job stability. Initially, this may be done in groups where general questions may be answered, but each employee who is affected should be interviewed individually. (3) During the interview the reason for the lay-off should be particularly emphasized, especially if the subjective method was used. If a recall is possible, advise the employee when he can expect to return to work. Also, the manager should get answers to questions that the employee may have regarding such things as employee compensation, and company and union benefits. (4) After the employee leaves the organization, it is a good policy to keep in touch with him. Keep him interested. Tell him what is going on. Have him willing and able to come back to work when he is needed.

When a person is *fired* from the job, there is no way to tell how the exit interview will go. Some people take being discharged calmly, others become emotional and practically uncontrollable. When possible, these general rules should be applied: (1) The interview should be planned and the manager should work out his comments in advance. This should include the points he wants to make and the employee's possible reactions. (2) The manager should be frank and tell the employee why he is being fired. Of course this is normally known already, but it should be reestablished in the interview. Also, the employee is to be told whether he will be given a recommendation. The points should be stated as clearly and as precisely as possible, and no point should be argued. (3) Again, since the employee will be another ambassador, he should leave with as good an attitude toward the company as possible. This may be partly achieved if the manager emphasizes that he and the organization are not infallible, and he is only judging the action, not the person. The manager should then wish him well.

After the exit interview, a form is required by some organizations on which the manager may make comments. If this is not the case, the manager may wish to make notes for his own file.

KEY POINT SUMMARY

1. One of the most effective and versatile tools the manager has at his disposal is the informal and formal interview.
2. To use the formal interview effectively the manager should consider:
    a. The approach
    b. The plan
    c. The technique
3. There are three approaches the manager can use:
    a. The direct approach
    b. The indirect approach
    c. The patterned approach
4. In planning the interview the manager should consider:
    a. The background of both the employee or applicant to be interviewed and the problem or situation.
    b. Setting up the situation, to include determining questions to be asked and the employee's response to the questions as well as making arrangements for the time and place of the interview.
5. The technique concerns how the interview is actually conducted and includes four steps:
    a. Developing rapport between the manager conducting the interview and the person being interviewed
    b. Gathering and interpreting information
    c. Deciding upon a course of action
    d. Closing the interview
6. There are five types of interviews the manager may use in handling special situations. The types are:
    a. The preemployment interview

b. The performance interview
c. The counseling interview
d. The disciplinary interview
e. The exit interview

7. The purpose of the preemployment interview is to assist the manager in selecting the right man for the right job. Special factors to consider are:
   a. Job requirements
   b. Applicant's background

8. The performance interview is a systematic way to review with the employee the employee's past performance, reassess job requirements, and establish goals. An effective pattern to follow in this type of interview is the result-oriented approach, which involves four steps:
   a. Discuss the employee's duties and responsibilities and agree on priorities.
   b. Review the employee's past performance and establish performance objectives.
   c. Discuss how the employee's performance is to be measured.
   d. Make a joint commitment to obtain desired results.

9. In the counseling interview the manager attempts to assist the employee in solving a problem that is affecting the employee-manager relationship. Special features to consider in this type of interview are:
   a. Getting the employee to talk freely to reveal the facts concerning the problem.
   b. The manager recognizing his limitations in helping the employee.

10. The disciplinary interview is used to correct some aspect of the employee's unacceptable behavior. Special features to consider are:
    a. Have interview when calm.
    b. Discipline should be administered promptly, fairly, and consistently.
    c. Use the least amount of punishment to correct the undesirable behavior.
    d. Use discipline to correct, not to punish.

11. The exit interview is used under three conditions: When an employee quits, is laid off, or is fired. The common factor of this interview is:
    a. To maintain the employee's good will toward the company.

DISCUSSION QUESTIONS

1. Why is the interview an important supervisory skill? How can it be used?
2. What are the three factors of an effective interview?
3. What is the best approach to use in conducting an interview?
4. In planning an interview, what factors should be considered, and why is each factor necessary for an effective interview?
5. Why is it necessary that a manager develop rapport with the person being interviewed, and how can this be done?
6. What is the best way to gather information during the interview? Relate the technique of questioning an employee to the employee's possible response.
7. What is a key factor in deciding upon a course of action?
8. What factors should be considered in closing the interview?
9. What are the five types of interviews? What is the purpose of each type?
10. Why is knowing job requirements and an applicant's background important in selecting a person for a job? How can this information be obtained, and what should be considered?
11. In rating an employee's performance, how can the manager make his rating less subjective? Relate relating an employee's performance and the four-step method of conducting a performance review with making job performance requirements understood as discussed in Chapter 14.
12. What special factors should the manager consider when counseling an employee, and what is the significance of each factor? Relate unacceptable behavior and identifying and solving employee problems discussed in Chapter 14 to employee counseling.
13. What should the manager consider in using the interview to discipline? Relate the disciplinary interview with taking disciplinary action discussed in Chapter 14.
14. What are the special factors to consider when interviewing an employee who is leaving the organization when:
    a. The employee is quitting
    b. The employee is being laid off
    c. The employee is being fired
15. What general relationship is there between the manager's leadership style and how he conducts and uses an interview?

CASE PROBLEMS

Case 15–1

A young lady stopped the personnel manager as he walked by her department. She was obviously upset. With her eyes full of tears, she said, "I would like to ask you something."

"Yes, what is it," he asked.

"Is it the policy of this company just out of nowhere to offer a transfer to a person?" she asked.

"You have been offered a transfer and you feel it was out of nowhere?" the personnel manager asked.

"It's worse than that. It's the same as being fired—that's what it is." she said.

"You feel you're being fired?" he asked.

"I certainly do. Everything was O.K. when I went home last Friday. In fact, everything has been O.K. for two years. Got three merit raises during that period. I came in this morning, and all of a sudden I was told that I'm not handling my job as I should and they have in mind getting another girl. It's like a dream; I just can't believe it. I know I'm not the most perfect person in the world, but my performance rating has always been above average. Besides, when I was hired my supervisor told me that the job was mine as long as I wanted it. Now, he offers me a transfer to a menial job. I don't care what you say, it's the same as being fired. So I'm quitting." she said.

Questions

1. *What human relations factors are involved in this case?*
2. *What is the relationship between this case and the performance interview and the disciplinary interview?*
3. *If you were the personnel manager, what interviewing principles and practices would you use in handling this employee's problem?*

Case 15–2

A young manager of a fairly large department has the following routine personnel problems that he must solve:

1. Mary Adams, a mediocre employee, is leaving the organization to take a job with another organization.
2. He has several applicants for Mary's job with whom he must talk.
3. Several employees have complained to him about Mary Baker, a sensitive middle-aged widow, who has a body odor problem.
4. Jake Salley, a practical joker who has been warned about this action before, heated the handle on the men's room door causing an employee to burn his hand severely. He has to do something about Jake.
5. Jane Berry, who is a high producer but who talks incessantly, spreading rumors, and who is occasionally late for work, is due for a performance rating.

Questions

1. *If you were this manager, what type of interview would you use in each of the situations above?*

a. Make an outline of the major items you would include in each interview.
b. Discuss how each interview should be handled.

SELECTED REFERENCES

HARITON, THEODORE, *Interview,* Chap. 2. New York: Hastings House, Publishers, 1970.

HEPNER, HARRY W., *Perceptive Management and Supervision,* Chap. 17. Englewood Cliffs, N.J.: Prentice-Hall, Inc., 1961.

———, *Psychology Applied to Life and Work* (4th ed.), Chaps. 7 and 8. Englewood Cliffs, N.J.: Prentice-Hall, Inc., 1966.

MORGAN, JOHN S., *Getting Across to Employees,* Chaps. 9, 16, and 23. New York: McGraw-Hill Book Company, 1964.

IV

Management Techniques

In the process of carrying out his duties, the manager finds that certain situations require special attention. These situations are normally "spin-outs" resulting from his routine day-to-day operation, or they may be in the form of special requirements given to him by his immediate supervisor. In any event, when these special situations occur, they should be dealt with promptly and properly. To do this, the manager needs to develop certain management techniques (working methods). Therefore, it is the purpose of this part to discuss some of the more common techniques that the manager can use in handling these special situations. However, it is to be recognized that although each of these techniques can be taught as a separate course, primary attention is given here to outlining and discussing only those essential elements of each technique sufficient for the manager to develop a pattern to follow in applying the technique on the job. With this purpose in mind, this part includes these topics:

How to Solve Problems
How to Develop a Training Program
How to Hold Group Discussions
How to Simplify and Improve Work
How to Manage Paperwork

16

How to Solve Problems

A fundamental technique that must be acquired by all managers is that of solving problems. A problem can be defined as the difference between what a situation is and what it should be. Consequently, problem solving is the technique of bringing the two elements into alignment by making a decision among various alternatives. Every day, the manager is confronted with many problems that require decisions. When these problems involve one individual or are limited to a single situation, they can be handled routinely by the manager using his supervisory skills. But some situations are so complex and involved that they require special attention and treatment.[1] This makes it necessary for *exceptional situations* to be handled by a separate process, called problem solving, which in this chapter is discussed under the following major topics: (1) problem-solving pattern, (2) studying information, (3) habit and problem solving, (4) conflict and problem solving, and (5) group approach to problem solving.

PROBLEM-SOLVING PATTERN

To solve a problem effectively, three elements are involved. First, the manager must withhold judgment until he has considered all possible aspects of the problem and all possible solutions. Secondly, he must make a decision as to the best possible course of action. Finally, to have meaning, the manager must take action. If left to chance it is doubtful that adequate

[1] These special situations are often identified as a result of the controlling process discussed in Chapter 2.

consideration would be given to these key factors, if done at all. Therefore, the need for a pattern or system that the manager can logically and systematically follow is apparent. A pattern commonly used is the scientific method of problem solving.[2] This system, so called since it closely follows the scientific pattern of investigation, consists of five phases or steps arranged in a logical sequence. These steps are:

1. Recognizing and identifying the problem
2. Gathering and analyzing data
3. Listing possible solutions
4. Testing possible solutions
5. Selecting a final solution

Before discussing these steps in more detail, it should be understood that in actual practice the steps do not always follow a definite and orderly sequence. The steps may overlap, as indicated in Figure 30.

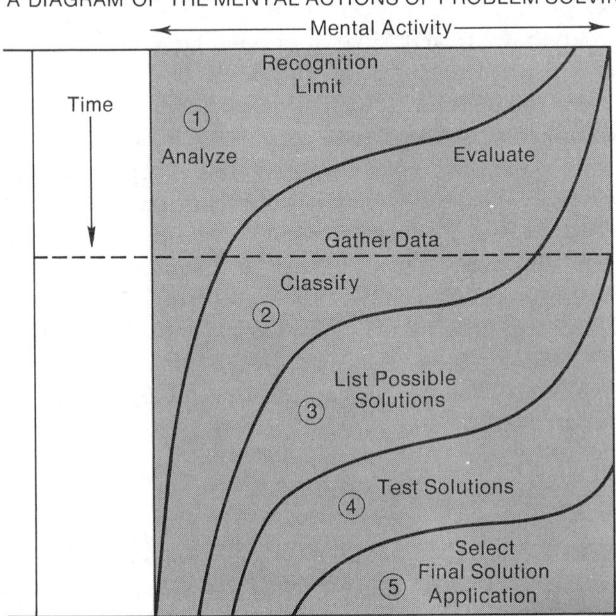

Figure 30 **Interrelations of Problem-solving Pattern (Courtesy of U.S. Air Force Department.)**

[2] See Howard L. Timms, *Introduction to Operational Management* (Homewood, Ill.: Richard D. Irwin, Inc., 1967), p. 71.

As shown in this illustration, more than one step may be considered at one time; or developments at one step may cause the manager to reconsider a previous step. For example, the data he collects may force the manager to redefine his problem. Similarly, while testing solutions, he may think of a new solution, or in the process of selecting a final solution, he may discover a need for additional information. The steps, as outlined, should be considered only as a checklist to bring order to the mental processes. They are not a guarantee that a problem will be solved successfully. With this in mind, the five steps are discussed below.

Recognizing and Identifying the Problem

This is considered the most important phase in problem solving. No problem can be solved until it is recognized and clearly identified. A manager normally recognizes that he has a problem when some phase of his operation is not going according to plan or when he fails to meet one or more of his objectives. Once this situation is recognized, the manager must then identify the particular obstacle causing the problem. This requires limiting the problem and reducing it to a manageable size. To do this the manager should analyze the whole problem, then each part. If, for example, a manager discovers that he is not meeting critical scheduling deadlines, he should first analyze all possible situations that may be causing the problem and examine each part until he discovers the specific obstacle blocking his goal. His analysis may reveal, for example, that the problem is the work backlog in one unit, and by removing this obstacle he can solve this deadline problem. In this case he has limited the problem and reduced it to a manageable size.

Gathering and Analyzing Information

Once the manager has recognized and identified the obstacle causing the problem, he must then collect information concerning the problem. There are many ways in which information can be gathered. He may research the records, interview the people involved, consult other departments, make studies, prepare questionnaires, or observe the situation. Regardless of how it is obtained, the information must be analyzed to determine the possible cause of the problem. An analysis of the information gathered by the manager having the deadline problem may reveal, for example, that the backlog is caused by lack of material, poor scheduling, improperly trained employees, low morale, or insufficient personnel. By discovering the cause, the manager is of course in a better position to find a solution to the problem. However, before the information can be used to solve the problem, it should be valid. Therefore, the manager should pay particular attention to the reliability of the source of his information.

Listing Possible Solutions

In this step, the manager's experience, intelligence, and judgment are applied. The data collected are used to suggest solutions to the problem. Normally, there are several possible solutions that should be identified and listed. In the backlog problem, for instance, there are several possible solutions. Better scheduling, closer supervision, more training, obtaining more people, and better use of present employees are examples of long-range solutions. On a short-range, temporary basis, having employees work overtime to overcome the immediate backlog should be considered. But the point is that most problems have several possible solutions that should be listed.

Testing Possible Solutions

After the possible solutions have been listed, each solution should be analyzed. The appropriateness of each possible solution in getting the job done, the cost involved, and the required resources should be mentally tested by matching one against the other.

Selecting a Final Solution

The final solution should emerge as the logical result of the above process. It requires the manager to make a decision as to which solution or combination of solutions would produce the best results.

Taking Action

In theory, the process stops when the manager makes a decision by selecting his final solution. But for the process to be effective, action must be taken. Of course, the specific action will depend on the nature of the problem. In any case the manager's action should not only correct the immediate problem, but be such as to preclude a similar problem from happening again.

As pointed out earlier, these steps in themselves do not solve problems or assure accurate or "right" decisions. But when used either by the individual manager or in a group, they can serve as a systematic means by which judgment can be withheld until all aspects of a problem have been logically considered. In studying these steps, it should again be remembered that they are listed sequentially for convenience of discussion. Like most processes pertaining to management, in actual practice this sequence is seldom as definite as it appears here. Figure 30 illustrates this point. In addition, it is well to realize that in the process of solving one problem, several related problems may be revealed. Consequently, the problem-solving pattern is a continuous cycle, literally without end.

STUDYING INFORMATION

A vital part of the problem-solving process is information. To draw a conclusion (decision) on which action can be taken, the information must not only be complete and accurate, but the method of study must be valid. Some common ways in which information can be studied are through *generalizing, hypothesizing, seeking causes for effects,* or through a combination of these three ways. These three ways to study information and the typical types of information used in each are briefly discussed below.

GENERALIZATION. In generalization, inference is drawn and conclusions made about classes or groups of people or things after studying only a part of the group or class. A common method of obtaining information used in generalization is the sampling technique. This technique, which can be used for people and things, consists of selecting only a relatively few of a class or group either by mathematical statistics through questionnaires, quantitative analysis and the like, or by direct observation and the recording of facts. In management, morale and communication surveys and random count in inventory control are examples of this technique. By having a limited number of employees fill out a questionnaire pertaining to their feelings about certain aspects of their company, job, and supervisors, management attempts to draw conclusions regarding the morale of the total organization. Or by counting a certain number of items at random of the total stock of a warehouse and then comparing this count with the records, management can draw a conclusion as to the validity of its inventory control system. The danger of this approach is called *hasty generalization.* It simply means that if too few samples are used, or if the samples taken are not representative of a group or class, the results will lead the manager to an inaccurate conclusion by hasty generalization.

HYPOTHESIS. In this method of studying information, the manager starts with a theory or proposition as a possible conclusion (hypothesis) and then tests the validity of his hypothesis against facts and opinions. A hypothesis can help the manager select information for study and can give directions for solving the problem. He can start with a tentative conclusion in the form of a statement and then try to prove or disprove the statement by studying the evidence. For example, a manager may make the hypothesis that inventory records are inaccurate, then take a sample to either prove or disprove this statement. Or from the hypothesis that morale is good, a morale survey may prove the hypothesis to be right or wrong. Of course, the danger here lies in being unwilling to accept information that disproves the hypothesis and slanting information to prove a hypothesis that is incorrect.

CAUSE AND EFFECT. When using this method, study is made of some occurrence or act of human behavior in an effort to discover the cause. If the study shows that a certain problem was caused by a certain thing, it may then be argued that the same cause will always cause that effect. The validity of this method depends on the interrelationship of circumstances. If all the circumstances in all similar problems are identical with the one used in the study, cause and effect are possibly valid. On the other hand, if circumstances are not constant in all cases, then this method will not work. Cause and effect lends itself better to mechanical things than to problems in which human behavior is involved. For example, if through scientific techniques of trouble shooting the cause of an engine failure was found due to a faulty part, it can be reasonably assumed with a fairly high degree of accuracy that this cause will affect all like engines in a similar manner. However, problems involving human behavior cannot be related to cause and effect in a similar manner. In the first place, the cause cannot be as precisely isolated since there are no accurate trouble-shooting techniques for people. And secondly, even if the cause is isolated successfully, the human mechanism does not function with the same degree of predictability as mechanical devices. What applies to one individual or one group can seldom be applied universally. In recognizing these limitations, the manager can then use cause and effect in the problem-solving process.

HABIT AND PROBLEM SOLVING

A major factor influencing the manager's problem-solving ability is habit. The tendency toward a condition that by repetition has become a standard is a dictionary definition of habit. On a day-to-day basis, habit is useful since it allows routine duties and responsibilities to be handled without too much thought or effort. But since problems are exceptions to routine, habit tends to hinder a manager's problem-solving ability.

Perception is the mental process by which an individual collects, stores, sorts, and interprets information. To be useful this information is interpreted by the individual according to his background and experience, and made to conform to a certain pattern by habit. By this process, habit tends to limit the information to certain prescribed and approved applications. This procedure is necessary for an individual to process and apply the vast amount of information he is exposed to, but it is a deterrent to his problem-solving ability since it tends to place limitations on the way information can be used.

Perceptual Dimensions

To solve a problem, the manager must be able to see and examine it from as many dimensions or angles as possible. Often his ability to do this is restricted by the habit of conformity. When applied to problem solving, habit tends to establish fixed patterns of thought and action that impose imaginary boundaries on the manager's ability to see a problem in its many dimensions. This can be illustrated by the frequently used dot problem shown in Figure 31.

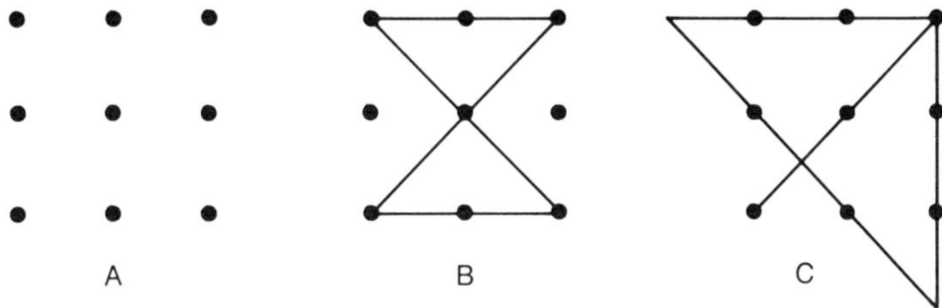

Figure 31 Dot Problem

When asked to connect the dots (*A*) by using four straight lines, most people try to solve the problem by following the imaginary line formed by the dots (*B*), when the problem can only be solved by increasing their perceptual dimension of the problem beyond the imaginary boundaries (*C*).

Like the dots, the solution to most problems is found outside the imaginary boundaries mentally fixed by the habit of conformity. Only by increasing his perceptual dimension beyond the boundaries can a manager view a problem from its many possible angles.

Perceptual Stereotypes

The world presented through the individual's senses is a vast, jumbled confusion of sensation. To cut these down to size where they can be useful, the human brain sorts these variable bits and pieces of information into categories, and assigns names to the categories.[3] These categories take on functions or characteristics consistent with the background and experience of

[3] See James Deese, *The Psychology of Learning* (New York: McGraw-Hill Book Company, Inc., 1958), p. 291.

the individual. Often the individual's perception of the functions and characteristics of these various categories, whether objects or people, become fixed by habit into stereotypes. Stereotype thinking restricts the manager's problem-solving ability since it makes it hard for him to see any other function or characteristic in his dealings with objects or people.

If the manager sees the characteristics of women, for instance, as being inherently inferior to those of men, this perceptual stereotype could preclude him from considering a qualified woman employee in solving the problem of filling a critical managerial position. This would restrict his ability to solve the problem since it would limit this potential resource. Similar examples could be applied to occupational categories, racial groups, or any number of categories often perceived as stereotypes, thus precluding them from honest consideration.

Objects such as machines, materials, equipment, and even processes and procedures are often seen as having only one or a limited number of functions. Actually, most items have many uses other than the ones for which they were designed. A small item like a paper clip, for example, with the obvious use of holding paper, has been shown to have more than a hundred different uses other than its intended function. Stereotype perception of the functional use of objects not only limits the manager's problem-solving ability, but restricts the use of by-products resulting from the problem-solving process. A procedure developed for one process may very well be adapted to another, or a report resulting from the solution to a particular problem may have many uses.

Perceptual habit is a product of the individual's fears, superstitions, beliefs, and total background and experience, conditioned by the habit of conformity. Consequently, to solve problems effectively a manager should train himself to analyze his perceptual habits and make necessary adjustments when required.

CONFLICT AND PROBLEM SOLVING

Another factor bearing on problem solving is concerned with the conflict involved when making a decision between alternates and taking action on a problem. Psychologists have found that when an individual is faced with a situation having both positive and negative values, his reaction to the situation follows an established pattern. This pattern is called the approach-avoidance conflict and according to N. E. Miller has four principles: [4]

[4] See James Deese, *The Psychology of Learning,* p. 32.

1. The tendency to approach a goal is stronger the nearer the subject is to the goal.
2. The tendency to avoid an unpleasant task is stronger the nearer the subject (person) is to the goal.
3. As the subject (person) nears the goal (pleasant and unpleasant tasks) the subject's avoidance tendency is stronger than the approach tendency.
4. The tendency to either approach or avoid the goal is influenced by the subject's drive (desire) to reach the goal.

The approach-avoidance conflict principles apply to both the manager making a decision and his taking action after the choice among alternate solutions has been reached. As these principles indicate, although tasks (decision or action) that are pleasant or have positive values are easier to approach than those that are undesirable, the tendency to avoid the task altogether is easier than approaching it. This simply means that, either good or bad, there is a strong tendency for an individual to avoid making a choice or taking action. The human tendency to avoid making a choice has long been recognized in the sales field. Closing the sale by getting a prospective buyer to commit himself by signing an agreement or contract is considered by most experienced salesmen as the most difficult part of selling. So it is with management decision making. Often after alternate solutions to a problem have been reduced to the extent that only a "yes" or "no" is required, the manager delays making a final choice. In taking action, the tendency to avoid direct involvement is stronger than taking positive steps to implement a decision. Even action of positive value is often delayed.

The reasons people are reluctant to make a choice and take action are as varied as the individuals involved. Fear of being wrong, the inexactness of the future, and the inherent resistance to change are possible causes. Ways to overcome this reluctance are equally varied and inexacting. However, some answers are implied in Miller's principles of the approach-avoidance conflict hypothesis. First, since goals with positive value are easier to approach than those with negative value, reducing the negative aspect involved in the decision or action will make his choice easier. This can be done by clarifying the negative aspects and by developing the necessary skills for coping with them, and by reducing the magnitude of the decision or action to a manageable size. The second answer implied in these principles is that the manager's strong desire or drive to reach the goal will make his approach to it less reluctant. This implies that if a manager is highly motivated, making decisions and taking action become less difficult. Finally, simply by recognizing the conflicts indicated in the four principles, the manager is better prepared to analyze the reason for his indecisiveness.

THE GROUP APPROACH TO PROBLEM SOLVING

In formal organizations, most operational problems are solved by their managers on an individual basis, but some problems can best be approached by people working in groups. The group approach has the obvious advantage of using the ideas of more people and employing more of the organization's resources to solve a problem. On the other hand, this approach has disadvantages. One disadvantage is the failure of the group to withhold judgment until all aspects of the problem have been logically considered. Also, pinpointing individual responsibility for making and carrying out the decision of the group is easily omitted. Often judgment is hastily made, and "decision by committee" sometimes fails due to lack of authority and a plan to carry out the decision. Despite these disadvantages, the group approach can be used to solve many organizational problems.

In the group approach, people and resources of an organization can be organized in several ways to solve problems. Two of the more common ways are the *creative method* and *the quantitative method.*

The Creative Method

The creative method to problem solving is employed in a conference situation where individual members of the group are encouraged to use their imaginations and their creative abilities to solve a problem. To do this, several techniques have been developed.[5]

THE BRAINSTORMING TECHNIQUE. Brainstorming is a conference technique by which a group attempts to find a solution to a specific problem by amassing all the ideas spontaneously contributed by its members. This technique was developed by Dr. Alex Osborn and is possibly one of the most widely used creative approaches to problem solving.[6] According to Dr. Osborn, "No conference is a brainstorming session unless the deferment of judgment principle is strictly followed." He gives four basic rules:

1. Criticism is ruled out. Ideate here, evaluate later.
2. "Free wheeling" is welcomed. The wilder the idea, the better.

[5] For a more analytical summary of these techniques, see Charles S. Whiting, "Operational Techniques of Creative Thinking," in *Readings in Management,* 3rd ed. (Cincinnati, Ohio: South-Western Publishing Company, 1969), Chap. 19.

[6] See Alex F. Osborn, *Applied Imagination* (New York: Charles Scribners Sons, 1953).

3. Quantity is wanted. The greater the number of ideas, the more likehood of useful ideas.
4. Combinations of ideas and improvement are sought.

In addition to providing a climate for encouraging the flow of ideas and freedom of expression, the brainstorming technique has the advantage of creating enthusiasm and developing a spirit of competition. Also, studies show that "free association" of ideas of adults is more numerous in group action than by an individual working alone.

THE GORDON TECHNIQUE. This technique was developed by William J. Gordon of Arthur D. Little, Inc., a research and consulting firm of Cambridge, Massachusetts. It is a variation of the Osborn (brainstorming) technique, but has some important exceptions. While the brainstorming method seeks many possible ideas, the Gordon technique is looking for only one new—best—idea, and only the chairman or leader of the group knows the problem. The chairman starts the discussion by giving the basic concepts associated with the problem, but withholds the actual problem until the group is nearing a satisfactory solution. Other than these exceptions, the brainstorming rules apply.

THE CATALOGUE TECHNIQUE. In this technique, a catalogue such as Sears, Spiegel, or the yellow pages of a telephone book are used by the group to get ideas. These ideas will in turn suggest other ideas for solving a problem. (This technique may be used in the Brainstorming Technique.)

THE CHECKLIST TECHNIQUE. One of the most commonly used and simplest forms of creative problem solving is the checklist. Checklists can be developed for a special problem by listing items that make up its components. The items can be compared against the problem or subject under consideration. Ideas for solving the problem can be sought by using one or more of nine basic categories: (1) put to other use, (2) adapt, (3) modify, (4) magnify, (5) minify, (6) subordinate, (7) rearrange, (8) reverse, or (9) combine.

The checklist method has the disadvantage of wasting time by considering questions that are not necessary for solving the problem, and it relies on the historical background of the problem, which may exclude new information from being considered.

In using any of the above techniques, it should be understood that the solution to a problem depends on more than inspiration and bright ideas. For ideas to be useful, they must be organized and applied within the framework of the problem-solving pattern so that appropriate judgment as to their value can be systematically analyzed and action taken.

The Quantitative Method

With the advent of the electronic digital computer, which is capable of performing mathematical calculations in enormous quantities and with fantastic speed, mathematical or quantitative problem-solving techniques have been developed. Due to its specialized and scientific nature, this method will not be discussed in detail here. But one technique becoming widely used by many organizations should be at least noted. The technique is called *operations research.*

In the operations research technique to quantitative problem solving, the variables involved in a problem are expressed as values in a set of equations or "mathematical models." A mathematical model can involve the use of any of a number of mathematical or statistical tools.

> In order to make the discussion of mathematical models more meaningful, an algebraic model utilizing the technique of differential calculus in its solution is illustrated here. An understanding of calculus is not necessary to appreciate the role it serves in the model. As a simplified example, suppose the quality of customer service in a particular department store increases with number of employees only up to a point, and then actually decreases, and the store manager wants to know what that point is. Further suppose that the relationship between quality of customer service and the number of employees can be represented by the equation $Y = 14X - \frac{1}{2}X^2$. The equation, then, is the mathematical model representing the situation being studied.[7]

These models are normally developed by a team of specialists, technicians, engineers, scientists, and so on. It is the role of the manager to work with this team to interpret the problem to the specialists. He must also be alert to see that the model closely represents actual conditions. Once the model has been developed, it is then transferred to computer programs where it can be used to solve the particular problem or problems for which it was designed. Types of specific problems are included in Chapter 20, where the computer is discussed.

KEY POINT SUMMARY

1. A *problem* can be defined as the difference between what a situation is and what it should be, whereas a *decision* is the choice among alternatives to bring the two into alignment.

[7] See Leonard J. Kazmier, *Principles of Management* (New York: McGraw-Hill Book Company, 1964), pp. 52-53.

2. To solve a problem effectively, three elements are involved:
    a. Withholding judgment until all possible aspects and all possible solutions have been considered
    b. Making a decision as to the best course of action
    c. Taking action
3. The pattern commonly used to solve problems is called the scientific method and includes six basic steps.
    a. Recognizing and identifying the problem
    b. Gathering and analyzing information
    c. Listing possible solutions
    d. Testing possible solutions
    e. Selecting a final solution
    f. (Taking action, although not a step, must be included)
4. Problem solving requires the manager to study information. Three ways in which this can be done include:
    a. Generalizations—drawing inference and conclusion after studying only a part of a group or class
    b. Hypothesis—starting with a theory or proposition as a possible conclusion, and then testing the validity of the theory or possible conclusion against fact or opinion
    c. Cause and effect—making a study of some occurrence, or act of human behavior, to discover the cause
5. Habit, the tendency toward a condition that by repetition has become standard, is useful in handling routine duties but is a drawback to problem solving since habit limits the manager's perception of the problem.
6. Perceptual limitations are of two major types:
    a. Perceptual dimension
    b. Perceptual stereotypes
7. The tendency to avoid making a decision or taking action is called the approach-avoidance conflict and in problem solving has two applications:
    a. Either good or bad, there is a strong tendency for an individual to avoid making a decision or taking action.
    b. By clarifying the reasons for his indecisiveness, being motivated, and by developing the necessary skills to cope with the problem, the avoidance conflict can best be overcome.
8. While most problems are solved by individual managers, sometimes problems can best be solved by the group approach. Two common methods of this approach are:
    a. The creative method
    b. The quantitative method

9. The creative method involves ideas and imagination to solve a problem and includes:
   a. The brainstorming technique
   b. The Gordon technique
   c. The catalogue technique
   d. The checklist technique
10. The quantitative method uses mathematical equations or models to solve a problem and operations research is the most common technique.

DISCUSSION QUESTIONS

1. What is the process of aligning what a situation is and what is should be? Explain.
2. What are the steps in the scientific approach to problem solving? Why are these steps necessary? Discuss.
3. What is the relationship between studying information and problem solving? Explain.
4. What are the three ways in which information can be studied? Explain.
5. Why is perceptual habit a hindrance to problem solving? What is meant by perceptual dimensions and perceptual stereotype? Explain each.
6. What are the four principles associated with H. E. Miller's approach-avoidance conflict theory? How do these principles affect an individual's problem-solving ability? Explain.
7. What are the advantages and disadvantages of the group approach to problem solving?
8. In the creative method of problem solving, what are four common techniques? Explain each.
9. What is operations research and what role does the manager play?

CASE PROBLEMS

Case 16–1

Manager Jim Wells is called in by his boss to discuss the low production of his department. After listening to his boss, Jim says, "Well, I know what the problem is. It's that new woman that personnel made me take. I told them that I had tried a woman on that job before and she didn't work out."

Questions

1. What are the factors in this case:
   a. In relation to studying information?

b. *In relation to habit?*
c. *In relation to withholding judgment?*

2. *How should Jim have handled his low production problem? (Discuss how each step of the problem-solving pattern could have been applied.)*

Case 16–2

In a large organization, rejections of finished products were the cause of so many late orders and customer complaints that the situation was called to the attention of the production superintendent. In observing the situation, he found that the handling of rejections had fallen so far behind that the only way to solve the problem was to have everyone in the department work on rejections to clear the backlog. After the backlog was cleared, he followed it for several days and when everything seemed to be going smoothly, he dismissed it from his mind. About a month later, the problem was again brought to his attention. This time he talked with the supervisor of the department and the employees doing the work, stressing the importance of their jobs. To clear the backlog he again stopped production and had all employees work on rejections. This time he kept close check on the operation for more than a month before assuring himself that the problem was solved and did not need special attention. About three months later, the situation occurred once more.

Questions

1. *What are the factors in this case?*
2. *What steps in the problem-solving pattern were missing in the way the superintendent handled the problem?*
3. *What are the possible reasons for the situation recurring after the superintendent stopped giving the department special at tention?*
4. *Could the group approach to problem solving be applied in this case?*

SELECTED REFERENCES

Coleman, James C., *Personality Dynamics and Effective Behavior,* Chap. 12. Chicago: Scott, Foresman, and Company, 1960.

Osborn, Alex F., *Applied Imagination.* New York: Charles Scribners Sons, 1953.

Timms, Howard L., *Introduction to Operations Management,* Chap. 3. Homewood, Ill.: Richard D. Irwin, Inc., 1967.

Whiting, Charles S., "Operational Techniques of Creative Thinking," in *Readings in Management* (3rd ed.), Chap. 5, Article 19. Cincinnati, Ohio: South-Western Publishing Company, 1969.

17

How to Develop a Training Program

One of the basic responsibilities of a manager is to modify and shape the behavior of his employees so that they can perform as members of an organization. A fundamental way in which behavior can be changed is through training. Training can be conducted informally through everyday experience or by the job instruction method as previously discussed. However, training is more effective if it is organized to meet certain objectives in a formal training program. Basically, the technique of developing a training program involves identifying the training needs, selecting the best course of action to meet these needs, and evaluating the results. The specific course of action will depend on the type of training, the number of employees to be trained, the learning level of those to receive the training, and a host of other factors that the manager must take into consideration. This makes it obvious that no single approach can apply to all training situations, nor is there one best approach or a standard training program that applies in all cases. However, by following a systematic pattern and recognizing the various options open to him, the manager's chances of selecting the best course of action to meet his training needs will be greatly enhanced. In this chapter, this process is discussed in 9 parts: (1) the characteristics of learning, (2) identifying training needs, (3) training objectives, (4) training methods, (5) training material, (6) training techniques, (7) scheduling training, (8) instructions, and (9) evaluation.

CHARACTERISTICS OF LEARNING

Learning can be defined as a change in behavior as a result of experience. Since the purpose of formal training is to provide an individual with an organized series of experiences directed toward some specific objective, learning is the crux of any training program. This being so, before training is discussed as such it is well that the manager be aware of some of the factors and principles associated with the learning process.

Types of Learning

Psychologists have classified learning in several ways, but for practical purposes learning can be divided into two basic types, skills learning and conceptual learning.

SKILLS LEARNING. Skills learning can be either mental or motor (physical). It is the simplest kind of learning and can be taught by rote, through practice, or a combination of the two. For example, a manager may teach an employee how to fill out a certain form by having the employee memorize (rote) the sequence in which the information is to be entered, then actually fill out the form until he is proficient (practice). Or, a manager may have an employee commit to memory the proper steps in setting up and operating a particular machine and then let him perform the operation until he learns the skill.

Whether motor or mental, the process is much the same in that learning follows a certain curve or pattern. A typical learning curve for skills training is shown in Figure 32.

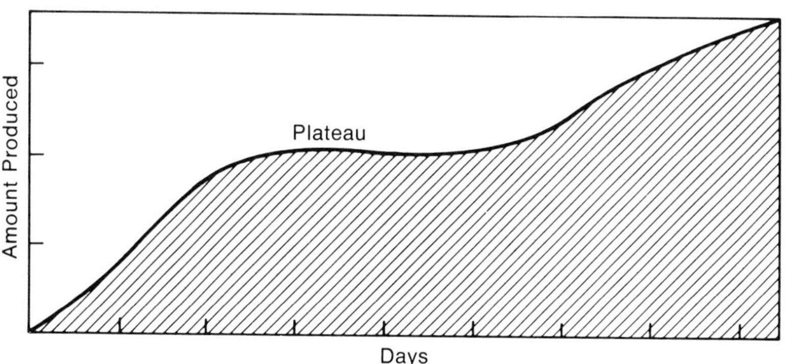

Figure 32 Typical Learning Curve for Motor Skills with Plateau

As this curve indicates, the first trials are slow, then there is rapid improvement followed by a leveling off that may remain level for a period of time. The leveling off slope of the curve is called a *learning plateau.* Plateaus frequently, but not always, occur in skills training, and some research supports the theory that since they occur at approximately the same time, they are caused by lack of motivation. For example, when an employee is learning a task and reaches a point where he shows no improvement for a period of time, he may become so discouraged that he will stop trying to improve his performance. Individual attention, changing the method of practice, or charting the individual's work and showing him his day-to-day progress are ways in which plateaus may be overcome or avoided. Rest periods are another means by which skills learning may be improved. Studies show that short rest periods given at frequent intervals increase the employee's performance in learning certain tasks. Consequently, whereas plateaus do occur, they do not indicate that learning has ceased.

CONCEPTUAL LEARNING. This type of learning deals with the individual obtaining a mental picture of abstract ideas or facts about a class of particular things. It first involves learning a set of principles or facts, then using these principles or facts as clues to associate them with a larger picture or idea. Concepts are drawn from the individual's experience and training and may represent concrete objects (machines, procedures, specific rules, and so on) or abstract ideas (philosophy of management, leadership, human nature). This type of learning involves a process called concept formation. In this process, through experience the individual builds up identification of various categories of things. Consider how a child forms his concept of DOG. First, he learns that the family collie is a DOG. This DOG has four legs, long fur, long snout, short upright ears, and a long bushy tail. It barks and is friendly. It is also quite large (bigger than he is, but smaller than his father). Secure in his notion of DOG, the child then confronts a bulldog and finds he must adjust his concept. Dogs can be different sizes. They may have short hair and almost no tail. They may have short, ugly snouts. They still bark, are friendly, and have upright ears. Then one day the child learns that there is such a dog as a Mexican hairless. An almost radical change occurs in his concept of DOG, but the resulting picture is a more valid view of the whole class. Eventually, of course, the child gets a wide range of experiences and his concept of DOG is complete. He reaches the point where he can see new animals and correctly classify them as dogs or not-dogs. He knows a dog when he sees one. Once a concept is formed, the individual may then learn to generalize by seeing the relationship between two or more concepts, thereby widening his mental picture of classes of ideas or objects. Closely associated with thinking and problem solving, conceptual learning, unlike skills learning, cannot be as readily observed.

In the section above, the two basic types of learning are discussed separately for convenience. This does not mean that the two types are not interrelated or should be taught as individual entities. In most situations training can be made more effective if both skills and conceptual learning are taken into account. For example, a student studying auto mechanics may be learning to perform a specific operation, such as changing a carburetor on a certain car. In the process, he is learning new concepts and generalizations, perhaps learning new applications of mechanics principles. He increases his interest in internal combustion engines. He learns something about the engine in general. So, his experience results in changes in his ways of seeing, feeling, thinking, and doing, although his instructor may have been primarily concerned with his ability to change a carburetor. However, it should be recognized that due to individual differences, the extent to which skills and concepts are learned is predicated on the employee's ability (aptitude). It may be found that some employees possess the mental capacity to comprehend only the simplest concepts but at the same time have extraordinary coordinative ability to master a motor skill. On the other hand, an employee may be endowed with exceptional intellectual ability but with little capacity to learn a motor skill. Although the two examples are possibly exaggerated, the point to remember is that all employees do not have equal ability to learn either skills or concepts, and both mind and muscle must be considered.

Principles of Learning

Despite the wide array of research on the topic, actually little is known about how people learn. However, over the years, experimental and educational psychologists have advanced many theories and from these theories certain principles or generalizations have emerged that can be applied in most training situations. Since the application of these principles is included later in the chapter, they will only be identified at this time:

1. People learn best when they are ready to learn and have a reason for learning.
2. People learn best when they are shown immediate results or feedback of their progress.
3. People learn best through participation.
4. People learn best when they are rewarded for correct responses or desired behavior.
5. People learn best when material is distributed in parts over a period of time rather than when it is scheduled continuously.
6. People learn best if the learning experience is pleasant and their first experiences are positive and successful.
7. People learn and remember best when the experience is vivid, dramatic, or exciting, and is meaningful.

8. People learn best when new ideas, subjects, topics, or exercises can be related to their present knowledge and past experiences.
9. People learn skills best through practice and repetition.
10. People learn concepts best when built from the "ground up" with relationships between elements clearly established and linked to the individual's experience and training.

In applying these principles to a training situation, the manager must also realize that people learn best when training is organized and material is presented in a logical sequence with the purpose and specific goals of the training clearly defined. Moreover, it should be remembered that these principles only help establish the optimum conditions for learning; they do not assure that learning will take place. Learning is an individual process and occurs only when the individual wants to learn and is self-motivated to change his behavior.

IDENTIFYING TRAINING NEEDS

Obviously, before training can be conducted, the need for training must first be identified. Training needs can be classified in two basic categories: (1) The need for initial training, and (2) The need for continuing training. The first category concerns the need for new job training, whereas the latter pertains to developing employees in their present jobs or preparing them so they can progress to other jobs. In either case, the need for training is the difference between the employee's current level of proficiency on one hand and the desired level on the other.[1]

Initial Training Needs

In identifying training needs for a new job, the requirements may be determined through job analysis and the job description discussed in Chapter 10. If no job analysis has been made, the manager may make his own analysis by preparing a job breakdown. A job breakdown can be made by systematically listing all tasks involved in the job, and then indicating the knowledge and skills required for each task. A sample job breakdown for a warehouseman is shown in Figure 33.

[1] See Joseph Tiffin and Ernest J. McCormick, *Industrial Psychology,* 5th ed. (Englewood Cliffs, N.J.: Prentice-Hall, Inc., 1965), p. 287.

JOB BREAKDOWN	
Position: Warehouseman Function: Receive, store, and issue material.	
TASKS	JOB QUALIFICATION REQUIREMENTS
1. Unpack incoming mail	Knowledge of nail pullers, box slitters, claw hammers, wire and metal cutters, and other tools used in opening a variety of types of containers. Knowledge of methods of salvage of cartons, crates, packing material, etc.
2. Identify items and count for invoice verification	Knowledge of nomenclature of item by use of catalogs, past experience, or illustrations. Knowledge of units of measure such as: gross, reams, bbls, cwt, rods, grams, etc. Ability to read, write, and make simple mathematical calculations; e.g., add, subtract, etc. Knowledge of interchangeability of items for receipt or issue purposes.
3. Inspect for obvious damage	Ability to spot water damage, broken items in unopened cartons, crates, etc. Knowledge of effects of corrosion on items not packed according to shipping instructions.
4. Establish stock locations	Knowledge of space utilization and stock arrangement; e.g., use of 4-inch items in bins having multiple of this width (12, 16, etc.). Knowledge of access of space to various heat, cold, and humidity conditions and placement of items in relation to the properties of the items to be affected by such conditions. Knowledge of flammability of items and types of care to be given various items for fire protection. Knowledge of inventory age and methods of "LIFO" (Last in-First out), and "FIFO" (First in-First out) receipt and distribution patterns. Knowledge of items needing turnover to protect or preserve; e.g., turning of certain materials for aging, mixing.
5. Others	

Figure 33 Typical Job Breakdown

After the job breakdown has been made, the training needs can be determined by matching the skills of the employee with the requirements of the job. This method is particularly applicable in determining the training needs for inexperienced employees in low skilled jobs where skills and knowledge can be easily and readily observed and deficits of employee qualifications are apparent. For new jobs of a more complex nature and for employees with experience, training needs are less obvious and may have to be assessed over a period of time. In either case, a job breakdown or job description is a basic tool for determining new job requirements on which training needs can be based.

Continuing Training Needs

In most departments, changing circumstances create a need for continuing training, either for certain individuals or groups of employees. These needs are less obvious than those for initial training, and no method for precisely determining continuing training needs has yet been devised. Observation of certain factors, however, often provides the manager with clues of training needs. High absenteeism and turnover, low production, frequent accidents, excessive waste, and poor work quality are common indicators. Skills inventory, work count, and work distribution study, discussed in other chapters, are useful in assisting the manager in identifying training needs of his department. Also, individual training needs may be identified during the performance review or the counseling interview.

TRAINING OBJECTIVES

Once needs have been identified, the manager should next develop objectives for his program. Objectives give direction to the training and establish the results expected. Therefore, they should be specific and when possible stated in measurable terms. This will depend on the nature and type of training, but it means that when developing the objectives for the program, the manager should decide as closely as possible what the outcome is expected to be. For example, if the training is to improve production of a department, the manager may establish an objective for that department of so many units per day, week, and so on and then plan the training program to meet that objective. Or in the case of training individual workers, if the requirement is fifty units per worker per day and a worker is only producing forty-five units, the objective may be stated this way: To increase production five or more units per day by training in work procedures, skills, or whatever the case may be. In these examples, objectives may be stated in specific and measurable terms since the desired results can be factually determined through record keeping. Work factors that can be stated in this manner are turnover, absenteeism, errors, accidents, production quotas, or other factors where records are kept and the results expected can be stated in measurable terms. In most skills training, the objectives can also be stated specifically and in measurable terms. If, for example, the training is to teach a worker or a group of workers to operate a certain machine, the objective may be stated like this: The objective of the training is for each worker to learn how to operate the (name of machine) through demonstrated performance. In the above example, the training objective can be stated specifically since the results can be determined through objective evaluation. Some training is of such a nature that objectives cannot be determined and stated precisely nor can the results be measured objectively. Training to improve overall effectiveness, to improve attitudes or morale, sales training, and management and supervisory development are examples of such training. Since the objectives of training programs of this general type are concerned with employee development, they can be stated in these terms: To improve work habits; to improve human relations, and so on. Although the results expected cannot be expressed in measurable terms, the overall desired results may be related to more concrete objectives. For example, the improvement of work habits may lead to improved performance; the improvement of human relations may influence turnover, absenteeism, errors, accidents, and the like. Although the specific results of such training may be intangible, the results may be manifested in other areas. Therefore, the objectives of employee development training may be stated in the expected improvement in other areas. Whether objectives are specific or broad, in program planning they should serve as the fundamental guide for organizing the program and evaluating results.

TRAINING METHODS

When training needs have been identified and stated in terms of well-defined training objectives, the manager should consider the best approach to use in producing the desired results. This involves identifying the method by which the training is to be conducted.

The manner in which the training is to be conducted is referred to as the training method. There are many methods that the manager can use, but four of the methods most often used are listed below.

On-the-job Training

On-the-job training is the most common method used to train workers to do a job. On-the-job training (OJT) is conducted in the work area under actual working conditions. It may be used to teach a specific job or used in connection with a job rotation plan. OJT is economical since the worker is producing as he learns, and no special equipment or facilities are required. This type of training can be conducted by the manager or assigned to an experienced worker. In the case of teaching a specific job, OJT works best in developing skills rather than concepts. When used as a part of a job rotation plan, OJT is more effective when it is integrated with other methods.

Vestibule Training

This method is similar to OJT, except that the training is conducted away from the work area. In this method, mock-ups of actual machines, equipment, or processes are set up for demonstration, practice, and review. Vestibule training is appropriate when training is of a continuing nature due to a high turnover or work expansion, and when the training on the actual equipment is hazardous or when the work is such that little production could be gained in the process of the training. Vestibule training is normally conducted in groups, but as individuals reach the desired level of proficiency, they should be assigned to their particular jobs where their training may be continued by OJT.

Apprenticeship Training

Although this type of training is more a system than a method, it is discussed here since it is a means by which the manager can train his employees. The purpose of apprenticeship training is to assist an individual in learning a particular trade or craft. It involves both classroom and on-the-job training. It is a cooperative effort of management, government, and if applicable, the union, and involves obtaining approval and agreement of all concerned. Apprenticeship training is for a specified duration and is best used in building a labor force of skilled craftsmen (machinists, carpenters, printers, plumbers) who will be needed over a long period of time.

Guided Group Discussion

When the objective of the training is to shape attitudes, disseminate information, or to develop concepts through the interchange of knowledge and ideas, this method is appropriate. Group discussion may be used as a separate method or in combination with one of the other methods. In this method, employees are allowed to criticize and discuss topics presented under controlled conditions, the degree of control depending on the nature of the topic and background of the employees.[2]

[2] How to lead a group discussion is covered in Chapter 18.

TRAINING MATERIAL

The topics, data, subject matter, principles, practices, techniques, and other information that the employee of the training program needs to know, understand, and apply are called materials. For this information to be meaningful to the employee, the material must be carefully selected and logically organized.

Material Selection

Obviously, the material selected should be of such nature to meet the objective of the training. This being so, no attempt will be made here to belabor the kinds of material that should be considered in developing individual programs. However, in selecting material these criteria may prove useful:

The employees' intellectual level and experience level should be taken into account. This means that before the material is selected, the manager must make an assessment of the individuals who will receive the training. Whereas this should be axiomatic, it is often overlooked. Too frequently, programs are developed based on incorrect assumptions. If, for example, the manager is an expert in the subject himself, he may make the erroneous assumption that his employees should have equal knowledge and select material far above the level of his employees. On the other hand, if the assumption is made that the employees know nothing about the subject, it is possible that the training will be ineffective since it will be teaching something they already know. Selecting the material that strikes the right balance is therefore a key factor in program development.

The material selected should support one or more of the program's objectives. In applying this criterion, the material can be weighed against each objective by asking the question: Will the material help the employee achieve the desired behavior change sought by the objective? This simple test will permit the manager to reject extraneous material and select material that is both appropriate and useful.

The third and final criterion for selecting material is determining whether it is appropriate and useful. This criterion involves a summation of the two mentioned above. Here, the manager should look over the topics he has selected and make a final determination as to whether they meet the two criteria previously established. If the material takes into account the level of the employees, it is appropriate. If it can be applied to support the program's objective, it is useful. The two taken together constitute the basis for material selection.

Material Organization

In organizing the material for the training, the manager should consider both the sequence in which the material is to be presented and how it will be distributed over the training period.

SEQUENCE. For material to be meaningful, it should be organized in a logical sequence to support the learning objectives. This means that main points should relate to other main points, and each subpoint should add meaning to the main point it supports, so the total integrated pattern supports the training objectives. The detailed design for such a pattern will of course depend on the method and type of training. However, most job-oriented training can be arranged according to three levels or phases to form a logical sequence.

At the *introduction* level, the employee should become keenly aware of the specific objective and the general topic of the training. This level should introduce information that sets the stage for more important material, create the conditions of the program or lesson, or is motivational in nature. The employee should become familiar with the basic nature of the material, understand the objective, and become motivated to learn.

At the *development* level, the employee should gain knowledge of the material and understand its relationship. This includes introducing material specifically related to the subject to: (1) Build the necessary knowledge so the employee can recall facts and specific information concerning the who's, what's, when's, and where's about the subject, and (2) develop the necessary understanding of the subject so the employee can develop concepts and relate the material to previous experience and training. What is sought here is for the employee to become so thoroughly knowledgeable with the material that it will become part of his thinking and action pattern. To do this, the material may be organized in one of the following ways: (1) *From the past to the present.* This is a good way to sequence material when history or background of the topic is important. Discussing the history of the organization in a new employee orientation program is an example. (2) *From the simple to the complex.* This sequence should lead the learner from the fundamental element of a subject to an understanding of involved relationships and concepts. In filling out a form, for example, the material may be sequenced to first show the use of the particular form, then how the form is applied to a particular operation, and finally, how the operation is related to the whole organization. (3) *From the known to the unknown.* The final sequence starts with something that is already known as a point of departure, then the material is organized to lead the learner into new ideas and concepts. For example, if the training is to teach skilled workers how to be "trouble shooters," the material may begin with the employees' background based on the subject and then be sequenced to teach trouble detection and problem solving.

At the *application* level, the employee should be able to use previous physical or mental learning. Physical application involves the employee's ability to perform the particular skill being taught. On the other hand, mental application includes the employee's ability to develop ideas and concepts, or to apply principles in solving problems. To instruct application of physical skills, the employee should be given material that will allow him to perform operations under supervision. Conversely, to instruct mental skills, the employee should be given material that will allow him to demonstrate his ability to relate principles to real or hypothetical job situations.

Within the framework of the three levels, the material for most training programs can be organized in a format consistent with the type of training. This may consist of a single plan to teach one man a simple job in one session, or a series of courses or programs to develop employees over a long period of time. In any event, the levels of learning are important in sequencing the material in a logical way. However, it should be understood that the intensity at which each level is stressed and the degree in which it is to be presented to the employees should be directly related to the objectives of the training and the ability of the employees. For example, if the objective of the training is to teach a simple skill for immediate application to a worker with limited conceptual learning ability and moderate muscular aptitude, the emphasis would be on introduction and skills application with the development phase being stressed to a far lesser degree. On the other hand, if the material is to convey principles and concepts in a program to teach senior workers how to be "trouble shooters," the emphasis would be on development and concept application. Other examples could be cited, but the point should be clear that in organizing material into a learning design, both the employees and the objectives must be closely considered. Moreover, it should be understood that although each level is presented separately, material may be organized in such a way that more than one level is presented. Examples of this will be given in some of the techniques discussed elsewhere in this chapter.

DISTRIBUTION. For material to be meaningful, not only must it be presented in a logical sequence, but properly distributed as well. As used here, distribution refers both to the manner in which the material is spaced over the training period and the breakdown of the material within the training designed. Therefore, to determine how the material should be distributed, the manager may seek the answer to the question: "Is it better to teach material continuously without a rest period (break), or will breaks increase learning?" The answer to this question depends on the type of learning. For example, in learning a physical or mental skill many studies show that rest periods have a positive affect on learning. These studies indicate that when tasks are continuous over a period of time without a rest period (mass practice), learning decreases, and when rest periods are given, learning improves. These studies also indicate that spacing rest periods at frequent intervals increases learning still further. On the other hand, when learning is conceptual or when the learning of skills is sequential, rest periods tend to break up the learning pattern and thereby decrease learning. Consequently, it can be concluded that in learning a mental or physical skill requiring repetition (such as memorizing a list of terms, typing, producing a single part on a machine) it is best that the material be organized to allow breaks or other activities. However, when learning a concept such as general principles of human behavior or the interrelations of the parts of an internal combustion engine, the material should be organized and distributed as a related whole or block.

TRAINING TECHNIQUES

Once the manager has selected and organized the material best suited to meet a particular training need, he can then select the technique or a combination of techniques for getting the information, concepts, or the skills to be learned across to the employee. There are many techniques the manager can use. Six of the more common techniques are identified and briefly discussed below.

Demonstration–Performance

This is a common technique widely used in teaching an individual or a group how to perform certain skills. It is based on the principle of learning by doing and is the fundamental technique applied in on-the-job, vestibule, and apprenticeship methods of training. The demonstration-performance technique puts theories and concepts into action where employees learn physical and mental skills under supervision. It can be applied in teaching simple administrative procedures, such as filling out a form, or more complex mechanical tasks. Skills requiring the use of tools, machines, and equipment are particularly suited to this technique.[3]

Role Play

Another technique of learning by doing is the role-play. As the title implies, it involves the manager having the employee assume the role of a particular person under a certain set of circumstances, and then having the employee

[3] The four-step job instruction method, discussed in Chapter 12, applies here.

act out the role. This technique is best suited to the guided group discussion. It is especially suitable in teaching principles of interpersonal relations, since it allows both the group observing the role-play and the participants to gain insight into their own behavior. In selecting the role-play technique, the manager should be astutely aware of his employees so he can determine their reactions if asked to participate.

Case Study

The case study is a technique that requires the employee to participate actively in problem solving, which may be either hypothetical or real. The case is first presented to the employee or group in the form of a situation or instance that contains essential data concerning the problem. The employee or group then analyzes the data, evaluates the problem, decides on the applicable principles, and finally recommends a solution. The case study technique is based on the premise that if the employee can solve problems in a conference situation, he will be able to solve similar problems on the job. This technique is suitable in teaching the application of selected principles or to simulate conditions related to the job.

The Lecture Technique

In the lecture technique, the instructor presents and interprets the information to be learned. Since it is based on one-way communications, allowing little or no feedback from the employee, used alone it is a very poor technique of instructing. Therefore, the lecture technique is more effective when used with other techniques, or when it is used separately, providing the employees with the opportunity to question the material presented. The lecture technique is useful in introducing a new subject, summarizing ideas, showing relationships between concepts and practices, and reemphasizing main points. The lecture technique is also useful when dealing with employees with little experience, when there is a large group involved, or when some general information on new policies, methods, and procedures is to be explained and placed into operation immediately.

Programmed Instructions

An emerging technique in employee training is the use of programmed instructions. Programmed instructions, first developed by Harvard University psychologist B. Frederick Skinner, are based largely on reinforcement (rewarding the student for correct responses) by having the employee respond to a frame of information and then providing him with immediate feedback (knowledge of how well he is doing). An example of programmed instructions is shown in Figure 34.

Page 21

Your answer: 52.5

Good. Now you know how to compute centile rank. Memorize the formula:

$$\frac{\text{Below} + \frac{1}{2}\text{ tied}}{\text{Total}} = \text{Centile rank}$$

Another way of expressing a relative score is by means of Rank Order. We are now ready to compute it. Rank order is just another way of showing the relative position occupied by any individual in the group. It is expressed as a fraction in which the denominator indicates the number in the group; the numerator is the individual's position from the top of the group. For example, 3/75 tells us that this person is third highest in a group of 75 people.

In order to compute rank order we must first arrange the raw scores, as we did for centile rank, from the highest to the lowest, including all duplicate scores. The following are the raw scores for a group of nine students:

38, 36, 35, 34, 32, 29, 27, 26, 22

What is the rank order for the person whose raw score is 29?

	Page
A. 4/9	24
B. 6/9	18
C. 1/3	27

You came from page 20.

Page 18

Your answer: 6/9

Good! You are on to the mechanics of the method and it isn't difficult to count down. However, all cases aren't as easy as this one.

When you have more than one person at any given score it would be unfair to assign different ranks to each of them. We must arrive at just one rank order for these three people as no one of them ranked higher or lower than the other two. We do this by determining which positions these scores would hold in the sequence of scores and average them. For example; if the score 84 was held by three people and there were eight other scores higher, these three would actually occupy positions 9, 10, and 11 in the sequence of scores (the eight higher scores would have used up positions 1 through 8). We would then average 9, 10, 11 $\frac{(9 + 10 + 11)}{3}$ and get 10.

This is the one rank order we would assign to *each* of the scores, 84. If there were 40 people in the group we would report this rank order, 10/40.

Try this:

In the following distribution of raw scores,

73, 68, 69, 74, 74, 67, 74, 70, 71, 75

what is the rank order for a score of 74?

	Page
A. 8/10	19
B. 4/10	23
C. 3/10	26
D. 2/10	30

You came from page 21.

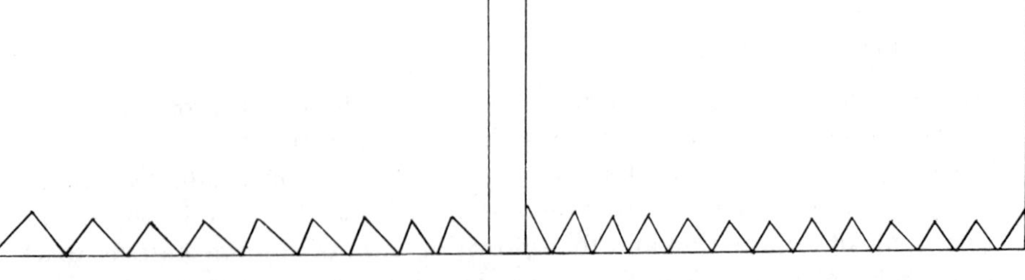

Page 24

Your answer: 4/9

You must have started counting from the bottom instead of from the highest score down.

Page 21 is your destination.

Page 27

Your answer: 1/3

Your mathematical instinct fouled you up. This is one computation where you never reduce fractions.

You probably know the basic methods but go back to page 21 and be sure.

Figure 34. Typical Example of Programmed Material (Courtesy of U.S. Air Force Department.)

As this figure shows, the material is designed so that the successful completion of information takes the employee one step closer to the learning objective (desired behavior change). The material is presented either by machine or in book form and is available commercially for many industrial and business subjects, or some organizations prefer to develop their own. This technique can be used separately or with other techniques in groups or on an individual basis. Since programmed instructional material allows an employee to learn at his own rate, the technique is particularly suited when one or a small number of employees are to be trained by self-instruction, or when there is a wide variance of learning levels within the group.

Using Training Aids and Devices

An overlapping technique in getting information across is the use of aids and devices. Unlike the techniques mentioned above, aids and devices are not self-supporting. Their primary use is to support, supplement, or reinforce other techniques and may be visual or aural, or a combination of both. Aids and devices include motion pictures, film strips, slides, and transparencies that can be used in various types of projectors. Also included are models and mock-ups, charts, graphs, illustrations, and other visual material. Another aid becoming widely used in employee training is television. Although sometimes used as a separate technique, since television does not permit feedback or an interchange of information between the instructor and the student it is more effective when used as an aid to supplement instruction rather than as a separate entity. Therefore, like other aids, the use of television should be made an integrated part of the total learning experience.

TRAINING SCHEDULE

As the term implies, scheduling is the process of selecting the time and place for conducting the training. Although this is a very important phase of program development, it is contingent upon so many variable and extenuating circumstances that the discussion here is limited to only some basic factors that apply to most training programs.

Possibly the most important factor to consider is making time for the training. Many worthwhile training programs simply never get started. The reasons for this are twofold. First, most training is normally conducted on organization time, therefore, it is both costly and inconvenient. It is costly since it ties up employees and takes them away from their work, and it reduces productivity. It is inconvenient since it disrupts routine. Second, whereas most organizations and managers alike play "lip service" to training, some actually feel that it is a waste of time. These organizations and managers may develop training programs and discuss training needs but never have it scheduled. Therefore, the manager should make training a continuing part of his routine schedule and be convinced himself and be able to convince others that the training will be worth the cost. Also, unless the manager is convinced that the program will be given, the program should never be developed in the first place.

The second factor that should be considered in scheduling training is the employees involved. When possible, training should be scheduled for a time that is convenient for the employee, and his personal needs should be taken into account. This is particularly important when the training is scheduled on the employee's time. Also, in this case, whether the employee will be paid for the time spent in training should be clarified, not only for the personal satisfaction of the employee but from the legal aspect as well. (Laws concerning this subject are very complex and may require expert interpretation.)

The final basic factor to consider is the place of the training. This includes both the facility where the training is to be given and the equipment and devices to be used in the training. This is the "make ready" part of scheduling, and how well it is done may influence the training outcome. Although things will never be ideal, such things as poor lighting, too little or too much heat, noise, poor acoustics, inadequate and badly organized training aids and equipment should be avoided whenever possible. A systematic way in which this can be done is by making a checklist. The checklist can include those things mentioned above, plus any other items that apply to a particular program.

After the manager has considered these basic factors, he should develop a schedule consistent with the program requirements.

INSTRUCTIONS

The manner in which training is to be carried out is referred to as the instruction phase. Since the success of the training program will depend in large measure upon the quality of instructions, in developing the program the manager should give careful consideration to two important factors: (1) Who should conduct the training, and (2) The qualifications of the trainer.

Who Should Conduct the Training?

The answer to this question depends on the circumstances. The manager may want to conduct the training himself or have others do the training for him. In some instances, it may be best that the training be conducted by an outside consultant or through the assistance of training and educational institutions such as vocational or trade schools, colleges, or universities. Further, if the organization has a training department, the instructor may be provided through that department. (However, it should be noted that the primary role of a training department is to train trainers and provide assistance to the manager in developing, improving, and evaluating his program, not to do the training.) All these sources should be considered, but the best person to do the training is the employee's immediate supervisor. This is true for several reasons. First, since the purpose of the training is to change or modify behavior, the immediate supervisor is, in the final analysis, the person who determines how the employee should behave. Therefore, he is in the best position to set the atmosphere where the behavior change can take place. Secondly, by virture of his position, the employee's immediate supervisor should be better prepared to recognize individual differences, personal goals, and other individual characteristics that are important to learning. Finally, the employee's immediate supervisor is the best person to blend the contents of the training plan with the experience and expected performance on the job. Despite the fact that the immediate supervisor is the best person to do the training, this does not make his selection as an instructor automatic. To be effective, he must be qualified as a trainer.

Trainer Qualifications

A common fallacy in selecting a trainer is making the assumption that a man who knows the job or subject can automatically teach others. Although job or subject knowledge is important, other equally important factors must be considered if the training program is to be successful. Like leadership, traits and characteristics that constitute the qualifications of a good trainer are inexact and difficult to define. But in selecting a trainer for a program, the following list of qualifications may be used as a guide:

1. He should command the respect of the employees with whom he deals.
2. He should have a first-hand knowledge of the job and problems of the employees.
3. He should speak the language of the employees and use expressions most commonly used by all of them.
4. He should be interested in the employees, be sympathetic and understanding.
5. He should develop the ability to stimulate employees to do their own thinking and to express their own ideas.
6. He should learn to ask thought-provoking questions.
7. He should possess a good sense of humor.
8. He should be quick in his reactions—quick to analyze, quick to observe, quick to think.

9. He should be tactful and patient, diplomatic at all times, and firm when necessary.
10. He should strive to develop a personality that appeals, attracts, and wins confidence and respect.

As pointed out previously, some organizations have training departments to train their trainers in the skills of motivating employees to learn, making the instructions fit the needs of the individuals, and encouraging employee participation. If this is not the case, such skills can be learned by taking a "How to Instruct" course offered by an educational institution.

EVALUATION

When developing a training program for a department, provisions should be made to evaluate the effectiveness of the training. Although the trainer should be perceptive of individuals during the training, the program as such should be evaluated in terms of the overall results. Specifically, program evaluation should help the manager answer the question: Did the training produce the desired results?

Since results are manifested in both tangible and intangible forms, getting exact answers to this question is no easy matter. But possibly the best way is the "before" training and "after" training correlation technique. In order to evaluate training by this method, it is necessary that existing conditions be recorded before training begins. By recording such things as turnover, absenteeism, grievances, quality and quantity of employee output, or job training time at the beginning of the program, a base is available upon which an evaluation can be made. At the termination of the program, when enough time has elapsed for significant results to be shown, the conditions can then be recorded in the same manner as before. This "before" and "after" training information can then be compared and the results evaluated. While this method works best for training where data can be indicated quantitatively, by using morale and attitude surveys and questionnaires to show "before" and "after" information, this method can be used to a limited degree to evaluate the results for such programs as human relations training and sales training.

The best way of obtaining "before" and "after" information is by examining existing records. Of course the extent that this can be done will depend upon the adequacy of records and the type of training. But records common to many organizations that the manager can use in obtaining information to evaluate most training programs include the following: (1) Individual performance records, (2) Safety and health records (dispensary visits and frequency and severity accident records), (3) Quality records, (4) Turnover records, (5) Absenteeism, (6) Grievances, (7) Cost, (8) Suggestions,

(9) Morale and attitude surveys, (10) Termination or exit interviews, and (11) Wage incentive, earnings or output.

KEY POINT SUMMARY

1. An effective way for a manager to modify and shape the behavior of his employees so they can perform as members of the organization is by developing a training program for his department.
2. Basically, developing a training program involves the process of identifying training needs, selecting the best course of action to meet these needs, and evaluating the results. A systematic method of doing this involves these steps:
    a. Understanding how people learn
    b. Identifying training needs
    c. Developing training objectives
    d. Selecting a method of training
    e. Selecting and organizing the material
    f. Selecting the training technique
    g. Scheduling the training
    h. Selecting the instructor
    i. Making provisions for evaluating the training
3. To understand how people learn, two factors should be considered:
    a. Types of learning, both skills and conceptual
    b. The principles of learning including ten common factors (see page 291).
4. The need for training can be identified by comparing the difference between what the employee knows and what he should know. This can be done for both initial training needs and continuing training needs as follows:
    a. Initial training needs can be determined by comparing the employee's skill with a job description or job breakdown.
    b. Continuing needs can be identified by observing certain indicators such as high absenteeism and turnover, low production, frequency of accidents, and so on.
5. Because objectives give direction to the training program and furnish a means by which results may be evaluated, they should:
    a. Be stated in measurable terms, where possible.
    b. When this is not possible, objectives should be indirectly related to some measurable and tangible results.

6. In selecting the manner in which the training is to be given, one or more of four common methods may be used:
    a. On-the-job training
    b. Vestibule training
    c. Apprenticeship training
    d. Guided group discussion

7. In order for the material to be meaningful, it must be carefully selected and logically organized.
    a. In selecting the material, the manager must consider the educational and experience level of the employee.
    b. For best results, material should be organized in a logical sequence and properly distributed.

8. The common technique that the manager may use to get the material across to the employee includes:
    a. The demonstration–performance technique
    b. The role play technique
    c. The case study technique
    d. The lecture technique
    e. Programmed instructions
    f. Training aids and devices

9. To schedule training effectively, the manager should consider:
    a. Making time available for training
    b. Selecting a time convenient to the employee involved
    c. The facilities where the training will take place and the equipment and devices involved

10. Since the success of any training program will depend on the manner in which the material is presented, prime consideration should be given to the quality of instructions. Therefore, the manager should consider:
    a. Who should conduct the training
    b. The qualifications of the instructor

11. Although there is no foolproof way in which training can be evaluated for all training situations, the "before" and "after" method should be used when possible. This method involves two steps:
    a. Review and record the conditions before the training begins.
    b. Compare the same information with the conditions after the training has been completed when sufficient time has elapsed to show results.

DISCUSSION QUESTIONS

1. In developing a training program for his department, what basic process should the manager use? Relate this process to planning and problem-solving.
2. When selecting a course of action, what specific steps should the manager consider?
3. In reference to skills and concept learning, what are their basic differences and how are they interrelated when applied in a training situation?
4. What relationship is there between each of the ten principles of learning and the following factors: (a) motivation, (b) individual differences, and (c) the communications process.
5. In developing a training program, why is it necessary to identify training needs, how can needs be divided, and how can needs be identified?
6. In reference to objectives, what is the relationship between training objectives and the functions of planning and controlling?
7. What training method would be most appropriate to use in the following situations:
   a. To train a group of experienced salesmen in the use of a new product?
   b. To instruct a select group of technicians to be supervisors?
   c. To teach one clerical worker how to operate a new machine (cash register, adding machine, or others)?
   d. To develop a group of trade school welding graduates?
8. In reference to the four situations indicated in the question above, answer the following questions:
   a. Which of the situations would involve more conceptual learning? Skills learning?
   b. In which situation would the Plateau of Learning phenomenon most likely occur and how should it be handled?
9. In developing a training program, why is the selection and organization of material important and what factor should the manager consider in each area?
10. In reference to getting the material across to the employee, which technique or combination of techniques could the manager use in each of the situations indicated in Question 8?
11. In scheduling a training program, what three factors should the manager consider and why is each important?
12. Why is the employee's immediate supervisor the best person to use as an instructor, and why can't he be used in all cases?
13. What is the most effective method to use in evaluating the results of training. Relate evaluation to the program's objectives.

CASE PROBLEMS

Case 17–1

Lex Tabor, a department manager in a large retail chain store, has received numerous complaints from customers concerning the way they were treated by his sales personnel. The employee makeup of the department consists mostly of housewives working to supplement their family incomes and girls on their first jobs, with students from the local high school distributive education program being used on a part-time basis. Since none of his regular employees has had any training except being shown how to do his particular job, Lex decided that formal training would help solve the customer complaint problem in his department. In addition to customer relations training, Lex knew that his employees also needed training in such things as the proper preparation of sales slips, cash register operation, housekeeping, and the general principles of good selling.

Questions

1. *How should the objectives of Lex's training program be stated?*
2. *What methods would be most appropriate to use?*
3. *What factors should Lex consider in selecting and organizing his material.*
4. *What techniques would work best in getting the material across?*
5. *What possible scheduling problems would Lex have?*
6. *What would be the advantage of Lex instructing the program himself versus getting an instructor from the local high school?*
7. *How can Lex evaluate the results of his program?*
8. *Should the part-time high school students be included in the training program?*

Case 17–2

A small manufacturing organization hired a number of "hard-core" disadvantaged employees under the "JOBS" program sponsored by the National Alliance of Businessmen. After these employees were given a thorough orientation, they were assigned to the various departments for further job training. Two of the employees were assigned to Ben Alexander's department for training as assemblers. These two particular assembly jobs consist of fitting a cover plate over an opening and machine riveting the plate in place. While the duties are not hard to learn, they are repetitious, monotonous, and boring. In fact in the past, Ben has had a problem keeping the jobs filled.

Questions

1. *What factors should Ben consider when deevloping a training program for these two employees, particularly in the following areas:*

a. The method to use
b. The technique to use
c. The principles of learning a skill
d. The principles of learnıng
e. The distribution of material

SELECTED REFERENCES

AMRINE, HAROLD T., JOHN A. RITCHEY, and OLIVER S. HULLEY, *Manufacturing, Organization, and Management* (2nd ed.), Chap. 7. Englewood Cliffs, N.J.: Prentice-Hall, Inc., 1959.

ECKER, PAUL, JOHN MACRAE, VERNON OUELLETTE, and CHARLES TELFORD, *Handbook for Supervisors,* Chap. 7. Englewood Cliffs, N.J.: Prentice-Hall, Inc., 1959.

GILMER, B. VON HALLER, *Industrial Psychology,* Chap. 7. New York: McGraw-Hill Book Company, 1961.

TIFFIN, JOSEPH, and ERNEST J. MCCORMICK, *Industrial Psychology* (5th ed.), Chap. 10. Englewood Cliffs, N.J.: Prentice-Hall, Inc., 1966.

18

How to Hold Group Discussions

An effective means of managing people is through group discussions. As indicated in previous chapters, the group discussion is not only useful in allowing employees to participate in decisions that affect them, but is also an effective method to use in certain training situations and when applying the creative approach of problem solving. Group discussions can be formal (as in the case of a conference) or informal. The formal discussion or conference is planned and organized around a specific topic with a definite objective in mind, whereas the informal discussion is less structured with the purpose of allowing the group to release pressure. In this chapter, techniques for holding a formal group discussion are discussed. However, since it is obvious that conference leadership can only be learned through actual practice, this chapter is primarily concerned with outlining the procedure and providing some fundamental techniques the manager can use to make his group discussions more effective. With this in mind, the following topics are examined: (1) role of the discussion leader, (2) planning the meeting, (3) pattern for leading a discussion, (4) how to use questions, (5) how to use the chalk board or chart pad, (6) how to handle problem individuals, (7) how to handle problem conference situations, and (8) evaluating the discussion.

ROLE OF THE DISCUSSION LEADER

The basic role of the manager as a discussion leader is to guide and control the discussion. The degree to which this is required depends on the type and nature of the discussion. There are three general types of group discussions or conferences.

Informational Type

In this type of discussion, the role of the leader is to impart information. It may be in the form of an address or a lecture, or it may be of a visual nature, using motion pictures, film strips, slides, drawings, and printed material. In conducting a discussion of this type, the leader's control is greatest. He guides the meeting closely along predetermined lines. The leader attempts to gain group acceptance by allowing the participants to assist in developing the topic, and by permitting the group to discuss and criticize the material presented. Conclusions are largely predetermined but not forced on the group.

Opinion Seeking Type

This type of discussion is used when the manager needs the advice and opinions of others in making a decision. In this case, the leader clearly defines the topic, establishes limits for the discussion, and selects those who attend for their knowledge and experience concerning the subject, or employees who are capable of analyzing the topic and offering opinions and suggestions. The leader allows free discussion of the topic within the framework he has established, and encourages group members to offer their opinions and suggestions. Final decision, however, is left to the leader-manager.

Problem-Solving Type

In this type of meeting, the leader serves as the chairman or coordinator of the conference. In this capacity, the leader need not be an expert in all phases of the topic being discussed, nor need he be an accomplished public speaker. His role is to: (1) Introduce and present the topic for discussion, (2) Stimulate the free exchange of knowledge and experience, (3) Keep the objective of the discussion clearly before the group, and (4) Guide the discussion toward the objective by assembling and evaluating facts and opinions necessary to draw conclusions or impart factual information. Like the opinion-seeking conference, participants should have knowledge of the topic or be capable of analyzing the topic being discussed. One of the creative approaches to problem solving may be used in this type of conference.[1] The group draws its own conclusions, and participants have complete freedom in discussing the topic.

Before leaving the role of the discussion leader, it should be noted that most conferences are not purely of one type. The types tend to overlap, and

[1] See Chapter 16.

all three types may be evident in one conference. Also, it is important to note that regardless of the type of meeting, the less control the leader exercises over the group, and the more he encourages and permits employee participation, the better are the chances of the group accepting the conclusions and ideas derived from the meeting.

PLANNING THE MEETING

The key to the success of any group discussion is proper planning, but before a meeting can be properly planned, the manager should ask himself some fundamental questions. These include: (1) What is the specific objective of the meeting? (2) Could some other less costly method be used to achieve the objective? (3) Is the topic of general interest? (4) Who should attend? (5) What type of conference should be used? (6) Will the results be worth the cost? After the manager has convinced himself that a group discussion is the best way to handle a particular situation, the meeting can be planned according to certain guidelines.

The Discussion Outline

The discussion outline is the leader's plan for conducting the conference. It is the most basic and most important element in discussion planning. It permits the leader to think the topic through in detail, and allows him to anticipate in advance the participants' responses or reaction to the topic. Depending on the type of discussion, the outline can be formal or informal, detailed, or simply a set of notes. To be an effective instrument for leading a conference, the outline should include these elements:

1. The objective of the conference.
2. A brief outline of the topics to be discussed, arranged in a logical sequence with a time schedule.
3. Key points to be covered.
4. Questions to be asked.
5. Aids and materials to be used.
6. Summary and conclusion.

A formal discussion plan is shown in Figure 35.

As this outline indicates, a discussion plan is not a script of a prepared speech, but a working guide that allows flexibility. In preparing an outline such as the one shown, the discussion leader can use the top portion to state the objective of the discussion and develop a topical outline and time allotted for each topic. On the right side, he can briefly outline his introduc-

DISCUSSION PLAN

Discussion Topic: ____________________

Objectives:

1. ____________________

2. ____________________

Topical outline and time schedule: Minutes

1. ____________________ ________

2. ____________________ ________

3. ____________________ ________

4. ____________________ ________

(Summarize major points in bold outline form on this side of sheet.)

Introductory Remarks

____

____

(Continue with draft of your discussion, setting down all necessary information.)

____

____

Summary

____

____

Aids and Materials

(List aids that you will require.)

____

____

Figure 35 Typical Discussion Plan

tory remarks, list essential information, outline his summary, and note the required aids and materials. On the left side, he can list key words and phrases, questions to be asked, illustrations, and references to the conference aids.

Have Materials Ready

The next step in planning a discussion is to prepare the materials to be used in the discussion. The materials may include any aids and devices that will assist the discussion leader in conducting the meeting. Such materials as slides, handouts, film, mock-ups, and demonstration models may be effective aids for some conferences, but basic to any group discussion is the chalkboard or chart pad. These materials can be used to: (1) Direct thinking to a specific topic, (2) Record key information, and (3) Summarize the discussion. The chalkboard has the advantage of providing greater flexibility since it can be erased and ideas reconstructed. On the other hand, the chart pad provides a permanent record, may be displayed, or duplicated and returned to the group. The chalkboard or chart pad should be positioned where it can be clearly seen by all members of the group and arranged to avoid glare.

Arrange Time and Place

Once the discussion plan has been prepared and materials have been made ready, the leader should next arrange the time and place for the meeting. This step involves: (1) Selecting a time most convenient to everyone, and assuring that those who are to participate are notified well in advance of the meeting, (2) Seeing that the facility is properly lighted, well ventilated or heated, and free from distractions, and (3) Seeing that ample seating and workspace are available, ash trays are provided, and that the participants will be as comfortable as possible. When possible, the tables and chairs should be arranged to form a "U" or a three-quarter "Box" rectangle. This seating arrangement affords each participant maximum visibility and the discussion leader better control over the meeting.

PATTERN FOR LEADING THE DISCUSSION

Before discussing the various techniques the manager can use in leading a conference, the pattern to follow should be first understood. Although each group discussion will be different, making it impossible to discuss specific situations in detail, the following general pattern can be applied to most conference situations and serve as a guide for understanding the techniques discussed later in the chapter.

Introduction

In many ways the introduction is the most important step because it sets the attitude of the group. The introduction determines how well the group is willing and able to participate later.

In opening the conference state the objective clearly and give a brief description of each topic to be discussed and its importance.

Use chalk board or chart pad for general guidance by entering the general heading of the topic or problem and adding subheadings and columns as discussion develops.

Show a film introducing the subject if applicable.

Drawing-Out

It is at the drawing-out stage that the discussion really starts. The entire meeting can be made or broken here. The leader must introduce material that the group can understand and discuss without fear of embarrassment or ignorance. Well-planned questions will be of considerable help. The following points should be considered:

Guide the discussion toward the conference objective by: (a) questioning those points that do not seem pertinent, (b) helping members to express or clarify their thoughts, (c) calling for illustrations, diagrams, cases to clarify points, and (d) establishing new objectives that come from the group.

Relate the outline on the board or pad to the conference objective by entering the essential facts, points, or ideas that may lead to solution of the problem. If necessary, get group agreement on restatement of item; when several points are offered at once, ask members to hold the contributions for further consideration.

Acceptance and Control

Acceptance and control are the most distinctive characteristics of a discussion. Many different and conflicting opinions may have been expressed up to this point. Now the discussion leader must organize and compromise. He may have to reason and hold discussion with individual members. This is a true test of leadership, for he must get members of the group to reconcile their views and accept a basic set of ideas. The points to be considered are:

Discourage faulty thinking, biased judgments, or narrow viewpoints expressed by conferees; use "pro and con" analysis; list advantages and disadvantages of a course of action; analyze causes and remedies of a difficulty.

Keep the discussion "on the beam" through restatement of the original problem; postpone side issues until the main point has been settled; question why a seemingly irrelevant remark is being made if it has nothing to do with the problem under discussion.

Influence the discussion by: (a) "speed-ups"—discuss a specific case that will provoke interest; make entries on chart promptly; raise suggestive questions, and (b) "slow-ups"—clarify a point through injection of illustrative cases; question whether all sides of the problem have been considered; summarize the opinions expressed on the point at issue.

Deal with the "problem" members of the group. The leader must consider peculiar characteristics of group members and deal with them as individuals.

Summation

Having obtained acceptance, the group leader now summarizes the highlights of the discussion and emphasizes the major conclusions that have been agreed upon. He may also review the actions or steps that will be taken as a result of the meeting.

Closing

Close the meeting at the time established in the outline. Invariably certain members will want to continue the meeting after the discussion has been summarized. Under no circumstances should the discussion leader allow a few individuals to monopolize the time of the majority of the group. He should close the meeting tactfully by inviting the ones who have questions to remain after the meeting. However, if a majority of the group is interested in further discussion, another session should be arranged.

HOW TO USE QUESTIONS

One of the most effective means of directing and stimulating employees' participation is the use of questions. Questions can be used in the following situations.

1. To open the discussion.
2. To stimulate interest.
3. To provoke thinking.
4. To accumulate information.
5. To get individual participation.
6. To develop subject matter.
7. To determine a member's knowledge.

8. To change the trend of the discussion.
9. To arrive at a conclusion.
10. To terminate or limit discussion.

Some specific examples of questions and how they can be used are shown in Figure 36.

QUESTIONS

Type of Question	Example
1. Leading questions suggest answers	Would you fire or transfer that person in this case?
2. Factual seeks facts, data, etc.	What is the cost of repairing this typewriter?
3. Direct directed at specific person	Mr. White, what are your men doing?
4. General or Overhead directed at entire group, anyone to answer	What is the meaning of good supervision?
5. Ambiguous two or more meanings	Is it a good policy to "ride" a worker?
6. Controversial two or more answers	Are leaders born or made?
7. Provocative to incite answers	What do you think of the statement: "Most supervisors drive their men too hard?"
8. Redirected directed at leader, but returned to the group	Mr. Clark asks,'What is meant by "seniority?"' Conference Leader: 'Mr. Jones, how would you define "seniority?"'
9. Yes or No calls for "yes" and "no" answers	Did you attend the last conference?
10. Why, When, Where, What Follows "yes" and "no" type used alone to stimulate thinking	What kept you from attending the last conference? Why is promptness important?

Figure 36 Types of Questions and Examples

In addition, questions can be categorized and used for specific purposes.

Directed Questions

Directed questions are aimed at a specific member of the group. This type of question can be used to lead off a discussion or redirect the discussion along certain paths. Also, directed questions are useful to involve members who are reluctant to participate. However, the leader should use caution to avoid embarrassing the timid member or using this questioning technique too excessively.

Overhead Question

The overhead question is directed at the group in general to provoke or channel group thinking or to stimulate discussion. For example, if the discussion begins to drift from the topic or if the group as a whole is slow to participate, the overhead question can be used to focus attention on the topic and stimulate group thinking and participation.

Reverse Question

Using the reverse question, the leader directs the question back to the person who asked it. This technique can be used effectively when the leader is convinced that the participant knows the answer, is using the question as a means of expressing his own opinion, or to put the discussion leader on the spot. Also, when the topic pertaining to the question has been fully covered, the reverse question can be used to encourage the group member to think more constructively. In using the reverse question, the leader should be well aware of the particular individual's personality and his probable reaction. This technique should be used sparingly. If participants feel that they will be called on to answer each question they ask, they may become convinced that it is better to keep quiet.

Redirected or Relay Questions

Questions addressed to the discussion leader may be redirected to another member or to the total group. This type of question is useful to obtain group opinion, to get acceptance of the answer through group responses, or when the leader feels a participant has special knowledge of the topic. Whereas it is a good practice and often necessary for the discussion leader to occasionally answer questions himself, he is primarily concerned with stimulating group discussion. The redirect or relay questioning technique is a good means for allowing members to do their own thinking and the leader to avoid answering too many questions.

HOW TO USE THE CHALKBOARD OR CHART PAD

As pointed out earlier, the chalkboard or chart pad is an effective aid to direct thinking, record key information, and summarize the discussion. To do this the major topic of the discussion may be written across the top of the chalkboard or chart pad followed by major points as they are developed, and at various points of the discussion the group's conclusion can be summarized. If the chart pad is used, the sheets can be retained for future reference. Since this is not possible with a chalkboard, the discussion leader should assure that the information is understood by all concerned before it is erased. When using the chalkboard or chart pad the following points have proved helpful.

Rephrase the information in as few words as possible. While the group is discussing a point, the time can be used to condense the discussion into a word or a short phrase. In doing this, do not quibble over words, but use words familiar to the group.

Know what is to be written before turning to the chalkboard or chart pad. Record information promptly, legibly, and rapidly. This will increase the tempo of the meeting and stimulate participation.

Do not block the view of members by standing in one spot. By moving from side to side, you give each participant a better opportunity to see the information.

Talk while writing by reading what is being written, elaborating on the point, or asking the group to respond to the information.

Talk to the group, not to the board or pad. Stand sideways and maintain frequent eye contact with the group. If the discussion leader turns his back to the group he loses temporary control.

The chalkboard or chart pad can also be used for prepared outlines, charts, graphs, or other visual illustrations. These devices are particularly applicable in the informational type of conference. When prepared illustrations are used, they should be of high quality, simple, and adapted to be an integrated part of the overall discussion.

HOW TO HANDLE PROBLEM INDIVIDUALS

Human nature being what it is, in most groups certain individuals require special attention. Although the problem individuals usually are few in number, unless properly handled, they can have a devastating effect on the conference. Some common situations that develop with the problem individual and suggested ways the discussion leader can handle them are identified and briefly outlined here.

The Member Who Talks Too Much

This type of individual will monopolize the discussion unless he is controlled. The methods to consider in handling this individual are:

1. Seat him near the front, either to the left or right of the leader where he can be conveniently ignored.
2. Avoid direct eye contact.
3. Tactfully ask another member's opinion concerning the topic being discussed.
4. Establish a limit on the amount of time one member can talk.

The More Experienced Member Who Knows All the Answers

Often, this type of individual can be of great value to the conference if properly handled. To do this, the leader may:

1. Let him know that his opinion is respected, but the discussion is to obtain everyone's point of view.
2. Use him as the anchor man for the discussion.
3. Direct technical questions to him that need further explanation.
4. Talk to him privately and solicit his support.

The Participant Who Is Argumentative and Critically Opposes the Views of the Leader and Other Members

This type of individual can wreck a meeting because he is interested in only his own views. He is very hard to handle, but may respond to this treatment:

1. Try to discover why he is hostile.
2. Treat his questions and comments as if they were sincere and normal.
3. Reword his contributions so they appear more acceptable.
4. Relay his questions to the entire group or reverse the question for his answer.
5. Allow the group to express their dissatisfaction with his behavior.

The Individual Who Talks Too Little

These individuals are of two types: The timid and the disinterested. The leader may use these techniques to encourage participation:

1. Ask directed questions pertaining to his work.
2. Ask a question that he will be able to answer.
3. Praise him whenever possible.
4. If feasible, ask him to help in some phase of the meeting such as putting up charts, distributing handouts, and so on.

The Member Who Starts a Conversation with His Neighbor

This situation is impossible to avoid and unless carried to the extreme, it should be tolerated. But if prolonged, the leader can use the following to bring those involved back into the discussion:

1. Interrupt and ask a direct question.
2. Ask one of the members to repeat his remarks to the group.
3. If the leader is talking he can stop, if he is sitting he can stand or make some movement that will attract attention.
4. Forcefully but tactfully call for order.

HOW TO HANDLE PROBLEM CONFERENCE SITUATIONS

The most effective way to prevent problems in leading a group discussion is by proper planning and by recognizing some of the "don'ts" in conference leadership. These "don'ts" include: (1) Don't argue, (2) Don't ridicule, (3) Don't take sides, (4) Don't lecture, (5) Don't talk too much, and (6) Don't try to dominate the thinking of the members. These techniques will prevent most problems, but in many group discussions the leader will be confronted with certain problem situations that he did not anticipate. Some common problem situations and suggested ways the leader may handle them are identified and outlined below.

Group Will Not Participate

A passive group is one of the most common problems in leading a group discussion, especially if the group members are unacquainted with each other, or if the members are not directly involved in the topic being discussed. When this situation occurs, the leader may try one or more of these techniques:

1. Diverge slightly from the main topic to introduce some topic of more general interest that can then be related to the main theme.
2. Start a discussion or stimulate an exchange of views by directing a question to someone who knows the answer.
3. Use a "yes" or "no" question, then follow up with a "why" question.
4. Address an overhead question to the group, preferably of a provocative nature.
5. Show by your questions that you are alert and interested.

6. Do not use questions that may antagonize the group or put a member on the spot.
7. Make an intentional misstatement that members will challenge, or temporarily take a positive stand on a controversial point.
8. Relax the group by telling a pertinent story.

Discussion Wanders from the Topic

Occasionally a well-planned discussion will wander from the topic. When this happens the following are suggested:

1. Using a direct question, ask how this discussion is related to the problem at hand.
2. Gradually tie in the remote conversation with the main topic.
3. Introduce new material closer to the central theme.
4. Summarize what has been discussed up to this point.
5. Use the time to take inventory of the progress of the conference or to plan the next step.
6. Avert such digressions by carefully planning the conference, announcing the plan to the group, and adhering to it.

Group Refuses to Accept Conclusion of Discussion Leader

In the problem-solving conference, the conclusion drawn by the discussion leader may differ from that of the majority of the group. If this occurs, the following are suggested:

1. The leader may have to compromise.
2. Guide the discussion closely so that the same conclusion comes from the group in different words.
3. Encourage those participants who agree with the discussion leader to take his side and talk.
4. Use the relay question. When a participant challenges the leader's statement, have another participant answer the challenge.
5. Take a poll of the participants.

The Discussion Lacks or Loses Tempo

When the discussion runs out of steam, the leader may speed up the discussion by these methods:

1. Cite specific cases that will provoke discussion.
2. Ask the group to give special examples from their experiences.
3. Take an opposite or controversial point of view.
4. Ask directed questions.
5. Ask overhead questions.

The Discussion Is Moving too Fast, or the Leader Is Losing Control

In groups where the interest is intense, members may get carried away by the discussion causing the leader to sense that he is losing control. In this situation, the leader may:

1. Get the group's attention by standing up, asking a directed question, or calling on the participants to repeat their statements.
2. Summarize the discussion up to that point.
3. Introduce a new phase of the topic.
4. Tell a "that reminds me" type of story.

EVALUATING THE DISCUSSION

After each group discussion it is a good policy for the leader to evaluate his performance. This should be done after each conference. Only by practice and critical evaluation can he master these five essential elements: (1) Being prepared, (2) Getting off to a good start, (3) Keeping the discussion on the topic, (4) Obtaining full cooperation and participation of the members, and (5) Summarizing the discussion so that the participants feel that something has been learned or accomplished. The self-rating scale included below can be used to assist the discussion leader in evaluating his performance. By indicating a "yes" or "no" response to each statement and by multiplying the number of "yes" responses by five, his overall effectiveness may be determined. A score of below seventy-five is considered poor, whereas a score of ninety-five is excellent.

LEADER'S SELF-RATING SCALE

No.	*Statement*	*Yes*	*No*
1.	Necessary preparations for the meeting were properly handled.	___	___
2.	The meeting started on time.	___	___
3.	There was good discussion—all members participated.	___	___
4.	Questions were well planned, properly asked, and provoked discussion.	___	___
5.	Discussion seemed to be spontaneous and not forced.	___	___
6.	Discussion was progressive; it kept on topic and was directed toward the attainment of the objectives.	___	___
7.	Offering my own personal opinion, lecturing, or domineering was avoided	___	___
8.	An attempt was made to get participants to recognize and respect the opinion of others.	___	___

9. I did not take sides in any discussion. ___ ___
10. I refrained from answering questions, referring them back to group. ___ ___
11. Expressing of opinions and ideas on my part was avoided. ___ ___
12. Rephrasing was used only when it was necessary, using the simplest words possible and being brief. ___ ___
13. Control was maintained over the conference at all times. ___ ___
14. Frequent summaries of the discussion were made to crystallize group thinking. ___ ___
15. A chalkboard or chart pad was used effectively. ___ ___
16. All essential topics or phases of the outline, excluding application, were covered. ___ ___
17. Interest was maintained throughout the meeting. ___ ___
18. The group left with something to think about, so thinking would continue after the conference was over. ___ ___
19. A final summary was made with the help of the group. ___ ___
20. The meeting closed on time. ___ ___

KEY POINT SUMMARY

1. The group discussion is an effective means to:
   a. Allow employees a degree of control over their work
   b. Train employees
   c. Solve problems
2. The role of the manager as a discussion leader is to guide and control the discussion within the framework of three general types of meetings:
   a. The informational type
   b. The opinion-seeking type
   c. The problem-solving type
3. The key to successful conference leadership is proper planning and involves three steps:
   a. Preparing a discussion outline
   b. Having materials ready
   c. Arranging for time and place
4. The general pattern for leading a discussion includes these steps and should be understood by the manager.
   a. The introduction
   b. The drawing out
   c. The acceptance and control
   d. The summation
   e. The closing

5. One of the most effective means of guiding and controlling group discussions is the questioning technique. Questions are of the following types:
   a. The directed question—to a specific member of the group
   b. The overhead question—to the group in general
   c. The reverse question—back to the member who asked it
   d. The redirected or relay question—leader switches question back to another member or to the entire group

6. Another effective device in leading a conference is the chalkboard or chart pad. When using this tool the leader should remember:
   a. To rephrase the information in as few words as possible
   b. To know what is to be written before turning to the board or pad
   c. Not to block the view of the group
   d. To talk while writing
   e. To talk to the group, not to the board or pad

7. Though few in number, the discussion leader should be able to recognize and handle the problem individual. These include:
   a. The member who talks too much
   b. The member who knows all the answers
   c. The member who is argumentative and contrary
   d. The individual who talks too little
   e. The member who starts a conversation with his neighbor

8. In addition to the problem individual, the discussion leader may be confronted with certain problem conference situations. These include:
   a. Group will not participate
   b. Discussion wanders from topic
   c. Group refuses to accept the conclusion of the conference leader
   d. Discussion lacks or loses tempo
   e. Discussion moves too fast, or leader loses control

9. To determine his effectiveness as a discussion leader, the manager should rate his performance.

DISCUSSION QUESTIONS

1. What is the purpose of a group discussion?
2. What are the three major types of group discussions, and what is the role of the manager-leader in each type?

3. What are the steps in planning a conference and what does each step involve?
4. What are the steps or phases in leading a discussion, and what should the discussion leader consider in each phase?
5. What are the basic types of questions the conference leader can use in guiding and controlling a meeting? Give an example of each.
6. In leading a conference, how can a chalkboard or chart pad be used?
7. In using the chalkboard or chart pad, what points should the discussion leader remember?
8. Who are the problem individuals that a leader must identify, and what are some of the techniques the discussion leader can use in handling each type?
9. What are some common problem situations with which the discussion leader is often confronted, and how can each be handled best?
10. Why should a manager evaluate his performance after each discussion he leads?

CASE PROBLEMS

Case 18–1

A manager of a large department has been notified of a major reorganization that will affect approximately two-thirds of his employees. After thinking the situation over, the manager decides that he will hold a group discussion to:

1. Inform his employees of the change.
2. Obtain their suggestions as to how the change can best be brought about.
3. Solicit their cooperation in making the change and ask the help of his senior members in solving certain problems that he can foresee.

Questions

1. *What type of group discussion would best serve in this particular situation?*
2. *Who should be asked to attend the meeting? All employees? Only those directly affected?*
3. *In planning the meeting, what factors should be considered?*

Case 18–2

After leading his first group discussion, a young manager made an analysis of his performance using the self-rating scale on page 325 as a guide. Although he was generally satisfied with the way the meeting was conducted, his analysis showed a need for improvement in five areas. In relation to the statements on the checklist, these areas were:

No. 3. There was good discussion—all members participated. (Some members of the group did not participate at all, whereas a few talked too much, and some seemed to know all the answers.)

No. 4. Questions were well planned, properly asked, and provoked discussion. (Questions did not stimulate discussion.)

No. 6. Discussion was progressive. It kept on the topic and was directed toward the attainment of the goal. The discussion frequently wandered from the topic, and members talked among themselves.)

No. 13. Control was maintained at all times. (Occasionally, he felt that he did not have command of the situation, and at times the meeting moved too fast or too slow.)

No. 15. A chalkboard or chart pad was used effectively. (He had trouble summarizing the discussion, and he would temporarily lose control when he turned to write on the chalkboard.)

Questions

1. *What factors are involved in each of the above situations?*
2. *How could the manager have handled each situation effectively?*

SELECTED REFERENCES

Conference Leadership, Manual of Instruction prepared by Technical Aids Branch, Office of Industrial Resources, International Cooperation Administration, Washington, D.C.

Conference Leadership Training, Technical Bulletin No. 21. Office of Industrial Resources, International Cooperation Administration, Washington, D.C.

Suggestions on the Conduct of Small Group Discussions, New York: American Management Association.

19

How to Simplify and Improve Work

Work simplification has been defined as the organized use of comomn sense to find easier and better ways of doing a job. Stemming from the pioneer work of Frank and Lillian Gilbreth, the primary objective of this technique is to increase productivity and reduce cost. Actually, it is nothing new. The first wheel, the first plow, the first sail, are age-old examples of work simplification. Work simplification is a tool through which management may measure, predict, analyze, and make better decisions. It is a process that can be used anywhere by any manager. It can be used with success not only in industrial plants but also in offices, stores, laboratories, and service industries. It can apply to people, material, or processes. By knowing and applying the fundamental principles, processes, and practices discussed in this chapter, the manager can make better use of his resources. An understanding of these techniques will be developed under these topics: (1) pattern for work simplification, (2) flow process chart, (3) layout diagram, (4) motion economy, and (5) an integrated approach to work simplification.

PATTERN FOR WORK SIMPLIFICATION

About a half century ago the father of the scientific approach to management, Frederick Taylor, was charged with increasing the productivity of a giant steel company. He started by observing how a crew of shovelers went about their work. After watching and observing dozens of different shovelers doing various kinds of shoveling from light pea coal to heavy iron ore, he came out with one conclusion that may be considered the fundamental element in methods as applied to the factors of production. That conclusion was that there is "one best way" to do a given job. For the shovelers, he found a shovel load of approximately twenty-one pounds produced the highest production with the least worker fatigue.

As a result of his observation on the example just cited, he concluded that for each step in a productive process, there is always a "one best way." This observation of Frederick Taylor's did not come about by chance. He made actual observations that stimulated him to find better ways to improve services, lower operating costs of companies, and raise production. And again he concluded that there is always one best way in any productive process.

For the manager to find the "one best way" to perform an operation, he needs to use a pattern. A uniform pattern is required in all work simplification effort.

Selecting the Job to Be Improved

In the first step of work simplification, careful consideration should be given to the job to be improved. Common sense probably will indicate the operation, task, or process that is causing the most trouble and therefore where the need for improvement is greatest. However, a careful study of the following factors will provide hints of where jobs in need of improvement may be found:

1. Work that involves the most expenditure of money, man-hours, and use of machines.
2. The major work being done to accomplish the mission of the activity.
3. The anticipated length of time the work will be done. Will the work be done for only a few weeks or months, or will it last for a long period of time?
4. Work involving many workers.
5. Work that involves highly skilled people may require simplifying so that less skilled persons can do it.
6. Failure to meet performance requirements, which results in backlogs and requires overtime work.
7. Work not meeting required standards of quality.
8. Work that results in waste of energy, material, and time.
9. Work that results in numerous accidents or is dangerous. Work that results in near accidents.
10. Work that involves great physical activity and must be done with frequent rest periods.
11. Work that is undesirable because of extreme conditions, such as dust, noise, fumes, temperature, and other unfavorable conditions.

Breaking Down and Recording the Job Details

The next step in the pattern of work simplification is to break down the job and record every detail. This is a very important step. Unless this is done accurately and completely, the task, operation, or process cannot be soundly analyzed. Information should be sufficient to allow questioning of any detail that may affect the total process. In applying this step it is important to remember not to omit seemingly insignificant information. It may be found later that these minute data are important in developing an improved method. Also, the sequence in which the work is being done is important. Details should be recorded in the order of occurrence to avoid confusion when making the analysis.

Analyzing the Job Details

In analyzing the job, each detail should be questioned. The most important question that should be asked over and over is: *Why is it necessary?* This question may lead to the elimination of details, or even major parts of the job being analyzed. There is little value in improving a job that is unnecessary. After asking the basic question—Why?—the following ones should be applied:

1. *What* is the purpose of each detail? Why?
2. *Where* should each detail be performed? Why?
3. *When* should each detail be done? Why?
4. *Who* should do each detail? Why?
5. *How* should each detail be accomplished? Why?

Because some of the information will come from other individuals, it is wise to be sure that this information is based on facts and reason, not opinions and excuses. Only factual data will form the sound base for developing a new and improved method.

Developing a New and Improved Method

In this step of the work simplification pattern, new and improved methods of doing the task, operation, or process should be developed. The answers to the questions in the previous step should furnish clues to possible improvement. For example, the overall question—Why is it necessary?—may show that a particular task or a portion of a job can be eliminated. Answers to other questions may suggest that related details be combined in a single process, or that changing the sequence of a process may reduce the time and cost of the task and increase productivity. This may in turn result in further elimination and combination and permit simplifying necessary details. Therefore, *eliminate, combine, change the sequence,* and *simplify* are key words in developing a new and improved method. Also, making the work easier and safer is important. Once the new method is developed, it should be worked out on paper. If approval is required before the new method is installed, which is often the case, the write-up should be in the form of a proposal. A typical proposal sheet is shown in Figure 37.

In developing the proposal sheet, the workability and practicality of the new method should be clearly demonstrated. This means that although the proposal should be kept brief, proof that the new method will produce better results must be shown. Contrasting the new and old methods in a "before" and "after" fashion is an effective means of presenting a proposed method.

WORK-SIMPLIFICATION PROPOSAL SHEET

TO: ____________________ __________
(Supervisor) (Date)

FROM: ____________________ __________
(Organization Unit)

WORK STUDIED: ____________________

PROPOSAL:

SAVINGS INSTALLING COST

Figure 37 Typical Proposal Sheet

Installing the New Method

The final step in the work simplification process is getting the new method accepted and putting it into effect. In taking this step, the human factor should be considered.

Possibly the greatest human factor to overcome is resistance to change. As noted in previous chapters, people generally resist change of any kind. This is particularly true if criticism of past methods is implied in the new improvement. To avoid resistance to change as much as possible, the manager should: (1) Allow the employee being affected by the change to participate in developing the new idea, (2) Ask the opinion and advice of this employee and encourage him to develop work simplification suggestions of his own, (3) Convince him that the new method will make work easier, simpler, or safer, and (4) Assure the employee that no criticism of past methods is implied. Also, it is a good idea to coordinate the proposed method with others who may have useful suggestions or who will be directly involved in the change. In all cases, give credit where credit is due.

FLOW PROCESS CHART

A valuable tool in applying the work simplification pattern is the flow process chart. This chart is shown in Figure 38. Not only is the flow process chart useful in breaking down the work in detail, but it can serve as an aid in analyzing the details as well.

Chart Preparation

In preparing this chart, after the information in the upper left hand corner has been completed, each step in the process should be recorded sequentially and identified according to five basic symbols: operation, transportation, inspection, delay, and storage. These symbols and a brief description of each are included in Figure 39. When taking this step, details should be as clear and concise as possible since the symbols are not substitutes for written steps. Distance should be entered on the chart when transportation is used. Quantity and time should be listed with operations, inspections, and delays. A standard unit of time should be used throughout. After all steps have been recorded and identified, a line should be drawn from one symbol to the next, thus connecting each step in the process. This will help the symbols to serve as a guide in analyzing a process and in developing or installing improvements.

FLOW PROCESS CHART		NO.	PAGE NO.	NUMBER OF PAGES
PROCESS				
☐ MAN OR ☐ MATERIAL				
CHART BEGINS	CHART ENDS			
CHARTED BY	DATE			
ORGANIZATION				

SUMMARY						
ACTIONS	PRESENT		PROPOSED		DIFFERENCE	
	NO.	TIME	NO.	TIME	NO.	TIME
○ OPERATIONS						
⇨ TRANSPORTATIONS						
□ INSPECTIONS						
D DELAYS						
▽ STORAGES						
DISTANCE TRAVELED (*Feet*)						

STEP NO.	DETAILS OF METHOD ☐ PRESENT ☐ PROPOSED	OPERATION / TRANSPORTATION / INSPECTION / DELAY / STORAGE	DISTANCE (*In feet*)	QUANTITY	TIME	ANALYSIS (*Why?*) WHAT? WHERE? WHEN? WHO? HOW?	NOTES	ANALYSIS CHANGE: ELIMINATE COMBINE SEQUENCE PLACE PERSON IMPROVE
		○⇨□D▽						
		○⇨□D▽						
		○⇨□D▽						
		○⇨□D▽						
		○⇨□D▽						
		○⇨□D▽						
		○⇨□D▽						
		○⇨□D▽						
		○⇨□D▽						
		○⇨□D▽						
		○⇨□D▽						
		○⇨□D▽						
		○⇨□D▽						
		○⇨□D▽						
		○⇨□D▽						
		○⇨□D▽						
		○⇨□D▽						
		○⇨□D▽						
		○⇨□D▽						
		○⇨□D▽						
		○⇨□D▽						

Figure 38 Flow Process Chart

Analysis

When all details are recorded, a systematic analysis of the data on the chart should be made by asking the questions: Why? When? Where? Who? and How? Answers to the questions may suggest steps in the process that could be eliminated, combined, rearranged, or simplified. In analyzing each step,

FLOW PROCESS CHART SYMBOLS

OPERATION ○	Wrapping Part	Drill Hole	Typing Letter
	An operation represents the main steps in the process. Something is created, changed, or added to. Usually transportations, inspections, delays, and storages are more or less auxiliary elements. Operations involve activities such as forming, shaping, assembling, and disassembling.		
TRANSPORTATION ⇨	Move Material by truck	Persons Moving Between Locations	Move Material by Carrying (messenger)
	Transportation is the movement of the material or man being studied from one position or location to another. When materials are stored beside or within two or three feet of a bench or machine on which the operation is to be performed, the movement used in obtaining the material preceding the operation and putting it down after operations are considered part of operation.		
INSPECTION □	Examine for Quality and Quantity	Review for Accuracy	Checking for Information
	Inspection occurs when an item or items are checked, verified, reviewed, or examined for quality or quantity and not changed.		
DELAY D	Material Waiting in "in" Basket	Person Waiting in Line	Waiting for Signature
	A delay occurs when conditions do not permit or require immediate performance of the next planned action.		
STORAGE △	Suspense Copy in File	Material in Warehouse	Filed for Permanent Record
	Storage occurs when something remains in one place, not being worked on in a regular process, awaiting further action at a later date, permanent storage or disposal.		

Figure 39 Flow Process Chart Symbols

potential changes may be noted on the right hand side of the chart. The summary in the upper right corner may be completed by recording each action under "Present" column. After the analysis has been completed, a new chart can be prepared showing the proposed improvements.

LAYOUT DIAGRAM

Another useful method in simplifying work is the layout diagram. This diagram indicates the relationship of the flow of work, the physical movement of people, and the placement of furniture, machines, and equipment to the physical facility. The purpose of making a layout diagram is to provide the greatest physical ease to the greatest number of workers, and to provide the shortest and straightest distance possible in the processing and travel of material, documents, and personnel.

Diagram Preparation

A layout diagram is a plan or a sketch of the physical facilities of an office, department, shop, warehouse, store, or other work place upon which the flow of work is placed. To make a layout diagram, graph paper is best, but if this is not available ordinary paper will do. In drawing the diagram, all doors, windows, utility outlets, and other permanent fixtures that will affect the placement of furniture, machines, and equipment should be considered. Each piece of equipment should be indicated on the chart and labeled as to what it is, who uses it, and so on. When the diagram is prepared, the work flow can be traced on the diagram by showing distance and direction of flow. Different colored lines may be used to show different processes if the diagram is complex.

Analysis

Although the ideal layout may be impractical to achieve due to facilities, cost, and other conditions, most work situations can be simplified and improved through systematic analysis. In analyzing the layout diagram, where possible, the following factors should be considered:

1. Work flow should follow straight lines with a minimum of backtracking and cross-travel.
2. Persons having the most frequent contact should be located near each other.
3. Files, cabinets, and other records and material should be located conveniently near those who use them most.

4. Surplus facilities, such as furniture, tools, and so on, should be released to provide space for other purposes.
5. The allocation of space should be in keeping with the requirements of the work—that is, the best lighted and ventilated space should be used for work requiring closest attention and concentration, where possible.
6. The arrangement of men and equipment should facilitate supervision.
7. Persons using the same equipment should be grouped together.

After the layout has been analyzed, a new diagram can be made showing the proposed changes. The new chart will assist in putting the proposed method into effect. Also, when coupled with the present layout, it will show a "before and after" picture, which will be useful in getting the new proposal approved. A "before and after" chart is shown in Figure 40.

MOTION ECONOMY

An important factor in work simplification is motion economy. Motion economy prescribes the area in which a person can work more efficiently, and the fundamentals to be followed in accomplishing tasks with a minimum of physical effort. While associated with the field of industrial engineering, the manager does not have to be a methods engineer to apply motion economy to the job. He needs only to be familiar with certain fundamental principles which should be observed and some techniques for analyzing the basic motions related to the details of a job.

Work Areas

In applying motion economy to work simplification, the manager should first recognize that there is a *maximum* and *normal* work area for a person doing hand work. Work areas are shown in the illustration in Figure 41.

The maximum work area can be determined by having the employee extend each arm from the shoulder and making a circular sweep with the shoulders as the pivotal points. The overlapping areas formed by the arcs of the right and left hand make a zone beyond which two hands cannot work close together without moving the body.

The normal work area can be determined by tracing an arc in a similar manner. In this case, however, only the forearm is extended, with the elbows held close to the body. The overlapping area forms the zone in which work requiring the use of both hands can be done more conveniently. Also, eye travel is at a minimum within this area.

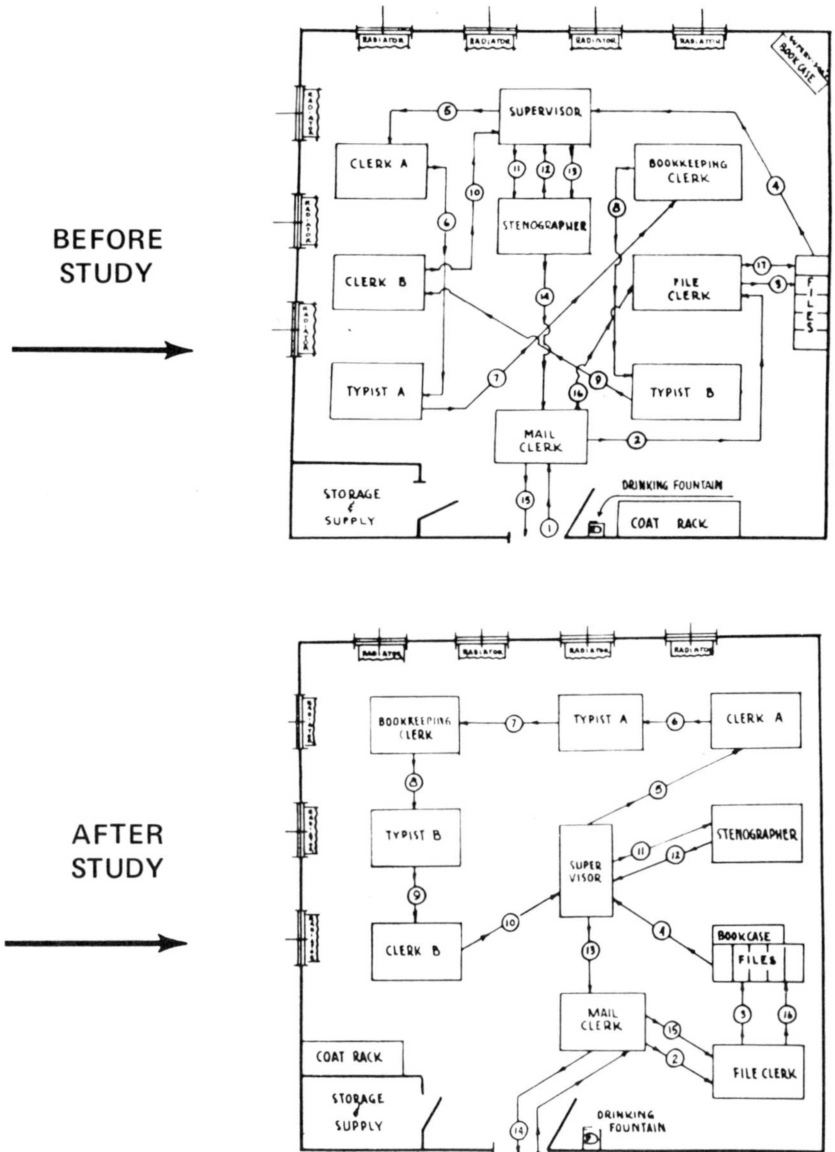

Figure 40 Before and After Floor Diagram for Office

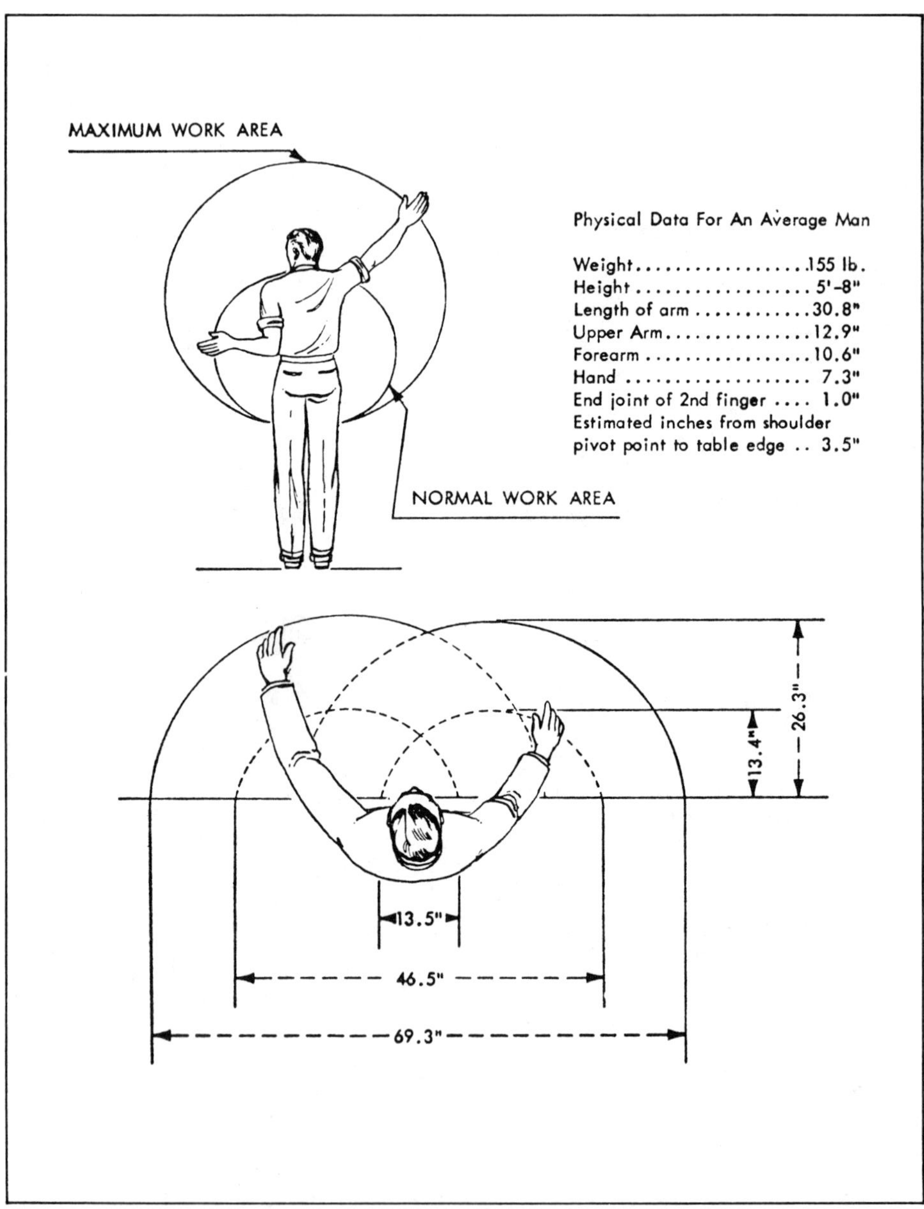

Figure 41 Minimum and Maximum Work Areas (Courtesy of U.S. Air Force Department.)

Fundamentals of Motion Economy

The number and type of basic motions involved in an operation will depend on the particular job. In production operations such as assembling, sorting, washing, repairing, and the like, the basic motions will be very small and detailed. In office and other general types of operations, the motions may include only such movements as walking, stooping, filing, sitting, and working. However, these motions should be observed and identified where possible. In doing this, these eleven fundamental principles apply:

1. Both hands should begin movements simultaneously.
2. Both hands should complete their movements at the same instant.
3. Both hands should not be idle at the same instant except during rest periods.
4. Motions of the arms should be in opposite and symmetrical direction and should be made simultaneously.
5. Hesitation should be studied and its cause eliminated whenever possible.
6. Hand motions should be as simple as possible to provide the fastest motions. Motions are classified from fastest to slowest as follows:
    a. Finger motions only
    b. Finger and wrist motions
    c. Finger and wrist, and forearm motions
    d. Finger, wrist, forearm, and upper arm motions
    e. Finger, wrist, forearm, upper arm, and body motions (This class requires a change in position whereas the first four do not.)
7. Material and equipment should be located as nearly as possible within the normal grasp area.
8. Sliding, rolling, and pushing, rather than carrying, is usually quicker for transporting small objects.
9. Straight-line motions requiring sudden changes in directions are not so desirable as continuous curved motions.
10. The sequence of motions should be so arranged that they increase the possibility of automatic rhythm.
11. Work equipment and materials should be put in place before work begins; their position should be settled to reduce the operations of searching, finding, and selecting.

Analysis

To assist the manager in analyzing a particular job and improving the motions involved, in addition to the basic questions of Why? What? Where? When? Who? and How? more specific questions may provide additional clues for improvement.

1. Are the simplest motions being used? Can they be made automatic?
2. Are desks, files, or workbenches arranged to permit efficient work flow?
3. Is work stored within easy reach?
4. Is there too much walking back and forth for tools? Materials? Finished products?
5. Is there jumping up and down to accomplish a task?
6. Are the right tools or equipment being used?
7. Can mechanical equipment replace manual work?
8. Is the most efficient means of transportation being used?
9. Has the comfort of the workers been considered?

AN INTEGRATED APPROACH TO WORK SIMPLIFICATION

Although the flow process chart, the layout diagram, and motion economy can be used separately, they are often more effective if integrated in a system consistent with the work simplification pattern discussed at the beginning of this chapter. This approach may be applied by using the following guide:

1. Review the work and select a task, operation, or process to be improved. Consider work where the improvement will result in the greatest savings and best use of resources.

2. Make a flow process chart and layout diagram. Consider all details.

3. Analyze the chart and diagram by questioning each detail. Consider motion economy principles.

4. Determine action. Consider eliminating any part or detail of the task, operation, or process, and combining or rearranging details that will simplify the job.

5. Make a new flow process chart and layout diagram for the proposed method. Consider ideas of the worker doing the job, supervisors doing related work, and ask for staff assistance if required.

6. Write up the proposal sheet. Consider and briefly state the advantages of the proposal, what resource savings will be realized, and how the new method will be placed into effect.

7. Submit work simplification project for approval. Consider this arrangement pattern: (a) Proposal sheet, (b) Flow process chart (present), (c) Layout diagram (present). (d) Flow process chart (proposed), and (e) Layout diagram (proposed).

8. Install the new method. Consider ways in which employee resistance to change may be overcome.

KEY POINT SUMMARY

1. Work simplification is the organized use of common sense to find easier and better ways of doing a job.
2. In applying work simplification, a uniform pattern consisting of five steps has proved effective. These steps are:
    a. Selecting the job to be improved. Use common sense, cost, time, and workload as criteria.
    b. Breaking down and recording job details. Consider all details and record them in the sequence in which they occur.
    c. Analyzing the job details. Question all details by asking Why? What? Where? When? Who? and How?
    d. Developing a new and improved method. Where possible eliminate, combine, change the sequence, and simplify details before writing up the new proposal.
    e. Installing the new method. Consider the human factor.
3. A basic tool for breaking down and analyzing a job to be improved is the flow process chart. Preparation of a flow process chart involves the following steps:
    a. Determine process, subject, and scope.
    b. Briefly describe each step.
    c. Apply the symbols (operation, transportation, inspection, delay, and storage).
    d. Record time, distance, and quantity where applicable.
    e. Summarize, analyze, improve, and make new chart showing improved method.
4. Another useful tool of work simplification is the layout diagram of the work area. In developing a layout diagram the following steps apply:
    a. Draw a floor plan sketch of the work area to include all equipment, furniture, machines, and permanent installations such as doors, windows, and so on.
    b. Trace the work flow on the diagram showing distance and direction of flow.
    c. Analyze the diagram for possible improvement in the work flow and space utilization.
    d. Make a new diagram showing improved method.

5. In all work simplification projects, the manager should consider motion economy by:
    a. Recognizing and observing maximum and normal work areas.
    b. Recognizing and observing the eleven principles of motion economy.
    c. Analyzing the basic motions involved in a particular operation, task, or process with respect to the overall process, the worker, and the machines, and make improvements where possible.

6. To integrate the flow process chart, layout diagram, and motion economy with the five-step work simplification pattern, the following guide can be used:
    a. Select the job to be improved.
    b. Make a flow process chart and layout diagram.
    c. Question each detail.
    d. Determine action.
    e. Make a new flow process chart and layout diagram.
    f. Prepare a proposal sheet.
    g. Obtain approval.
    h. Install the new method.

DISCUSSION QUESTIONS

1. What is meant by *work simplification?* Where and by whom can work simplification be applied?
2. What are the five basic steps for improving an operation, task, or process?
3. In selecting work for improvement, what factors should the manager consider?
4. When breaking down a job, why should all details be taken into account, and why should they be listed in the sequence in which they occur?
5. By asking the questions—Why? What? Where? When? Who? and How?—in analyzing the job, what clues should the answers to these questions suggest in developing a new and improved method?
6. What work and safety principles should be observed in developing a new and improved method? How should the work simplification project be presented for improvement?
7. In installing a new work method what factors should the manager consider?
8. What is the purpose of a flow process chart and how is it prepared and analyzed? Discuss.

9. What is the purpose of a layout diagram and how is it prepared and analyzed? Discuss.
10. What are the basic principles of motion economy and how can these principles be applied to work simplification? Discuss.
11. How can the flow process chart, layout diagram, and motion economy be integrated with the basic pattern for work simplification? Discuss.

CASE PROPLEMS

Case 19–1

After finishing a work simplification course, Al Berkley decided to apply the principles and techniques he had learned to his department. In studying the work of his department, Al discovered that the job that needed improvement most was being done by one of his senior employees, a woman who had been doing the same operation in the same way since she started working with the organization fifteen years ago. Despite this, Al decided to continue with his plan.

Questions

1. *In addition to selecting the job to be improved, what other steps should Al take?*
2. *In installing his improvements, what problems would Al possibly have?*

Case 19–2

In an operation where a worker is assembling heavy manuals (books), a manager observes this situation:

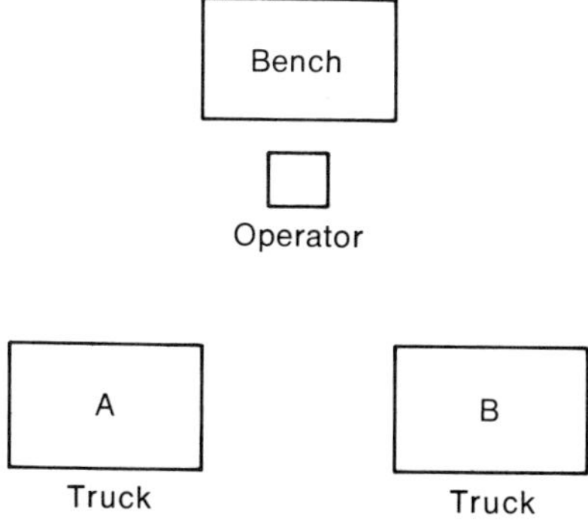

1. The layout of the operation consists of a bench on which the manuals are assembled, a hand-truck containing the unassembled material, and a hand-truck for the completed manuals. The operator has the trucks placed behind him at a distance of four feet as shown below:

2. Truck *A* contains the material to be assembled, and Truck B holds the completed manuals. When the worker assembles a manual, he picks it up, looks it over to assure that it is properly assembled, turns around, carries it to Truck *B,* and places the manual on that truck. Then he walks to Truck *A,* picks up a set of material to be assembled, turns around and walks back to the bench again.

Question

1. *How can this operation be improved? (In answering this question apply Steps 2 through 7 of the integrated approach to work simplification on page 342 of the text.)*

SELECTED REFERENCES

BROWN, MILON, *Effective Work Management,* Chap. 11. New York: The Macmillan Company, 1960.

LEHRER, ROBERT N., *Work Simplification,* Chaps. 16 and 22. Englewood Cliffs, N.J.: Prentice-Hall, Inc., 1957.

Paperwork Simplification, Technical Bulletin No. 86. Technical Aids Branch, Office of Industrial Resources, International Cooperation Administration, Washington, D.C.

Time and Motion Study, Technical Bulletin No. 90. Technical Aids Branch, Office of Industrial Resources, International Cooperation Administration, Washington, D.C.

20

How to Manage Paperwork

With the advance of technology, wider diversification, decentralization of industry and business, the increase of governmental controls, and a host of other factors too numerous to mention, today's manager—line or staff, top, middle, or first-line—is confronted with an increasing amount of paperwork. As distasteful as it may be to some, no manager can avoid this necessary if often burdensome task. Paperwork furnishes the manager with the information on which most of his decisions are made and his action taken. This being so, no book on management would be complete without discussing this subject. Therefore, in this chapter some techniques and principles will be discussed with the purpose of not only making the manager's job easier but more important, making his paperwork more effective. This discussion covers the following topics: (1) classification of paperwork, (2) guide to effective writing, (3) guide to effective reading, and (4) guide for understanding computers.

CLASSIFICATION OF PAPERWORK

In management, paperwork can be defined as documented information. As information, paperwork should be managed and controlled. Before it can be managed properly, how paperwork is classified should first be understood. At the individual managerial level, paperwork can be classified in one of three ways. First, there is the paperwork that the manager must prepare himself or is responsible for preparing. This includes letters, memos, reports, forms, and the like, which are necessary for the information system of his department. The second type of paperwork is that prepared by others on which the manager is responsible for taking action. This includes orders, requests, and other paperwork that the manager must process, manage, and control. The third and final type of paperwork is that which is to keep the manager informed. Informative paperwork may include plans, procedures, and other paperwork that may pertain to his department or the organization in general. Also included in this classification are professional and technical publications containing information that the manager needs to know to keep current in his field.

Within the framework of the three general classifications, paperwork can be further classified as recurring and nonrecurring, internal and external. Recurring information is usually thought of as that which is generated at intervals at least once a year. This includes such things as daily attendance reports, employee appraisals, and nearly all accounting, production, inventory, and sales reports. On the other hand, nonrecurring paperwork includes such things as one-time reports or studies of a special nature. Internal paperwork is that which is generated or developed by those in the organization and can include most of the types indicated above. External paperwork pertains to that which is generated by outside sources and may include such things as orders for goods or services from customers or people the organization is designed to support, or directives, regulations, policy from higher echelons, or governmental agencies that require compliance.

In addition to the above classifications, paperwork can be further classified according to information systems. The systems are to handle major types of information (paperwork) entering, leaving, and circulating through an organization. Major information systems common to all organizations include financial information, personnel information, and logistical information. As the title implies, a financial system concerns the flow of paperwork pertaining to money (budgets, pay checks, credit and collection, financial statements, and the like), and the personnel system pertains to the flow of paperwork about the people of the organization (personnel records, appraisals, absenteeism and turnover files, and employee payrolls and benefits included). Logistical records concern the paperwork about the physical flow of goods through an organization. (Information pertaining to procurement, distribution, and production is involved.) A fourth type of system, and one of the most important in many organizations, is marketing. The paperwork involved in this system varies widely among organizations. (Customer profiles, advertising effectiveness, and sales records are examples.) Although there are other types of information systems, these are the more common ones that the manager may be required to either support or manage.

To sum up, it can be seen that the paperwork a manager must deal with includes that which he must generate himself and that which is generated by others; it can be recurring and nonrecurring, internal and external; and these classifications can be part of a system. In short, the effectiveness of most organizations relies heavily on the flow of its paperwork. This makes it clear that understanding and developing techniques to manager paperwork are required of every manager.

GUIDE FOR EFFECTIVE WRITING

As indicated in the discussion above, one of the major categories of paperwork is that which he develops himself. This makes it only logical that the first technique that the manager should develop is the ability to write effectively. However, for obvious reasons no attempt will be made to discuss the intricacies of how to write. The aim here is to provide the manager with a fundamental guide that he can use to judge the effectiveness of his writing in general and to develop better reports.

Test of Effective Writing

The manager can use his best English grammar; he can punctuate precisely according to the rules; he can construct flowing sentences; but whether it is a letter, a memo, or a report, this will not make his writing effective. Like all types of communications, writing is effective only if the message intended by the writer is understood by the reader. Business writing is effective if it meets this four-way test:

1. Is it clear?
2. Is it appropriate?
3. Is it direct?
4. Is it correct?

To determine if his writing meets the four-way test of clarity, appropriateness, directness, and correctness, the manager may use the checklist shown in Figure 42.

Note that the checklist contains a key question in parentheses after each checkpoint. The manager should first try to answer honestly, in his own mind, each key question. If he can answer all of them with a firm, confident "yes," he may have little need of the other questions on the checklist.

However, if he cannot be positive about some of them, he should go through the checklist and try to answer the other questions. In some cases he may not be able to answer the questions with a definite "yes" or "no." If not, he should check the "I don't know" column to indicate areas that might need improvement.

After the checklist has been used to identify areas that need improvement, the manager can proceed immediately to work on them. Many times he knows how to write better, and if so, the appraisal will guide him as he

A. CLARITY: (Did you communicate clearly?)	YES	NO	I DON'T KNOW
1. Does your main message come through easily? 2. Are your ideas logically organized? 3. Have you supported and developed your ideas? 4. Have you weeded out unnecessary details?			
B. APPROPRIATENESS: (Does the writing fit its environment?)	**YES**	**NO**	**I DON'T KNOW**
1. Does the general tone suit the subject matter? 2. Have you considered who your reader will be? 3. Have you considered his knowledge level? 4. Does your writing style seem to fit you?			
C. DIRECTNESS: (Do your ideas come into focus quickly?)	**YES**	**NO**	**I DON'T KNOW**
1. Have you avoided long, involved sentences? 2. Have you chosen simple words, rather than flowery or unusual ones? 3. Will the reader understand all the technical terms? 4. Did you use active verbs whenever possible? 5. Did you use personal pronouns where appropriate?			
D. CORRECTNESS: (Have you met the standards of accepted usage?)	**YES**	**NO**	**I DON'T KNOW**
1. Are you sure about your spelling? 2. Do your subjects and verbs agree? 3. Have you punctuated correctly and where necessary? 4. Are your pronouns in the right case? 5. Have you capitalized correctly?			
Totals			

Figure 42 Checklist for Effective Writing (Courtesy of U.S. Air Force Department.)

edits and rewrites. Editing and rewriting cannot be overemphasized as a method of writing improvement. The world's finest writers often rewrite their material many times before they are satisfied with it. The manager can profit by their example if he makes it a habit to rewrite all of his own material at least once, and even more if necessary.

Of course if the manager does not have the basic knowledge he needs to correct the weaknesses in his writing, he must find help from others. In many cases, he can get the help he needs from an authoritative reference book. A good dictionary is also helpful, especially on questions of correctness and usage. In addition, the manager should have access to a reputable guide or handbook on writing. If he feels the need for a more complete review of basic fundamentals, he should either enroll in a writing course or undertake self-study. In any event, the checklist should help make the writing more effective.

Reports

Because of the complexity of modern organizations, a manager cannot always take time to gather all the information he needs. He must depend largely upon the reports of others. Since information presented orally is not always sufficient, often it needs to be written. Therefore, reports become a major source of the paperwork that the manager must handle. This being so, reports deserve special attention.

Types and Purpose of Reports. In management, a report is more or less an official document that presents facts for information of an interested reader. In the simplest terms, it is or should be an objective, impartial presentation of facts. In addition to being factual and objective, a report is aimed at a specific audience, adapted to the needs of that group or person, and designed to be used to make decisions and take action. Reports may take many forms. They may be in the form of codes or rules, recommendations, statements of policy, bulletins, manuals, pamphlets, booklets, folders, leaflets, press releases, and more. Reports, also, may be in the form of memos or letters. However, for memos and letters to be reports, they must meet the definition of a report. For example, a sales letter is like a report in that it is designed for a particular audience, should be based on factual information, and is designed to help the readers make decisions and take action. But since the intent of the sales letter is to persuade, it is not objective and therefore does not meet the definition of a report. In addition to the above, there are other reports designed for special purposes. Staff and technical reports fall within this category. It can be seen then that reports take many forms—from the simple memorandum to the more highly designed technical report—but regardless of its form all reports should serve one purpose: *to help the manager make a decision and/or take action.*

REPORT DEVELOPMENT. If this were a course in report writing, this would be the appropriate space to devote considerable time to the detailed preparation of the various types of reports about which a particular group of managers would be particularly concerned. But since this is not the case, an attempt will be made here only to outline basic principles and factors that can be used by most managers for developing most reports.

As indicated previously, the purpose of a report is to help the manager who receives it make a decision and/or take action. This means that he does not want to be bothered with facts or problems that do not concern him. This being the case, all reports have one thing in common: *The reader wants to be shown as precisely as possible what is expected of him.* In short, he wants answers to some specific questions.

What is the subject? The first step is to identify the subject so that the reader will know at once the subject matter of the report. Then include enough detail to show the nature of the problem. This can usually be accomplished in the opening sentence. Don't include minor details that have no bearing on the subject.

Why should I be interested? Or the question may be: What difference does that make to me? The answer to this question brings the reader into the report by showing how it affects him. If the report is going to the right man, the relationship between the subject matter of the report and his interests can be quickly shown.

What is the story in a nutshell? All the pertinent facts should be stated. Do not shorten the report to the extent of omitting necessary information. Consider the previous knowledge the reader has on the subject. Remember that he must have all the background facts or history to understand the problem. Arrange these facts in a related flow. A haphazard listing of facts may be misleading.

What action is recommended? The real purpose of most reports is to get the reader to do something about the matter discussed in the report, or furnish information the reader can use. Given the facts, the reader now wants to know if he is expected to make a decision, approve the action already taken, or simply note the information. He will also want to know the reasoning used in arriving at the conclusion. It may be helpful to list the advantages of the proposed solution and show how these advantages outweigh the disadvantages.

Who else is interested? Frequently the action the manager recommends will affect other activities. He should be certain that the report shows the relationship between these activities and his recommendation or information. If the material is so voluminous that it makes the report unwieldy and breaks its continuity, as much as possible of this material should be placed in an attachment to the report.

Developing detailed answers to these five questions will provide the material for most reports. In developing the answers, it will be helpful if the manager follows a systematic work schedule. A step-by-step work schedule is shown in Figure 43.

Although this is a schedule for developing the most complicated report, it can be adjusted for simpler tasks.

COMPLETED STAFF WORK. All paperwork used to report information should represent completed staff work. This simply means that the person preparing the paperwork—either staff or line—should make every effort to assure that the information is complete in every detail. The reason for this is that busy executives do not have the time to verify the information they must use. They must depend on their staff to furnish them with factual and timely information. To illustrate this point, consider the case of Ralph, a division manager of a major company, as reported by a team who visited his office:

> There is a never-ending pile of paperwork that goes with Ralph's job, plus the continuous task of planning ahead farther than you can see and then revising long and short-range plans every time conditions change. Friday morning we found Ralph at his desk going through a stack of mail. "Routine," he explained. "First thing every day I read all my mail and route a good deal of it to staff supervisors—in the laboratory, engineering, personnel, accounting, inspection, production planning, purchasing, etc.—asking for the special information required to answer each inquiry. When these reports come in, I will answer the letters." [1]

The scene above is typical of executives (major and minor) in every field and in every type of organization (large or small). Thousands of Ralphs are literally snowed under with mountains of paperwork on which they need to take action, and to do this they rely on their staff (middle and first-line managers) to produce information that will provide them with answers. To be useful the information must be valid, for in a real sense the executive's professional reputation and career are based on the accuracy of the information he receives from his subordinates. Therefore, the final test of completed staff work is this: *If you were the boss, would you stake your professional reputation on the information contained in the report?* If the answer is "no," the manager should take it back and start over. It is not yet completed staff work.

[1] See Chester R. Anderson, Alta G. Saunders, and Francis W. Weeks, *Business Reports,* 3rd ed. (New York: McGraw-Hill Book Company, Inc., 1957), pp. 2-3.

STEPS IN PREPARING A REPORT

Step A

1. Through discussion and/or correspondence with superiors, define the main purpose of the report.

2. Form a tentative but clear statement of the scope.

3. Form a tentative but clear statement of the procedure to be followed, including latitutde allowed you in changing the procedure.

4. Record all mutual understandings about the deadline, costs, and fees (if any).

Step B

1. Assemble further data needed.

2. Divide, classify, and roughly arrange the data.

3. Tabulate and graph all data that can be treated in this way.

Step C

1. Check all calculations, tables, curves, graphs, and quotations.

2. Select from your material the facts that must go into the report.

3. Decide which facts belong in the report proper, which belong in an attachment.

4. Interpret these facts--seeing what conclusions they point to--even though the conclusions may not be those finally decided upon.

5. Draw recommendations from the conclusions if recommendations are wanted.

6. Determine where and how to preserve the other facts you have gathered.

Step D

1. Phrase a topic sentence that states the purpose of your report as you have finally settled upon it.

2. Make a preliminary outline or at any rate a preliminary table of contents.

3. Get the report down on paper.

Step E

1. Double-check the organization of your report by:

   a. determining whether you have actually carried out your announced purpose and plan.

   b. determining whether any final summary you use agrees with your topic sentence.

(continued)

Figure 43 Report Preparation Work Schedule (Courtesy of U.S. Air Force Department.)

c. making sure that text, tables, and illustrations do not needlessly duplicate one another but instead complement one another.

2. Double-check the proportions of the report allowed for different subtopics.

3. Read the report aloud, preferably to someone else.

Step F

1. Revise the report, perhaps several times.

2. Prepare the final table of contents and list of illustrations and tables.

3. Copyread the manuscript.

4. Correct all errors and retype when necessary.

5. Present the report.

Figure 43 (cont'd.)

GUIDE FOR EFFECTIVE READING

In addition to preparing paperwork, the manager must read what is written by others. Therefore, to manage paperwork the manager must become an effective reader. As in the case of writing, it is not the purpose here to present a course in reading improvement, but only to point out its importance and give some fundamental tips that the manager may use as a guide to improve his reading effectiveness.

Most people can develop the ability to increase reading rate and comprehension. The key to efficient reading practices is the adaptability or flexibility in adjusting reading rate to the material and to the purpose in reading. The main causes of slow reading are a short span of recognition, regressing, subvocalizing, and an inadequate vocabulary. Everyone can increase his reading rate without reducing comprehension. The following ten tips will help each manager improve his reading.

1. Try to get something out of reading. Read with a purpose.
2. Read at a forced pace to eliminate daydreaming.
3. Vary reading rate to suit purpose. Types of material dictate reading speeds.
4. Look for main ideas in reading to aid comprehension.
5. Do not read words one at a time—read groups of words for key thoughts.
6. Be word-conscious—a large vocabulary enables one to be a more efficient reader.
7. Try to keep from regressing; the efficient reader concentrates on the material.

8. Eliminate movement of lips and throat muscles when reading. Subvocalization restricts reading speed to rate of speech.
9. Read more to develop broader interests, to become a better reader.
10. Be relaxed when reading.

GUIDE FOR UNDERSTANDING COMPUTERS

By the discussion so far, it can be seen that management must be kept informed by reliable up-to-date information if it is to operate at top efficiency, and that this information is prepared for management in the form of reports that become the basis for administrative action. With the avalanche of paperwork required in the operation of most organizations and because of the length of time required to prepare information, manual methods often fall far short of meeting management requirements. To solve this problem, many organizations—large and small—are turning to the services of computers. Therefore, the computer is today and will become more so in the future a major management tool in most organizations. This means that on a day-to-day basis, much of the paperwork that the manager must process, analyze, manipulate, or otherwise manage will directly or indirectly involve a computer. Although no manager should feel overwhelmed by those who understand the mechanics of a computer any more than he may feel embarrassed because he does not understand the inner workings of any electronic/mechanical device, he should at least have a working knowledge of a computer's basic functions and the generalities of application. Therefore, the purpose of this section is to answer two questions: How does the computer work and how is it used?

How a Computer Works [2]

When a computer is applied in a business operation, it should be understood that several pieces of equipment other than the computer are involved. Such a group of hardware is referred to as an electronic data processing system (EDPS). These systems are made by many manufacturers (IBM notwithstanding) and come in various sizes to accommodate a wide array of operations, but all are basically the same. Therefore, the animated system shown in Figure 44 can be used to understand the workings of most computer systems.

As this illustration indicates, an electronic data processing system consists of five units: (1) an input unit, (2) a storage unit, (3) an arithmetic

[2] Adapted from *Introduction to the Statistical, Analysis, Data Processing, and Programming Career Field,* Course 6812, Extension Course Institute, Air University, Department of United States Air Force.

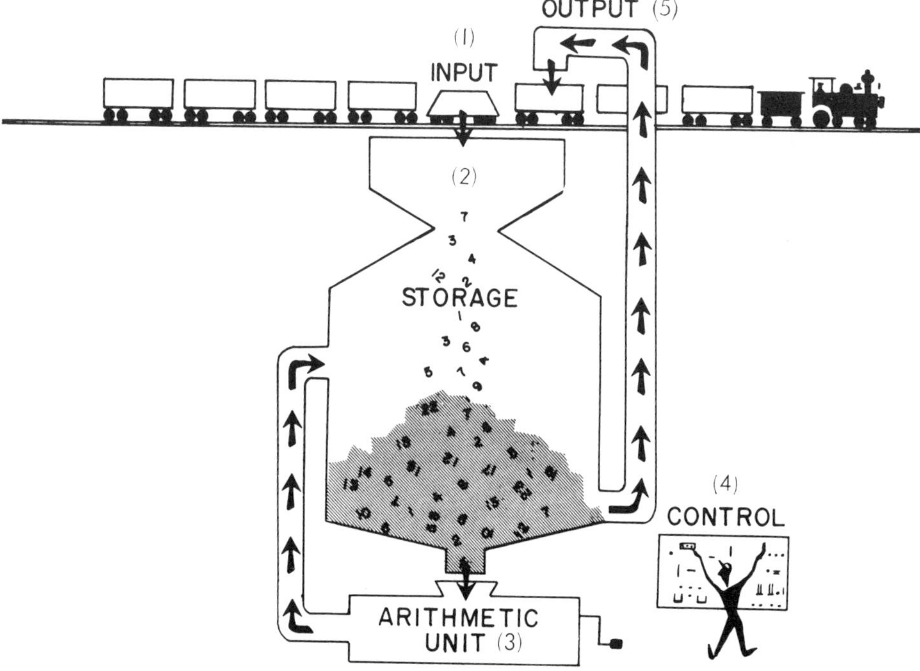

Figure 44 Animated Model of Electronic Data Processing System (Courtesy of U.S. Air Force Department.)

unit, (4) a control unit, and (5) an output unit. Although only the storage, arithmetic, and control units are normally referred to as the computer, since the computer depends on the input and output units, the way a computer works can best be understood when studied as a system.

The *input component* facility is a vital part of this system since the computer must have information given to it from some physical medium in order to handle, read, and process the data. This information comes in the form of bundles of new facts. Dependent upon the particular type of electronic data processing system being used, this information can be fed in by just about any common language media, such as cards or tapes (either paper or magnetic), keyboard input, and so on.

The *storage component* of a computer consists of a group of electromechanical or electronic devices. There, information is stored until the computer is ready to use it. It is readily accessible, it can be referred to once or many times, and it can be replaced whenever desired. The information held here can be original data, intermediate answers, or instructions.

The *arithmetic component* in this equipment is capable of performing addition, subtraction, multiplication, and division whenever it is directed to do so. The speed at which these computations are made must be measured in millionths of a second.

The *control component* actually is the nerve center of the electronic computer system. It prescribes a chain of instructions (a program) for every bundle of new facts that enters the system. It can request stored data whenever it is needed during the program cycle. It can examine the results of any one step of the program in order to select the following step or steps. When one bundle of facts has been processed, orders then can be issued by this control component to start all over again with the next set of facts. Different types of machines require different means of instructional entry.

It should be mentioned at this point that a computer is not an electronic brain. Each problem that is fed into the machine is completed by progressing through a series of prearranged steps, called a program. This device is a simple set of instructions or steps that tells the computer exactly how to handle a complete problem, such as payroll, production scheduling, finding a lost item in an inventory, or whatever other solution may be needed. Without these instructions, the computer cannot add one and one. Most programs include alternate steps or routines to take care of variations of procedure that may be encountered during calculations. Generally, program steps form a complete cycle; that is, each incoming bundle of facts (unit of information) sets off the whole cycle from start to finish. Each of the succeeding units sets the cycle off again, and this procedure continues until the desired program has been completed. However, the system cannot do anything it has not been directed to do by programmers—persons who prepare programs.

Programmers are scientifically and technically trained personnel who plan the whole operation from input to output and set the control section to handle it during the electronic data processing. Therefore, contrary to popular belief, the programmer, not the machine, is the "brain."

The *output component* of the computer system is the portion of the equipment that furnishes the answers. These may be answers to mathematical problems, such as those involved in research—statistical, analytical, or accounting figures, or production schedules, or whatever solution the initial problem called for. These answers may be given in the form of numbers, words, or symbols and can be punched into a card, recorded on tape, or printed on finished paper forms, such as orders, bills, checks, payrolls, reports, and others.

How the Computer is Used

In recent years, newspapers, magazines, and even television programs have reported amazing feats performed by computers. This has included everything from mate matching to moon launching. But on a day-to-day basis, managers use computers to solve everyday problems. Therefore, with its fantastic speed, its incredible accuracy, and its capability to make complex and complicated calculations, the computer has become the "work horse" instead of the "glamour boy" in many organizations. The computer can be used to perform a wide range of tasks in practically every field. Some examples are identified and discussed below.

LENGTHY DATA PROCESSING PROBLEMS. The high speed of the electronic computer makes possible the rapid processing of great amounts of clerical data. Computers can drastically cut the time and cost spent on functions such as payroll processing, inventory control, billing, shop order writing, sales analysis, and hundreds of other operations of a clerical or accounting nature. Processing clerical data is an area in which the computer has been the most widely and profitably used. The reason for this is twofold. First, it provides management with accurate up-to-date information on which decisions can be made, and second, it reduces the clerical personnel and paperwork that would otherwise be involved. It can be added that prior to the computer, much of the information needed by managers to operate the various departments of the operation simply could not be obtained accurately and timely, if at all. Therefore in this one area, the computer has proved an invaluable tool of management and an asset to all managers at all levels.

PRODUCTION PROBLEMS. In the area of production, the computer has been used to solve many everyday problems. For example, the computer can be used in such areas as:

Machine shop scheduling—finding the number of each item to be produced by each station in a machine shop to minimize delays and overtime and to shorten delivery time.

Production scheduling—designing schedules to meet expected sales, and varying these schedules in accordance with sales fluctuations.

Blending or mixing problems—finding the best combination of ingredients or raw materials.

Reduction of trim losses—forming, shearing, slitting, or punching rolls and sheets of material to produce various sizes, while at the same time minimizing waste.

Until the computer, the best that managers could do was to make an educated guess among many alternatives. Now, a high-speed computer can examine all the factors, explore all possible choices, and come up with the solution that will yield the best results.

Transportation and Distribution Problems. Illustrative of these problems is a business that operates a fleet of trucks. The transportation manager wanted to find out the most economical routes for them to follow. The factors that had to be considered included among others mileages, traffic congestion, toll roads, and load capacities. In just a few hours, a computer analyzed 10 million possible route combinations and found the best ones. Without a computer, it was estimated that it would have taken twenty years to solve that problem. Obviously, during that time, the manager would not have been able to save his company several thousands of dollars per year as he is now doing.

Similarly, computers can be used in forecasting sales and demand—performing market research by determining sales probabilities in different geographical areas for different products, and many other distribution problems.

Retailing Problems. Besides being used to help handle such retailing problems as inventory control, accounting, credit and collection, pricing, tagging, and reporting, the computer has helped managers in the retailing field in making decisions as well. For example, a large ladies' wear chain rented a computer for inventory control. One day the buyer of ladies' sweaters decided he would like to know which sizes were most popular. This is a simple computer problem, and the information was readily available. Then he wanted to know about the popularity of various colors, and was given the answer. Then he wondered if bright colors were better in small sizes than large. This goes on and on, until the buyer is so well equipped with information that he can perform with far greater efficiency. At this point it is foolish to compare the cost of the computer with the salaries of the clerks it replaced, since the information the device supplies is far more important than the job it was originally installed to do.[3]

The above are only a few examples of the many applications a computer has in an organization. Managers may use the computer to solve management analyses and engineering problems of a very complex nature. Many of the techniques used to solve these problems have been developed by the relatively new field of Operations Research mentioned in Chapter 16. But the above example clearly indicates that the computer can be used to help managers solve their day-to-day paperwork problems. Therefore, all managers, including middle and first-line, should be constantly on the lookout for areas in their operations where the computer can be used effectively. Since computers are expensive, whether rented or purchased outright, areas of application should be selected with discretion. The use of a computer can be best justified in processing information that is voluminous

[3] For a complete discussion on how the computer is used in retailing, see Gerald Pintel and Jay Diamond, *Retailing* (Englewood Cliffs, N.J.: Prentice-Hall, Inc., 1971), pp. 386-87.

and repetitious, when speed is an important factor, or when accuracy is required.

KEY POINT SUMMARY

1. Today a major factor that influences the manager in managing his operation is paperwork, and paperwork can be classified in many ways.
2. At the individual managerial level, paperwork can be classified in three ways:
    a. That which the manager prepares himself
    b. That which is prepared by others on which the manager is responsible for taking action
    c. That which the manager needs to keep himself informed
3. In addition, paperwork can be classified as:
    a. Internal
    b. External
    c. Recurring
    d. Nonrecurring
4. When applied to an organization, paperwork can be classified by major operational systems to include:
    a. Financial information
    b. Personnel information
    c. Logistical information
    d. Marketing information
5. To manage his paperwork effectively, the manager should develop certain techniques to include:
    a. Writing effectively
    b. Reading effectively
    c. Understanding the use of computers
6. For business writing to be effective, it must meet this four-way test:
    a. Is it clear?
    b. Is it appropriate?
    c. Is it direct?
    d. Is it correct?
7. An essential type of paperwork in all organizations is the report: an objective impartial presentation of facts.

8. For a report to be effective, it should:
   a. Help the manager make a decision or take action.
   b. Show the reader as precisely as possible what is expected of him.
   c. Represent completed staff work.
9. To process the mass of paperwork, the manager should learn to read effectively. The main causes of poor reading are:
   a. Short span of recognition
   b. Regression
   c. Subvocalizing (moving lips)
   d. An inadequate vocabulary
10. In recent years more and more organizations are using electronic computers to assist in managing paperwork. Although computer systems vary widely, they have in common these basic configurations:
    a. An input component
    b. A storage component
    c. An arithmetic component
    d. A control component
    e. An output component
11. On a day-to-day basis the manager can use the computer in many ways to help solve his paperwork problems, particularly in these areas:
    a. Voluminous work
    b. Repetitious work
    c. Where accuracy is required
    d. Where speed is important

DISCUSSION QUESTIONS

1. How can the increase in the amount of paperwork needed to manage an organization be explained?
2. How is paperwork that affects the operation of an organization classified? Relate the flow of information within and without an organization to the upward, downward, and across communications pattern disscussed previously.
3. What is the test of effective business writing? Relate the factor of appropriateness to the guide to effective communications discussed in Chapter 4.
4. If a manager discovers that his writing needs improvement, what steps should he take?
5. In management, what is the basic purpose of reports? Relate reports to the problem-solving process discussed in Chapter 16.

6. In preparing reports, what factors should the manager consider?
7. What is meant by completed staff work? How can the manager determine if his staff work is complete?
8. Why is being able to read effectively a technique that a manager should acquire?
9. In reference to the ten tips for effective reading, how would you rate yourself in each area?
10. Why is it necessary that a manager have a basic understanding of computers?
11. In actual operation, what components make up an electronic data processing system, and what are the basic functions of each?
12. What is the role of programmers in relation to computers?
13. What are some common uses of a computer in managing paperwork?
14. What are the advantages of using a computer to manage paperwork?
15. Under what circumstances should the use of a computer be considered?

CASE PROBLEMS

Case 20–1

This case is in two parts.

Part I

All supervisors of a small organization received this memo from their general manager:

"Effective on or about March 1st all supervisors including department heads are requested to make a weekly report very briefly in writing on the housekeeping in their departments. Generally speaking this report should be brief and yet include all improvements or changes that have been made in the interim between the previous week's report and the report in question. It is important that those reports are made regularly and on time and any failures to do so will be dealt with individually because of the importance of these reports. Your earnest cooperation is solicited and we know it will be forthcoming."

Part II

In reply to this request, one supervisor submitted this report:

"In reference to your recent memo, I have taken this matter into account and hope to have some improvement to report at a later date. Meanwhile, I have made my employees cognizant of good housekeeping practices and have developed procedures to implement same. In addition, I have talked with Bill in the next department to see if he can do something about the mess that his employees create during their lunch break. You know that I am a 'nut' about housekeeping and will support the program to the hilt."

Questions

1. *Does the memo in Part I meet the four-way test of effective writing?*
2. *Is the report in Part II consistent with the five basic questions indicated in the text?*
3. *Is the report completed staff work?*
4. *How could both the request and the report be improved?*

Case 20–2

A small manufacturing firm that produces and markets a variety of products has rented a computer for inventory control. After the inventory control system was installed and functioning properly, it was found that the minimum time covered by the rental agreement was not being used. To take advantage of this excess time, the general manager asked each of his department managers to meet with a representative from the computer rental firm, to attempt to identify areas where the computer could be used in their departments. In addition to the representative from the computer service, the managers of the following departments were present:

1. Personnel
2. Accounting and Finance
3. Marketing and Sales
4. Production
5. Transportation and Distribution

Questions

1. *Considering each of the five departments separately, what possible areas could be identified?*
2. *After the areas are identified, what factors can be used as criteria in establishing the priority for using the computer?*

SUGGESTED REFERENCES

ANDERSON, CHESTER R., ALTA G. SAUNDERS, and FRANCIS W. WEEKS, *Business Reports,* Chaps. 1 and 13. New York: McGraw-Hill Book Company, Inc., 1957.

DALE, ERNEST, and L. C. MICHELON, *Modern Management Methods,* Chap. 13. Cleveland, Ohio: The World Publishing Company, 1966.

DEARDEN, JOHN, and F. WARREN MCFARLAN, *Management Information Systems,* Chap. 1. Homewood, Ill.: Richard D. Irwin, Inc., 1966.

Getting Your Ideas Across Through Writing, Training Manual No. 7. U.S. Department of Health, Education, and Welfare, Washington, D.C. 44 pages.

Index